CLOSER WALK

365 DAILY DEVOTIONALS THAT NURTURE A HEART FOR GOD

CLOSER WALK

BRUCE H. WILKINSON
EXECUTIVE EDITOR

MICKEY R. HODGES
EDITOR

PAULA A. KIRK
GENERAL EDITOR

WALK THRU THE BIBLE MINISTRIES, INC.
ATLANTA, GEORGIA

ZONDERVAN PUBLISHING HOUSE
GRAND RAPIDS, MICHIGAN

Closer Walk
Copyright © 1992 by Walk Thru the Bible Ministries
All rights reserved

Published by Zondervan Publishing House

Requests for information should be addressed to:
Walk Thru the Bible Ministries   or   Zondervan Publishing House
4201 North Peachtree Road   Grand Rapids, MI 49530
Atlanta, GA 30341-1362

Library of Congress Cataloging-in-Publication Data

Closer Walk: 365 daily devotions that nurture a heart for God / Walk
Thru the Bible Ministries, Atlanta, Georgia
    p. cm.
    Includes index
    ISBN 0-310-54221-9 (pbk.)
    1. Devotional calendars. I. Walk Thru the Bible (Educational
Ministry)
BV4810.C5387   1992
242 c3.2—dc20   92-8296
                                                              CIP

Interior design by Michelle Beeman
Illustrations by Lewis A. Wallace
Cover photo by The Image Bank

Printed in the United States of America

92 93 94 95 96/ DH /10 9 8 7 6 5 4 3 2 1

*D*edication

*C*hrist entered a new level of intimacy with His disciples when He told them, "I have called you my friends." His statement was based on the depth of spiritual truth they were experiencing together. In that vein, Deen Day Smith has over the years become a true friend to Walk Thru the Bible Ministries. She has stood by us, supported us, prayed for us, hosted us, spoken for us, advised us, and most of all, been a friend to us. I can think of little that one would desire in a friend that she has not been to us, and therefore affectionately dedicate *Closer Walk* to Deen Day Smith.

Bruce H. Wilkinson

*A*cknowledgments

*C*loser Walk is a team effort, and many people have contributed to make it a reality. Walk Thru the Bible Ministries would like to thank the following people for their part in the creation and production of this book: Robyn Holmes, Kyle Henderson, Bobby McCann, Meg Anderson, John Hoover, Jim Gabrielsen, Calvin Edwards, and the late Shildes Johnson. We would also like to acknowledge the excellent assistance of Mary McCormick, our editor at Zondervan.

*I*ntroduction

*C*loser Walk is a new compilation of daily devotional readings taken from Walk Thru the Bible's monthly devotional guide of the same name. With this book you can gain practical devotional insights directly related to a specific passage in God's Word, and at the end of one year you will have read the New Testament at an easy, manageable pace. But more than that, you will find your relationship with the Lord deepening as you spend time meditating on His Word.

As a result of using Closer Walk as a devotional guide, you will see the New Testament in a new light as you find practical answers to the perplexing problems you face each day. From great men and women of faith you will learn how to worship God in an intimate and personal way . . . how to handle your heartaches . . . how to praise God through prayer and biblical meditation. In short, you will develop a heart for God.

We at Walk Thru the Bible Ministries are pleased to join with Zondervan Publishing House to make this devotional book available to you. May it increase your love for God.

Bruce H. Wilkinson
President and Executive Editor
Walk Thru the Bible Ministries

Walk Thru the Bible Ministries

Walk Thru the Bible Ministries (WTB) began in the early 1970s in Portland, Oregon, when a young teacher named Bruce Wilkinson developed an innovative way of teaching surveys of the Bible. By enabling people to actively participate in the learning process through memorable hand signs, the Word of God came alive for them and lives were changed.

From these small beginnings emerged the multifaceted Bible-teaching outreach that Dr. Wilkinson officially founded as a nonprofit ministry in 1976. In 1978 WTB moved to its current home in Atlanta, Georgia. Since then, WTB has grown into one of the leading Christian organizations in America with an international ministry extending to 30 countries representing 22 languages. International branch offices are located in Australia, Brazil, Great Britain, Singapore, and New Zealand.

By focusing on the central themes of Scripture and their practical application to life, WTB has been able to develop and maintain wide acceptance in denominations and fellowships around the world. In addition, it has carefully initiated strategic ministry alliances with more than one hundred Christian organizations and missions of wide diversity and background.

WTB has four major outreach ministries: seminars, publishing, leadership training, and video training curricula. Since it began its seminar ministry two decades ago, WTB has instructed more than one million people worldwide through seminars taught by more than two hundred highly qualified, well-trained teachers. People of all ages and religious persuasions have developed a deeper understanding of the Bible through these unique Old and New Testament surveys, and many have come to know Christ in a new and more personal way.

WTB's publishing ministry began in 1978 with the launching of *The Daily Walk* magazine. Since then, WTB Publishing has continued to develop additional publications that enable individuals, families, and churches to maintain a regular, meaningful habit of daily devotional time in the Word of God. The publications include *Closer Walk, Family Walk, LifeWalk, Quiet Walk,* and *Youthwalk.* WTB is one of the largest publishers of devotional magazines in the Christian community.

The third strategic ministry of WTB is the training of Christian leaders and communicators. Launched in the late 1980s, the Applied Principles of Learning (APL) training conference for teachers, pastors, and parents has rapidly become the most widely used interdenominational teacher training program in North America. Dozens of certified WTB instructors regularly conduct this life-changing course in schools, churches, businesses, and colleges. In addition, WTB's Leadership Dynamics curriculum is an integral part of the regular and ongoing discipleship training in hundreds of churches.

The newest ministry of WTB is the Video Training curriculum. In just a few short years, the WTB creative team has developed a number of leading video courses that have enjoyed widespread distribution. *The Seven Laws of the Learner,* featuring Dr. Bruce H. Wilkinson, focuses on the needs of the student and helps teachers learn to communicate in the most effective and compelling manner possible. *The Seven Laws of the Teacher*, featuring Dr. Howard G. Hendricks, equips church school teachers, parents, and others to effectively prepare and teach Bible lessons that capture attention and change lives. *Master Your Money*, a six-part presentation by Christian financial planner Ron Blue, trains people to maximize their effectiveness as stewards of God's resources. Thousands of churches use these and other fine WTB videos with their congregations each year.

WTB has had a consistent history of strategic ministry from its beginning. The organization strives to help fulfill the Great Commission in obedience to the Lord's call. With this mission in mind, WTB lives out its commitment to excellence with the highest standards of ethical conduct and integrity, not only in the ministry but also in its internal operational policies and procedures. No matter what the ministry, no matter where the ministry, WTB focuses on the Word of God and encourages people of all nations to grow in their knowledge of Him and in unreserved obedience and service to Him.

For more information about Walk Thru the Bible's publications, videos, or seminars in your area, write to Walk Thru the Bible Ministries, 4201 North Peachtree Road, Atlanta, GA 30341-1362 or call (404) 458-9300.

How to get the most out of Closer Walk

Closer Walk is conveniently arranged for daily Bible reading 365 days of the year. Each devotional reading is dated with the month and the day of the year and contains the following:

• *Worship from the Heart* provides a springboard for meditation, prayer, and personal worship as you begin your devotional time or as a platform for personal commitment as you conclude.

• *Walk Thru the Word* directs you to the daily passage and will lead you through the entire New Testament in one year. A corresponding Old Testament passage adds insight on the day's theme.

• The *key verse* focuses the day's devotional on one idea from the Scripture passage.

• *Walk with a Christian Leader* provides inspiration for today from the writings of faithful Christian teachers and leaders of the past.

• *Walk Closer to God* is a challenge to deepen your relationship with God through obedience and personal worship.

In addition, short biographies of some of the great Christian leaders of the past will give you insight into the lives of men and women whose faith and walk provide inspiration for us.

Every feature of *Closer Walk* is designed to help you get the most out of your devotional times. It's the tool you have been looking for to help you develop your heart for God!

Contents

Discipleship: Following the Master's Footsteps

In the book of Matthew Jesus entrusts the Great Commission to all those who confess Christ as their Savior.

Matthew presents Jesus Christ as the long-awaited Messiah ("Anointed One") of Israel. Writing to a Jewish audience, Matthew draws heavily on Old Testament prophecies to convince his readers that Jesus is the Christ, the Son of the living God.

But you needn't be Jewish to benefit from reading Matthew's gospel. This tax-collector-turned-disciple presents some distinct impressions about Jesus of Nazareth. He was a worker of miracles, a preacher of parables, a lover of people. Everywhere He went, He taught people what right living was all about, modeling His teaching with His own life.

Jesus chose a twelve-member team of traveling companions—called disciples—who followed Him everywhere and learned much from Him. Their lives changed dramatically as they came in contact with the life-changing Savior. But discipleship is just as important for your own personal life. After all, you as a follower of Jesus Christ are also His disciple. Such an assignment must not be taken lightly. Jesus often spoke of the high price of being His disciple—alienation from family, self-denial, loss of earthly possessions, physical abuse, even martyrdom!

Jesus knew that being His disciple would demand nothing short of a transformed life. Furthermore, before His departure from this earth, Jesus commanded His followers to "make disciples of all nations" (Matthew 28:19). Disciple-making, in other words, is a continuing responsibility; the Great Commission has been entrusted to all those who confess Christ as their Savior.

This should be an exciting month in God's Word—a month of change, of growth, of becoming more like Jesus. It will be a month to help you develop a heart for God.

God present in touchable form

JANUARY 1 ❑ DAY 1

"And they will call him Immanuel"—which means, "God with us" (Matthew 1:23).

*W*hat does a greeting have in common with a good-bye?

Simply this: *Good-bye* is short for "God be with you." And that's who is introduced in the first chapter of Matthew—Immanuel, whose name means "God with us." For Jesus Christ is the God-man, the long-awaited Messiah.

Centuries earlier, God had promised through the prophets to come and dwell among men. John Calvin describes how Jesus fulfilled that promise.

Walk with John Calvin

"Scripture often speaks in terms of God being with us when His help and favor are by us, and when He reaches out in His power to protect us.

"In Christ the presence of God was tangibly displayed to the people, no longer in shadows. He would certainly be no true Mediator if there were not in Him an undivided bond of each nature, human and divine, to tie people to God.

"Which again brings home to us that Christ was God revealed in the flesh, and it is right that He puts on the title 'Immanuel.' So this name must make us think first of the divine majesty of Christ, to bring us to reverence it, as is due to the one and everlasting God.

"As often as we see God and man in the one person of Christ, we may be certain that we possess God, if by faith we are joined to God."

Walk Closer to God

Today you begin reading the remarkable account of how the Son from heaven came to live as a man on earth, and His every word, every work, every step is worthy of note.

Think of it! Jesus began His earthly life as a baby, yet He existed in the beginning with God. At birth, He was laid in a manger, yet He created the tree it was made from.

Jesus Christ is God's "good-bye" gift to you, that you might greet each new day with the words, "Hello, Lord!"

Have you done that yet today?

Worship from the Heart

Try to imagine the anger and distress which must surely have warred with protectiveness and love in Joseph's emotions. Though they will never be of the same magnitude, we too will have loved ones drop emotional "bombs" on us. Rejoice today in the example of Joseph, the sufficiency of God's grace, and the peace which will "guard your hearts and your minds [emotions] in Christ Jesus" (Philippians 4:7).

Walk Thru the Word

New Testament Reading
Matthew 1
Old Testament Reading
Isaiah 43:1-7

In the path of the Magi

On coming to the house, they saw the child with his mother Mary, and they bowed down and worshiped him (Matthew 2:11).

*P*arts of the Christmas story are anything but idyllic. For example: the cold night, the stable full of livestock, the rough feeding trough as a crib. But parts of that dramatic occasion can scarcely be exaggerated. For instance, the angelic visitors and the wise men who came to worship the infant King.

John Chrysostom will help you appreciate the mystery and majesty of that first Christmas.

Walk with John Chrysostom

"Let us follow the Magi; let us separate ourselves from our worldly desires that we may see Christ, since they too—had they not been far from their own country—would have missed seeing Him. Let us depart from the things of earth.

"Let us rise up and run to the house of the young Child; though kings, though nations, though tyrants interrupt our path, let not our desire pass away.

"The Magi, too, would not have escaped their danger from the king unless they had seen the young Child. Before seeing Him, fears and dangers and troubles pressed upon them from every side; but after the adoration, there is calm security.

"Do thou therefore likewise leave the pomp of this world, and hasten to Bethlehem, where is the house of the spiritual Bread.

"Only let your coming be to honor and adore, not to spurn the Son of God. Do this with trembling and joy."

Walk Closer to God

The greatest gift given on that first Christmas came from God Himself—the priceless treasure of His Son. And the wonder of that gift is still reason enough for you to bow in adoring worship today and sing these familiar lines:

> *O come, let us adore Him,*
> *O come, let us adore Him,*
> *O come, let us adore Him,*
> *Christ, the Lord.*

Worship from the Heart

King Herod experienced the visit of the Magi, heard the prediction of Scripture, knew of the sign in the heavens, and obtained the opinion of the scholars. Still he thought he could thwart God's plan. Ask God to make you sensitive to any blind spots in your ability to see His plans unfold in your life. Praise Him for His constancy and power; rejoice that nothing confounds Him or catches Him off guard.

Walk Thru the Word

New Testament Reading
Matthew 2
Old Testament Reading
Psalm 95:1-7

A heritage in God's family

"This is my Son, whom I love; with him I am well pleased" (Matthew 3:17).

*I*n Matthew 3, a man named John bursts upon the scene, looking and sounding like Elijah the prophet. According to the Old Testament, that was precisely as it should have been.

Another Man named Jesus came to be baptized by John. Coincidence? Or the long-awaited Messiah (Anointed One)? The audible voice of God supplied the answer.

Matthew Henry, prolific 18th-century Bible commentator, reveled in the Christian's privileges in Christ. If you are "in Him," you enjoy a rich heritage in God's family, as Mr. Henry explains.

Walk with Matthew Henry

"Jesus is God's 'beloved Son,' not only 'with whom' but 'in whom' God is well pleased. God is pleased with all who are in Christ and are united to Him by faith. Hitherto God had been displeased with the children of men; but now His anger is turned away, and He has made us 'accepted in the Beloved.' Outside of Christ, God is a consuming Fire, but in Christ He is a reconciling Father.

"This is the sum of the whole gospel: God has declared by a voice from heaven that Jesus Christ is His beloved Son. With this we must by faith cheerfully concur and say that He is our beloved Savior, in whom we are well pleased."

Walk Closer to God

What is your heavenly heritage? Forgiveness. Acceptance. Salvation. Indescribable wealth in Jesus Christ, all because you are "born again" into God's family, giving you the right to call God your Father. That's your legacy. You are rich in Christ . . . but do you live as a King's heir?

You are forgiven, but do you nurture feelings of guilt? You are accepted, but do you try to "repay" God for what He has given as a free gift?

It's hard to live like a pauper when you know you're as rich as a king. And focusing on your heritage in the family of God can be exciting.

Don't be surprised if something changes when you do. And don't be content until it does.

Worship from the Heart

"The world in its whirl of sin is sometimes like a cold wind that chills to the bone. I was once an orphan, blown along deserted streets by that wind. But, Jesus, You took me in and adopted me as Your own child. How I praise You for the security and acceptance that I have found in Your presence."

Walk Thru the Word

New Testament Reading
Matthew 3
Old Testament Reading
Isaiah 9:6

4

Jesus answered, "It is written: 'Man does not live on bread alone, but on every word that comes from the mouth of God' " (Matthew 4:4).

*O*h, for a word that, when spoken, would automatically
   ... wash the dishes
   ... write the report
   ... heal the pain
   ... sweep away the problem.

In the desert, Satan tempted Jesus to "say the word" and so satisfy His hunger. But Jesus chose instead to speak another word, a word more powerful than any magic formula—the Word of God.

Charles Spurgeon describes the scene and its implications for the modern-day Christian.

Walk with Charles Spurgeon

"Our Lord was led into the wilderness, where the Devil adapted the temptation to the circumstances: He tempted a hungry man with bread.

"He put it very cunningly. One single word, and the hard stone of the desert would be bread. But out flashed the sword of the Spirit, the Word of God. Our Lord will fight with no other weapon.

"He could have spoken new revelations, but He chose to say, 'It is written . . . ' There is power in the Word of God which even the Devil cannot deny.

"Our life and sustenance are not dependent upon the visible. We live 'not by bread alone,' though it is the usual means of support. The Word of the Lord which made the heavens can assuredly support all it has made.

"Jesus would not distrust the providence of God, but would wait His Father's time for feeding Him. He would by no means be driven to an act of unbelief and self-reliance."

Walk Closer to God

"I have hidden your word in my heart that I might not sin against you" (Psalm 119:11).

Oh, for a word which, when spoken, would cause Satan to flee.

Such a word exists! Three times Jesus employed it, declaring, "It is written . . . " You dare not confront your wily Enemy without it.

Relying solely on the Word of God

Worship from the Heart

With Jesus, Satan struck first at a weak point, then at a strong point, and finally at the heart of the matter. He attacked the physical, the spiritual, and finally the relationship Jesus had with His Father. Praise God that though the first Adam was tempted and failed, the last Adam triumphed. What cause for rejoicing to know that you too can stand against the onslaughts of the Enemy when you stand in Christ!

Walk Thru the Word

New Testament Reading
Matthew 4
Old Testament Reading
Job 23:12

Getting right with God and others

Worship from the Heart

C. S. Lewis said, "I can hardly imagine a more deadly spiritual condition than that of a person who can read the [Sermon on the Mount] with tranquil pleasure." When something in today's reading "hits you where it hurts," don't ignore it. Stop and let the Holy Spirit expose any sin. Confess, repent, and begin again as you take this opportunity to praise God for the ability to live in a way that pleases Him.

Walk Thru the Word

New Testament Reading
Matthew 5
Old Testament Reading
Genesis 45:4-5, 14-15

"Leave your gift there in front of the altar. First go and be reconciled to your brother; then come and offer your gift" (Matthew 5:24).

*D*uring the Sunday morning service, the pastor suddenly steps down from the platform and approaches a member of the congregation . . . and asks forgiveness for something he had said earlier in the week.

Unusual? Perhaps.

Uncomfortable? Probably.

Biblical? Absolutely!

Such openness and honesty in obedience to one of Christ's commands is rare today. But the importance Jesus places upon restored relationships is highlighted in the Sermon on the Mount.

G. Campbell Morgan explains why.

Walk with G. Campbell Morgan

"God seeks and values the gifts we bring Him —gifts of praise, thanksgiving, service, and material offerings. In all such giving at the altar we enter into the highest experiences of fellowship.

"But the gift is acceptable to God in the measure to which the one who offers it is in fellowship with Him in character and conduct; and the test of this is in our relationships with our fellow men.

"We are thus charged to postpone giving to God until right relationships are established with others.

"Could the neglect of this be the explanation of the barrenness of our worship?"

Walk Closer to God

It's not easy to sing praises to God when you're angry with the person sitting next to you.

Or you feel the eyes of one you have wronged glaring at you.

Or you sense that a wrong relationship with a brother or sister is getting in the way of a right relationship with your Father.

Before you attempt to show your love for God by singing, praying, or searching His Word, go to someone you've treated wrongly, and deal with the grievance.

The heart that yearns to stay right with God will not resist His command to get right with others.

"This, then, is how you should pray: 'Our Father in heaven' " (Matthew 6:9).

*F*amiliar prayers can sometimes become taste-less substitutes for an unmotivated heart. But "the Lord's Prayer" is more than a formula; it is a pattern by which you can model your own times of talking with your heavenly Father.

Martin Luther offers these insights about those very familiar words.

Walk with Martin Luther

"This prayer covers all matters and affairs. The first three petitions ask for such grand and heav-enly blessings that no heart can ever exhaust their meaning.

"The fourth petition presents, as in one little package, all the interests of state and home, all bodily and temporal needs.

"The sixth petition combats the Devil and his temptation to sin.

"Truly, this prayer was made by a wise Man, whom no one can imitate, for the Lord has com-posed the Prayer for us in this compact manner and has included in it every need that may arise.

"In addition, we should be drawn to prayer because God anticipates us and arranges the form of prayer for us.

"He puts into our mouths the very manner and matter of the prayer which He wants us to offer, so that we may see how He is concerned about our need, and may never doubt that this prayer is pleasing to Him and will certainly be answered."

Walk Closer to God

If prayer has become a tedious chore in your walk with God, perhaps you've lost sight of . . .

- the *object* of prayer ("Our Father in heaven")
- the *privilege* of prayer ("Hallowed be your name")
- the *power* of prayer ("your kingdom come")
- the *provision* of prayer ("Give us today our daily bread")
- the *protection* of prayer ("Deliver us from the evil one").

There's only one thing left to do: *pray!*

*T*he pattern for coming to God in prayer

*W*orship from the Heart

People measure each other by outward appearance and actions, possessions and status. But God is concerned with getting your inner life in tune with Him. Meditate on these facts as you read Matthew 6:19-24, 33. Compare your earthly treasures to what you've already laid up in heaven. Rejoice that time, money, and effort poured into God's kingdom make the wisest investments.

*W*alk Thru the Word

New Testament Reading
Matthew 6
Old Testament Reading
1 Kings 8:22-25, 38-40, 56-61

Safely removing the plank in your eye

JANUARY 7 ❏ DAY 7

"You hypocrite, first take the plank out of your own eye, and then you will see clearly to remove the speck from your brother's eye" (Matthew 7:5).

*A*sk an individual to characterize a neighbor, boss, or a pastor, and chances are good the description will "major" on negative aspects. But turn the spotlight on yourself, and it's amazing how the dark spots suddenly become blind spots.

Thomas à Kempis discusses the attitude that every Christian needs when confronted by the shortcomings of others.

Walk with Thomas à Kempis

"Those things that one cannot improve in himself or in others, he ought to endure patiently, until God arranges things otherwise.

"Nevertheless when you have such impediments, you ought to pray that God would help you, and that you may bear them kindly.

"Endeavor to be patient in bearing with the defects of others, whatever they are; for you also have many failings which must be borne by others.

"If you cannot make yourself be as you would like to be, how can you expect to have another person be to your liking in every way?

"We desire to have others perfect, and yet we do not correct our own faults. We would allow others to be severely corrected, and will not be corrected ourselves. We will have others kept under by strict laws, but in no case do we want to be restrained.

"And so it appears that we seldom weigh our neighbor in the same balance with ourselves."

Walk Closer to God

There will always be applicants for the position of "Splinter Inspector" in the lives of others. But the real need is for Christians who are willing to become "Plank Removers" in their own lives.

Would you trust your teeth to a dentist who has no teeth? Or your car to a mechanic who couldn't keep his own car running? Of course not!

Would you trust a Christian whose life showed no evidence of the power of God at work?

It's a question worth asking. And the first person to ask is yourself.

Worship from the Heart

A foundation must do two things: It must bear the weight of the structure, and it must withstand the onslaught of the elements. God has revealed that hearing and doing His Word forms the only foundation that will bear the building of life and will withstand the storm of circumstances. Rejoice in His precious assurance that if the foundation of your life is indeed hearing and doing His Word, then you will stand any test.

Walk Thru the Word

New Testament Reading
Matthew 7
Old Testament Reading
Psalm 119:33-40

The centurion replied, "Lord, I do not deserve to have you come under my roof. But just say the word, and my servant will be healed" (Matthew 8:8).

A centurion with a sick servant admits his own unworthiness of Jesus' healing attention, and in the process highlights his belief in the Master's power—a belief so strong that it amazes even Jesus Himself (8:10)!

Humble faith is a commodity highly prized and praised by God. Albert Barnes probes the relationship between humility and faith.

Walk with Albert Barnes

"The case of the centurion is a strong instance of the nature and value of humility. He had no exalted conception of himself.

"Humility is an estimate of ourselves as we are. It is a view of ourselves as lost, poor, wandering creatures.

"In the centurion's case we have an equally beautiful exhibition of faith. He had unwavering confidence in the power of Jesus. He did not doubt that Jesus was able to do just what he needed, and what he wished Him to do. This is faith.

"Humility and faith are always connected. The one prepares the mind for the other. Having a deep sense of our weakness and unworthiness, we are prepared to look to Him who has strength.

"Compared with Him, we see our unworthiness. Seeing His strength, we see our feebleness. Seeing His strength exerted to save creatures impure and ungrateful as we are, we gain an increased sense of our unfitness for His favor."

Walk Closer to God

"Unworthiness . . . feebleness . . . unfitness for His favor." Not a very encouraging picture if you are drawing near the throne of God with a prayerful request. Unless you are approaching God in the name of One who is infinitely worthy . . . strong . . . and fit to be your Mediator.

Let the centurion's humble words be your model for approaching the Almighty One with confidence, there to "find grace to help us in our time of need" (Hebrews 4:16).

The link between humility and faith

Worship from the Heart

Peter's mother-in-law was perhaps too sick even to realize that Jesus was in her home. But when Jesus healed her, she rose and served her guests. What a beautiful picture this is of Jesus' thoroughly healing touch. Consider several occasions in your life when He has healed and restored you, whether it was physically, emotionally, or spiritually. Praise Him that He does nothing halfway, but is tender and thorough in His mighty touch.

Walk Thru the Word

New Testament Reading
Matthew 8
Old Testament Reading
2 Chronicles 7:13-15

Seeing the depths of another's need

Worship from the Heart

Imagine for a moment that you were a paralytic in Jesus' day facing total immobility, complete dependence on others, and hopelessness that your condition would ever change. Now consider this fact: Sin, like paralysis, makes every human being helpless. Regardless of your physical condition today, praise God that Jesus died to release you from the paralysis of sin into the freedom of life in Him.

Walk Thru the Word

New Testament Reading
Matthew 9
Old Testament Reading
2 Kings 13:23

When he saw the crowds [Jesus] had compassion on them (Matthew 9:36).

The word *compassion* comes from a root meaning "to suffer together with another."

In Matthew 9, the Greek word translated "had compassion" refers to a stomach-churning grief at the plight of others.

Gazing at the multitudes, Jesus recognized the depth of their spiritual need . . . and what He saw caused Him physical pain.

To know that Jesus suffered can become a source of comfort as you suffer, for He truly can identify with your pain. His words ring true when He says, "I know how you feel." Allow A. B. Simpson to explain.

Walk with A. B. Simpson

"He [Jesus] is able to 'sympathize with our weakness.' The word *sympathize* expresses a great deal. It means that our troubles are His troubles, and in all our afflictions He is afflicted.

"There is much help in this for the tired heart. Suffering is the foundation of His sacrifice, and God meant that it should be to us a source of unceasing consolation.

"Let us realize our oneness with the One who suffered, and cast all our burdens on His great heart of love.

"As the mother feels her baby's pain, as the heart of friendship echoes every cry from another's woe, so in heaven our exalted Savior—even amid the raptures of that happy world—understands in His spirit what all His children bear."

Walk Closer to God

The compassionate Christ "suffers together with" you when the need arises and comforts and strengthens you as you overcome each challenge in your day.

If it is true that misery loves company, it is even more true that suffering needs company.

Rest confidently in the knowledge that your Savior knows what you are going through . . . and He also knows what assistance you need to emerge "more than conqueror" as a result (see Romans 8:37).

*S*haring in the mystery of Christ

"There is nothing concealed that will not be disclosed, or hidden that will not be made known. What I tell you in the dark, speak in the daylight" (Matthew 10:26-27).

*A*s a child of God, you are privileged to know "the secrets of the kingdom of heaven" (Matthew 13:11). And one such mystery is the "mystery of Christ" (Colossians 4:3)—the Good News of eternal life in Him.

F. B. Meyer has these thoughts concerning the rewards and responsibilities of sharing in that mystery.

Walk with F. B. Meyer

"Our Lord is constantly taking us into the dark, that He may tell us His secrets, great and wonderful, eternal and infinite.

"The eye, which has become dazzled by the glare of earth, becomes able to behold the heavenly constellations; and the ear to detect the undertones of His voice, which is often drowned out amid the tumult of earth's strident cries.

"But such revelations always imply a corresponding responsibility—to speak in the light—to proclaim upon the housetops. We are not meant to linger always in the dark, or stay in the closet; presently we shall be summoned to take our place in the rush and storm of life. And when that moment comes, we are to speak and proclaim what we have learned.

"God has a purpose in it all. He has drawn His child to the higher altitudes of fellowship, that he may hear God speaking face to face, and bear the message to his fellows at the mountain foot."

Walk Closer to God

Devotees of mystery novels have been known to stay in dimly lit rooms for days reading volume after volume. But the mystery of Christ is one story that wasn't meant to be kept in obscurity. God has clearly revealed Jesus as the Savior of humankind.

Someone near you is in the dark about the Light of the World, Jesus Christ. You hold the key to dispel that darkness; you have the clues to help that person "solve" the mystery of life. Show a friend the solution today.

*W*orship from the Heart

If you are timid or fearful about your reception when you share your faith, meditate on Christ's instructions to His disciples in Matthew 10. Appropriate His strength and be encouraged with the thought of His ultimate words of commendation: "Whoever acknowledges me before men, I will also acknowledge him before my Father in heaven" (Matthew 10:32).

*W*alk Thru the Word

New Testament Reading
Matthew 10
Old Testament Reading
Deuteronomy 29:29

A yoke designed with comfort in mind

"Take my yoke upon you and learn from me, for I am gentle and humble in heart, and you will find rest for your souls. For my yoke is easy and my burden is light" (Matthew 11:29-30).

*B*easts of burden require "breaking" before they are of any use to their master. In the same way, the Christian must be broken if he is to be of any use to his Master. He must come under the yoke of Christ.

But no one—animal or human being—readily takes to the yoke, bit, or bridle. And yet, all three are designed by the Master to be a blessing, not a burden.

John Chrysostom describes the benefits of a well-yoked life.

Walk with John Chrysostom

"Virtue's yoke is sweet and light. Therefore, do not be afraid or draw back from the yoke but put yourself under it with all forwardness, and then you shall know well the pleasure thereof.

"For it does not bruise your neck at all, but is put on you only to persuade you to walk seemly, and to lead you unto the royal road, and to deliver you from the precipices on either side, and to make you walk with ease in the narrow way.

"Since then so great are its benefits, so great its security, so great its gladness, let us with all our soul and with all our diligence draw this yoke, that we may both here 'find rest for [our] souls,' and attain unto the good things to come."

Walk Closer to God

Wearing the yoke of Christ means that you have Christ for your Guide. And as John Chrysostom says, that can give you a great sense of security that leads not to a burden of work, but to a "burden" of rest.

Anxiety is the by-product of failing to wear His yoke; contentment comes from walking in concert with Him.

Accept His invitation right now to "take [His] yoke upon you." You'll quickly discover which burden is lighter: His yoke or your problems!

It's no contest!

*W*orship from the Heart

By earthly standards Jesus had little to be thankful for in His prayer (Matthew 11:25-26), for He was experiencing rejection and disappointment. But He still rejoiced in God's method: "Yes, Father, for this was your good pleasure." Let the words of Isaiah 55:8 sink into your spirit, and worship today by placing your confidence in God's ways, especially when they differ from your expectations.

*W*alk Thru the Word

New Testament Reading
Matthew 11
Old Testament Reading
Isaiah 53:4-5

He who does the kinsman's part

"For whoever does the will of my Father in heaven is my brother and sister and mother" (Matthew 12:50).

Family. It's been called many things: the natural and fundamental unit of society . . . the nucleus of civilization . . . the bond that can never really be broken. But there is also a "family of faith"—kith and kin in the household of God.

And in a remarkable way, the ties to your spiritual family can be stronger than those to your physical one. Often the fellowship with spiritual kin is sweeter than that of a natural family.

Matthew Henry enumerates the benefits of being members of the family of God.

Walk with Matthew Henry

"Christ's disciples, who had left all to follow Him and embrace His doctrine, were dearer to Him than any kinsmen according to the flesh.

"They had preferred Christ before their own relatives. And now to make amends, and to show that there was no love lost, He preferred them before His relatives.

"All the saints have this honor. All obedient believers are near kin to Jesus Christ. They wear His name, bear His image, have His nature, are of His family. He loves them, freely converses with them as His relations. He bids them welcome to His table, takes care of them, provides for them.

"When He died, He left them rich legacies; now that He is in heaven, He keeps up a correspondence with them, and will have them all with Him at last. He will in nothing fail to do the kinsman's part."

Walk Closer to God

If it is true about families that "blood is thicker than water," how much more binding is the blood of Jesus Christ, that "purifies us from all sin" (1 John 1:7)!

Jesus' blood is a "family tie" that binds you close to your heavenly Father and makes you "heirs of God and co-heirs with Christ" (Romans 8:17).

Think back over your heavenly heritage: "honor . . . name . . . image . . . nature."

Then thank your Father that you can say with the saints of old, "We are family!"

Worship from the Heart

As the Master shapes us as clay in His hands, His imprint should be apparent on our lives. Make Adelaide Pollard's hymn a prayer of dedication:
"Have Thine own way, Lord! / Have Thine own way! / Thou art the Potter, / I am the clay! / Mold me and make me after Thy will, / While I am waiting, / Yielded and still."

Walk Thru the Word

New Testament Reading
Matthew 12
Old Testament Reading
Isaiah 64:8

13

A happy ending in view

"Then the righteous will shine like the sun in the kingdom of their Father" (Matthew 13:43).

*F*or cynics, happy endings can only be found in fairy tales. The end of life, they say, is no better than the beginning or the middle. But these cynics fail to take into account the triumphs of the Christian life. Like the hero riding off into the sunset, the Christian has a happy ending in view.

Peter Abelard, medieval teacher who suffered much for his Lord, looks ahead in this hymn to a happier time.

Walk with Peter Abelard

O what their joy and their glory must be,
Those endless Sabbaths the blessed ones see;
Crown for the valiant, to weary ones rest;
God shall be All, and in all ever blest.

Truly Jerusalem name we that shore,
"Vision of Peace," that brings joy evermore;
Wish and fulfillment can severed be never,
Nor the thing prayed for come short of the prayer.

We, where no trouble distraction can bring,
Safely the anthems of Zion shall sing;
While for Thy grace, Lord, their voices of praise
Thy blessed people shall evermore raise.

Low before Him with our praises we fall,
Of whom, and in whom, and through whom are all;
Of whom, the Father; and through whom, the Son;
In whom, the Spirit; with these ever One.

Walk Closer to God

It's a lift to the spirits when, after a week of cloudy weather, the first sunbeams break through the gloom and drive away the thought of rain.

Much the same will be your arrival in heaven after your years on Planet Earth. The brightness and warmth of God's glory will greet you, a sharp contrast to the troubles of earth.

In the meantime, you have plenty to look forward to. That's reason to join with Abelard in praise to the One who has made a happy ending possible.

*W*orship from the Heart

In heaven we'll experience the fullness of joy in Christ's presence. We'll also enjoy the fellowship of other believers throughout eternity. As you have joyful interaction with fellow Christians today and in your quiet time with the Savior, be sensitive to the fact that this is but a foretaste of what eternity will hold. Praise God for what lies ahead.

*W*alk Thru the Word

New Testament Reading
Matthew 13:1-52
Old Testament Reading
Psalm 16:9-11

But when he saw the wind, he was afraid and, beginning to sink, cried out, "Lord, save me!" (Matthew 14:30).

A cry for help from a child in a swimming pool brings adults running. One dives in fully clothed to snatch the child from danger.

If humans are galvanized into action by a single cry for help, how much more your Father in heaven heeds the cries of His children!

Desperate circumstances tend to produce the sincerest—and shortest—of prayers, as in the case of Peter in Matthew 14. Allow Charles Spurgeon to explain.

Walk with Charles Spurgeon

"Sinking times are praying times with the Lord's servants. Peter neglected prayer at starting upon his adventurous journey. But when he began to sink, his danger made him quick to pray, and his cry—though late—was not too late.

"Short prayers are long enough. There were but three words in the petition that Peter gasped out, but they were sufficient for his purpose. Not length but strength is desirable.

"Our most desperate times are the Lord's opportunities. Immediately a keen sense of danger forces an anxious cry from us which the ear of Jesus hears; and with Him ear and heart go together, and the hand does not linger long.

"At the last moment we appeal to our Master, but His swift hand makes up for our delays by instant and effectual action.

"When we can do nothing, Jesus can do all things; let us enlist His powerful aid upon our side, and all will be well."

Walk Closer to God

No doubt you have turned to the Lord in moments of crisis, just as Peter did. But what about the times when your life was relatively trouble-free?

"Lord, rescue me!" An honest, brief prayer from a child in need.

"Lord, renew me!" An honest, brief prayer you may wish to pray right now. Neither prayer will your Father in heaven ignore.

When short prayers are long enough

Worship from the Heart

David's prayer in Psalm 40:13-17 may remind you of Peter's. Whether danger appears imminent or your life seems trouble-free, "Blessed is the man who makes the Lord his trust" (Psalm 40:4). Praise God today that He is always accessible and ready for you to come to Him in prayer.

Walk Thru the Word

New Testament Reading
Matthew 13:53–14:36
Old Testament Reading
Psalm 40:13-17

*T*he supreme authority on the human heart

*W*orship from the Heart

Sometimes sin goes unconfessed, strangling fellowship with God. No sin is acceptable to Him. If that's where you find yourself right now, use the words of Psalm 51:1-10 as your own heartfelt prayer of confession. Rejoice in the fact that your loving Father is waiting to cleanse your heart.

*W*alk Thru the Word

New Testament Reading
Matthew 15
Old Testament Reading
Psalm 51:1-10

"But the things that come out of the mouth come from the heart, and these make a man 'unclean' " (*Matthew 15:18*).

*A*n amateur detective working on a case correctly anticipated the criminal's moves, and so solved the case. When asked how he knew the criminal mind so well, the clergyman-detective responded, "My own heart is sinful; thus, I knew what the criminal would do."

This fictitious incident illustrates well the point Jesus made about the Pharisees: Internal attitude determines external actions.

Oswald Chambers outlines the argument many people offer to excuse their wicked hearts, and suggests the only genuine solution to the problem.

Walk with Oswald Chambers

"We begin by trusting our ignorance and calling it innocence, by trusting our innocence and calling it purity. And when we hear these rugged statements of our Lord's, we shrink and say: 'But I never felt any of those awful things in my heart.'

"Either Jesus Christ is the supreme authority on the human heart or He is not worth paying attention to. Am I prepared to trust His judgment or do I prefer to trust my innocent ignorance?

"As long as I remain under the refuge of innocence, I am living in a fool's paradise. The only thing that safeguards is the redemption found in Jesus Christ. Purity is too deep down for me to get to naturally; but when the Holy Spirit comes in, He brings into the center of my life the very Spirit that was manifested in the life of Jesus Christ—the Holy Spirit, who is unsullied purity."

Walk Closer to God

Brushing one's teeth and gargling with mouthwash may be as close as many people ever come to getting clean on the inside. But brushing and gargling do not come close to reaching the heart of the problem. Instead, what Jesus prescribes is a "heartwashing"—the cleansing work of the Holy Spirit (Titus 3:5).

And a clean heart is the only cleanliness that can truly lead to godliness!

16

He asked, "Who do you say that I am?" Simon Peter answered, "You are the Christ, the Son of the living God" (Matthew 16:15-16).

*P*ublic opinion concerning Jesus was divided. Some suggested He was John the Baptist or Elijah; others assumed He was Jeremiah or another one of the prophets (16:14). The Pharisees even thought Jesus was in league with Satan.

But the question still confronts every thinking individual today: Who in your estimation is Jesus of Nazareth?

Alexander Maclaren calls attention to the importance of the inquiry.

Walk with Alexander Maclaren

"This Christ has a strange power, after nineteen hundred years, of coming to each of us with the same persistent interrogation. And today, as then, everything depends on the answer we give.

"Many answer by exalted estimates of Him, like these varying replies which ascribed to Him prophetic authority. But they have not understood His own name for Himself, nor comprehended the meaning of His self-revelation, unless they can reply with the full-toned confession of Peter, which sets Him far above and apart from the highest and the holiest.

"He is the Messiah, but He is more than what a Jew meant by that name; He is 'the Son of the living God,' which is a statement not to be watered down.

"True, Peter did not know all which lay in his words. But do we?"

Walk Closer to God

Until you are ready to agree with Peter that Jesus is in fact the Son of the living God, your estimation of Him falls far short of reality. But once you acknowledge Him as Lord, then you will discover the imperative of obeying Him as Lord.

Peter didn't understand the full scope of his own words when he testified of Jesus, "You are the Christ, the Son of the living God." But he started in the right place. The same place you may need to start . . . right now.

Who do you say Jesus is?

Worship from the Heart

Praise God for so clearly setting forth the principles of His kingdom and the laws of life. As you read Matthew 16: 24-26, ponder the principle that we save by losing and we lose by saving. Praise God for the comforting knowledge that if you love Him with your entire being and put Him and His concerns first, you will not lose in the end, but will receive great gain.

Walk Thru the Word

New Testament Reading
Matthew 16
Old Testament Reading
Daniel 2:19-23

17

In holy harmony

Just then there appeared before them Moses and Elijah, talking with Jesus (Matthew 17:3).

*I*f a 20th-century historian could spend an hour with George Washington . . . or a writer with Shakespeare . . . or a painter with Michelangelo . . . the odds are good he wouldn't talk about the weather!

On the Mount of Transfiguration, Jesus met briefly with Moses and Elijah. Their conversation revolved around Jesus' impending sacrifice (Luke 9:31), a subject of eternal significance.

Listen as F. B. Meyer reviews the great subjects discussed that day.

Walk with F. B. Meyer

"They 'spoke about his departure [decease], which he was about to bring to fulfillment at Jerusalem.'

"Moses would remind Him that if as God's Lamb He must die, He would thus redeem countless myriads. Elijah would dwell on the glory that accrues to the Father.

"These thoughts were certainly familiar to the mind of our blessed Master, yet they must have gladdened and strengthened Him, as they fell from other lips: the more so when they conversed about the splendor of the resurrection morning that would follow His death.

"And what greater subjects could there have been than His wondrous death and His glorious resurrection? Here the travail of creation meets with its answer and key.

"We must often climb the mountain of transfiguration in holy reverie; for the nearer we get to the cross, the closer we shall come into the center of things and the deeper will be our harmony with ourselves and with God Himself."

Walk Closer to God

It has been well said, "What makes individuals great is their ability to decide what is truly important, and then to focus all their attention on that."

Dwelling on Christ's death and resurrection is one good way to cultivate a heart for God. And when you do, you'll be in good company!

Worship from the Heart

As Jesus instructed His disciples about His death and resur-rection, they couldn't comprehend and were "filled with grief." Think quietly about the times you don't quite understand how or why God is leading you in an uncharted direction or is placing you in a dark circumstance. Praise Him for toler-ating your human-ness in the dark, doubting times; then rejoice that the Resurrection enables all believers to look to Jesus, the Light.

Walk Thru the Word

New Testament Reading
Matthew 17
Old Testament Reading
Exodus 25:21-22

18

Then Peter came to Jesus and asked, "Lord, how many times shall I forgive my brother when he sins against me? Up to seven times?" Jesus answered, "I tell you, not seven times, but seventy-seven times" (Matthew 18:21-22).

*F*orgive and forget. Peter was certainly comfortable with that principle. After all, hadn't Jesus taught him already that if he forgave others when they sinned against him his heavenly Father would also forgive him? And hadn't the sacrificial system he had grown up with taught him that God forgives the sins of His people?

Yes, Peter was certainly comfortable with forgiveness—seven times. But seventy-seven times?

Unfortunately, all of us are like Peter in this respect—all except one. John Flavel reminds us to imitate Him who is infinite forgiveness.

Walk with John Flavel

"Labor for meek forgiving spirits. I shall propose two reasons for doing so: for the honor of Christ, and for your own peace. His glory is more than your life, and all that you enjoy in this world. Oh, do not expose it to the scorn and derision of His enemies. Let them not say, 'How is Christ a lamb, when His followers are lions? How is the church a dove, that smites and scratches like a bird of prey?'

"Consider also the quiet of your own heart. What comfort can you have in all that you possess in the world as long as you do not have possession of your own soul? If inside you are full of tumult and revenge, the Spirit of Christ will become a stranger to you; that Dove delights in a clean and quiet heart. Oh, then imitate Christ in this excellency also!"

Walk Closer to God

The rest of the chapter is the parable of the unmerciful servant who refused to forgive as he had been forgiven. Note that he was "turned . . . over to the jailers to be tortured" (Matthew 18:34).

Are you "tortured" by an unforgiving spirit? Ephesians 4:32 has the answer: Meditate on Christ's forgiveness. There is no better way to cultivate your own.

*G*od forgave my sin in Jesus' name

*W*orship from the Heart

If you don't forgive people who have hurt you, bitterness can quickly take root in your life, causing great harm. Ask the Holy Spirit to reveal any area of bitterness in your life. Are you willing to forgive those who caused the hurt? God will give you the grace to forgive—but the desire and the actual act of forgiving can only come from you, a step of obedience and faith.

*W*alk Thru the Word

New Testament Reading
Matthew 18
Old Testament Reading
1 Samuel 26:1-12

19

Putting allegiance in all the wrong places

"It is easier for a camel to go through the eye of a needle than for a rich man to enter the kingdom of God" (Matthew 19:24).

If this life is but a pilgrimage of a few short years when compared to eternity, the question remains: Why carry so much along if you can't take it with you?

In chapter 19, Jesus exhorts the rich young man to lighten his load, but his attachment to material wealth is too strong.

John Wesley examines the subtle shift of allegiance that can—and frequently does—take place when wealth is present.

Walk with John Wesley

"From atheism there is an easy transition to idolatry; from the worship of no God to the worship of false gods. In fact, a person who does not love God will instead love some of God's works; he will love the creature, not the Creator.

"But to how many species of idolatry is every rich man exposed! What continual and almost insurmountable temptations is he under to 'love the world' in all its branches—'the desire of the flesh, the lust of the eyes, and the pride of life.' What innumerable temptations will he find to gratify the 'lusts of the flesh'!

"Understand this correctly. It does not refer to one only, but to all the outward senses. It is equal idolatry to seek our happiness in gratifying any or all of these."

Walk Closer to God

The rich young man was not guilty of sensational sins, such as murder or adultery or robbery. The command he tripped over was the first: "You shall have no other gods before me" (Exodus 20:3). His gold had become his god and he was not willing to give up his idolatry.

Many today follow in his tragic footsteps—people whose lives are just comfortable enough to draw attention away from eternal concerns.

Are you like that? Then you dare not miss the disciples' question in 19:25, "Who then can be saved?" or Jesus' answer in 19:26, "With God all things are possible."

Worship from the Heart

It's evident from this chapter that concern for children is a priority in God's kingdom. Mentally list the children and young people whose lives touch yours in some way and praise God for the simplicity, trust, and sincerity in the life of each one. Thank Him for the joy these children add to your life as you lift each of them before Him in prayer.

Walk Thru the Word

New Testament Reading
Matthew 19
Old Testament Reading
Deuteronomy 6:10-13

*C*lay doesn't argue with the potter

"Don't I have the right to do what I want with my own money? Or are you envious because I am generous?" (Matthew 20:15).

*O*ur world bears an invisible mark of owner-ship that reads, "Property of Jesus Christ."

Why? Because "by him all things were created" (Colossians 1:16). He has rights of ownership and has the last word about how His property is used. But it's easy to forget that fact, as the laborers learned in Matthew 20.

Matthew Henry offers these profound observations about God's authority.

Walk with Matthew Henry

"God is the owner of all good; His right in it is absolute, sovereign, and unlimited. So He may give or withhold His blessings as He pleases.

"What we have is not our own, and therefore it is not lawful for us to do what we will with it; but what God has is His own.

"When God takes from us that which was dear to us, we must silence our discontent with this thought: May He not do what He will with His own? He has taken away, but He originally gave. It is not for such depending creatures as we are to quarrel with our Sovereign.

"There is a counsel in every will of God, and what seems to us to be done arbitrarily will appear at length to have been done wisely.

"But God is sovereign over all and may do what He will with His own. This is enough to silence all murmurers and objectors. We are in His hand as clay in the hands of a potter; and it is not for us to advise Him or argue with Him."

Walk Closer to God

For those who presume to question the Creator of the universe, God has a penetrating question: "Where were you when I laid the earth's foundation?" (Job 38:4).

Rather, come humbly before your Creator God acknowledging, "Father, I am Yours. You know best. Use me as You will."

Then rest assured the Potter is well able to fashion the clay for His intended purpose.

*W*orship from the Heart

The crowd was unresponsive when the blind men cried for mercy, but Jesus stopped and granted their request (vv. 30-34). Reflect on times when your feelings of compassion have been modified or sub-dued by the crowd you were with. May such reflections lead you to praise God for His unfailing kind-ness and for His mercy which reached you even while you sat blind and hope-less in the darkness of sin.

*W*alk Thru the Word

New Testament Reading
Matthew 20
Old Testament Reading
Psalm 24

21

*T*he ministry of mercy and judgment

Seeing a fig tree by the road, he went up to it but found nothing on it. . . he said to it, "May you never bear fruit again!" Immediately the tree withered (Matthew 21:19).

*W*hen Jesus cursed a fig tree and caused it to wither because it bore no fruit, His action seemed out of character . . . impulsive . . . hard to explain. But when you probe beneath the surface you discover the incident is no mere temper tantrum, but a stern warning for Christians of all generations. G. Campbell Morgan explains.

Walk with G. Campbell Morgan

"Christ's ministry of mercy merges into that of judgment when individuals refuse to submit themselves to His mercy. Of course, this is to recognize and to abide by the truth of man's responsibility.

"Christ seeks to provoke men and women to fruit-bearing for the satisfaction of God. He comes seeking righteousness. He comes to make it possible for men and women to live the life of judgment and righteousness. But if a person refuses, the ministry of Jesus is intended not merely to be a ministry of pity, but a ministry that provokes us to the realization of God's underlying purpose for us. To imagine that He came simply to plead for pity upon those who fail is false to the whole teaching of the New Testament.

"He came to reveal sin to be what it is: active, willful, definite, positive rebellion against God. And He came to deal with men and women, so that their wills should be turned in the direction of the will of God."

Walk Closer to God

Have you ever wondered, "Why did God create me . . . and send His Son to die for me?"

Look no further than Jesus' own words: "You did not choose me, but I chose you and appointed you to go and bear fruit—fruit that will last" (John 15:16).

Fruit-bearing is not an option; it is the very reason you were created (Ephesians 2:10).

You have experienced God's power in your life; are you fulfilling God's purpose for your life?

*W*orship from the Heart

The chief priests and the scribes, not able to see the sin and hypocrisy in their own lives, became indignant at the praises of the children (vv. 15-16). They protested rather than praised. Picture yourself as a child in the presence of the King. Your duty today is to recite Psalm 8 aloud to Him. Do that now, and let your heart and voice swell with the excitement of praise.

*W*alk Thru the Word

New Testament Reading
Matthew 21
Old Testament Reading
Psalm 8

"A king . . . prepared a wedding banquet for his son. He sent His servants to those who had been invited . . . but they paid no attention and went off" (Matthew 22:2-3, 5).

*I*n Matthew 22 Jesus compares the kingdom of heaven to a wedding feast. But the invited guests do not attend; they have more important things to do . . . things they consider more "worthy" of their time.

But as Richard Baxter shows, they are only deluding themselves.

Walk with Richard Baxter

"It is a most lamentable thing to see how most people spend their time and their energy for trifles, while God is cast aside. He who is all seems to them as nothing, and that which is nothing seems to them as good as all.

"It is lamentable indeed, knowing that God has set mankind in such a race where heaven or hell is their certain end, that they should sit down and loiter, or run after the childish toys of the world, forgetting the prize they should run for.

"Were it but possible for one of us to see this business as the all-seeing God does, and see what most men and women in the world are interested in and what they are doing every day, it would be the saddest sight imaginable. Oh, how we should marvel at their madness and lament their self-delusion!

"If God had never told them what they were sent into the world to do, or what was before them in another world, then there would have been some excuse. But it is His sealed word, and they profess to believe it."

Walk Closer to God

You will always have time for what is most important to you. Employment . . . investments . . . recreational pursuits . . . relationships with family and friends . . . a growing walk with God.

You may offer excuses or fill your schedule with matters of secondary importance. But in the end, the real loser is you.

The business of heaven is serious business. Do you have the time to "be about it" today?

Worship from the Heart

"Father, I know that no human life remains untouched by grief at some time. I praise You now for the liberating, comforting knowledge that You are 'not the God of the dead, but of the living.' I thank You for my loved ones who are already in Your presence and for all those we will fellowship with in eternity. In the name of the risen Lord, Amen."

Walk Thru the Word

New Testament Reading
Matthew 22
Old Testament Reading
Hosea 9:17

Dwight L. Moody (1837-1899) Giver of the Gospel

*I*n the latter part of the nineteenth century, revivals occurred on both sides of the Atlantic. And, more than any other person, the man responsible for the success of those revivals was a former shoe salesman whose formal education ended at the age of thirteen. The accomplishments of Dwight L. Moody show the faithfulness of God at work in an obscure but dedicated servant.

Born in 1837 in Northfield, Massachusetts, Dwight Moody's early years were marked by hardship. His father died suddenly when Moody was only four years old, leaving his mother to raise nine children. In his late teens, Moody left home to work for his uncle in Boston as a shoe salesman.

Moody demonstrated one remarkable quality: an abundance of energy. He could—and often did—work long hours. While in Boston, he became involved in a church where he was led to a saving knowledge of Christ by his Sunday school teacher.

Moving on to Chicago, Moody excelled as a shoe salesman while at the same time devoting himself more and more to church activities. He began a Sunday school class that soon had over 1,500 children attending. By the outbreak of the Civil War, Moody had decided to forsake shoe-selling for soul-winning; he was twenty-three years old.

During the Civil War, Moody ministered to the soldiers and was involved in the Y.M.C.A., becoming its president in 1865.

Widely sought as a preacher and evangelist, Moody never completed his formal education and was never ordained.

A trip to England in 1873 marked the beginning of several highly visible and successful evangelistic speaking tours on both sides of the Atlantic. It is estimated that during his lifetime Moody traveled over one million miles, preached to more than one hundred million people, and counseled over seven hundred thousand men and women—all before the invention of the airplane or television! He continued his evangelistic efforts until his death in 1899 at the age of sixty-two.

Moody did much more than travel and preach. He began several schools to provide for others the education he never received, the best-known being Moody Bible Institute (founded as the Chicago Evangelization Society). He started a book service to provide low-cost Christian literature. Whatever he did, Dwight Moody threw himself into the endeavor with all his energy and enthusiasm.

Moody's heart for ministry is a model for the twentieth century. His sermons were filled with vivid illustrations and fast-paced stories that helped clarify and apply spiritual truths. He not only evangelized, but he encouraged countless others to do the same. He stressed the love of God in his gospel preaching. Some preachers said that he was the only man who had the right to preach about hell, because he shed tears every time he mentioned the word. Though he didn't live to see the twentieth century, Moody's influence is perhaps more extensive today than it was during his lifetime.

Uneducated but enthusiastic, Dwight Moody touched two continents for God. Let his life encourage you to seek ways you can spread the good news of God's redeeming love in the lives you touch every day.

A Lesson from the life of

Dwight L. Moody

By sharing the gospel in an enthusiastic and loving way, I can touch others for Jesus Christ.

*H*ealer of the broken-hearted

"O Jerusalem, Jerusalem . . . how often I have longed to gather your children together . . . but you were not willing" (Matthew 23:37).

*W*onder adhesives. Miracles glues. With all of our twentieth-century know-how, you'd think we could fix anything. But science has yet to discover a product strong enough to mend a broken heart.

For that you'll have to go to the Savior who specializes in such matters.

He's the one who, in the final days of His life on earth, surveyed the city of Jerusalem . . . and what He saw made Him weep.

Evangelist Dwight L. Moody offers some thoughts about the Savior's tears.

Walk with Dwight L. Moody

"From Adam's day to ours, tears have been shed, and a wail has gone up from the broken-hearted.

"And it is a mystery to me how all those broken hearts can keep away from Him who has come to heal them.

"Jesus often looked up to heaven and sighed. I believe it was because of so much suffering around Him.

"It was on His right and on His left—everywhere on earth. And the thought that He had come to relieve the people of their burdens, yet so few would accept Him, made Him sorrowful.

"Do you think there is a heart so broken that it can't be healed by Him? He can heal them all. But the great trouble is that people won't come."

Walk Closer to God

Jesus wept over a city. Not for its buildings, but for its people. People like you—with broken hearts and broken spirits. People in need of repentance and repair.

Though He wept, He can tenderly wipe the tears from your eyes. For He is the mighty physician, capable of healing every wounded heart brought to Him. But you must be willing to put yourself under His care. He has so much to give. But so few are willing to receive. Let those few include you.

*W*orship from the Heart

In compassion and love, the Savior has swung the door of grace widely open. One moment you were outside; the next moment you were inside. Ponder what that open door has meant to you since you became a Christian. Rejoice that Jesus is the Door of the sheepfold.

*W*alk Thru the Word

New Testament Reading
Matthew 23
Old Testament Reading
Exodus 34:6-7

"Therefore keep watch, because you do not know on what day your Lord will come" (Matthew 24:42).

$\mathcal{S}$ome events bring sudden, unexpected, surprising joy; others are enjoyable only when you have advance notice.

In Matthew 24 Jesus gives all the advance notice you will ever need to get ready for His return.

John Calvin highlights some of the appropriate preparations every alert Christian makes in anticipation of that day.

Walk with John Calvin

"Matthew says: 'Keep watch.' Luke is more particular: 'Be careful, or your hearts will be weighed down with . . . the anxieties of life.'

"Anyone who lives intemperately and has his senses swamped with food and wine will never think of heaven. As there is no desire of the flesh that does not intoxicate a person, we must attend to all these and not sink into the world if we want to make haste to the kingdom of Christ.

"Note that the uncertainty of the time of Christ's coming ought to be a stimulus to our attention and watchfulness. God deliberately wished it kept hidden from us, that we should never be so carefree as to neglect our unbroken lookout."

Walk Closer to God

In Matthew 25:1-13, Jesus tells a parable about being ready for His return. Heed His warning and you will be able to sing with the hymn writer:

> *Rejoice, rejoice, believers,*
> *And let your lights appear;*
> *The evening is advancing,*
> *And darker night is near.*
>
> *See that your lamps are burning;*
> *Replenish them with oil;*
> *And wait for your salvation,*
> *The end of earthly toil.*
>
> *The watchers on the mountain*
> *Proclaim the Bridegroom near,*
> *Go meet Him as He cometh,*
> *With alleluias clear.*

*B*eing alert for Christ's return

*W*orship from the Heart

Regardless of your view of when the second coming of Christ will occur, the indisputable fact is this: Jesus will come again. Make these words of Charles Wesley your song of praise today: "Lo, He comes with clouds descending,/ Once for favored sinners slain;/ All the many saints attending/ Swell the triumph of His train:/ Alleluia! Alleluia!/ God appears on earth to reign."

*W*alk Thru the Word

New Testament Reading
Matthew 24
Old Testament Reading
Deuteronomy 4:9

The certainty of His coming

"Therefore keep watch, because you do not know the day or the hour" (Matthew 25:13).

Q uestion: What do defeated politicians and slumping athletes have in common?

Answer: "Don't worry, I'll be back."

Some do in fact recapture success. But for many more, their comeback is only a wishful dream.

Jesus also promised a "comeback," and He made good on His promise when He rose from the dead. But His second "comeback" is now a 2,000-year-old promise. However, G. Campbell Morgan makes it clear that there's no reason to give up hope.

Walk with G. Campbell Morgan

"That Jesus Christ is coming again He plainly declared, and all the New Testament writers affirmed the truth. That certainty falls upon all the darkness of the processes through which the victory of the kingdom of God is to be won.

"Nothing will be completed until He comes, but everything is working to that consummation. Nothing is more explicit in His references to that glorious end than the declaration that the day and hour are not revealed.

"The hiding of that time is part of the divine counsel. To seek to discover it is to attempt to be wiser than our Lord intends that we should be. Our attitude is to be that of those who watch. To know the day or the hour would make watching largely unnecessary, and this would rob us of that alertness which is the very essence of true discipleship.

"Knowing beforehand both the strangeness of the period of our waiting, and the certainty of His coming, we are to be so occupied about His business that when He comes we shall be neither surprised nor ashamed."

Walk Closer to God

You do not know the day of Christ's return, but you do know how He wants you to live each day.

Knowing Him. Serving Him. Keeping His commands. There's plenty to keep you busy in the Master's work. The wait will seem shorter when you have much to do between now and then.

Worship from the Heart

Though some rabbis thought Scripture spoke of two Messiahs, the truth is that one Messiah would come twice. He came the first time to die for the sins of mankind; He will come a second time to reign as King. He kept His promise the first time. Without doubt He will keep His second promise as well. Rejoice!

Walk Thru the Word

New Testament Reading
Matthew 25:1-30
Old Testament Reading
Jeremiah 23:5-6

"Then they will go away to eternal punishment, but the righteous to eternal life" (Matthew 25:46).

*E*verlasting punishment is the penalty for failing to do what is right in the sight of God. It is the result of—not the remedy for—falling short of God's glory.

But God has provided a path to peace through personal faith in His Son, Jesus Christ. But only you can choose that path, as Jonathan Edwards explains.

Walk with Jonathan Edwards

"That you may escape the dreadful and eternal torments, you must embrace Him who came into the world for the purpose of saving sinners from such torments. He alone has paid the whole debt due to the divine law, and has exhausted eternal sufferings.

"What great encouragement it is that you are exposed to eternal punishment, that there is a Savior provided who offers to save you from that punishment, and that He will do it in a way which is perfectly in keeping with the glory of God. In fact, it is more to the glory of God than it would be if you should suffer the eternal punishment of hell.

"Those who are sent to hell will never pay the whole of the debt which they owe to God. Justice can never be actually satisfied in their damnation; but it is satisfied in Christ. Therefore He is accepted of the Father, and all who believe are accepted and justified in Him."

Walk Closer to God

The course of your life is determined by the choice you make in life—a choice centering around the person of Jesus Christ.

You can ignore Him, or embrace Him. But you cannot avoid Him . . . or the consequences of your choice.

Jonathan Edwards preached eloquently of the horrors of hell because he realized what was at stake in the lives of his listeners.

If you haven't as yet realized what is at stake in your own life, "be entreated to flee and embrace Him."

The choice that determines the course of life

Worship from the Heart

One truth embedded in the parable of the talents is this: We are responsible for what we have, not for what we don't have. Honestly assess the talents God has given you, whether they are in the form of money, power, position, or abilities. Humbly thank God for trusting you with each "talent" and thank Him also for the knowledge that each one can be invested in His kingdom.

Walk Thru the Word

New Testament Reading
Matthew 25:31-46
Old Testament Reading
Malachi 4

29

S haring the burden of another's soul

"My Father, if it is possible, may this cup be taken from me. Yet not as I will, but as you will" (Matthew 26:39).

Never be afraid to do what God tells you to do—it's always good.

But be certain your will is in neutral first so that God can shift it.

After enjoying a last meal with His disciples, Jesus made His way to the Garden of Gethsemane. He went, not to relax, but to wrestle in prayer. Not to while away the moments, but to urge His disciples to watch with Him in prayer.

Alfred Edersheim provides insight into the struggles of the Savior just before His death.

Walk with Alfred Edersheim

"Alone, as in His first conflict with the evil one in the wilderness, the Savior entered into the last contest. On His knees, prostrate, His agony began. His prayer was that—if it were possible—the hour might pass away from Him.

"Fallen man is born with the taste of death in his soul. Not so Christ. It was He who had no experience of it. His going into death was His final conflict with Satan for man, and on man's behalf.

"At the close of that hour His sweat—mingled with blood—fell in great drops on the ground. And while He lay in prayer, the disciples lay in sleep."

Walk Closer to God

Christ yearned for support in prayer during His darkest hour.

It's possible—even probable—that someone near you is wrestling in prayer to discover God's will or overcome the Enemy. That person knows the way ahead may be painful, yet he yearns to do God's will. But the battle for his will is raging and the issue is undecided.

You can slumber indifferently, like the disciples. Or you can kneel at that person's side and share his or her burden. That's one of the privileges—and the responsibilities—of being a brother or a sister in Christ. Someone near you is struggling. Wake up. Move alongside. Pray.

Worship from the Heart

Come to the Father today with the burdens of your family members, friends, and co-workers.
As you know their situations and the hardships they face, lift each of them before God in prayer. Praise Him for the opportunities you have to encourage and minister to them.

Walk Thru the Word

New Testament Reading
Matthew 26:1-46
Old Testament Reading
Job 1:21

Turning tears of guilt into tears of joy

Then Peter remembered the word Jesus had spoken: "Before the rooster crows, you will disown me three times." And he went outside and wept bitterly (Matthew 26:75).

*Y*ou have failed someone who was counting on you. Guilt is written all over your face. You lower your head in shame and remorse.

Guilty! That's the unspoken verdict for many individuals who have faced failure in the service of the Lord. But as the apostle Peter discovered and Hannah Whitall Smith describes, God's forgiveness is as near as a prayer.

Walk with Hannah Whitall Smith

"A little girl once asked if the Lord Jesus always forgave us for our sins as soon as we asked Him, and I had said, 'Yes, of course He does.'

" 'Just as soon?' she repeated doubtfully. 'Yes,' I replied, 'the minute we ask, He forgives us.'

" 'Well, I cannot believe that,' she replied deliberately. 'I should think He would make us feel sorry for two or three days first. And then I think He would make us ask Him a great many times, and not just in common talk. And I believe that is the way He does, and you need not try to make me think He forgives me right at once, no matter what the Bible says.'

"She only said what many Christians think, and what is worse, what a great many Christians act on, for then the emotions of discouragement and remorse make them feel further from God than their sin would have done."

Walk Closer to God

When you can no longer lift guilty eyes to God, you can rest assured God is still looking at you. Not with the peeved expression of an irritated parent, but with compassion, tenderness, and unfailing love.

When you least expect Him to forgive, He reaches out in grace—reminding you that you are His own . . . wiping away the tears of remorse . . . encouraging you to try again.

If your eyes are clouded with tears of guilt and failure today, run to your Father's waiting arms. He's ready to turn your weeping into tears of joy.

Worship from the Heart

"Father, sometimes I'm like the little girl in this story— doubtful that You really forgive me right away, as soon as I ask. Increase my faith in Your loving forgiveness, extended to me through Your Son, Jesus, my Savior. Amen."

Walk Thru the Word

New Testament Reading
Matthew 26:47-75
Old Testament Reading
Ezra 9:1-5

*F*orgiveness: yours for the asking

"I have sinned," [Judas] said, "for I have betrayed innocent blood." . . . So Judas threw the money into the temple and left. Then he went away and hanged himself (Matthew 27:4-5).

*A*fter a particularly embarrassing moment, the thought might cross your mind: "I wish I could just die."

It's a thought you really don't mean. But for Judas, knowing that he had betrayed the Lord so filled him with remorse that he sought escape through death. Rather than seek forgiveness and a new start, Judas decided to give up and end his own life.

The special circumstances of Judas's life and death provide lessons you can profit from. Alexander Maclaren shares his thoughts on the nature of sin and forgiveness.

Walk with Alexander Maclaren

"I do not suppose that Judas was lost because he betrayed Jesus Christ, but because, having betrayed Jesus Christ, he never asked to be forgiven.

"I pray you to learn this lesson: You cannot think too blackly of your own sins, but you may think too exclusively of them; and if you do, they will drive you to madness of despair.

"My dear friend, there is no remorse which is deep enough for the smallest transgression; but there is no transgression which is so great but that forgiveness for it may come. And we may have it for the asking, if we will go to that dear Christ who died for us.

"If Judas died without hope and pardon, it was not because his crime was too great for forgiveness, but because the forgiveness had never been asked."

Walk Closer to God

Judas could not forgive himself. But God could. "[God] does not treat us as our sins deserve or repay us according to our iniquities. . . . as far as the east is from the west, so far has he removed our transgressions from us" (Psalm 103:10, 12).

Forgiveness is yours for the asking when you take God at His word.

*W*orship from the Heart

Judas died in misery. David, on the other hand, confessed his sin and went on to write many psalms of praise. Be a David today! Confess your sin and continue, cleansed and rejoicing, in your walk with God. His forgiveness is one of the greatest treasures you can have. And your willingness to forgive others for their offenses is one of the most powerful forces in the kingdom of God.

*W*alk Thru the Word

New Testament Reading
Matthew 27:1-31
Old Testament Reading
Psalm 32:1-5

When they had crucified him . . . they kept watch over him there (Matthew 27:35-36).

*T*he Roman soldiers who crucified Christ had become accustomed to the grisly ordeal. No doubt they had attended to many such executions.

To them, Jesus was no different from other criminals or political prisoners. They could sit down and watch Him die with calm, professional detachment. All in a day's work.

But it was to be a day—and a crucifixion—unique in history. Alexander Maclaren paints a word picture of the Cross of Calvary.

Walk with Alexander Maclaren

"How possible it is to look at Christ's sufferings and see nothing! The rude legionnaires gazed for hours on what has touched the world ever since, and saw nothing but a dying Jew. They thought about the worth of the clothes, about how long they would have to stay there.

"In the presence of the most stupendous fact in the world's history, they were all unmoved.

"We too may gaze on the Cross and see nothing. We too may look at it without emotion, because we are without faith, or any consciousness of what it may mean for us.

"Only they who see there the sacrifice for their sins see what is really there. Others are as blind as, and less excusable than, these soldiers who watched all day by the Cross seeing nothing, and tramped back to their barracks at night utterly ignorant of what they had been doing."

Walk Closer to God

It's hard to be deeply moved by words that are comfortably familiar. But now relive the awful events history records as "Good Friday."

Six hours of excruciating agony. Abuses hurled from onlookers. Forsaken by God. Abandoned by friends. A death totally undeserved . . . for sinners totally undeserving.

Gaze at the Cross with eyes of gratitude, and you—like the centurion—will respond, "Surely he was the Son of God!" (Matthew 27:54).

To say anything less is to have closed the eyes of your heart and seen nothing at all.

*W*hat do you see when you look at the Cross?

*W*orship from the Heart

When you next worship with other believers be mindful of the events surrounding the Crucifixion. Praise God that because of Jesus' willing sacrifice, Satan's apparent triumph was actually his defeat, and that Christ's "defeat" was actually His victory—and yours!

*W*alk Thru the Word

New Testament Reading
Matthew 27:32-66
Old Testament Reading
Amos 6:1-6

*D*eclare His glory, proclaim His wonders

*W*orship from the Heart

As you absorb the meaning of Matthew 28:11-15 and Acts 6:7, praise God that every attempt to disprove or discredit the resurrection of Jesus Christ has been futile. Beginning with the fact that He is your risen, living Lord, praise Him now for six other aspects of Jesus you've seen as you've studied the book of Matthew.

*W*alk Thru the Word

New Testament Reading
Matthew 28
Old Testament Reading
Psalm 96:1-5

"All authority in heaven and on earth has been given to me. Therefore go and make disciples of all nations" (Matthew 28:18-19).

*M*atthew 28:18-20 puts great authority at the disposal of Christ's disciples. *But notice who holds the power!* "All authority is given to me."

When you have Jesus, you have the powerful promise of His abiding presence. And along with that power comes the responsibility to use it the way *He* intended. Oswald Chambers offers these challenging words on using God's power properly.

Walk with Oswald Chambers

"When the disciples returned from their first mission, they were filled with joy because the demons were subject to them, but Jesus said, 'Don't rejoice in successful service; the great secret of joy is that you are rightly related to Me.'

"The great essential for the Christian is to remain true to God's call, and realize that his one purpose is to disciple men and women to Jesus.

"The believer's challenge doesn't come because people are difficult to get saved, or that backsliders erect barriers of callous indifference. Instead, the challenge is along the line of his own personal relationship to Jesus Christ: Do I know my risen Lord? Do I know the power of His indwelling Spirit? Am I wise enough in God's sight to base my life on what Jesus Christ has said?

"If I take up any other method or motive, I depart altogether from the methods laid down by our Lord—'All authority has been given to me . . . Therefore go.' "

Walk Closer to God

As you think back over Matthew's gospel, take a moment to catalog all you have learned:

Your *relationship:* You are a child of the King.

Your *authority:* Nothing less than the power of the resurrected Lord.

Your *responsibility:* To spread the news that men and women can become a part of His family.

Your *challenge:* To know and make known your risen Lord.

Your *response:* _____ .

34

In the Savior's School of Servanthood

Mark shows us that the call to service is rarely a call to convenience.

Mark, the shortest and simplest of the four Gospels, provides a vivid, action-packed account of the life of Jesus Christ. Names and places change rapidly, and Mark keeps the account brisk by using words like "immediately" and "at once" more than forty times. Just when you think you've caught up with the Savior, He moves on again.

Writing to a Roman audience, Mark presents Jesus primarily as a servant, who ministers first as a servant to the crowds (Mark 1–7), then as a servant to the disciples (Mark 8–10), and finally as a servant to all humanity by giving His life as a ransom (Mark 11–16; see especially 10:45). In the final analysis, however, Jesus was a servant of His heavenly Father, sent forth to do His will.

The call to service is rarely a call to convenience, and Jesus' life of servanthood was not easy. Note how Isaiah describes the role of the Servant-Messiah centuries before Jesus' birth (Isaiah 52:13–53:12). Mark frequently describes the difficult life of the servant. You'll see Jesus interrupted as He spends time in prayer. You'll feel the eager crowds pressing in to tap His power. You'll sense His compassion for those in need and His anger at those using traditions as an excuse to avoid serving others. And you'll sense His resolute commitment to face the cross in spite of its agony and shame. Truly Jesus is the supreme model of servanthood.

Your call as a disciple is likewise a call to servanthood. Do you place your Master's will ahead of your own? Does your heart respond with compassion at the sight of needy people? Do your actions speak louder than words? Active, compassionate, obedient service to the Master—that's your joyful privilege today and every day. Are you ready to enter the Savior's school of servanthood?

Follow faithfully to be used fully

At once they left their nets and followed him (Mark 1:18).

"Come, follow me," Jesus said, " and I will make you fishers of men" (1:17).

When Peter, Andrew, James, and John heard Jesus' call, their response was immediate. And after meeting the Master, their employment and interests would never be the same.

H. A. Ironside reminds us that the Lord calls different people to different tasks.

Walk with H. A. Ironside

"The Lord called the four fishermen to become fishers of men. He saw they were expert at and diligent in their work on the Sea of Galilee, and He called and equipped them for higher and nobler service.

"They turned from whatever they had in the way of earthly prospects, and He made them valiant and competent workmen in the great task of winning souls to Himself.

"We are not to conclude from this that all who follow the Lord Jesus Christ will become great soul-winners. Some are called to serve in a much humbler capacity.

"But each one is called to serve in whatever place the Lord puts him, even if it is only to suffer for His sake. All can participate in the ministry of prayer and thereby be a real help to those to whom is committed the preaching of the Word.

"We may be assured that all who follow Him faithfully will be used of Him in some way that would not be true otherwise."

Walk Closer to God

The attitude God wants you to exhibit is one of delight in His calling—regardless of the assignment He gives.

Not complaining.

Not comparing.

Simply consenting to the task He has set before you—whatever it may be.

Learn a lesson from these fishers of fish who became fishers of men. When Christ calls you by name, rest assured He has made no mistake.

Worship from the Heart

Satan is malicious and determined to destroy. As he did with Jesus, he will suggest appealing courses of action that are not in line with God's will. Praise God that though you have an Enemy, you also have an Advocate (1 John 2:1) and that God will "not let you be tempted beyond what you can bear. But when you are tempted, he will also provide a way out so that you can stand up under it" (1 Corinthians 10:13).

Walk Thru the Word

New Testament Reading
Mark 1:1-20
Old Testament Reading
1 Samuel 3:1-10

No other guarantee needed

The people were amazed at his teaching, because he taught them as one who had authority, not as the teachers of the law (Mark 1:22).

*I*n straightforward language, Mark relates all that transpired in one remarkable day in Capernaum.

Notice how the people responded: They were astonished and amazed. Some questioned; others spread Jesus' fame.

Notice too how Jesus accomplished it all; He taught, rebuked, commanded, healed, ministered, and moved with authority.

Alexander Maclaren profiles the most authoritative Teacher the world has ever known.

Walk with Alexander Maclaren

"Christ quoted no one. He spoke of His own authority: 'Yes, I say to you.'

"Other teachers explained the law; He is the Law-giver. Others drew more or less pure waters from cisterns; He is in Himself a well of water from which all may draw.

"He does not argue; He affirms. He seeks no support from others' teachings; He alone is sufficient for us. He not only speaks the truth, which needs no other confirmation than His own lips, but He is Himself the truth.

"We may canvass other people's teachings and distinguish their insights from their errors; we have but to accept His. He teaches all ages, including our own, with authority.

"The guarantee for the truth of His teaching is Himself. 'Yes, yes, I say to you.' No other man has a right to say that."

Walk Closer to God

Jesus spoke with authority. God is His Father, and the words He spoke were none other than the very words of God.

Some—such as the scribes—attacked His authority; others—such as the disciples—bowed before it. Some listened and obeyed; others listened and turned away.

All who have heard the teachings of Jesus have had to make their choice regarding His authority; you must make yours.

Worship from the Heart

When the leper implored Jesus to help him, Jesus responded, "I am willing." No less responsive to our pleas, Jesus still is willing to heal those separated from God by sin; to restore those cut off from family and friends by bitterness and anger; to comfort those who are lonely and depressed by circumstances. As you hold your arms up to Him today, praise Him that He is always willing to receive you.

Walk Thru the Word

New Testament Reading
Mark 1:21-45
Old Testament Reading
Exodus 24:3

Combining faith with friendship for a miracle

"That you may know that the Son of Man has author-ity on earth to forgive sins . . . I tell you, get up, take your mat and go home" (Mark 2:10-11).

A man is suffering from incurable paralysis. Four of his friends, not content simply to send flowers, take decisive action to demonstrate the depth of their concern.

How? By tearing a hole in the roof of a house!

Why? Because the One who could do good for their friend was under that roof.

As Johann Peter Lange notes, their faith in Christ helped to accomplish far more than the healing of paralyzed legs.

Walk with Johann Peter Lange

"The healing of the palsied man gives us, in one sense, the key to all the miraculous works of our Lord, for in it the physical healing is defi-nitely based upon the healing of the heart, the forgiveness of sins, awakening, and regeneration.

"Because Christ Himself was the new Man from heaven, He is the principle of regeneration to sinful mankind. All the miraculous energies for the renewal of life issue from Him.

"The regenerating principle works in the regenerate person gradually, and in almost invis-ible, leaven-like influence and transformation.

"But as surely as the regeneration of the heart is brought about, so the seed of renewal in the whole life is present.

"Too often we've separated the external mira-cle from the internal. It is the power of Christ over the whole life that is regeneration—the great and abiding miracle."

Walk Closer to God

It's likely the faithful friends of the paralytic were thinking only of his physical needs when they brought him to the Savior. But Jesus was aware of the man's greater need for a clean, whole life in the sight of God.

You may know of friends who are in the same predicament—who need to see what faith cou-pled with friendship can do. And you probably don't need to remove a roof to demonstrate a faith in Christ that can make every person whole.

Worship from the Heart

Is there someone in your life who has played a role similar to that played by the four friends of the paralytic—someone who through prayer, through concern, or maybe even by foot-ing the bill for some roofing tiles brought you into the presence of Christ? Thank God now, by name, for those friends who took a risk for you.

Walk Thru the Word

New Testament Reading
Mark 2
Old Testament Reading
Job 2:11-13; 6:14

He appointed twelve . . . that they might be with him and that he might send them out to preach (Mark 3:14).

Called with a commission to go and to serve

Following Christ has always been a come-and-go proposition.

First, come and be with Him. Develop an intimate, personal relationship with Him. Learn to share heart to heart.

Then, go, sent out by Him in grateful service.

Put them together and you have a powerful program for on-the-job discipleship training.

G. Campbell Morgan shares from experience what it means to be called and commissioned as a servant of Christ.

Walk with G. Campbell Morgan

"The same Lord is still choosing, calling, and appointing. I cannot choose to be a missionary or a Christian minister. I must be chosen.

"The restfulness of this consideration lies in the fact that His choices and His calls are vindications. If He has called me, I know it; and if He has called me, He has chosen me.

"Every day that I live I wonder more why He called me; but I know He did, and therein is my rest, my peace.

"My brothers and sisters within the Christian church, you cannot elect to serve. But if He has elected and called you, a solemn responsibility rests upon you.

"I urge you: Be of good cheer, for if He calls, it is because He has chosen, and your responsibility is only that of yielding."

Walk Closer to God

Unlike the U.S. Marine Corps, God is not just "looking for a few good men" to serve Him. Rather, He wants all His children to hear and heed His call to action.

But like a Marine, the disciple of Christ needs time in training in order to be ready for action—time spent with Jesus in preparation for time spent serving Jesus.

Take it from twelve men who ought to have known: You cannot impart to others what you do not possess yourself.

Worship from the Heart

The multitudes came to Jesus because they had heard about the changed lives from friends and neighbors. Worship God today by sharing with a neighbor, friend, family member, or co-worker what He has done for you. As you share your personal relationship with the Lord, people will come who need similar help. Honor the Lord by telling what He has done for you.

Walk Thru the Word

New Testament Reading
Mark 3:1-19
Old Testament Reading
Isaiah 42:6-7

Blind eyes and hard hearts reap destruction

And the teachers of the law who came down from Jerusalem said, "He is possessed by Beelzebub! By the prince of the demons he is driving out demons" (Mark 3:22).

In Mark 3 the Jewish leaders are confronted by the fact of Jesus' power to heal. But unwilling to acknowledge the claims that accompany that power, they grope for an excuse to explain it away!

Albert Barnes notes that the obstinate attitude of the scribes and Pharisees is still visible today in the feeble excuses men and women offer God.

Walk with Albert Barnes

"People are greatly prone to ascribe all supernatural religion to the Devil. Anything that is unusual, anything that confounds them, anything that troubles their conscience, they ascribe to fanaticism, overheated zeal, and Satan.

"It has always been so, for it is sometimes an easy way to stifle their own convictions and bring religion into contempt.

"However, like the Pharisees, unbelievers must account for revivals of religion, for striking conversions, and for the great and undeniable effects which the gospel produces.

"How easy it is to say that it is delusion, and that it is the work of the Devil!

"What pains people will take to secure their own destruction, rather than admit that it is possible that Christianity is true!"

Walk Closer to God

The Pharisees of Jesus' day—and the pharaoh of Moses' day—share a similar spelling of names. They also exhibit a similar hardness of heart and blind stubbornness.

The Pharisees were confronted by countless unexplainable events at the hands of Jesus: storms stilled, food multiplied, diseases cured, death reversed. But they refused to believe that Jesus was the Son of God, sent as their Messiah.

The pharaoh of Egypt saw his land devastated by ten plagues from the God of Israel. But he opposed God by refusing to submit to His will.

What conclusion have you reached concerning the Man of Galilee?

Worship from the Heart

The words of a popular chorus make this claim: "I'm so glad I'm a part of the family of God." As you assemble with other believers on the weekend, remember that having a "family" relationship with Jesus Christ is not based on physical ties but on doing the will of God (Mark 3:35). Thank God for leaders who, by their obedience, keep the "family" growing and reaching out to those who have not yet heard the gospel.

Walk Thru the Word

New Testament Reading
Mark 3:20-35
Old Testament Reading
Exodus 4:28–5:2

When he was alone, the Twelve and the others around him asked him about the parables (Mark 4:10).

*P*arable: A short, descriptive story designed to teach one central truth.

The teacher who uses a parable usually expects his students to draw conclusions and make applications as they meditate upon his vivid word picture. So it must have taken some courage for the disciples to approach their Teacher asking for an explanation of the "parable of the soils."

Oswald Chambers explores the significance of Jesus' exposition of this parable when He was alone with His closest followers.

Walk with Oswald Chambers

"Watch Christ's training of the Twelve. It was the disciples, not the crowd, who were perplexed.

"If you are going on with God, the only thing that is clear to you, and the only thing God intends to be clear, is the way He deals with your own soul.

"There are areas of stubbornness and ignorance to be revealed by the Holy Spirit in each one of us, and it can only be done when Jesus gets us alone.

"Are we alone with Him now, or are we taken up with little fussy notions, fussy comradeships in God's service, fussy ideas about ourselves?

"Jesus can expound nothing until we get through all the noisy questions of the head and are alone with Him."

Walk Closer to God

Finding answers to perplexing questions is difficult even under the best of circumstances. In the middle of a crowd it can be nearly impossible. The bustle and noise drown out not only your own voice, but often God's as well.

Many things can come between you and a deeper communion with your Lord. They are called distractions, diversions, hindrances. You must learn to crowd them out before they crowd out your time with God!

What questions do you have for the Master? Today find a quiet place where you can be alone with Him to ask humbly—and wait patiently—for His answers.

*T*he necessity of being alone with the Lord

*W*orship from the Heart

The parables in this chapter help us to see that even though things look ordinary and uneventful, we live in a time of promise. The farmer has thrown in the seed, which is developing in its stages according to its nature. One day the harvest will be ready. Rejoice with confidence that Jesus' work, now as then, is moving toward a climax when all people will worship Him.

*W*alk Thru the Word

New Testament Reading
Mark 4:1-20
Old Testament Reading
Psalm 131

The secret of restful sleep

Jesus was in the stern, sleeping on a cushion (Mark 4:38).

Few things are as tiring as a sleepless night— except perhaps a sleepless night filled with worry!

The disciples' problem during their storm-tossed crossing of the Sea of Galilee was more than an inability to fall asleep; they also faced an inability to stop worrying. "Teacher, don't you care if we drown?" they asked.

Christ's answer reveals how intensely He wanted them to learn to exercise faith in the midst of life's storms.

Charles Spurgeon offers this advice for getting a good night's sleep.

Walk with Charles Spurgeon

"Having left everything with His Father, our Lord did the very wisest thing possible. He did just what the hour demanded.

" 'Why,' you say, 'He went to sleep!' Indeed, that was the best thing Jesus could do, and sometimes it is the best thing we can do.

"Christ was weary and worn. And when anyone is exhausted, it is his duty to go to sleep if he can. The Savior must be up again in the morning, preaching and working miracles. And if He does not sleep, He will not be fit for His holy duty.

"Often when we fret and worry, we would glorify God far more if we literally went to sleep. To glorify God by sleep is not so difficult as some might think; at least, to our Lord it was natural.

"Go to bed, and you will better imitate your Lord than by putting yourself into ill humor and worrying other people."

Walk Closer to God

Insomnia. Some people try to combat it by taking pills, counting sheep, or drinking warm milk. But a better remedy is to leave your worries and struggles, your tossings and turnings with the One who specializes in calming storms.

When you find that stormy weather in your heart drives sleep away, remember the biblical prescription: a generous dose of prayer.

You'll wake up refreshed!

Worship from the Heart

God designed sleep for a purpose, and we thwart that purpose when we worry over things that are His business. Lie down to sleep with praises in your heart and on your lips. Let the One who never slumbers or sleeps keep watch over your life and your concerns.

Walk Thru the Word

New Testament Reading
Mark 4:21-41
Old Testament Reading
Psalm 127:1-2

Jesus . . . said, "Go home to your family and tell them how much the Lord has done for you, and how he has had mercy on you" (Mark 5:19).

*C*hildren and busy roads don't mix. Why? Because children, if unattended, often play in the road, heedless of danger. So until a child reaches maturity, the parent takes responsibility for the child's protection, guidance, and nurture.

Christian, do you sometimes think you know better than your heavenly Father which road is best for you? Listen as J. C. Ryle explains that your Father truly does know best.

Walk with J. C. Ryle

"The place where Christians wish to be is not always the best place for their souls. There are none who need this lesson so much as believers newly converted to God.

"Seeing everything in a new light, yet knowing little of the depths of Satan and the weakness of their own hearts, they are in the greatest danger of making mistakes. With the best intentions they may fall into mistakes about their plans, their choices, or their professions. They forget that what we like best is not always best for our souls.

"Let us pray that God would guide us in all our ways after conversion, and not allow us to err. It may not be quite what we like. But if Christ by His providence has placed us in it, let us not be in a hurry to leave it."

Walk Closer to God

Elijah supposed he was the only man left in Israel who worshiped God.

Moses was an obscure shepherd for forty years before he led God's people out of Egypt.

John lived out his life in exile on a desolate island while he wrote the book of Revelation.

That's because God's best sometimes comes wrapped in unpleasant circumstances and unexpected changes of plan.

Like the man from Gadara in Mark 5, don't hesitate to submit your plans to God's providence. Great things can happen when God's best becomes yours.

The best place to be is the place God chooses

Worship from the Heart

Jesus took a demonic, crazed individual and restored him to sanity —and the residents of Gadara then requested the Lord to leave! Praise God that in His power and sovereignty, He can—and does— dispense with the predictable.

Walk Thru the Word

New Testament Reading
Mark 5:1-20
Old Testament Reading
Psalm 46:1-3, 10-11

Looking to the One who is all you need

Then one of the synagogue rulers, named Jairus, came there. Seeing Jesus, he fell at his feet and pleaded earnestly with him (Mark 5:22).

*A*s a ruler of the synagogue, Jairus was responsible for leading the services. He was accustomed to giving orders, not taking them.

But seeing his daughter on the verge of death dramatically changed Jairus. He forgot the power of his position and threw himself at Jesus' feet.

Whether you are an influential leader like Jairus, or a citizen of little renown, Jesus has all you need because Jesus is all you need. Gipsy Smith explains.

Walk with Gipsy Smith

"You cannot do without Him. If you think you can, will you prove it by creating a planet and then go and live on it?

"Don't talk about doing without Him while you depend on Him for every breath you draw.

"No one is at his best till he is Christ's. No one can be, no one can do, what God means him to be and do till he belongs to Christ.

"You think it is a sentimental thing to be a Christian. Try it. It is a noble and brave thing to be a Christian.

"The strange and wonderful thing to me is that it does not matter who the person is or where he comes from; what his nationality, education, or breeding; what his culture or outlook may be, the moment he looks into the face of Jesus he says, 'My Lord and my God!'

"Every person sees in Him all he needs."

Walk Closer to God

A crisis doesn't make a man or woman; a crisis merely reveals what an individual is like already.

But you don't have to wait for a crisis in order to come to the Savior. Form the kind of life-sustaining habit that will carry you through any crisis by sharing your needs with Him every day. Then when a crisis comes, it will be the natural thing to turn to Him, fall at His feet, and find help.

Bring your concerns to Him. His ear is ever attentive; His door is always open.

Worship from the Heart

Imagine Jairus forging ahead as Jesus moves slowly through the crowd. His frustration builds when the crowds press in and Jesus stops. How often have you, in your desperation and deep hurt, overlooked another's need? After reading this chapter, praise the God who responds both to the bold faith of a Jairus and to a timid touch from the crowd. Rejoice that when you reach out in desperation, He responds.

Walk Thru the Word

New Testament Reading
Mark 5:21-43
Old Testament Reading
2 Chronicles 20:1-13

On hearing of this, John's disciples came and took his body and laid it in a tomb (Mark 6:29).

When grief strikes, the need is critical for someone to wipe away tears and restore confidence that what seems to be out of control is in fact still very much under control. The sudden martyrdom of John the Baptist threw his followers into confusion and sorrow. Jonathan Edwards spotlights Jesus' compassion when John's followers turned to Him for comfort.

Walk with Jonathan Edwards

"The grief-filled heart desires to pour out its complaint; but it seeks a compassionate friend to pour it out before. Christ is such a one, above all others.

"He was the most compassionate spirit that ever appeared in the world. No wonder John's disciples—bereaved of their teacher, their hearts full of sorrow—came to Him [Christ] for pity. He was one who wept with those that wept.

"No one ever came to Him with a heavy heart, sorrowful or in distress, but what He met that person with a kind and compassionate reception.

"And He has the same compassion now that He is ascended into glory; there is still the same encouragement for bereaved ones to spread their sorrows before Him."

Walk Closer to God

Before His ascension, Jesus anticipated the disciples' need for comfort. "I will ask the Father, and he will give you another Counselor to be with you forever. . . . I will not leave you as orphans; I will come to you" (John 14:16, 18).

The thought of God the Holy Spirit, the divine Comforter, being with you in troublesome times is comforting indeed. And God's comfort in your time of grief is not just to be accepted; it is also to be imitated: "The Father of compassion and the God of all comfort . . . comforts us in all our troubles, so that we can comfort those in any trouble with the comfort we ourselves have received from God" (2 Corinthians 1:3-4).

God's comfort: The quickest way to double it is to share it!

Comfort for us; comfort for others

Worship from the Heart

Herod didn't heed John's convicting message because he valued the opinion of evil men above justice and the approval of God. As you meditate on the tragic death of John the Baptist, ask the Holy Spirit to bring to light any weakness which makes you more anxious to please people than God. Praise God that though human hearts are deceitful, He will cleanse and renew them "by the washing with water through the word" (Ephesians 5:26).

Walk Thru the Word

New Testament Reading
Mark 6:1-29
Old Testament Reading
Isaiah 40:1-2

Meeting the Father in the place of prayer

After leaving them, he went up on a mountainside to pray (Mark 6:46).

The person who claims, "I'm too busy to breathe," would be met with skepticism. Of course you have time to breathe! Life depends on it.

The Christian who claims, "I'm too busy to pray"—is his claim any less ludicrous . . . or tragic?

No busier itinerary has ever existed than the one confronting the Son of God. Yet He found time—indeed, He made time—to pray.

J. C. Ryle shows the vital link between prayer and growth.

Worship from the Heart

How often do you recognize the giants of the faith, those people who step out on faith to test God's promises? Read Mark 5:27-29 and 6:56; then praise God for someone whose personal experience has encouraged you. Thank God for the example of that person's faith, and give back some encouragement with a note of thanks or a telephone call.

Walk with J. C. Ryle

"What time do we give to prayer in the twenty-four hours of the day? What progress can we mark, one year after another, in the fervency, fullness, and earnestness of our prayers? These are humbling inquiries, but they are useful for our souls.

"Our Master's strong crying and tears, His nights in prayer, His frequent withdrawals to private places for communion with the Father, are things more talked of and admired than imitated.

"We live in an age of hurry, bustle, and so-called activity. Men and women are tempted continually to cut short their private devotions and abridge their prayers. The church must learn to copy its Head more closely."

Walk Closer to God

There will often be twenty-five hours of valid demands on your twenty-four-hour day. Your temptation will be to label such requirements an excuse for prayerlessness—when in fact there is no better reason for prayerfulness.

Jesus "went up on a mountainside to pray" (6:46). When people temporarily interrupted His plans with their pressing needs, He reacted compassionately—then returned to His sanctuary of prayer.

There may not be another opportunity the rest of the day like the one right now to draw in a refreshing breath of prayer. So take a deep breath . . . and another . . . as you whisper the needs of your heart to your heavenly Father.

Walk Thru the Word

New Testament Reading
Mark 6:30-56
Old Testament Reading
1 Chronicles 16:8-13

"These people honor me with their lips, but their hearts are far from me" (Mark 7:6).

Inward strength that comes from joy

*C*an you tell the difference between mere tradition and living faith?

One pays lip service to God; the other enjoys a heart-to-heart relationship with the Creator. One teaches the opinions of mortals as unchangeable doctrine; the other lives by the quick and powerful Word of God.

George Müller recognized that proper conduct must be the result of the inward working of the Holy Spirit, not ceremony or custom.

Walk with George Müller

"The sort of clothes I wear, the kind of house I live in, or the quality of my furniture should not be the result of other people doing so or because it is customary among those with whom I associate.

"But whatever is done in these things in the way of self-denial or deadness to the world should result from the joy we have in God, and from the knowledge of our being His children, and from entering into our precious future inheritance.

"Not that I mean in the least by this to imply that we should continue to live in luxury and self-indulgence while others are in great need; but we should begin the thing in a right way. Aim after the right state of heart; begin inwardly instead of outwardly.

"Oh, how different if joy in God leads us to any little act of self-denial! How gladly we do it then! How much does the heart then long to be able to do more for Him who has done so much for us!"

Walk Closer to God

George Müller is remembered as a man who strove to be faithful to God in every area of life. Yet such a zeal did not prevent him from experiencing the joys of life.

Müller's concern was not so much keeping the law as it was meeting the Lawgiver.

The joy of knowing God led Müller to rejoice that he could serve God. Read back through Müller's wise words; rejoice that you too can serve God with joy.

Worship from the Heart

Doing right in God's sight requires far more than performing certain activities. God's standard is this: Love Him and love others. Rejoice today that God has promised to flood your innermost being with springs of living water. That which defiles you will be replaced with His own pure sweetness, enabling you to reach out to others in love.

Walk Thru the Word

New Testament Reading
Mark 7:1-23
Old Testament Reading
Psalm 5:11-12

Sighs that speak of sympathy and power

He looked up to heaven . . . with a deep sigh (Mark 7:34).

Deeply moved by the needs all around Him, Jesus responded in the best way possible—not with fine sounding words, but with a sigh of compassion followed by meaningful action.

A man who could neither hear nor speak . . . a multitude who had followed Jesus without eating for three days—each experienced His unspoken, yet unmistakable love.

Jesus sighed. Yet it was no mere sigh of resignation or frustration, as F. B. Meyer makes clear.

Walk with F. B. Meyer

"In this passage, along with Mark 8:12, Mark twice calls attention to the Lord's sighs. A sigh is one of the most touching and significant tokens of excessive grief. When our natures are too disturbed to remember to take a normal breath and must compensate for this omission by one deep-drawn breath, we sigh deeply in our spirit.

" ' He looked up to heaven . . . with a deep sigh.' As the deaf-mute stood before Him—an image of all the closed hearts around Him, of all the inarticulate unexpressed desires, of all the sin and sorrow of mankind—Jesus' sensitive heart responded with a deep-drawn sigh.

"But there was simultaneously a heavenward look which mingled infinite hope in it. If the sigh spoke of His tender sympathy, the look declared His close union with God, by virtue of which He was competent to meet the direst need.

"Jesus, in doing good, would look to heaven and sigh; but His sighs were followed by the touch and word of power. Let us not be content with a sigh of sympathy and regret."

Walk Closer to God

You, like Jesus, can couple a heartfelt sigh with effective action, looking to God for the power to start correcting that which made you sigh in the first place.

There's a sighing, dying world waiting for someone like you to take compassionate action. What will be your answer: A sigh or a shrug? Or a sigh and service?

Worship from the Heart

If you have no other way to show compassion for others you can at least pray. Praise God today that He has given you access to heaven's throne room and that through prayer you can always intercede for those who are hurting.

Walk Thru the Word

New Testament Reading
Mark 7:24-37
Old Testament Reading
Ezekiel 21:1-7

Jesus called his disciples to him and said, "I have compassion for these people" (Mark 8:1-2).

*H*ave you ever happened upon a scene of misfortune that caused you to . . .

Pity the poor victim?

Weep over the victim's plight?

Exchange places with the sufferer?

Mark 8 describes a scene in which pity was plentiful, but only compassionate action could meet the needs.

English clergyman John Henry Jowett contrasts pity—which tends to be passive—with compassion—which is active and often costly.

Walk with John Henry Jowett

"Jesus' compassion was part of His passion. It culminated upon Calvary, but it was bleeding all along the road.

"It was a fellow-feeling with all the pangs and sorrows of the race. Only a pity that bleeds is a pity that heals.

"As in Jesus' day, the multitude is around us still. There is the multitude of misfortune, the children of disadvantage. There is the multitude of outcasts, the vast army of modern-day publicans and sinners. There are the bewildering multitudes who have nothing to eat.

"How do I share the compassion of the Lord?

"Do I exercise a sensitive and sanctified imagination, and enter somehow into the pangs of their cravings?

"I must. For my Lord calls me to help."

Walk Closer to God

Pity looks and says, "How awful." Compassion weeps and says, "I'll help."

Pity looks on from afar. Compassion rolls up its sleeves and pitches in to help.

Pity waits for a convenient time. Compassion knows no office hours.

Pity is cheap and plentiful. Compassion is rare and priceless and costly.

Jesus looked on the multitudes and said, "I have compassion." Then He taught and healed, fed and forgave, and went to the cross to die.

What do you have?

A feeling, healing compassion

*W*orship from the Heart

Jesus' compassionate actions changed the course of many lives. As you praise God for His compassion toward you, make a short list of other words which describe what compassion is. Recall specific situations in which God has demonstrated that aspect of compassion in your life . . . and thank Him for it.

*W*alk Thru the Word

New Testament Reading
Mark 8:1-13
Old Testament Reading
Psalm 78:38

What way are we to follow?

"If anyone would come after me, he must deny himself and take up his cross and follow me. For whoever wants to save his life will lose it, but whoever loses his life for me . . . will save it" (Mark 8:34-35).

When Jesus spoke to His own about the demands of discipleship, the words were strong and foreboding.

"Deny . . . take up your cross . . . follow." Those are the words of Jesus.

"Pamper yourself . . . indulge . . . grab the gusto." Those are the words of the world.

Augustine reminds all Christians that genuine servanthood involves both a privilege . . . and a price.

Walk with Augustine

"It is good to follow Christ. But we must see by what way we are to follow.

"For when the Lord spoke the words of Mark 8, He had not already risen from the dead. He had not yet suffered, nor yet come to the cross, not yet felt the dishonoring, the outrages, the scourging, the thorns, the wounds, the mockeries, the insults, the death.

"Rough may be the way, but follow on. Where Christ has gone is worn smooth.

"Who would not wish to be exalted? Honor is pleasing to all. But humility is the path to it.

"The two disciples disliked taking this step of humility. They sought exaltation, one at the right hand and the other at the left.

"They did not see the cross."

Walk Closer to God

Christ's invitation to discipleship is an invitation to die. Die to self. To the world. To ambition.

It is a call to follow Jesus in His life. In His death. In His resurrection. It is a reminder that exaltation and elevation in God's sight are the by-products of humility.

Small wonder there is so seldom a crowd gathered at the cross. For few are willing to pay the price that discipleship demands.

But it's a price well worth paying. For a life of discipleship is the most fulfilling life of all.

Will you pay the price?

Worship from the Heart

Jesus' desire for His twelve disciples is His desire for us: He is actively working to transform us into His likeness. "And we, who with unveiled faces all reflect the Lord's glory, are being transformed into his likeness" (2 Corinthians 3:18). In your time with the Lord today, acknowledge the work He is doing to mold and shape your character. Praise Him for the attention He gives to the details of your life.

Walk Thru the Word

New Testament Reading
Mark 8:14–9:1
Old Testament Reading
Psalm 94:12-15

Faith: taking God at His Word

[Jesus said,] "Everything is possible for him who believes" (Mark 9:23).

*T*his is CWA flight 003 to tower. Request permission to land. We have an emergency situation. Cannot wait for the fog to clear. Over."

"Roger, CWA 003. We know you're blind in that soup out there, but you'll be okay. We'll get you down."

Trusting the control tower and a set of instruments is sometimes a must for pilots. But trusting our all-knowing God is also a must for believers when the fog rolls across life, causing the decision-making process to be difficult.

But, as Lettie Cowman explains, God has both the knowledge and the power necessary to get things done.

Walk with Lettie Cowman

"What should be the attitude of a Christian when placed in a difficult and trying situation —a place of severe testing? There can be but one attitude! A simple and unwavering trust in God.

"God is stronger than any temptation and danger; and the person who has God in his heart is unconquerable.

"It is true that God often seems to place His children in positions of profound difficulty, leading them into a tight corner from which escape seems impossible . . . contriving a situation which no human judgment would have permitted.

"During such periods, these words of Jesus take on added significance. It should be clearly understood that this kind of faith in God is the most practical approach to the problems and testing of life—it is not sense, or sight, or reason, but taking God at His Word."

Walk Closer to God

It has been said that life's greatest loss is the loss of faith. Jesus did not try to shield Peter from failure (Luke 22:31), but He did interfere between Peter and the loss of faith.

Are you trusting God today to bring your craft in safely—no matter what the weather? He always will when you give the controls to Him.

Worship from the Heart

Faith is being certain of what we do not see (Hebrews 11:1). Faith focuses on Jesus Christ and His trustworthiness. Praise God that Jesus walked among us so that we might know Him and learn to relate to Him. In your time alone with Him, tell Him what He means to you right now.

Walk Thru the Word

New Testament Reading
Mark 9:2-32
Old Testament Reading
2 Chronicles 20:20-30

Lettie Cowman (1870-1960) A channel for God's blessings

The first half of Lettie Cowman's life was filled with achievements that opened a new era of mission service for thousands of believers. But Lettie Cowman never rested on past accomplishments. In her sixties, she found that her past was merely preparation for continued service.

Born late in the lives of rich and cultured parents, Lettie Burd seemed destined to lead a life of luxury. And when, at age fifteen, she fell in love with seventeen-year-old Charles Cowman, a young telegraph dispatcher, it seemed that the two of them would work to maintain the life to which Lettie had been born. Married in 1889, the young couple moved first to Colorado and then to Chicago where Charles rose rapidly to a position of leadership in Western Union.

But God had plans for this young couple, and in December, 1893 Lettie accepted Jesus as her Savior and purposed to follow Him—even if she had to walk alone. But within a few months, Charles too, met Jesus and yielded his life to God.

Charles and Lettie Cowman were filled with zeal. While Charles continued working, they began preparation for missionary service at Moody Bible Institute.

And so it was that in 1901 Charles and Lettie Cowman left their life of privilege to begin a work of faith in Japan. In the seventeen years they spent in Japan they founded the Oriental Missionary Society and undertook to systematically reach every home in Japan with the gospel in printed form—the first Every Home Crusade.

Eventually the expanding work took a dreadful toll on Charles's health, and at the ages of forty-seven and forty-nine, the couple returned to the U.S. to train workers and supervise the growing mission society.

As Charles's heart attacks increased in frequency, Lettie cared for him and battled for his life, both in the physical and in the heavenly realms. For her own strength and inspiration and to encourage Charles, she mined God's Word and the writings of dear saints from across the centuries. Later she sent these gleanings forth to bless her missionary friends around the world. She called her little book *Streams in the Desert.*

In 1924, Charles Cowman went to be with the Lord, and at age fifty-four, Lettie was alone. During the next four lonely years, Lettie adjusted—to being without Charles, to a new dependence on Jesus, to waiting on God to reveal the next step. And what a step it was.

With Charles's death, Rev. Ernest Kilbourne had become president of the Oriental Missionary Society. But at Rev. Kilbourne's sudden death the Society faced a crisis. So Lettie, at age fifty-eight, was appointed president of the mission.

An able administrator, she continued to write, inspire, preach, and encourage. During this time, *Streams in the Desert* was translated into numerous languages and distributed around the world. Then God laid a new call for evangelization on Lettie's heart, and from age sixty-six she concentrated on getting a printed portion of the gospel to every home on the planet, systematically blanketing cities and nations.

Mrs. Charles E. Cowman died in 1960. Her book, *Streams in the Desert,* is still a best seller among devotional books. The mission society she and Charles founded is now known as OMS International and continues to send people to minister in countries around the world.

A Lesson from the life of Lettie Cowman

Age is no barrier to usefulness in God's mission to reach every person in the world for Christ.

*H*umility that leads to healing

"If anyone wants to be first, he must be the very last, and the servant of all" (Mark 9:35).

*I*magine that in your favorite store, you are waiting to be "waited upon"—when someone mistakes you for an employee.

Are you flattered or embarrassed? Do you laugh, or are you offended?

Being mistaken for a sales clerk can be humorous. It might also be highly revealing!

In Mark 9 and 10, Christ had more to say about serving than He did about being served.

Dwight L. Moody, whose ministry often placed him in prominent positions, shares two examples of the stature of the servant.

Walk with Dwight L. Moody

"There is a story told of William Carey, the great missionary, who was at a party attended by the governor-general of India. Also present were some military officers who looked down upon the missionaries with contempt.

"One of those officers said at the table: 'I believe that Carey was a shoemaker, wasn't he, before he took up the profession of a missionary?'

"Mr. Carey spoke up and said: 'Oh, no, I was only a cobbler. I could mend shoes, and wasn't ashamed of it.'

"The one prominent virtue of Christ, next to His obedience, was His humility. And even His obedience grew out of His humility.

"In His lowly birth, His submission to His earthly parents, His contact with the poor and despised, His entire submission and dependence upon His Father, this virtue—consummated in His death on the cross—shines out."

Walk Closer to God

Isn't it strange how many vie to be first when, according to Jesus, the prize goes to the one who is last!

William Carey was not ashamed to be a mender of soles and heels, if only by that he might find opportunity to be a mender and healer of souls.

"Only a servant. . . " Some would call that an insult. What would you call it?

*W*orship from the Heart

"Father, I praise You that Jesus humbled Himself and took on the form of a servant. Help me to see the people I meet as persons of great worth because You have made and loved them. May my humility toward those I meet be a service to You."

*W*alk Thru the Word

New Testament Reading
Mark 9:33-50
Old Testament Reading
Proverbs 16:19

*G*reatness according to God's definition

"Whoever wants to become great among you must be your servant" (Mark 10:43).

*A*s part of a select group, James and John witnessed great spectacles on the Mount of Transfiguration and at the raising of Jairus's daughter. Now they asked the Master for a great favor—seats of honor alongside Christ—and in the process incurred the great wrath of the other disciples!

A. W. Tozer writes perceptively about how Jesus firmly put greatness into perspective.

Walk with A. W. Tozer

"From the words of Jesus to His disciples we may properly conclude that there is nothing wrong with the desire to be great, provided (1) we seek the right kind of greatness; (2) we allow God to decide what greatness is; (3) we are willing to pay the full price that greatness demands; and (4) we are content to wait for the judgment of God to settle the matter at last!

"It is vitally important, however, that we know what Christ meant when He used the word great in relation to people. No one whose heart has had a vision of God will ever consent to think of himself as being great.

"There are two kinds of greatness recognized in the Scriptures: an absolute uncreated greatness belonging to God alone, and a relative and finite greatness achieved by or bestowed upon certain friends of God and sons and daughters of faith, who by obedience and self-denial seek to become as much like God as possible."

Walk Closer to God

Rather than clamoring for the honor and recognition which by rights were His, Jesus "humbled himself and became obedient to death—even death on a cross!" (Philippians 2:8).

That one supreme act of service has caused His name to be spread throughout the world. And yet, His motive was not fame but faithfulness to the will of His Father.

Consider carefully the full price that His kind of greatness demands!

*W*orship from the Heart

In chapter 10, the children wanted Jesus' touch, and they received His blessing. Praise Him for His willingness to welcome you as He did the children when your only desire is to be in His presence.

*W*alk Thru the Word

New Testament Reading
Mark 10
Old Testament Reading
1 Kings 3:4-14

The secret that transforms a market into a temple

Jesus entered the temple area and began driving out those who were buying and selling there. He . . . would not allow anyone to carry merchandise through the temple courts (Mark 11:15-16).

*P*rofit-minded individuals had turned the temple into a marketplace and had set up shop in the sanctuary. But Jesus upset the status quo in this thieves' paradise. There would be no "business as usual" in His Father's house.

Commenting on Mark 11, John Henry Jowett offers this insight on how to cultivate a reverent attitude of worship.

Walk with John Henry Jowett

"It was a teaching of the old rabbis that no one should make a thoroughfare of the temple, or enter it with dust upon his feet.

"Let me not enter the temple as a mere passage to something else. Let me not put on the garments of worship in order that I may readily fill my purse. Let me not make the sanctuary a shortcut to the bank! And let me not carry the dust of the world onto the sacred floor.

"Let me wipe my feet. Let me sternly shake off some things—all frivolity, indifference, the spirit of haste and self-seeking. Let me not defile the courts of the Lord. And let me remember that the whole earth is full of His glory. Everywhere, therefore, I am treading the sacred floor!

"Lord, teach me this high secret! Then shall I not demean the temple into a market, but I shall transform the market into a temple."

Walk Closer to God

Jesus' actions in the temple reflect His attitude toward worshiping God properly: He wants your undivided attention.

True worship begins when you leave other concerns behind and prepare your heart to enter into the presence of the living God.

And after you have worshiped the Lord reverently, allow the flavor, the quality, of that time together to accompany you into the world's marketplaces, transforming you into the kind of person who can turn the world upside down for Jesus Christ.

Worship from the Heart

Just as Jesus cleansed the actual temple of that which defiled it, He wants to cleanse the temple of your life as well. If you let Him, He will do so as a Master Builder, lovingly renovating the structure He inhabits. The heart is your place of rendezvous with your Savior. Let it be a place of beauty and purity.

Walk Thru the Word

New Testament Reading
Mark 11:1-19
Old Testament Reading
Hosea 6:6

"Whatever you ask for in prayer, believe that you have received it, and it will be yours. And . . . if you hold anything against anyone, forgive. . . . " (Mark 11:24).

*P*rayer has been defined as . . . putting feet to the promises of God . . . the gymnasium of the believer . . . the heartbeat of a holy life.

Most Christians can enumerate what prayer includes: confession, praise, thanksgiving, worship. But at the center of prayer is petition: asking God to intervene according to His will.

Martin Luther emphasizes the primacy and practicality of asking in faith.

Walk with Martin Luther

"It is a great matter when in extreme need to take hold on prayer. I know that, whenever I earnestly prayed, I have been amply heard and have obtained more than I prayed for. God sometimes delayed, but at last He came.

"O how great a thing, how marvelous a godly Christian's prayer is! How powerful with God that a poor human creature should speak with God's high majesty in heaven and know that God smiles upon him for the sake of Christ, His beloved Son.

"The ancients ably defined prayer as a 'climbing up of the heart' unto God. The heart and conscience in this act of praying must not recoil backwards because of our sins and unworthiness or stand in doubt, or be scared away. When we pray, we must believe that we are already heard in that for which we pray, with faith in Christ."

Walk Closer to God

Would you say your prayer life more closely resembles that of a heart climbing up to God or a head bumping against the ceiling?

If the latter, you need this reminder: "This is the confidence that we have in approaching God: that if we ask anything according to his will, he hears us. And if we know that he hears us— whatever we ask—we know that we have what we asked of him" (1 John 5:14-15).

With that as your invitation, spend some time right now speaking confidently, yet humbly, to your Majesty on high.

*H*earts that rest in the presence of God

*W*orship from the Heart

Holding on to past wrongs produces bitterness and magnifies the pain of the original hurt. God, who knows what's best and who desires our good, instructs us to forgive others as He forgives us. If someone you need to forgive comes to mind as you read today, don't waste a minute. On your knees before God, forgive that person and put yourself in the path of restored fellowship with God.

*W*alk Thru the Word

New Testament Reading
Mark 11:20–12:12
Old Testament Reading
Lamentations 3:40

Giving with groans or with gratitude

"They all gave out of their wealth; but she, out of her poverty, put in everything—all she had to live on" (Mark 12:44).

*A*s Jesus rested near the temple treasury, He watched how the worshipers gave their offerings, not how much they gave. And as He did, a certain poor widow caught His attention.

She gave two of the smallest coins in circulation at that time. But her gift—though insignificant in measure—revealed a sacrificial heart filled with faith in God.

A. W. Tozer draws upon that widow's example to show that attitude is more important than amount in God's account.

Walk with A. W. Tozer

"In God's sight, my giving is measured not by how much I give, but by how much I have left after I make my gift. Not by its size is my gift judged, but by how much of me there is in it. No one gives at all until he has given all! No one gives anything acceptable to God until he has first given himself in love and sacrifice.

"While Christ was the perfect example of the healthy, normal man, He did not live a normal life. He sacrificed many pure enjoyments to give Himself to the holy work of moral rescue. His conduct was determined not by what was legitimate or innocent, but by human need.

"He pleased not Himself but lived for the emergency; and as He was, so are we in this world!"

Walk Closer to God

If God is more concerned with how you give than what you give, that places a whole new sense of importance on what you do with your ... body... mind ... talents ... possessions ... ambitions.

Giving may be done grudgingly or gratefully. The millionaire who groans while giving a thousand dollars has actually accomplished less than the widow who is thankful to give two cents.

The One who owns the cattle on a thousand hills does not need your gift—no matter how great it may be. But you need to learn the joy of giving all you have with a grateful heart.

Worship from the Heart

The tabernacle was to be furnished through the gifts of God's people. As you read Exodus 35:21-29, note the repeated description of the manner in which the people gave: with stirred-up hearts and willing spirits. God desires no less today. Worship Him by giving willingly, cheerfully, meaningfully. Praise Him that in just such a manner He gave us His Son.

Walk Thru the Word

New Testament Reading
Mark 12:13-44
Old Testament Reading
Exodus 35:21-29

"Now learn this lesson from the fig tree: As soon as its twigs get tender and its leaves come out, you know that summer is near" (Mark 13:28).

*J*esus pointed to a fig tree to illustrate to His disciples that reading the signs of the times can be as objective as discerning seasonal changes.

John Calvin looks deeper into Christ's illustration and suggests how spiritual development parallels natural growth.

Walk with John Calvin

"In winter the trees, contracted by the severe cold, show greater vigor; but in spring they lose their toughness and appear more feeble, even as they open up a passage for fresh twigs. In a similar way the afflictions which seem, according to the perception of the flesh, to soften the church, do not impair its vigor.

"The inward sap diffuses through the tree, and after producing this softness, collects strength to throw itself out for renovating what was dead. So too the Lord draws from the corruption of the outward man the perfect restoration of His people.

"The general instruction conveyed is that the weak and frail condition of the church ought not to lead us to conclude that it is dying, but rather to expect the immortal glory for which the Lord prepares His people by the Cross and by afflictions.

"For what Paul maintains in reference to each of the members must be fulfilled in the whole body, that if the outward man is decayed, the inward man is renewed day by day."

Walk Closer to God

Fall, winter, spring, summer. Can you identify the seasons of your spiritual life?

John Calvin knew that the harsh afflictions of winter contribute toward growth and maturity, both in the physical world and in the spiritual life. So if you are battling what seems to be an unwelcome "storm," remember the lesson of the fig tree!

Long periods of deep inner preparation in winter weather always precede summer's arrival. And come warmer weather, you'll be amazed at your fruitfulness.

*S*easons of growth and renewal in the soul

*W*orship from the Heart

Today's Old Testament reading reminds us that God brought the Jews through fire and water even though the going was tough. Maybe you've not yet reached the point where you can look back as the psalmist did to see God's plan. Maybe you're right in the middle of the furnace. If so, take heart and rejoice that God's refining process is going on in your life.

*W*alk Thru the Word

New Testament Reading
Mark 13:1-31
Old Testament Reading
Psalm 66:8-12

Broken hearts that overflow with love

"She did what she could. She poured perfume on my body beforehand to prepare for my burial" (Mark 14:8).

The heart can break because its love, when offered, is rejected by another. Or it can break because it cannot contain the overflowing love it feels for another.

Robert Murray McCheyne describes Mary's sacrificial gift—a broken vial revealing a broken heart.

Worship from the Heart

Jesus clearly tells us that history is moving toward an end and that He is involved in both its course and its culmination. As current events cause concern or dismay, cling to the clear promise of Scripture: Jesus is coming back. In anticipation, may it be your desire today to be about your Father's business.

Walk with Robert Murray McCheyne

"Many seem to think that to be a believer is to have certain feelings and experiences, forgetting all the time that these are simply the flowers, and that the fruit must follow. Holy fruit is the end for which we are saved.

"Now we see Mary not only as a contemplative believer, but as an active believer. Jesus had saved her soul, and she felt that she could not do too much for Him. She brought an alabaster box of ointment, very costly, and broke the box and poured it on His head.

"This is what we should do. If we have been saved by Christ, we should pour out our best affections on Him. It is well to love His disciples, well to love His ministers, well to love His poor. But it is best to love Him. It was not the ointment Jesus cared for, but the loving heart, poured out upon His feet; it is the praise, love, and prayers of a believer's broken heart that Christ cares for."

Walk Closer to God

Have you learned the beauty of brokenness?

It was through broken pitchers that God provided light for Gideon's army (Judges 7:19-21).

It was broken bread that satisfied the hungry thousands (Matthew 14:19-21).

It was a broken jar that yielded the precious fragrance to anoint the Savior (Mark 14:3-9).

And it is a broken body that provides salvation for all who believe (Isaiah 53:5-6).

Hearts—unlike pitchers—are more easily filled when they are broken. Let love for God break your heart. Then God can enlarge it to allow more of His love to flow through you.

Walk Thru the Word

New Testament Reading
Mark 13:32–14:11
Old Testament Reading
Joshua 22:1-6

Going a little farther, he fell to the ground and prayed that if possible the hour might pass from him (Mark 14:35).

It's only human to want to avoid carrying heavy loads. But there is one burden too heavy for even the whole race to bear—the burden of sin.

H. P. Liddon elaborates on the weight of Christ's labor of love.

Walk with H. P. Liddon

"Christ was, so to speak, mentally robing Himself for the great sacrifice; He was folding round His sinless manhood, laying upon His sinless soul, the sins of a guilty world.

"To us the burden of sin is as natural as the clothes we wear; it sits on us so comfortably it may be we think nothing at all about it.

"But to Him the touch which we take so easily was an agony even in its lightest form.

"And when we consider the weight and magnitude, the subtle, penetrating poison, the dreadful burden He willed to bear; when we think of that festering accumulation of the ages, the sins of the people before the flood, the sins of Egypt and of Babylon, the sins of Sodom, of Moab, of Philistia, the sins of Rome, sins of disobedience and stubbornness, sins of scorn and ingratitude, sins of cruelty and hypocrisy—when we think of all that was suggested to the mind of the Son of David as He looked up from the mount there in Gethsemane, and beheld the city that was rejecting Him—can we wonder that His bodily nature gave way, that His passion seemed to have been upon Him before its time, and that His sweat was, as it were, great drops of blood falling to the ground?"

Walk Closer to God

"Father, I am reminded that the only thing heavier than my burden of sin was the weight of love that removed it. Sharpen my awareness of sin. Deepen my agony when I tolerate it, and my joy when I avoid it.

"Help me to sense the enormous privilege of calling Your Son my Burden-Bearer. In His Name I pray. Amen."

Love weightier than the burden of sin

Worship from the Heart

Imagine the conflicting emotions that must have been in the Lord's heart as He spoke the words of the New Covenant at that final Passover meal. He knew death would not pass over Him, but would, at the cross, make its final stop. Meditate on the fact that Jesus is both the Door to the sheepfold and the Lamb of God. Is His blood sprinkled on the doorposts of your life?

Walk Thru the Word

New Testament Reading
Mark 14:12-42
Old Testament Reading
Leviticus 4:13-21

Second chance straight from God's heart

Worship from the Heart

As you prepare once more to read of Jesus' crucifixion and death, remember that now, as then, God is seated on His throne. Just as He limits the boundaries of the sea, He also limits the course of evil. As you find the forces of darkness closing in on your life, praise God that the Enemy can only go to a certain point. Rejoice that the reality of a situation is often not what we see, but what we know by faith.

Walk Thru the Word

New Testament Reading
Mark 14:43-72
Old Testament Reading
Judges 16:4-5, 16-31

But [Peter] denied it. "I don't know or understand what you're talking about," he said, and went out into the entryway. (Mark 14:68).

*Y*ou also were with that Nazarene, Jesus " "This fellow is one of them."

These were two simple statements Peter would never forget. For as he looked into the servant girl's eyes, his faith crumpled.

Jesus had already warned Peter about what would happen (14:30). But the impetuous apostle declared that he would never deny his Lord and Master (14:31).

As Alexander Maclaren notes, Peter let down his faithful Friend, but the reverse was never true.

Walk with Alexander Maclaren

"Though Peter's grasp of Christ had relaxed, Christ's grasp of him had not. Peter might cease for a time to prize his Lord's love; he might cease either to be conscious of it or to wish for it. But that love would not change.

"Disowned, it still asserted its property in him. Being reviled, it blessed; being persecuted, it endured; being defamed, it entreated; patient through all wrongs and changes, it loved on till it had won back the erring heart. And is not that same miracle of enduring love that which is in Christ's heart for us?

"However real and disastrous may be the power of our evil in troubling the communion of love between us and the Lord, and in compelling Him to smite before He binds up, never forget that our sin is utterly impotent to turn away the tide that flows to us from the heart of Christ."

Walk Closer to God

David, Moses, Samson, Jonah—each experienced a crushing setback because of sin. Yet each man also enjoyed an equally great comeback when he obeyed the long-suffering, quick-forgiving God of the second chance.

You may think some failure in life has disqualified you from ever serving God again. If so, take it from an impressive group of ex-failures: The tide of God's love for you continues to run deep and wide.

Wanting to satisfy the crowd, Pilate released Barabbas to them. He had Jesus flogged, and handed him over to be crucified (Mark 15:15).

*I*n the case of *Jesus v. the Sanhedrin*, the choice was left up to Pilate to release Jesus or to condemn Him.

The evidence to support condemning the Messiah was flimsy. But the voice of the people was loud and insistent. Like most politicians, Pilate wanted to please the people.

Of course, Pilate's fateful decision is well known. But as F. W. Krummacher points out, his decision is one still faced today.

Walk with F. W. Krummacher

"The heathen governor would gladly have avoided the guilt of murdering the Righteous One. But he will not succeed in his desire.

"He must either decide for or against Jesus. He is compelled either to take the part of the Holy One to the setting aside of all private considerations, or to afford his sanction to the cruelest deed the world has ever witnessed.

"The case is similar with us. There is just as little room left for a neutral position as was left to Pilate.

"If we refuse to do Christ homage, we are compelled to aid in crucifying Him. We cannot escape the alternative of rejecting Christ if we will not decidedly devote ourselves to Him.

"If we wish to separate ourselves from Him, nothing is left for us but to say, in positive opposition, 'We will not have You reign over us!' God grant that this may not be the case with any of us, but may He enable us to exclaim with the apostle Thomas, 'My Lord and my God!' "

Walk Closer to God

The longer Pilate avoided the truth, the more difficult it became to act in accordance with the truth. The deceptive comfort of neutrality only helped to insure that when he finally made his choice, it would be the wrong one.

Whatever the decision you face, crowd out all voices but the small, insistent voice of God, and decide today . . . in His wisdom.

*C*hoose today whom you will serve

*W*orship from the Heart

Pilate thought it was politically advantageous to side with the crowd and allow Jesus to be executed. In our everyday world we too often have opportunities to be self-serving, or to do what is expedient. Praise God, we don't have to. Thank Him today that knowing Him gives you eternal perspective, that His Word gives moral and ethical guidance in a complex world, and that having His indwelling Spirit gives strength for making the right choices.

*W*alk Thru the Word

New Testament Reading
Mark 15:1-20
Old Testament Reading
1 Kings 11:1-13

Taking your stand beneath the cross

It was the third hour when they crucified him (Mark 15:25).

*J*esus' life was a matter of public record. He healed the sick, cast out demons, fed the hungry, comforted the grieving, preached the truth.

And, at the end of this full life of unselfish service, He was crucified as a troublemaker, a blasphemer, and a criminal.

But dying as a criminal was no accident. For by this greatest act of service, sin was conquered.

Let the words of Elizabeth Clephane's hymn, "Beneath the Cross of Jesus" take you back to that time when Christ Jesus offered His atoning sacrifice on the cross.

Worship from the Heart

Spend some time quietly meditating on Isaiah's prophetic portrait of the Lamb led to slaughter, the sin-bearing Servant. Then praise Him by singing or reading aloud the hymn on this page.

Walk with Elizabeth Clephane

Upon the cross of Jesus
  Mine eye at times can see
The very dying form of One
  Who suffered there for me;
And from my smitten heart with tears
  Two wonders I confess—
The wonders of His glorious love
  And my unworthiness.

I take, O cross, thy shadow
  For my abiding place;
I ask no other sunshine than
  The sunshine of His face;
Content to let the world go by,
  To know no gain nor loss,
My sinful self my only shame,
  My glory all the cross.

Walk Closer to God

The blood Jesus shed on the cross was the only acceptable payment for sin. "It was not with perishable things such as silver or gold that you were redeemed . . . but with the precious blood of Christ, a lamb without blemish" (1 Peter 1:18-19).

"In him we have redemption through his blood, the forgiveness of sins " (Ephesians 1:7).

Enslaved to sin, you were rescued by Christ.

Come now to the Cross. Take your stand there. Then kneel in grateful homage at His feet: Jesus paid it all!

Walk Thru the Word

New Testament Reading
Mark 15:21-47
Old Testament Reading
Isaiah 52:13–53:12

64

*"Don't be alarmed. . . . You are looking for Jesus
the Nazarene, who was crucified. He has risen!"
(Mark 16:6).*

*Y*ou celebrated Easter more than fifty times last
year! Jesus arose on the first day of the week—
Sunday. And since the days of the early church,
Christians have marked that glorious event by
meeting together for worship and celebration on
Sunday.

Martin Luther understood the significance of
the Resurrection, and penned the words of this
hymn to express his thankful praise.

Walk with Martin Luther

> Christ Jesus lay in death's strong bands,
>   For our offenses given:
> But now at God's right hand He stands
>   And brings us life from heaven;
> Therefore let us joyful be
>   And sing to God right thankfully
> Loud songs of hallelujah.
>
> It was a strange and dreadful strife
>   When Life and Death contended;
> The victory remained with Life,
>   The reign of Death was ended;
> Holy Scripture plainly saith
>   That Death is swallowed up by Death,
> His sting is lost forever.
>
> Then let us feast this Easter Day
>   On Christ, the Bread of Heaven;
> The Word of Grace hath purged away
>   The old and evil leaven.
> Christ alone our souls will feed.
>   He is our meat and drink indeed;
> Faith lives upon no other.

Walk Closer to God

A common greeting in the first-century church
was the triumphant announcement, "He is
risen!" To which the person being greeted would
reply, "He is risen indeed!"

Think of it! The "hello" of the first century was
a "Hallelujah—He is risen!" Indeed, He is risen.
Celebrate that fact today—and every day!

The Christ of Easter is always here!

Worship from the Heart

*Make this paraphrase
of Hebrews 10:19-22
your prayer today:
"How I praise You,
Jesus, that by virtue
of Your blood, I now
have confidence to
enter the holy place
which You have
opened up. Because
You are now the
High Priest over
God's household, I
draw near with full
confidence and a true
heart, knowing that
my inmost soul has
been purified by Your
blood. Amen."*

Walk Thru the Word

New Testament Reading
Mark 16
Old Testament Reading
Job 19:25-27

Jesus: Seeing, Seeking, Saving

In Luke's gospel we see Jesus' life changing interaction with all manner of people: young and old, men and women, infamous and religious, poor and rich.

After your brisk walk with Jesus in the gospel of Mark, it's time to take a slower-paced journey through the gospel of Luke, the longest book in the New Testament.

Drawing on carefully investigated details and eyewitness accounts, Luke writes "an orderly account" (Luke 1:3) of the life of Christ. As a divinely inspired investigative reporter, Luke unveils the undisputable facts about the Man from Galilee.

Luke's unique portrait of Jesus presents Him as God's Son who "came to seek and to save what was lost" (19:10). From the opening verses, Jesus emerges as the One who came to lead lost men and women out of their darkness and confusion.

Human interest stories abound in Luke's account, for he was interested in people—their hurts, fears, hopes, and joys. Throughout the book you'll meet individuals whose lives were touched by the power of God in Roman-occupied Palestine: the priest Zechariah, Elizabeth and Mary, an unnamed widow at Nain, diminutive Zacchaeus, two disciples on the road to Emmaus.

Jesus interacted with all manner of people: young and old, men and women, infamous and religious, poor and rich. Some came with physical needs, and He healed them with a touch. Others came with notorious reputations and found they were within the reach of His saving love. Some were called to be His disciples, and gladly left all to follow Him. Others came asking to become disciples and departed in dejection because of their unwillingness to pay the price that discipleship demanded.

This month, accompany Jesus on His mission to seek and to save lost people and learn how to read the needs of people. Let His example of sensitivity inspire you to reach out to others in the strength of His Spirit. When you do, Luke's purpose for writing will have been fulfilled in your life. So let's get started!

"I am the Lord's servant," Mary answered. "May it be to me as you have said" (Luke 1:38).

*I*n a remote village in Israel, an angel visited a young girl with what most would welcome as good news—she was going to have a baby!

But there were two problems. First, she was not married. Second, the man she was engaged to marry was not the father. How would you have responded to "good news" like that?

In Mary's case, she still considered it to be good news, because God was in control. F. B. Meyer explains Mary's example of utter obedience.

Walk with F. B. Meyer

"For this young, pure-hearted girl, the angel's message meant a great deal of misunderstanding and reproach. It was inevitable that clouds would gather around her character, which would sorely perplex the good man to whom she was betrothed.

"But as soon as she realized that this was ordained for her by God, she humbly acquiesced with the words of faith: 'May it be to me as you have said.'

"God's voice often speaks within our hearts, but we must test what seems to be His voice by these three corroborations: first, His Word; second, by the trend of outward circumstances; third, by the advice of Christian people.

"When these agree, we may take it that God has spoken, and we must respond. The responsibility may be a trusteeship for a dying friend, a charge of orphan children, an invalid, a difficult Christian ministry. But whenever it comes on us, imposed by the evident appointment of our Father, we must say as Mary did: May it be to me as you have said."

Walk Closer to God

If God appeared to you and said He was going to use your life to reveal His glory, how would you respond?

    a. "I'd like to think it over."
    b. "You've no business telling me what to do."
    c. "Let me see if I can fit it into my schedule."
    d. "Let it be to me according to Your word."
Only one answer will do.

*A*n example of obedience and faith

*W*orship from the Heart

Like Abraham and Sarah of old, Zachariah and Elizabeth must have believed that "nothing is impossible with God" (Luke 1:37). If there is an "impossible" situation looming in your life today, take it before the Lord in prayer. Then without asking for a sign as Zachariah did, honor God by accepting the answer He sends as being His will for you.

*W*alk Thru the Word

New Testament Reading
Luke 1:1-38
Old Testament Reading
Numbers 14:19-24

Words of praise focused on God's greatness

MARCH 2 ❑ DAY 61

Worship from the Heart

"O God of my salva-tion, as I ponder the cross of my beloved Savior, I see it point back to the awfulness of my past and for-ward to the magnifi-cence of my future. I join my voice to the praise songs of Your dear ones as we rejoice in Your love."

And Mary said: "My soul glorifies the Lord and my spirit rejoices in God my Savior" (Luke 1:46-47).

*I*t's always easier to magnify the negative than to accentuate the positive. For Mary, it would have been easy to murmur and complain about the unusual circumstances of her pregnancy. Instead, she chose to emphasize the positive and magnify (glorify) the Lord.

When your circumstances don't seem particu-larly praiseworthy, concentrate instead on God's character. Martin Luther points to the One who should be the first recipient of all your praise.

Walk with Martin Luther

"We must be on our guard, because we cannot do without God's good things while we live on earth; and therefore we cannot be without dis-tinction and honor. When people accord us praise and honor, we ought to profit by the example of Mary and at all times arm ourselves to make the proper reply and to use such honor and praise correctly.

"We should openly say, or at least think in our hearts: O Lord God, Thine is this work that is being praised and celebrated. Thine be the honor too.

"We should neither reject this praise and honor as though they were wrong, nor should we despise them as though they were nothing. But we should refuse to accept them as too precious or noble, and we should ascribe them to Him in heaven, to whom they belong.

"We should direct all praise to our praisewor-thy God for all the good we experience or have."

Walk Closer to God

Mary's focus indeed was firmly fixed on God.

"God my Savior . . . the Mighty One . . . holy is his name. . . . His mercy extends to those who fear him. . . . He has performed mighty deeds . . . he has scattered those who are proud. . . . brought down rulers . . . lifted up the humble. . . . filled the hungry with good things. . . . He has helped his servant Israel" (Luke 1:47-54).

What is "in focus" when problems come your way? Magnify the greatness of God, and watch how small your problems become by comparison.

Walk Thru the Word

New Testament Reading
Luke 1:39-56
Old Testament Reading
1 Samuel 2:1-10

68

Because of the tender mercy of our God (Luke 1:78).

*M*ercy. Everyone wants it when he or she least deserves it. Yet most hesitate to give it when another asks for it.

In Luke 1, mercy is mentioned five times. The One giving it is God; those who don't deserve it are men. And this mercy consists of God's becoming a man—the gift of Christ to sinners.

John Flavel explains that believers have the mercy of God in Jesus Christ.

Walk with John Flavel

"Jesus Christ is an incomparable and matchless mercy. You will find none in heaven or on earth to equal Him.

"He is more than all externals, as the light of the sun is more than that of a candle. He is more than life, as the cause is more than the effect. More than all peace and all joy, as the tree is more than the fruit.

"When you compare Christ with things eternal, you will find Him better than they. For what is heaven without Christ?

"If Christ should say to the saints, 'Take heaven among you, but I will withdraw from you,' the saints would weep, even in heaven itself, and say, 'Lord, heaven will not be heaven unless You are there, for You Yourself are the joy of heaven.' "

Walk Closer to God

Justice is receiving what you deserve. Mercy is not receiving what you deserve. Grace is receiving what you do not deserve.

All three come true in Jesus Christ (1:68-69, 77). His life and death provide redemption (that's justice—the price fully paid), remission (that's mercy—the guilt fully removed), and salvation (that's grace—eternal life freely given).

Giving others what's coming to them—that's only natural. Treating others with the mercy they don't deserve—that's supernatural.

Perhaps that's why Shakespeare wrote, "Earthly power doth show like God's when mercy seasons justice." Does that supernatural seasoning flow through your life to others?

*M*ercy: not receiving what you deserve

*W*orship from the Heart

Apart from Christ, each of us stands helpless before God, deserving only judgment. Yet He offers instead a balm of favor and forgiveness. By His strength today, show His mercy and kindness to someone who may only deserve your anger.

*W*alk Thru the Word

New Testament Reading
Luke 1:57-80
Old Testament Reading
Psalm 94:18-19

Is there room in your heart for Him?

And she . . . placed him in a manger, because there was no room for them in the inn (Luke 2:7).

*B*ethlehem was buzzing with out-of-town visitors who had come to obey Caesar's decree that all citizens register in their city of birth. But there was no room in Bethlehem for the Savior.

Emily Elliott's hymn beautifully expresses the believer's desire to make room for Him.

Walk with Emily Elliott

Thou didst leave Thy throne
  And Thy kingly crown
When Thou camest to earth for me,
  But in Bethlehem's home
Was there found no room
  For Thy holy nativity:
O come to my heart, Lord Jesus;
  There is room in my heart for Thee!

Heaven's arches rang
  When the angels sang,
Proclaiming Thy royal degree;
  But of lowly birth
Camest Thou, Lord, on earth,
  And in great humility;
O come to my heart, Lord Jesus;
  There is room in my heart for Thee!

Thou camest, O Lord,
  With the living word,
That should set Thy people free;
  But, with mocking scorn,
And with crown of thorn,
  They bore Thee to Calvary:
O come to my heart, Lord Jesus;
  Thy Cross is my only plea!

Walk Closer to God

In order for Christ to take His rightful place as Lord of your life, you need to make room for Him.

Make room in your work schedule, in your leisure activities, in your goals and priorities. To make room, the "furniture" may need to be rearranged. Some items may need to be thrown out so you can start over. But you'll never regret doing so.

Worship from the Heart

Though old in years, Simeon and Anna had their hearts set on the Lord. Imagine for a moment the overwhelming joy and satisfaction Simeon must have felt as he held the tiny infant in his arms and knew he was in the presence of the One for whom he had waited. Then praise God that a similar peace and joy can be yours continuously as you remain in His presence through the power of the Holy Spirit.

Walk Thru the Word

New Testament Reading
Luke 2
Old Testament Reading
Micah 5:2

Changing your mind and turning around

"Produce fruit in keeping with repentance."...
"What should we do then?" the crowd asked [John]
(Luke 3:8, 10).

For a prisoner, parole is an opportunity to convince the parole board that he has given up his life of crime. Unless he goes straight, he will soon find himself back in prison.

In Luke 3, John baptizes many people who profess to have changed their minds about sin. But the only way to prove that a change has occurred is by living a godly life.

Charles Hodge expands on John's call to repentance in both word and deed.

Walk with Charles Hodge

"The sure test of the quality of any supposed change of heart will be found in its permanent effects. 'By their fruit you will recognize them' is as applicable to the right method of judging ourselves as of judging others.

"Whatever, therefore, may have been our inward experience, whatever joy or sorrow we may have felt, unless we bring forth the fruit of repentance, our experience will profit us nothing.

"Repentance is incomplete unless it leads to confession and restitution; unless it causes us to forsake not merely outward sins, which others notice, but those which lie concealed in the heart; unless it makes us live not for ourselves but for God.

"There is no duty which is either more obvious in itself, or more frequently asserted in the Word of God, than that of repentance."

Walk Closer to God

"Repent and believe the good news!" (Mark 1:15). Repentance means changing your mind about sin . . . seeing it as God sees it . . . and turning from it.

A "straight" life is evidence of a mind and heart "straightened out" about sin. Anything less is not what Jesus and John preached.

The practice of righteousness is the proof of true repentance. If you had to convince a jury that you were serious about repentance, would there be enough evidence in your life to do it?

Worship from the Heart

The common people, the religious leaders, and the king himself were convicted of their sin by John's preaching and heard his call to repentance. As you worship with others this weekend, praise God for men and women in your community who are dedicated to declaring His truth regardless of the cost to themselves. Pray for their protection and continued courage.

Walk Thru the Word

New Testament Reading
Luke 3
Old Testament Reading
Isaiah 55:6-7

*Y*our sure defense when Satan comes calling

Jesus . . . was led by the Spirit in the desert, where for forty days he was tempted by the devil. . . . Jesus answered, "It is written: 'Man does not live on bread alone' " (Luke 4:1-2, 4).

*E*ve lived in a garden filled with good things to eat. Jesus had been in a desert forty days without food. Yet, when the temptation to eat the uneatable came, the One who needed it *most* resisted it *best*.

Under attack, Eve disobeyed God's Word not to eat; Jesus used God's Word to defend Himself.

The Word is still a sure defense against the wily schemes of Satan, as Martin Luther proclaims.

Worship from the Heart

As you ponder Jesus' response to Satan's demand for worship, remember that God has never annulled His commandments. He still desires to have a people who will worship Him as He rightly deserves. Rejoice that because of Jesus' life, death, and resurrection, you can come into God's presence, worshiping Him in spirit and in truth.

Walk with Martin Luther

"In every temptation simply close your eyes and follow the Word. Outside the Word there is nothing but tribulation and affliction. Through temptations and afflictions God proves the strength and virtue of His Word.

"Satan constantly tempts the heart. Therefore we must overcome the feeling of the flesh and adhere to the Word; for God does not forsake us but, like a mother, lovingly cherishes and carries us. Go to Christ, who is the sacrifice for our sins. In Him the Devil, sin, and death have been crucified.

"One way to conquer is to despise the thoughts suggested by Satan. The more you dwell on those thoughts in your mind, the more they oppress you. Once you lose sight of the Word, the ways and means of help are no more. But as soon as you lay hold of some saying of Scripture and rely on it as a holy anchor, the temptations are driven away."

Walk Closer to God

The Word of God is a sword with which you can defend yourself (Ephesians 6:17). But only if you carry it with you.

That doesn't mean wearing a sheath containing your Bible at your side. But it does suggest the need to know the Word of God intimately in your heart and mind.

This Sword of the Spirit is your sure defense when Satan comes calling; it is also your chief offensive weapon. Keep it sharp and ready to use at all times.

*W*alk Thru the Word

New Testament Reading
Luke 4
Old Testament Reading
Genesis 3:1-7

72

The product of prompt obedience

"Master, we've worked hard all night and haven't caught anything. But because you say so, I will let down the nets" (Luke 5:5).

*I*n spite of experience, skill, and effort, Peter had nothing to show for an entire night's work. Imagine how startled this professional fisherman must have been when the carpenter's Son told him to head into deeper water and lower his nets!

Where human skill and wisdom proved inadequate, humble obedience to the Master produced the catch of a lifetime.

George Müller observes how the *will* of God can be found in the *Word* of God.

Walk with George Müller

"To ascertain the Lord's will, we ought to use Scriptural means. Prayer, the Word of God, and His Spirit should be united together. We should go to the Lord repeatedly in prayer and ask Him to teach us by His Spirit through His Word.

"I say 'by His Spirit through His Word,' for if we should think that His Spirit led us to do so and so, because certain facts are so and so, and yet His Word is opposed to the step which we are going to take, we are deceiving ourselves. No situation, no business will be given to me by God in which I have not time enough to care about my soul.

"Therefore, however outward circumstances may appear, they can only be considered as permitted of God to prove the genuineness of my love, faith, and obedience. By no means are circumstances the leading of His providence to induce me to act contrary to His revealed will."

Walk Closer to God

The "fishing report" was bleak, but Christ's command was clear: "Let down the nets for a catch."

The fisher of fish obeyed the Fisher of Men . . . and the rest is biblical history!

When your own wisdom produces only frustration, perhaps it's time to listen to an Expert— to submit to the knowledge and counsel of One infinitely wiser than you.

And don't be surprised at the weight of blessing that results!

Worship from the Heart

At the Sea of Galilee Jesus called the disciples. They followed, leaving behind businesses and boats, possessions and previous lifestyles. Praise God that the invitation to follow the Savior is open to everyone. Then take a moment to examine the baggage of position and possessions in your life. Are you carrying excess baggage you need to lay aside? Remember, Jesus travels light.

Walk Thru the Word

New Testament Reading
Luke 5
Old Testament Reading
Daniel 4:1-3

Seeking the Father for expert advice

One of those days Jesus went out to a mountainside to pray, and spent the night praying to God. When morning came, he called his disciples to him and chose twelve of them, whom he also designated apostles (Luke 6:12-13).

I did it my way" is the way many important decisions in life are made. Right or wrong, wise or foolish—these make little difference as long as the final result is what I want.

Jesus, however, was concerned with making the *right* decision. He knew He needed His Father's counsel. And if the Son of God thought it important to consult His Father before making decisions, how much more should you do the same! James Hastings offers this insight in his Speaker's Bible.

Walk with James Hastings

"The ideal of the Christian life is certainly that we should naturally, spontaneously, and habitually carry every question we have to decide to God. This is not to abdicate our judgment or to disregard the faculties which God has given us to make decisions on practical questions of life. It is the sanctification of judgment.

"No one is in favor of a person acting thoughtlessly; why should we ever act prayerlessly? For the Christian, deliberation should be synonymous with taking counsel with God.

"We want to get rid of this wretched independence—independence of judgment, thought, action—and to feel that it is our privilege as the children of God to know the Father's will in everything and to embody that in utterance and in life."

Walk Closer to God

Many sad stories could be told of people who decided to forego the advice of an expert. Can you afford to ignore the guidance of the God who knows all things?

"Do not let this Book of the Law depart from your mouth; meditate on it day and night, so that you may be careful to do everything written in it. Then you will be prosperous and successful" (Joshua 1:8). A word *from* God and a word *with* God—there's no better way to make decisions in the will of God.

Worship from the Heart

What a refreshing truth to know that God never wearies in giving counsel. We need not worry about standing alone in a difficult decision. He is there to reveal His mind on the matter and to turn our thoughts and actions toward a godly path.

Walk Thru the Word

New Testament Reading
Luke 6:1-26
Old Testament Reading
2 Samuel 5:17-20

74

*F*reely giving what you can supply

"Do to others as you would have them do to you" (Luke 6:31).

*T*oday's popular version of the Golden Rule might go something like this: "Do unto others before they undo you!"—a sure sign of a society preoccupied with itself.

Focusing on the needs of others. That's fairly difficult when you're wrapped up in yourself. But for the Christian, the Golden Rule provides a ready remedy, as Matthew Henry explains.

Walk with Matthew Henry

"What we would want others to do to us, either in justice or love, if they were in our condition and we in theirs—that is what we must do to them. We must treat them as we should desire and justly expect to be treated ourselves.

"We must give to those in need, to everyone who is a proper object of charity, who lacks necessities which we have the means to supply.

"Give to those who are not able to help themselves. Christ would have His disciples always ready to distribute what is within their power in ordinary cases, and beyond their power in extraordinary ones."

Walk Closer to God

Living by the Golden Rule means your treatment of others is based on how you want to be treated in return.

Do you desire good? Of course! Then give good. Do you want others to forgive? Absolutely! Then be quick to forgive.

But here's the hard part: It is immaterial whether others actually treat you well or forgive you promptly. The point of the rule is: How would you want to be treated?

The Golden Rule was not given to society in general; that might explain its rather tarnished image. Rather, it was issued to the only group of people who were empowered to keep it—the people of God!

Whom do you know that needs a golden touch today? He or she may be surprised to learn that someone remembers the original rule, which is untarnished and still shines.

*W*orship from the Heart

"Father help me, in this selfish generation, to give other people the respect and courtesy that everyone created in Your image deserves. Help me to be thoughtful of others even at my busiest moments—because of Your love and kindness. Let me see any mistreatment that comes my way as an opportunity to express Your love. In the name of Jesus, who gave us the Golden Rule. Amen."

*W*alk Thru the Word

New Testament Reading
Luke 6:27-49
Old Testament Reading
Psalm 77:1-12

Believing faith makes the difference

When Jesus heard this, he was amazed at him, and turning to the crowd following him, he said, "I tell you, I have not found such great faith even in Israel" (Luke 7:9).

*F*aith is a concept more easily demonstrated than defined. You exercise faith when you fly in an airplane or visit a doctor. Chances are good that you couldn't land the airplane or diagnose your illness. Yet you rely on the strength and skill of someone who can. And that's faith!

In Luke 7, Jesus commends the great faith of a Roman officer—a commodity so scarce as to amaze even Jesus!

George Whitefield highlights the necessity of believing faith.

Walk with George Whitefield

"I am not against going to church, nor against the creed, the Lord's prayer, or the commandments. But believing is something more than those. It is coming to Jesus, receiving Him, rolling ourselves on Him, trusting in Him.

"I do not know of any one single thing more often repeated in Scriptures than believing. It is described as a coming, trusting, receiving, and relying, under a felt conviction that we are lost, undone, and condemned without Him.

"As a good old Puritan observed, we never come to Jesus Christ—the sinner's only hope—until we feel we cannot do without Him."

Walk Closer to God

Faith in Jesus Christ sets Christianity apart from religion.

Religion is based on what you do for God; Christianity is what God has done for you.

Religion is man's attempt to work his way to heaven; Christianity is God's good news that heaven is a free gift.

Religion involves trying; Christianity is relying.

Have you come to the point of realizing you can no longer do without the Savior, Jesus Christ? He's patiently waiting for you to come . . . receive . . . trust.

He's waiting for you to put your faith in Him. You cannot do without Him.

Worship from the Heart

"Lord Jesus, I come today knowing I can do nothing to save myself from my sinful condition. I can do nothing to gain fellowship with You or make my life worthwhile. But I do believe that You are able to do all those things. Take my life and make it pleasing to You. I know that You, Lord, are the only One who can."

Walk Thru the Word

New Testament Reading
Luke 7:1-35
Old Testament Reading
Genesis 15:4-6

76

*M*aking your heart Christ's home

Then he turned toward the woman and said to Simon, "Do you see this woman? I came into your house. You did not give me any water for my feet, but she wet my feet with her tears and wiped them with her hair" (Luke 7:44).

*W*hen you invite guests for dinner, it's not proper to ask them to take out the garbage or to tell them how much the meal is costing.

Such bad manners speak volumes about hosts: Simon's bad manners toward Jesus in his own house revealed an attitude of pride and selfishness. G. Campbell Morgan describes how Jesus set matters in their proper perspective.

Walk with G. Campbell Morgan

"This incident shows that Christ does notice neglect, and that He does appreciate devotion. Simon brought Him no water for His feet, gave Him no kiss, did not put oil upon His head. Yet Christ said nothing. But when the circumstances made it possible, He revealed the fact that He noticed the lack of hospitality.

"Another scene reveals the same truth. When Mary of Bethany anointed Jesus' feet, Judas said, 'Why wasn't this perfume sold and the money given to the poor? It was worth a year's wages.'

"All the disciples said the same thing. It was unanimous. Christ sharply rebuked them. 'Leave her alone. . . . It was intended that she should save this perfume for the day of my burial.' He valued her action. The aroma that filled Simon's house, and again when Mary brought it later on, was a sweet thing to the heart of Jesus Christ."

Walk Closer to God

A knock comes at your door. You open it to find Jesus standing at the threshold. You invite Him in.

Once He is comfortably seated, do you leave your Guest to entertain Himself? Or do you seek to make Him as welcome as possible?

Perhaps it depends on how much you want to know Him. The Pharisee didn't care to make Jesus welcome; the woman longed for her heart to be His home. In which manner will you welcome the One who stands at the door of your life and knocks?

*W*orship from the Heart

Phocas, a dear saint in the early history of the church, was renowned for his hospitality. He even invited for dinner the very men sent to kill him! Truly, one of the marks of genuine Christian love is hospitality to others. Praise God that He can warm our hearts and swing wide the doors of our homes so that He may be honored.

*W*alk Thru the Word

New Testament Reading
Luke 7:36-50
Old Testament Reading
Genesis 18:1-8

The cost of salvaging wrecked lives

Then all the people of the region of the Gerasenes asked Jesus to leave them (Luke 8:37).

*I*nstead of praising God for the wonderful restoration of an individual's sanity, the Gerasenes took offense because Jesus' healing resulted in financial loss for them.

But Jesus never let social pressure or popular opinion detour His rescue mission. As John Calvin points out, the Gerasenes would have welcomed Jesus if they had thought more of their salvation than they did of their swine.

Worship from the Heart

During Jesus' travels a group of faithful women provided materially for the group. They remained with Jesus to the end and were honored to be the first to see Him after His resurrection. In an age when the sexes compete in so many areas, ask God to give you a deep appreciation for the godly women who have made a difference in your life.

Walk with John Calvin

"We have here a striking proof that not all who perceive the hand of God profit as they ought to do by yielding themselves to Him in sincere godliness. They choose to be deprived of the salvation which is offered to them rather than to endure any longer the presence of Christ.

"And yet it is true that the Gerasenes' fear was partly caused by their loss. Even at the present day, people who believe that the kingdom of God is opposed to their interests have a depraved and carnal fear and have no relish for His grace.

"When He comes, they think that God does not regard them with favor, but rather with anger, and insofar as they are able, they send Him to another place.

"It is a mark of shame in those men that the loss of their swine gives them more alarm than the salvation of their souls would give them joy."

Walk Closer to God

You might say the Gerasenes were more pig-headed than open-minded about having God at work in their midst.

After all, what right did He have to help one man at the expense of their livelihood? Is *your* attitude any different? Will helping a needy person near you interfere with cherished plans? Will it cost you more than you are willing to pay?

Before you respond, think carefully about what it cost the Savior to salvage your life.

Then look around. That hillside in Galilee may be nearer than you think!

Walk Thru the Word

New Testament Reading
Luke 8
Old Testament Reading
Psalm 2:1-4, 10-12

He replied, "You give them something to eat"
(Luke 9:13).

*W*hat if you were close friends with an author
whose works you admired? Would you prize
his books over his friendship? Of course not.

The disciples were so concerned about finding
food for the crowd that they forgot they were in
the presence of the Bread of Life.

Mary Ann Lathbury wrote of our need for
daily spiritual food from the Word of God, which
reveals the living Word who is the Bread of Life.

Walk with Mary Ann Lathbury

Break Thou the Bread of Life,
Dear Lord, to me,
As Thou didst break the loaves
Beside the sea:
Beyond the sacred page
I seek Thee, Lord;
My spirit pants for Thee, O living Word.

Bless Thou the truth, dear Lord,
To me—to me,
As Thou didst bless the bread
By Galilee:
Then shall all bondage cease,
All fetters fall,
And I shall find my peace, My all in all.

Thou art the bread of life,
O Lord, to me;
Thy holy Word the truth
That saveth me:
Give me to eat and live
With Thee above;
Teach me to love Thy truth, For Thou art love.

Walk Closer to God

You wouldn't throw away a book just because
you knew the author. In fact, you would probably
strive to know him better by reading his works!

So as you read and meditate on God's Word,
expect to get closer to your Lord. And the next
time you see a loaf of bread, let it remind you of
your relationship with the One who is the Bread
of Life.

*G*etting to the Source of Life

*W*orship from the Heart

*"Savior, You are the
source of everything I
need. You are my
sustainer; You are
the creative force
behind anything good
that comes out of me.
Today I acknowledge
my need for You in
every situation. I am
nothing without
Your driving power
for good. Thank You
for making Your
love, Your provision,
and Your Truth
available to me.
Amen."*

*W*alk Thru the Word

New Testament Reading
Luke 9:1-36
Old Testament Reading
Psalm 104:10-15

Staying on the path to the kingdom

"No one who puts his hand to the plow and looks back is fit for service in the kingdom of God" (Luke 9:62).

Jesus had much to teach His disciples during His final weeks, and the events that transpired underscore the urgency of the task: John the Baptist's brutal murder . . . feeding the 5,000 . . . Peter's confession . . . the glorious event on the Mount of Transfiguration.

But now, beginning the long march to Jerusalem where certain death awaits the Master Teacher, it's time for the disciples also to put His teaching into practice and commit their lives. The time for turning back had passed. Jesus' face was set like a flint; the others could only follow, as F. B. Meyer comments.

Worship from the Heart

The world's distractions titillate our senses and beg us to look back. But praise be to God that He did not merely leave us a road map to eternity. He also gives us His precious Spirit as a traveling companion. Why not thank Him now for His kindness and grace?

Walk with F. B. Meyer

"The Master's steadfast face rebukes us. Whether we follow afar off or closely, that alert, eager figure is always in front, taking the upward path.

"We need to remember which kingdom we belong to. We have passed out of the sphere of force and war into the kingdom of the Son of God's love. It is a reversal of the divine plan to go back to the fire of vengeance. The only fire that we can invoke is that of the Holy Spirit.

"The Lord was ever acting as a winnowing fan, detecting the wheat and the chaff in human motive. Be prepared to follow your Lord through loneliness, homelessness, the rupture of tender ties, and the plowing of a solitary furrow. But keep your eye fixed on the eternal side of your life!"

Walk Closer to God

"If anyone would come after me, he must deny himself and take up his cross daily and follow me. For whoever wants to save his life will lose it, but whoever loses his life for me will save it. . . . For he who is least among you all—he is the greatest" (Luke 9:23-24, 48).

Sacrifice . . . humility . . . compassion—Jesus demonstrated the powerful reality of these lessons in His own life. The path where He leads may be long and demanding, but consider what waits at the journey's end, the "eternal side" of your life with God!

Walk Thru the Word

New Testament Reading
Luke 9:37-62
Old Testament Reading
Ruth 1:16

Finding the roots of love

" 'Love the Lord your God with all your heart and with all your soul and with all your strength and with all your mind'; and, 'Love your neighbor as yourself' " (Luke 10:27).

*I*n Luke 10, a lawyer challenged Jesus with tough, testing questions. Jesus did not dismiss the questions lightly, nor did He prescribe an easy course of action for inheriting eternal life. Instead, Jesus forced the lawyer to consider God's law and give his own interpretation of it.

This conversation left no doubts about the way of eternal life or how to identify a neighbor. Bernard of Clairvaux shares this meditation on how love for God enables us to love our neighbor.

Walk with Bernard of Clairvaux

"For our love of others to be wholly right, God must be at its root. No one can love his neighbor perfectly unless it is in God he holds him dear. And nobody can love his fellow man in God who loves not God Himself.

"We must begin by loving God; and then we shall be able, in Him, to love our neighbor too. For our nature is so constituted that it needs to be sustained, and He who made us is the One who meets that need.

"In this way man—by nature animal and carnal, loving himself alone—begins to learn that it is to his own profit to love God, because in Him alone (as He has often proved) can he do all things which it profits him to do; he is quite powerless apart from God."

Walk Closer to God

> Loving the world for me is no chore;
> My only problem's the person next door.

Is that a sentiment with which you find yourself in agreement? Do you find it relatively easy to love the world, but difficult to love your neighbor?

If so, Bernard's words can be an encouragement. Begin by loving God, and out of that relationship will grow an unfeigned love for others.

Love God completely; then you will find it easier to love your neighbor compassionately and you will love yourself correctly.

Worship from the Heart

As you mull over the attitudes and actions of the two people who failed to show compassion in the parable of the Good Samaritan, be aware that Jesus carefully chose His cast of characters. And as you meet people today, remember Jesus' last words to the lawyer. Clearly, God's "invitation" is for His children to live as He does— reaching out in compassion, love, and practical action.

Walk Thru the Word

New Testament Reading
Luke 10
Old Testament Reading
Psalm 15:1-3

81

*N*ourish your life with prayer

*W*orship from the Heart

Rejoice that the wall of partition has been broken down and you are free to seek God's presence at any time and in any situation. (See Ephesians 2:14.) The route to intimate communion with your King and fellowship with your Father is the path of prayer.

One of his disciples said to him, "Lord, teach us to pray" (Luke 11:1).

*J*esus' pattern of prayer had made an obvious impression on His men. Frequently they would find Him alone talking with His Father. At last, one curious disciple was prompted to ask, "Lord, teach us to pray."

In his classic devotional book, *My Utmost for His Highest,* Oswald Chambers considers the role of prayer in nourishing the spiritual life.

Walk with Oswald Chambers

"When a person is born from above, the life of the Son of God is born in him, and he can either starve that life or nourish it. Prayer is the way to nourish one's life with God. Our ordinary views of prayer are not found in the New Testament.

"We look upon prayer as a means of getting things for ourselves; the Bible's idea of prayer is that we may get to know God Himself.

"It is not so true that 'prayer changes things' as that prayer changes me and I change things.

"God has so constituted things that prayer on the basis of redemption alters the way in which one looks at things. Prayer is not a question of altering things externally, but of working wonders in one's disposition."

Walk Closer to God

Starvation in the spiritual life, as in the physical, is really quite simple. All you need to do is to do *nothing.* Stop feeding upon the Word. Stop breathing through prayer. Stop drinking in the refreshment of worship and fellowship with other believers.

Nourishing your spiritual life, on the other hand, is a daily challenge. The challenge comes in balancing time alone with God with time together with people.

Balance time to eat with time to exercise. Balance time in the Word with time in the world. Balance the times God wants to change you with the times He wants to use you to change others.

Perhaps you need to echo the plea of the nameless disciple: "Lord, teach me to pray!"

*W*alk Thru the Word

New Testament Reading
Luke 11
Old Testament Reading
Psalm 105:1-5

Staying alert and ready to run

"Be dressed ready for service and keep your lamps burning" (Luke 12:35).

Scene 1: The security guard sits with eyes glued to the screen . . . of his favorite TV program. Result: His attention is diverted, and a robbery goes undetected.

Scene 2: The disciple of Jesus Christ, called to be watchful in his Master's absence, becomes preoccupied with pursuits after the world's pleasures. Result: Embarrassment rather than eagerness when the Master returns.

In Luke 12, Jesus warns His disciples of the importance of staying alert—a theme Alexander Maclaren echoes in this insight.

Walk with Alexander Maclaren

"Prepare your minds for action, says the apostle Peter (1 Peter 1:13), echoing the Master's words. For the first condition of true service is that you shall do it with concentrated power.

"One reason why a man tucked his robe around his waist when he had anything to do that needed all his might was that it might not catch upon the things that protruded and so keep him back.

"Concentration, and what I may call detachment, go together. They are in effect two sides of the same thing. The girding up of our loins is not only the symbol of concentration and detachment, but of that for which the concentration and the detachment are needful—alert readiness for service.

"The servant who stands before his Lord with his belt buckled tight indicates thereby that he is ready to run whenever he is bid."

Walk Closer to God

Military troops must be ready to follow and fight on a moment's notice—Jesus demands the same preparedness from His followers.

Availability: The willingness to be "on call" any time, ready to perform any service for the Master.

Mobility: The willingness to go anywhere, leave familiar surroundings and comfortable circumstances, in obedience to the Master's bidding.

Are you "ready, willing, and able" to follow your Commander wherever He may lead today?

Worship from the Heart

You've already read several parables in the book of Luke, with more to come. In some way each one will be a lesson about what it means to follow Jesus, as well as a challenge to your own life. After you've read today's Scripture passage, thank God that the parables open your eyes to the opportunities you have as His child, both for service and accountability.

Walk Thru the Word

New Testament Reading
Luke 12
Old Testament Reading
Nehemiah 4:7-18

Asking questions to gain wisdom

Again he [Jesus] asked, "What shall I compare the kingdom of God to?" . . . Then Jesus went through the towns and villages, teaching (Luke 13:20, 22).

$\mathcal{S}$ome very bright minds in the church have been preoccupied with such "crucial" questions as . . . how many angels can dance on the head of a pin? Or, can God make a rock so big that He Himself cannot move it?

But Jesus came to teach, not to speculate. He answers questions that will change a person's life—questions such as the one asked by the rich young man: "Teacher, what good thing must I do to get eternal life?" (Matthew 19:16).

Johann Peter Lange points to the Master Teacher as an example for His children to follow.

Walk with Johann Peter Lange

"Here a bright light is thrown on the character of the King. We admire His wisdom in teaching, by which He brings the questioner back from the domain of unfruitful speculation to that of practice.

"In this the Savior is an unequalled example, especially for those in the church who would rather dispute about doctrine than listen to the personal requirements of faith and conversion; in a word, who continually are beginning, where on the other hand they ought to stand still and conclude. They need to turn to Deuteronomy 29:29.

"Unnecessary questions the gospel answers only to a certain degree; but to the one thing needful the answer is to be read: 'Believe in the Lord Jesus, and you will be saved' (Acts 16:31)."

Walk Closer to God

"The secret things belong to the Lord our God, but the things revealed belong to us and to our children forever, that we may follow all the words of this law" (Deuteronomy 29:29). God has the answers to questions you might never even think to ask, though nowhere does He promise to answer them if you do ask!

But He has given you the answers to the questions you *need* to ask about life—in His Word.

Are you looking in the right place to find the answers?

Worship from the Heart

Pray this prayer today: "Lord, let me find Thy light in my darkness, Thy life in my death, Thy joy in my sorrow, Thy grace in my sin, Thy riches in my poverty, Thy glory in my valley. In the name of Him who walks with me through every valley, Amen."
—Arthur Bennett

Walk Thru the Word

New Testament Reading
Luke 13
Old Testament Reading
Proverbs 3:31-32

The demands of being a disciple

"If anyone comes to me and does not hate his father and mother, his wife and children, his brothers and sisters—yes, even his own life—he cannot be my disciple" (Luke 14:26).

*C*onvicted felons, naturalized citizens, and those under the age of thirty-five are disqualified by law from being President of the United States.

In Luke 14, Jesus presents some "disqualifications" for being one of His disciples. There is a cost to be counted . . . priorities to be rearranged . . . allegiance to be sworn for all who would follow Him.

Andrew Murray explains why stringent qualifications are essential for discipleship.

Walk with Andrew Murray

"Why does Christ make the condition of discipleship such an exacting demand? Because the sinful nature we have inherited from Adam is indeed so vile that if we could see it in its true nature, we would flee from it as loathsome and incurably evil.

"The flesh is enmity against God; the soul that seeks to love God cannot but hate the old man which is corrupt through its whole being. It is not till we hate this life with a deadly hatred that we can give up the old nature to die the death that is its due.

"Christ claims all. In the path of following Him, learning to know and to love Him better, we shall willingly sacrifice all, self with its life, to make room for Him who is more than all."

Walk Closer to God

Probe your walk with God by asking yourself some pointed questions—the difficult kind Jesus specialized in asking:

What does your family think of your commitment to Christ?

What is it that makes others feel disapproving because you are a disciple of Christ?

What is limiting the possibility of your following Christ in total obedience today?

Such questions require thoughtful and perhaps painful answers. But better to deal with them now than to face the infinitely more painful verdict "Disqualified!" in the future.

Worship from the Heart

Spend a few seconds analyzing your eating habits. Consider the number of meals you eat each day, when you eat, the types of food that are part of your diet, what you snack on, and who you eat with and why. Then ask yourself those same questions regarding the spiritual nourishment you take each day. Is there a habit or pattern you need to change to strengthen your fellowship with Jesus?

Walk Thru the Word

New Testament Reading
Luke 14
Old Testament Reading
Psalm 51:15-17

The parable of the pouting sibling

The older brother became angry and refused to go in (Luke 15:28).

No doubt you've read the parable of the lost son in Luke 15 more than once. But don't miss the "parable of the pouting sibling" in the same chapter!

Outwardly, the older brother was a model son. But inwardly, his emotions seethed and eventually boiled over.

F. B. Meyer diagnoses the brother's root problem and applies his observations to today.

Walk with F. B. Meyer

"The elder brother is the dark contrast which heightens the glowing picture of the repentant prodigal.

"When we look at sin, not in its theological aspects but in its everyday clothes, we find that it divides itself into two kinds. We find there are sins of the body and sins of the disposition; or, more narrowly, sins of the passions, including all forms of lust and selfishness, and sins of the temper.

"The prodigal is the instance in the New Testament of sins of passion; the elder brother of sins of temper.

"One scholar did a careful analysis of the ingredients that went into that one spiteful speech. They were jealousy, anger, pride, uncharity, cruelty, self-righteousness, sulkiness, and touchiness.

"Let us carefully read our hearts, lest there be any trace of this spirit in us when others are pressing into the kingdom with joy."

Walk Closer to God

The language of the heart includes *attitude, belief, conduct,* and many other spiritual qualities.

After reading today's Scripture portion, pause for a moment to let the Holy Spirit "read" your heart as well. Does it hold resentment or bitterness toward anyone?

Ask God to renew your heart, to purify your inner spirit so that your external conduct will be governed by a heart filled with a sense of God's holiness.

Do that, and you'll have learned a worthy lesson from the life of the older brother!

Worship from the Heart

Picture yourself today as a lost sheep. Through misfortune, bad judgment, or disobedience, you have strayed from the flock. Stranded in a dark and lonely place, you are very frightened. Suddenly you hear the shepherd's voice. He is coming. He will carry you to safety. You have nothing to fear. Jesus is the Good Shepherd.

Walk Thru the Word

New Testament Reading
Luke 15
Old Testament Reading
Proverbs 4:23

Careful concern for the Master's goods

> " 'What is this I hear about you? Give an account of your management, because you cannot be manager any longer' " (Luke 16:2).

*I*t's a timeless tale of woe. A hardworking wage earner entrusts his savings to a financial trustee with instructions to invest only in safe, stable enterprises. Instead, the unworthy trustee follows a "hot tip" and soon the money has disappeared!

In Luke 16, Jesus uses a similar first-century scenario to show that the person God can trust doesn't gamble with what God has entrusted to him, but rather uses it for the maximum glory of his Lord. And John Wesley underscores the priorities of proper stewardship.

Walk with John Wesley

"We are now indebted to God for all we have. But although a debtor is obliged to return what he has received, yet until the time of payment comes, he is at liberty to use it as he pleases.

"It is not so with a steward. He is not at liberty to use what is lodged in his hands as he pleases, but as his Master pleases.

"This is exactly the case of everyone with relation to God. We are not at liberty to use what He has lodged in our hands as we please, but as He pleases, who alone is the Possessor of heaven and earth, and the Lord of all.

"And He entrusts us with these things on this express condition—that we use them only as our Master's goods, and according to the particular directions which He has given us in His Word."

Walk Closer to God

The behind-the-scenes role of a steward isn't exactly a glamorous job. But great rewards await faithful stewards who handle the owner's resources faithfully and diligently.

Stewards—trustworthy, diligent disciples—give their finest efforts to whatever task is set before them. The question remains: Do you pass the threefold test of a faithful individual?

Faithful in little things (16:10).

Faithful in money matters (16:11).

Faithful with others' things (16:12).

Worship from the Heart

The world offers enticements which appear desirable, beneficial, and perfectly harmless. But Jesus' warning to the Pharisees in Luke 16:15 still holds true. As you guard your heart against that which would entrap you, worship the Lord by acknowledging that His favor, His presence, and His power are worth far more than worldly success.

Walk Thru the Word

New Testament Reading
Luke 16
Old Testament Reading
Malachi 1:6

John Wesley (1703-1791) Preacher on Horseback and Founder of Methodism

*I*n our day many have concluded there can never be another revival. The times are too evil. Sin is too rampant. It's just too late.

But the history of the First Great Awakening shows that the worst of times is often the ripest of times for revival.

In 1662 the Industrial Revolution was in full swing, bringing sudden prosperity and, with it, low morality and religious indifference. Ministers were either ignored or subjected to scorn and ridicule.

Into this sin-filled scene John Wesley was born on June 17, 1703, at Epworth Rectory, Lincolnshire. The fifteenth of nineteen children, John became heir to a rich heritage of preachers: His father, grandfather, and great-grandfather were all ministers.

John's mother Susannah, herself one of twenty-five children, knew how to organize her large family so that each child received individual attention. Under her influence, John quickly developed in spiritual and academic matters.

At ten he began to learn Greek, Latin, and theology. At twenty-one he graduated from Oxford and three years later received his master's degree.

Returning to Oxford, John, his brother Charles, and George Whitefield became part of the "Holy Club"—a group dedicated to prayer, Bible study, and outreach.

J O H N   W E S L E Y

While Whitefield was preaching in England, John traveled to America, where for three years he labored with a growing sense of emptiness. In his journal Wesley wrote, "I went to America to convert the Indians; but Oh! who shall convert me?"

In 1737 he sailed back to England. Wednesday, May 24, 1738, was to be a destiny-shaping day in John's life. He describes it this way:

"In the evening I went very unwillingly to a society in Aldersgate Street, where one was reading Luther's preface to the Epistle of Romans. About a quarter before nine, while he was describing the change which God works in the heart through faith in Christ, I felt my heart strangely warmed. I felt I did trust in Christ, Christ alone for my salvation; and an assurance was given me that He had taken away my sins."

After his conversion Wesley took to the open air, preaching in the markets and mines, the fields and doorways of England.

During his life Wesley preached an average of 800 sermons a year — more than two a day — to crowds numbering as large as 20,000. By the time of his death in 1791, he had ridden an estimated 250,000 miles on horseback and had preached more than 40,000 sermons.

And what of the effect on the nation? "Religious revival burst forth . . . which changed in a few years the whole temper of English society. The church was restored to life and activity. Religion carried to the hearts of the people a fresh spirit of moral zeal. It purified their literature and manners . . . reformed the prisons, infused clemency and wisdom into the penal laws, abolished the slave trade, and gave the first impulse to popular education."

The same Word of God that transformed John Wesley's life — and through that life his world — is at work today, changing lives, mending homes, restoring morality, and removing idolatry.

Today and every day can be the beginning of a new revival in your life. But to obey God's Word, you must know it. And to know it you must read it.

Are you ready to begin a Great Awakening in your life?

A Lesson from the life of John Wesley

My unyielding obedience to God can make a difference in my world.

89

Gratitude that gladdens the heart of God

Jesus asked, "Were not all ten cleansed? Where are the other nine?" (Luke 17:17).

A certain man had three strikes against him. Strike one: He was an outsider living among the people of God. Strike two: He was a despised Samaritan. Strike three: He was a leper.

Then a miracle occurred. Ten lepers were cured of their dreaded disease by the Man from Galilee. But only one—the Samaritan outcast—returned to thank Jesus.

G. Campbell Morgan describes how one grateful heart brought more joy to the Savior than ten healed bodies.

Walk with G. Campbell Morgan

"Where are the nine? This question at once proves the value Jesus sets on praise. The glad outpouring of a grateful heart was acceptable to Him, and He missed that of the nine who were healed but did not return to express gratitude.

"One wonders whether our Lord has not been asking this question constantly, for we are all in danger of failing to give Him the adoration which is due Him.

"Sometimes we may be restrained by the feeling that our praise at its best is poor and unworthy. But we have no right, for any such cause, to withhold from Him what He values. So let us with the abandon of our utmost love go to Him constantly, telling Him of our joy and gratitude. All such worship is the incense which gladdens His heart, however amazing that may seem to us."

Walk Closer to God

A thankful spirit is one of life's beautiful but rare jewels.

Anyone who has experienced God's goodness has plenty of reasons to thank Him!

You can thank Him for the little things He's done for you throughout the week. And you can thank Him for the big things—for life, health, strength, friends, church, family, freedom— whatever comes to mind. And He will be worthy of all your praise!

Learning to be thankful in *everything* begins with learning to be thankful for *something*.

Worship from the Heart

"Spirit of love, help me love as Jesus loves. Give me His tenderness, compassion, humility, and peace. Keep me from causing anyone to stumble. May I be quick to forgive any who offend me and may I readily repent of any wrong that I do. May I honor You today by being a vessel through which Your light shines clear and bright in the darkness. Amen."

Walk Thru the Word

New Testament Reading
Luke 17
Old Testament Reading
Joel 2:26-27

Jesus took the Twelve aside. . . . The disciples did not understand any of this (Luke 18:31, 34).

As Jesus unfolded the details of His approaching death and resurrection, everything He said was misunderstood by His men. After three years of face-to-face communication, after more than thirty miracles and dozens of sermons, the disciples still lacked the understanding to grasp the significance of what was about to happen.

But understanding's not always necessary, as Oswald Chambers explains.

Walk with Oswald Chambers

"We are prone to say that because a person has natural ability, therefore he will make a good Christian. But God can do nothing with the one who thinks he is of use to God.

"As Christians we are not out for our own cause at all; we are out for the cause of God, which can never be our cause. We do not know what God is after, but we have to maintain our relationship with Him regardless of what happens.

"We must never allow anything to injure our relationship with God; if it does get injured, we must put it right. The main thing about Christianity is not the work we do, but the relationship we maintain and the atmosphere produced by that relationship. That is all God wants us to look after, and it is the one thing that is continually assailed."

Walk Closer to God

You brush to prevent cavities. You change the oil in your car regularly to keep it running well. You jog or walk and eat a balanced diet to keep your heart in shape. Preventive care helps you avoid future problems.

Your spiritual life also requires regular "preventive maintenance."

Confession ("Lord, I was wrong").
Communion ("Lord, I love You").
Petition ("Lord, I need You").
Meditation ("Lord, speak to me").

Attend to these, and even when Christ's ways seem unusual or inexplicable, your response will be trust rather than misunderstanding.

*K*eeping your relationship on the right track

*W*orship from the Heart

Nothing in any human heart is hidden from God, yet He loves us still. As He probes the recesses and dark corners of your heart today, He may convict you of areas which need growth or cleansing. As the Holy Spirit exposes these shadows to His light, may your commitment be to let the freshness of His presence sweep your life clean. Praise God, who is the Searcher of hearts.

*W*alk Thru the Word

New Testament Reading
Luke 18
Old Testament Reading
Numbers 13:26-30

The rewards of long and faithful service

" 'Well done, my good servant!' his master replied. 'Because you have been trustworthy in a very small matter, take charge of ten cities' " (Luke 19:17).

What would you think of a boss who had a habit of promoting
... stock clerks to managers?
... waitresses to vice-presidents?
... station attendants to oil company executives?

Luke 19 describes a series of promotions just as breathtaking as that of individuals who have been faithful with limited resources and who are suddenly "graduated" to positions of responsibility.

Read as A. B. Simpson comments on the tangible rewards of faithful service.

Walk with A. B. Simpson

"It is not our success in service that counts, but our faithfulness. Caleb and Joshua were faithful, and God remembered it when the day of visitation came.

"All of us are called in the crises of our lives to stand alone. And in this matter of trusting God for victory we will all be tested. Many of us have to stand alone for years witnessing to Christ's power and following Him wholly, even if alone. But this is the real victory and the proof of our uncompromising faithfulness.

"Let us not therefore complain when we suffer reproach for our testimony or stand alone for God, but thank Him that He so honors us, and stand the test so that He can afterwards use us when the multitudes are glad to follow."

Walk Closer to God

A crisis can be a lonely experience. Though others may wish to help, often the difficult decisions rest solely with you. You must act. You must confront. You must show where your confidence lies.

If you've developed the habit of faithfully trusting God over the years, you already know you can count on your Lord in an emergency. He is faithful. Like the faithful servant in the parable, He is calling upon you to remain true—even if it means standing alone.

You can count on Him; can He count on you?

Worship from the Heart

David was one of God's faithful servants who, for the most part, kept firm his trust in God and was rewarded. Today's Old Testament reading is David's song of praise for God's deliverance. Here David acknowledges that his faithfulness and God's blessings are interrelated. As you say "Amen" to that, praise God also for the infinite blessings which you have done nothing to merit.

Walk Thru the Word

New Testament Reading
Luke 19
Old Testament Reading
2 Samuel 22:1-4, 21-25

*T*he winner in the war of words

The spies questioned him: "Teacher, we know that you speak and teach what is right, and that you do not show partiality but teach the way of God in accordance with the truth" (Luke 20:21).

*J*esus was subjected to a relentless war of words, a barrage of questioning and accusation. Chief priests and scribes, Sadducees and spies—each came trying to trap Him in a slip of the tongue. "They were unable to trap him in what he said. . . . And astonished by his answer, they became silent" (20:26).

As John Calvin observes, even Christ's enemies acknowledged His excellence as a teacher and defender of God's truth.

Walk with John Calvin

"From the spies' words we obtain a definition of a good and faithful teacher, such as they believed Christ to be. They say that He is true, and teaches the way of God; that is, that He is a faithful interpreter of God, and that He teaches it in truth.

"Christ teaches rightly because He has no regard for the opinions of people. Nothing has more power to draw teachers from a faithful exposition of the Word than trying to please others.

"For it is impossible that anyone who desires to please people should truly devote himself to God. Some attention, no doubt, is due to people, but not so as to obtain their favor by flattery.

"In short, in order to walk uprightly, we must necessarily put away favoritism and partiality, which obscure the light and pervert right judgment."

Walk Closer to God

If someone challenged the who, what, and why of your beliefs, what answer would you give?

Truth is in short supply today. People would rather ignore it, or attack those who claim to have it, than search deeply for it. Many find it easier to deny that truth exists at all.

That's all the more reason why you need to be ready to explain the answers that hurting men and women need to hear. Be prepared at all times to tell why you believe in Christ.

*W*orship from the Heart

"Father, You have chosen me and others with whom I worship to know You personally, to believe You, to understand without any doubt that You are the only true God. Use us individually and collectively to be Your witnesses and to teach others Your ways. May our local congregation be a bright light for You in our community. In the name of the One who is the Light of the world. Amen."

*W*alk Thru the Word

New Testament Reading
Luke 20
Old Testament Reading
Isaiah 43:10-12

*W*hen small gifts become great treasures

*W*orship from the Heart

As you meditate on the widow and what Christ said of her, think about what He would have said if you had been the one to pass by the collection box. Evaluate your giving and acknowledge it as an opportunity to worship. Rejoice that God faithfully provides you an offering that you can return to Him.

"I tell you the truth," he said, "this poor widow has put in more than all the others" (Luke 21:3).

*H*ow is it possible to add together the offerings of countless rich men, and declare the total less than the two small copper coins of a poor widow? How is it possible for so little to amount to so much?

Jesus' arithmetic is not hard to comprehend when you understand as He did that the secret of giving is not in the amount that was given, but rather what was given up.

Attitude—not abundance—is the key. Bishop Ambrose discusses the kind of giving that really adds up.

Walk with Bishop Ambrose

"Liberality is determined not by the amount of our possessions but by the disposition of our giving.

"For by the voice of the Lord, a widow is preferred above all, of whom it was said: 'She has put in more than all.'

"The Lord teaches that none should be held back from giving through shame of their own poverty, nor should the rich flatter themselves that they seem to give more than the poor.

"The piece of money out of a small stock is richer than treasures out of abundance, because it is not the amount that is given but the amount that remains which is considered.

"No one gives more than she who has nothing left for herself."

Walk Closer to God

Giving is not a function of cold numbers, but the result of a warm heart.

A small gift humbly given is of greater value than a vast sum given out of pride, compulsion, or guilt.

The amount of your gifts may vary with your resources. But the attitude of your gift should remain constant—and commendable—even if you are a poor widow on a two-coin pension.

Peter Marshall said it well: "Help us to give according to our incomes, lest Thou, O God, make our incomes according to our gifts."

*W*alk Thru the Word

New Testament Reading
Luke 21
Old Testament Reading
Proverbs 13:7

A dispute arose among them as to which of them was considered to be the greatest (Luke 22:24).

*A*t the height of the most moving Passover meal ever celebrated, a bitter argument suddenly breaks out among the disciples. Human emotions and ambitions explode. "Who is the greatest?" the disciples demand.

Jesus, only hours away from crucifixion, could have rebuked His men harshly. Instead, He again explains the heavenly concept of greatness that has marked His ministry among them.

Albert Barnes expands the Master's important —and easily overlooked—definition of greatness.

Walk with Albert Barnes

"That the disciples should strive and contend about office and rank, just as Jesus was contemplating His own death and preparing them for it, shows how deeply seated the love of power is.

"The kings of the Gentiles, of the nations, or of the earth, do this and it is to be expected of them. But His kingdom was to be of a different character, and they were not to expect it there. He assures them that His kingdom is established on different principles from those of the world and that His subjects were not to expect titles, or power, or offices of pomp in His kingdom.

"He that would be most advanced in His kingdom would be he that was most humble."

Walk Closer to God

Ambition. Greed. The love of power. Such themes dominate the bookstore shelves today. But you will be hard pressed to find a volume that proclaims *"Suffer and Die in the Service of Others"* —though such a book does indeed exist. It's the Bible.

There you will discover that the real keys to greatness are few . . . and seldom used:

Humility (not glory-seeking);
Service (not lofty position);
Contentment (not greed);
Love of God (not love of money).

Take it from Someone who ought to know: Jesus Christ, the Author and Finisher of your faith, who "wrote the book" on true greatness!

*T*he last word on true greatness

*W*orship from the Heart

Imagine the joy of sitting at a holiday feast with Jesus as your host. In His presence there is the fellowship of shared life, the bond of a shared meal, and gratitude for all that God has provided both materially and spiritually. As you think about the Passover meal Jesus shared with His disciples, praise Him that He has made it possible for you to sit with Him at the marriage supper of the Lamb.

*W*alk Thru the Word

New Testament Reading
Luke 22:1-38
Old Testament Reading
Ecclesiastes 5:2-3

Ears that will hear the gospel

And one of them struck the servant of the high priest, cutting off his right ear. But Jesus . . . touched the man's ear and healed him (Luke 22:50-51).

*P*eter was armed and ready for action. Out came his sword, and off came Malchus's ear.

Then the Lord said, "Put your sword away!" Demonstrating compassion rather than vengeance, Jesus reached out to the wounded servant and healed him.

H. A. Ironside points out that "cutting off the listener's ear" is never an appropriate way to gain an audience for the gospel.

Walk with H. A. Ironside

"Peter made the mistake so many other servants of Christ make. We want to help people, to bring blessing to them; we want them to hear the Word of God, and yet we go about things in such a crude way. We cut off their ears and yet expect them to hear us.

"I cannot imagine Peter going to that man and asking him if he had put his trust in the Lord Jesus Christ as his Savior. I think Malchus would look at him and say, 'You come to talk to me about that? You, the man who cut off my ear!'

"We are often like that, and we hurt our own testimony. But our blessed, understanding Lord often corrects our failures.

"He so often overrules our failures and blunders and brings blessing out of that which otherwise would be a means of sorrow and disappointment."

Walk Closer to God

Think of the ways you've unknowingly or unintentionally prevented someone from receiving the Gospel message.

A frown. A cold look. An unkind word. Each can be as cutting as the sharpest sword. Who wants to listen to someone who is harsh and judgmental? Instead, try a smile, soothing words, and a genuine interest in someone's life.

Then observe how the way is prepared for the message of Christ. After all, you can surely plant more gospel seeds with a plowshare than with a sword!

Worship from the Heart

"Father, Your Son was betrayed by both His enemies and His friends. I live among the people who are His body. Help me to discern the times when I might unwittingly betray You by hurting another believer through insensitivity to emotional needs or by failing to help when help is needed. May I honor You by reaching out with Your love."

Walk Thru the Word

New Testament Reading
Luke 22:39-71
Old Testament Reading
Proverbs 15:23; 25:11

Viewing the greatest victory of all time

With one voice they cried out, "Away with this man! Release Barabbas to us!" (Luke 23:18).

At first glance it appears the raucous shouts of a bloodthirsty crowd caused Pilate to send Jesus to His death. But in fact, an unseen higher will was at work in and through the human actors in this moving drama.

Alexander Maclaren shares this fascinating sketch of the criminal Barabbas.

Walk with Alexander Maclaren

"This coarse desperado was the people's favorite because he embodied their notions and aspirations, and had been bold enough to do what every one of them would have done if he had dared. He had headed one of the many small riots against Rome. There had been bloodshed in which he had himself taken part.

"Jesus had taught what the people did not care to hear, given blessing which even the recipients soon forgot, and lived a life whose 'beauty of holiness' rebuked the common life of all.

"What chance did truth, kindness, and purity have against the sort of bravery that slashes with a sword and is not elevated above the mob by beauty of thought or character? Even now, after nineteen centuries, are the popular 'heroes' of Christian nations saints or teachers or humanitarians, whose Christlikeness is the thing venerated?

"The vote for Barabbas and against Jesus is an instructive commentary on human nature."

Walk Closer to God

Popularity is often a fleeting illusion. Today's bestsellers soon sit on the shelf unnoticed. Superstars only endure for a few brief seasons.

Society exalts winners and ignores losers. The world saw only a pitiful loss when Jesus went to the cross. In fact, they were viewing the greatest victory of all time.

When you think about it, who would remember Barabbas today if Jesus had not died and been raised?

Better to be condemned with Jesus than accepted with Barabbas. Wouldn't you agree?

Worship from the Heart

"Dear Savior, thank You for Your willingness to suffer the agony of Gethsemane for me. Thank You for desiring my salvation enough to endure the betrayal and abandonment of Your friends and family and, ultimately, the separation from God. Help me to keep Your sacrificial spirit always before me, that I too may strive to manifest that kind of love to others. Amen."

Walk Thru the Word

New Testament Reading
Luke 23:1-25
Old Testament Reading
Micah 7:18-19

A pattern for those who follow God wholly

There they crucified him. . . . Jesus said, "Father, forgive them, for they do not know what they are doing" (Luke 23:33-34).

People who are sentenced to die for crimes they did not commit rarely go to the gallows without loudly protesting their innocence. Much rarer are the ones who go to an undeserved death forgiving those who have treated them unjustly. But that is precisely how Jesus, who never did any wrong, treated His executioners.

To the end of His earthly life, Jesus never lost sight of the sinners He had come to save. He had taught them; He had healed them; now He would die for them. His whole life was a pattern for those who would follow God wholly. John Chrysostom points out that Christ taught by word and deed.

Walk with John Chrysostom

"Christ commanded all men to be lowly minded and meek, and He taught this by His words; but see how He also taught humility and meekness by His deeds. He showed how to practice these virtues. He took a towel, girded Himself, and washed the disciples' feet.

"Again He taught meekness by His acts. How so? He was struck by the servant of the high priest, and said 'If I said something wrong. . . . testify as to what is wrong. But if I spoke the truth, why did you strike me?' (John 18:23).

"Jesus admonished His followers to pray for their enemies; this also He taught by means of His acts. In pain on the cross He prayed, 'Father, forgive them, for they do not know what they are doing.' "

Walk Closer to God

The adage "Don't do as I do; do as I say" expresses the shortcomings of most human teachers. But Jesus Christ was no mere human teacher. Even at the moment of greatest personal suffering, He demonstrated the reality of His teaching.

On the evening before His arrest, Christ washed the feet of His disciples. From the cross, He forgave His killers. What more proof do you need of the difference God's power can make in *your* words and deeds—in both life and in death?

Worship from the Heart

From the moment of His birth until the moment the Roman nails pierced His hands, Jesus embodied truth and love. He literally "walked His talk." As you ponder the example Jesus set, rejoice that His desire is that you walk in His footsteps. Praise Him for the indwelling Holy Spirit who makes this possible.

Walk Thru the Word

New Testament Reading
Luke 23:26-55
Old Testament Reading
1 Samuel 24:10-12

98

A new chapter in cosmic history

"This is what is written: The Christ will suffer and rise from the dead on the third day" (Luke 24:46).

*T*wo discouraged, bewildered men trudged wearily along the road to Emmaus. Jesus was dead, and with Him had died the dreams of His followers. Now three days had passed. His body had mysteriously vanished from the tomb, and rumors were circulating that He had reappeared.

Suddenly a stranger fell in step with the men and joined in the conversation. As He spoke, their hearts began to burn with faith once again. Bewilderment at His death changed into wonderment at His resurrection. C. S. Lewis explains the significance of that event.

Walk with C. S. Lewis

"The Resurrection was not regarded simply or chiefly as evidence for the immortality of the soul.

"On such a view Christ would simply have done what all people do when they die; the only novelty would have been that in His case we were allowed to see it happening.

"But there is not in Scripture the faintest suggestion that the Resurrection was new evidence for something that had in fact been always happening.

"The New Testament writers speak as if Christ's achievement in rising from the dead was the first event of its kind in the whole history of the universe. He is the 'first fruits,' the 'pioneer of life.' He has forced open a door that has been locked since the death of the first man.

"He has met, fought, and beaten the King of Death. Everything is different because He has done so. This is the beginning of the New Creation: A new chapter in cosmic history has opened."

Walk Closer to God

Luke's last chapter marks the end of his book, but not the end of the story. The task of redemption was complete, but the spreading of those glad tidings had only begun. New chapters of encounters with the risen Lord have been written in every century. New chapters are still being written today.

A chapter is being written in your life. How does it read? How would you like it to read?

*W*orship from the Heart

In His resurrection, Jesus Christ was the "first fruits." And if you are His, you will follow Him in resurrection. You will awake one day to see His face. Spend some moments praising Him for His victory, and for your glorious future with Him. Then make time today to share the news of the Resurrection with someone who needs to hear it.

*W*alk Thru the Word

New Testament Reading
Luke 24
Old Testament Reading
Psalm 17:15

Eternity Invading Time

Having read Matthew, Mark, and Luke, you will find that the gospel of John requires a mental "shifting of gears." The first three Gospels emphasize Jesus's actions and events, with occasional parables and sermons interspersed. But in John's account, the works of Jesus take a backseat to His words. Only John, for example, captures the intimate conversation in the upper room just hours before Jesus' death, in which Jesus promises His disciples a divine Counselor, heavenly peace, and His abiding presence.

From the opening verses, John writes of One who was more than just a man. He was God, the Creator of all things, the source of light and the giver of life (John 1:1, 3–4, 9). He was the Word who became flesh (John 1:14); God had become a man. John continues this theme throughout the book. Those who came in contact with Jesus—John the Baptist, Nicodemus, the Samaritan woman, the man blind from birth, Mary, Martha, Peter, Thomas—all came to the same inescapable conclusion: God had visited the human race! At least eight times Jesus ascribes to Himself the name "I AM," the name God used to identify Himself to His people in Egypt (Exodus 3:14-15). Jesus said, "I am the bread, . . . the light, . . . the good shepherd, . . . the door, . . . the resurrection, . . . the way and the truth and the life, . . . the vine . . . ," and simply "I am."

John's gospel shows how Jesus' claims are authenticated by His miracles; His deeds prove His words.

Jesus' claims are authenticated by His miracles (called "signs"); His deeds prove his words. Only John describes the miracle of the man born blind receiving his sight; who but God can give sight to the sightless? Only John records the raising of Lazarus; who but God can give life to the lifeless?

This month you will listen to Jesus make startling claims to the gathered crowds, and then confirm those claims with dramatic demonstrations of His power. You will be confronted with the same question they faced: "Who is Jesus of Nazareth?" You will develop a bigger, brighter picture of God's Son—Jesus Christ. Are you ready to meet Him?

*P*erfect balance of grace and truth

The Word became flesh and made his dwelling among us . . . full of grace and truth (John 1:14).

*I*t takes a lot of scholars to write an encyclopedia in eighteen volumes. It takes the Spirit of God to write an encyclopedia in eighteen verses!

John's opening words form a virtual "encyclopedia" of truth. It will take you a lifetime—and more—to comprehend fully the depth and breadth of the person John writes about: Jesus Christ.

Listen as W. H. Griffith Thomas plumbs the depths of your matchless Savior.

Walk with W. H. Griffith Thomas

"The words *grace* and *truth* describe Jesus' personal character. By grace we are to understand His graciousness of attitude, speech, and action. Grace was manifest in everything He was and did.

"*Truth* is another marked characteristic of the life of Jesus Christ. His life was holy; His word was true; His whole character was the embodiment of truth.

"We cannot help noticing the perfect blend of grace and truth and their equally perfect proportion in the life of Jesus Christ.

"Grace by itself might be mere sentimentality. Truth by itself might be easily expressed in severity. But when grace is strengthened by truth, and truth is mellowed by grace, we have the exemplary character and true life of the perfect Man. For Jesus Christ is complete, balanced, and flawless."

Walk Closer to God

Do you think of yourself as: hardworking, popular, friendly, introverted, shy, easygoing, aloof, confident, dynamic, unobtrusive?

Or would you select from another list: loving, joyful, peaceful, patient, kind, good, faithful, gentle, and self-controlled (Galatians 5:22-23) —in a word, *Christlike?*

One month from now, if you keep on schedule, you will have traveled through John's entire gospel.

But there is an even more important consideration: *One month from now, how much of John's gospel will have traveled through you?*

*W*orship from the Heart

Take a glimpse at Revelation 1:10-18, and see the might of our Lord Jesus on His heavenly throne. The apostle who leaned on Jesus' breast in the book of John falls at His feet as if dead in the book of Revelation. Grace and truth are unleashed in full: "Hallelujah, what a Savior!"

*W*alk Thru the Word

New Testament Reading
John 1:1-34
Old Testament Reading
Exodus 33:12–34:6

*T*he witness of the Word

Philip found Nathanael and told him, "We have found the one Moses wrote about in the Law, and about whom the prophets also wrote—Jesus of Nazareth, the son of Joseph" (John 1:45).

*A*s fantastic as Christ's miracles may seem, plenty of eyewitnesses can testify to their truth. However, the problem has never been authentication, but rather acceptance: getting others to believe the words of the witnesses.

Nathanael's skeptical response to Philip is typical: "Nazareth! Can anything good come from there?" (1:46). C. S. Lewis clarifies some of the muddy thinking regarding those who would contend that seeing—and only seeing—is believing.

*W*orship from the Heart

Plagued with leprosy, Naaman was instructed by the prophet Elisha to wash seven times in the Jordan River (2 Kings 5). But Naaman balked at the simplicity of the requirement. Fortunately, he later followed through with the instructions and was healed. Perhaps there is a problem area in your life that can be corrected by following through with God's written instructions. Go ahead and take that step!

Walk with C. S. Lewis

"Believing things 'on authority' only means believing them because you have been told them by someone you think trustworthy.

"Ninety-nine percent of the things you believe are believed on authority. I believe there is such a place as New York. I could not prove by abstract reasoning that there is such a place. I believe it because reliable people have told me so.

"The ordinary person believes in the solar system, atoms, and the circulation of the blood on authority—because the scientists say so. Every historical statement is believed on authority.

"None of us has seen the Norman Conquest or the defeat of the Spanish Armada. But we believe them simply because people who did see them have left writings that tell us about them; in fact, on authority. A person who balked at authority in other things, as some people do in religion, would have to be content to know nothing all his life."

Walk Closer to God

Nathanael's disbelief quickly evaporated when Jesus told the skeptic where he had been sitting.

Nathanael believed because Jesus saw.

You may find it hard to believe all you read about the Son of God. But take it from the testimony of many witnesses: It's true. And that means you'd better believe it when *you* see it . . . in God's Word!

*W*alk Thru the Word

New Testament Reading
John 1:35-51
Old Testament Reading
Zephaniah 1:12-13

*C*ompletely committed in all areas of life

Many people saw the miraculous signs he was doing and believed in his name. But Jesus would not entrust himself to them, for he knew all men (John 2:23-24).

*A*fter turning water into wine at Cana, Jesus began to attract large crowds. But His head was not turned by His growing popularity.

Jesus saw right through the hangers-on. He knew they wanted a steady stream of spectacles, not the challenge of costly discipleship. So Jesus refused to commit Himself to them, for He knew their hearts too well. They failed to realize that the key to discipleship is relationship.

Allow G. Campbell Morgan to explain.

Walk with G. Campbell Morgan

"Many believed in His name (2:23), but their belief was not full commitment of themselves. It was really intellectual conviction produced by the signs He did. Seeing this was so, He did not commit Himself to them fully. He could not.

"This is a perpetual principle, for the law of relationship between Christ and individuals is always that of all for all.

"When our convictions are yielded to Him completely, He is able to give Himself to us in all His fullness. Until that is so, He cannot trust us.

"How true it is that we often miss the joy and strength of our Christianity because, by withholding ourselves from Christ, we make it impossible for Him to give Himself to us in all the fullness of His grace and truth."

Walk Closer to God

If you tell Jesus Christ, "All that I am and all that I have are Yours, my Lord," He will reply, "All that I am, and all that I have are yours, too, My child." By the same token, if you withhold compartments of your life from Him, don't be surprised if you have trouble hearing the still, small voice of God.

Perhaps the Indian believer Subodh Sahu captured it best when he said, "All that I had, He took; all that He has, He has given me in Jesus Christ."

Have you given Him *all?* It's a transaction you cannot enter into too soon . . . or too often!

*W*orship from the Heart

The world is an attractively wrapped package with lures aimed at even the most committed believer. The author of Hebrews gives us wonderfully practical advice on handling such distraction. "Lay aside every encumbrance, and the sin which so easily entangles us, and let us run with endurance the race that is set before us, fixing our eyes on Jesus" (Hebrews 12:1-2 NAS).

*W*alk Thru the Word

New Testament Reading
John 2
Old Testament Reading
Deuteronomy 10:12

God's solution: a new birth

"No one can see the kingdom of God unless he is born again" (John 3:3).

*B*eing "born again" is a popular slogan today. Consider:
- "Born-Again Bears Beat Tigers"
- "We Sell Born-Again Cars"
- "Born-Again Economy Moves into High Gear"

So you won't be confused by the world's clichés, John Wesley makes clear what Jesus meant when He preached the necessity of the new birth.

Walk with John Wesley

"The true, living, Christian faith is not only assent, an act of the understanding. It is also a disposition, which God brings about in a person's heart, a sure trust and confidence in God that through the merits of Christ his sins are forgiven and he is reconciled to God.

"This implies that one first renounce himself, for in order to be found in Christ and accepted through Him, he totally rejects all confidence in the flesh; that having nothing to pay, having no trust in his own works or righteousness of any kind, he comes to God as a lost, miserable, self-destroyed, self-condemned, undone, helpless sinner; as one whose mouth is utterly stopped, and who is altogether guilty before God.

"Such a sense of sin—together with a full conviction that through Christ alone does our salvation come—and an earnest desire for that salvation, must precede a living faith, a trust in Him, who paid our ransom by His death, and fulfilled the law in His life."

Walk Closer to God

Sin has led everyone astray; apart from the Savior one cannot hope to see the kingdom of God.

The answer to life's problems is not a fresh start, but a new life—a life made possible only through the merciful love of Jesus Christ.

Call upon Him, and the headline of your life will be far more newsworthy than any second-half comeback:

"Extra! Extra! Read all about it: Sinner Born Again Through the Savior's Sacrifice!"

*W*orship from the Heart

"Father, I thank You that my birth in Your kingdom rests solely on Your Son's finished work at Calvary. May I be faithful in sharing with others, as You did with Nicodemus, this life-changing truth."

*W*alk Thru the Word

New Testament Reading
John 3
Old Testament Reading
Ezekiel 11:19-20

Satisfy your spiritual thirst

"But whoever drinks the water I give him will never thirst. Indeed, the water I give him will become in him a spring of water welling up to eternal life" (John 4:14).

A day without rain is a delight; a month without rain is a drought. A year without rain is a calamity. Why? Because living things cannot survive without water, the precious liquid of life.

But strangely, in the spiritual realm, many try to quench their thirst with things that were never designed to satisfy. A. W. Tozer issues this challenge to those who thirst for God:

Walk with A. W. Tozer

"We do not need to have our doctrine straightened out; we are as orthodox as the Pharisees of old. But this longing for God that brings spiritual torrents of seeking and self-denial—this is almost gone from our midst.

"I believe that God wants us to long for Him with the longing that will keep us always moving toward Him, always finding and always seeking, always asking and always desiring.

"Dare we bow our hearts and say, 'Father, I have been a childish kind of Christian—more concerned with being happy than with being holy. O God, wound me with a sense of my own sinfulness. Wound me with compassion for the world, and wound me with love for You that will always keep me pursuing and always seeking and finding.'

"If you dare to pray that prayer sincerely, it could mean a turning point in your life. It could mean a great door of spiritual victory opened to you."

Walk Closer to God

Only those who have suffered drought know what it truly means to thirst. The dried husks of corn that will never be harvested. The blowing dust that only accentuates the need for relief.

Spiritual drought is no different. Drought in the soul only yields to the quenching that comes from the Fountain of life, Jesus Christ.

Drink deeply of Him. Discover for yourself the satisfaction no earthly beverage can rival.

Worship from the Heart

The Samaritan woman had set out simply to get water for household chores. But in the middle of her daily routine, her life was changed because of the time she spent with Jesus. The same can be true in your life. Think about Jesus, sing to Him, listen to Him, answer Him. Tell Him how much you appreciate the way your dullest routine is transformed by His companionship.

Walk Thru the Word

New Testament Reading
John 4:1-26
Old Testament Reading
Isaiah 12:2-6

Learning the blessedness of believing prayer

Worship from the Heart

The nobleman took Jesus at His word and departed, and his faith was rewarded. Praise God that His healing power is not diminished over time or through space. Thank Him for the resistance to disease and the healing capacity He creates in the human body. Thank Him specifically for any healing performed in your life or in the life of a loved one.

Walk Thru the Word

New Testament Reading
John 4:27-54
Old Testament Reading
Psalm 84

The royal official said, "Sir, come down before my child dies." Jesus replied, "You may go. Your son will live" (John 4:49-50).

There is something better than receiving from God what you prayed for.

That is receiving from God what you should have prayed for . . . but didn't! Ask the nobleman mentioned in John 4.

Alfred Edersheim shares this insight about the power and wisdom of God as seen in His marvelous answers to prayer.

Walk with Alfred Edersheim

"The supplication of the officer was an expression of imperfect faith.

"What the Savior denied was not the request for a miracle, which was necessary, but the urgent plea that He should come down to Capernaum for that purpose.

"The request showed ignorance of the real character of Christ, as if He were merely a rabbi endowed with special power.

"What Christ intended to teach this man was that He, who had life in Himself, could restore life at a distance as easily as by His presence; by the word of His power as readily as by personal application.

"So it is that when we have also learned this lesson we come to know both the meaning and the blessedness of believing prayer."

Walk Closer to God

Put yourself in the nobleman's place.

Your son is at home, lying near death from a raging fever. You've tried all the doctors and all the medicine available. Finally you come to the only Physician who might be able to help.

But He tells you to go home. Your son is already well.

You asked Him to come. He told you to go.

You came because your son was weak. He sent you home to show that He was strong.

You asked Him to do something great. He answered by doing something miraculous.

Aren't you glad God's answers are wiser than your prayers?

*W*aiting in the strength of hope

[In these porches] a great number of disabled people used to lie—the blind, the lame, the paralyzed (John 5:3).

*T*here are two types of waiting: waiting because you *have* to, and waiting because you *want* to.

The people around the pool at Bethesda waited because they had to; they needed to bathe in the healing waters. One man had waited years to be healed.

But when approached by Jesus, the man found himself being asked, "Do you want to be made well?"

Joseph Parker probes these two ways of waiting.

Walk with Joseph Parker

"The world is a hospital. The person who is in the most robust health today may be struck before the setting of the sun with a fatal disease. In the midst of life we are in death.

"Life is a perpetual crisis; it can be snapped at any moment.

"Blessed is that servant who shall be found waiting, watching, and working when his Lord comes.

"These folk were all waiting, groaning, sighing. A sigh was a prayer, a groan was an entreaty, a cry of distress was a supplication.

"All the people in the porches were waiting. Are we not all doing the same thing?

"We are waiting for help, waiting till our ship comes in, waiting for sympathy, waiting for a friend without whose presence there seems to be nobody on the face of the earth. Waiting.

"One method of waiting means patience, hope, contentment, assurance that God will redeem His promises and make the heart strong; the other method of waiting is fretfulness, impatience, distrust, and complaining—and that kind of waiting wears out the soul."

Walk Closer to God

"Father, teach me what it means to wait on You for my every need.

"You have promised to provide in Your time. Guard my heart from fretfulness and complaining, and make my heart strong to hope."

*W*orship from the Heart

Waiting, watching, working—biblical alliterations that suggest a servant fully in tune with God's will. As you pray for this weekend's worship service, remember your church leaders as they wait, watch, and work for the Lord Jesus Christ.

*W*alk Thru the Word

New Testament Reading
John 5:1-15
Old Testament Reading
Jeremiah 14:22

*C*arefully searching through His thoughts

*W*orship from the Heart

As you study the Scriptures today, make the promise of King David to God your own: "I meditate on your precepts and consider your ways. I delight myself in your decrees; I will not neglect your word" (Psalm 119:15-16).

"You diligently study the Scriptures because you think that by them you possess eternal life. These are the Scriptures that testify about me" (John 5:39).

*J*esus came claiming equality with God—a claim that was either brazenly arrogant, or true.

Jewish law required a minimum of two witnesses to validate any testimony (John 8:17). Jesus called upon no fewer than four: the witnesses of John the Baptist (5:32-35); Jesus' miraculous signs (5:36); God the Father (5:37); and the Scriptures themselves (5:38-39).

And as Charles Spurgeon underscores, the *fourth* is the key to discovering the other *three*.

Walk with Charles Spurgeon

"The Greek word rendered *search* signifies a strict, diligent search, such as men make when they are seeking gold, or hunters when they are in earnest after game.

"We must not be content with having given a superficial reading to a chapter or two of Scripture, but with the candle of the Spirit we must seek out the meaning of the Word.

"Holy Scripture requires searching—much of it can only be learned by careful study; for they are the writings of God, bearing the divine stamp and seal. Who shall dare to treat them lightly?

"The Word of God repays searching. God does not bid us sift a mountain of chaff with here and there a grain of wheat in it, but the Bible is winnowed corn. We have but to open the granary door and find it.

"Finally, the Scriptures reveal Jesus: 'These are the Scriptures that testify about me.' Happy is he who, searching his Bible, discovers his Savior."

Walk Closer to God

There are still more than 2,000 language groups in the world without a single Bible verse in print—two hundred million people without God's Word in their own language.

Compare that with millions of Scripture portions produced in the English language last year alone! Diligently, daily, discover Jesus for yourself.

*W*alk Thru the Word

New Testament Reading
John 5:16-47
Old Testament Reading
Psalm 119:11-16

A spiritually balanced view

When they had rowed three or three and a half miles, they saw Jesus approaching the boat, walking on the water; and they were terrified (John 6:19).

*S*tep onto a balance beam or a tightrope, and the concern to maintain balance becomes paramount. If you should lean too far in one direction, it quickly becomes necessary to compensate.

But overreacting can be just as dangerous. In trying to correct one mistake, you may in fact introduce another.

Martin Luther examines two extreme attitudes that are often exhibited toward God.

Walk with Martin Luther

"Both the hardness and the shyness of the human heart cannot be expressed in words.

"When there is no danger, the human heart is so immeasurably hard and callous that it regards neither the wrath of God nor His threatening. Although it hears for a long time that God will punish sin with eternal death and damnation, it goes on nevertheless, unimpressed, drowned in arrogance and avarice.

"When there is no trouble, we live on in security and sin, without any fear or awe. We stare like a stiff corpse. Speaking to us is like shouting at a cliff.

"On the other hand, when we feel our sin and are frightened at death, at God's wrath and judgment, then we, in turn, become rigid with great fear and sadness, and no one can comfort us again.

"In fact, we are frightened even by that which should comfort us, as the disciples were frightened by Christ, who came to them for the purpose of comforting and cheering them."

Walk Closer to God

The way to a balanced view of God is to do what the frightened disciples initially failed to do: *look* to Jesus and *listen* to His voice.

Only those with eyes to see and ears to hear will be tuned to Christ's words, "It is I; don't be afraid." Once you know the Savior, both paralyzing fear and demoralizing apathy seem strangely inappropriate.

*W*orship from the Heart

There is a fear that produces confidence (Proverbs 14:26). Not a fear of the unknown, but a reverential awe for our heavenly Father. We should fear our God, but not be afraid of Him.

*W*alk Thru the Word

New Testament Reading
John 6:1-24
Old Testament Reading
Proverbs 14:26-27

The treasure of His company

"Do not work for food that spoils, but for food that endures to eternal life" (John 6:27).

Ironic, isn't it, that the possessions you work a lifetime to acquire can be taken away from you in a moment of time? (Just think of the millionaire who stepped off the curb into the path of an oncoming bus!) Once death intrudes, no amount of money or possessions will have any real value.

The crowds misunderstood Jesus' motives. They thought He had come simply to provide for their physical needs. But the loaves and fish were given for a higher purpose: to show what Christ can do for hungry hearts and souls.

First things first—that's what Jesus calls for. John Chrysostom will help you set that heavenly agenda in your own life.

Walk with John Chrysostom

"We should learn to ask God for things which are suitable for us to ask. For neither the splendors nor the pains of the present life have much power in respect either to despondency or pleasure; they are contemptible and slip away very swiftly. By their very nature they do not long endure, but the things which are to come endure eternally, both those of punishment and those of the kingdom.

"Let us then in regard to these things use much diligence to avoid the first and to choose the last. For what is the advantage of this world's luxury? Today it is, and tomorrow it is not; today a bright flower, tomorrow scattered dust; today a burning fire, tomorrow smoldering ashes. But spiritual things are not so; they ever remain shining and blooming, and becoming brighter every day."

Walk Closer to God

"Do not store up for yourselves treasures on earth, where moth and rust destroy, and where thieves break in and steal. But store up for yourselves treasures in heaven . . . for where your treasure is, there your heart will be also" (Matthew 6:19-21). There is no greater treasure than an eternity with Christ. Treasure His company, and you will lack nothing.

Worship from the Heart

It is a temptation for Christians to return often to familiar, comforting verses of Scripture, skimming over the demanding passages. Do you take a mental "walk" when Jesus' words are difficult? Remember Peter's conclusion: "Lord, to whom shall we go? You have the words of eternal life." Rejoice that even though He demands much, Jesus is your source of life.

Walk Thru the Word

New Testament Reading
John 6:25-59
Old Testament Reading
1 Kings 3:5-15

From this time many of his disciples turned back and no longer followed him (John 6:66).

*H*ard sayings have a way of quickly thinning the ranks of lukewarm followers. In John 6 Jesus cut straight to the heart of the matter: "You are looking for me, not because you saw miraculous signs but because you ate the loaves and had your fill" (John 6:26).

Is it because of what you think He can do for you that you call Him "Lord"—or because of who He is? As James Stalker comments, wrong motives for following Christ often flow from faulty expectations about Christ.

Walk with James Stalker

"Jesus had heard of the tragic death of John the Baptist and immediately hurried to a desert place with His disciples to talk over the event.

"When moved by compassion for the helpless multitude, Jesus performed the stupendous miracle of feeding five thousand. The effect was overwhelming.

"The crowd became instantly convinced that this was indeed the Messiah. Having only one conception of what that meant, they endeavored to take Him by force and make Him a king, that is, force Him to be the leader of a messianic revolt.

"It seemed the crowning hour of success. But to Jesus Himself it was an hour of sadness and shame. This was all His work had come to? This was the conception they had of Him? Were they to try to determine the course of His future action instead of humbly asking what He would have them do?

"They were looking for a 'bread king' who would give them idleness and plenty, mountains of loaves, rivers of milk, every comfort without labor. What He had to give was eternal life."

Walk Closer to God

"No one can come to me unless the Father . . . draws him, and I will raise him up at the last day" (John 6:44).

"Lord draw me to You, that I too may know the One who is the resurrection and the life. I find my satisfaction in You, the bread of life."

*F*ollowing Christ for the right reasons

*W*orship from the Heart

"Father in heaven, only You know the motives that lie deep within the recesses of my heart. I truly want and need to serve You wholeheartedly with a purity of purpose. May my goals and expectations be not for me, but for You, my lovely Savior. I pray this in the name of Jesus, who never wavered in His purpose. Amen."

*W*alk Thru the Word

New Testament Reading
John 6:60-71
Old Testament Reading
1 Kings 18:17-22

111

*J*udgment that's free from prejudice

"Stop judging by mere appearances, and make a right judgment" (John 7:24).

*A*lthough the religious leaders who marveled at Jesus' teaching in John 7 had all attended the finest rabbinical schools, their formal training had not endowed them with true wisdom.

They were experts at debating the finer points of the law, but their practice left much to be desired. They were judges by *credential*, but crooks by *conviction*—a condition Jesus was quick to point out, with predictable results!

G. Campbell Morgan helps to explain the significance of "righteous judgment."

Walk with G. Campbell Morgan

"Our judgments of our fellow men must always be reserved.

"We should bear in mind that appearance may be deceitful; and therefore, with the love that hopes all things, we should be ready to give others the benefit of any doubt or uncertainty in our minds.

"It remains that within limits we are compelled to use the faculty of judgment, since our Lord uttered the positive word, 'Judge with righteous judgment,' as well as the negative.

"What then is righteous judgment? It is judgment that is free from prejudice, and which considers things as they are and then draws true conclusions. To form true conclusions, we need a mind free from all bias, and mastered by love."

Walk Closer to God

Jesus gave the best advice on judging in His Sermon on the Mount: "Do not judge, or you too will be judged. For in the same way you judge others, you will be judged" (Matthew 7:1-2).

That's another way of saying:

• When in doubt, don't judge.

• When you must, judge rightly.

• At all times, remember that you too have a Judge, One whose judgments are infinitely right and unerringly fair.

We can know very little about anyone beyond appearance, for the secrets of the heart and soul are hidden from all but God.

*W*orship from the Heart

Ministers tend to get a great deal of criticism thrown in their direction. Can you help turn the tables and think of at least one genuine praise you can give your pastor when you next see him? Perhaps you can even call with a word of encouragement or thanks for his ministry to you.

*W*alk Thru the Word

New Testament Reading
John 7
Old Testament Reading
Zechariah 8:14-17

*L*ight that pierces the spiritual gloom

When Jesus spoke again to the people, he said, "I am the light of the world. Whoever follows me will never walk in darkness, but will have the light of life" (John 8:12).

*T*ake away the sunlight which warms and illumines the world, and nothing would live for long. As the sun is to *physical* life, so the Son is to *spiritual* life. Without light, life is impossible; without Christ, a person walks in the darkness of spiritual death.

Jesus makes this clear when He calls Himself the "light of the world." Let Charles Wesley lead us to worship the Son for His ministry of light.

Walk with Charles Wesley

Christ, whose glory fills the skies;
   Christ, the true, the only Light,
Sun of Righteousness, arise,
   Triumph o'er the shades of night;
Dayspring from on high, be near;
   Daystar, in my heart appear!

Dark and cheerless is the morn
   Unaccompanied by Thee;
Joyless is the day's return
   Till Thy mercy's beams I see;
As they inward light impart,
   Cheer my eyes and warm my heart.

Visit, then, this soul of mine;
   Pierce the gloom of sin and grief;
Fill me, Radiancy divine;
   Scatter all my unbelief;
More and more Thyself display,
   Shining to the perfect day!

Walk Closer to God

Satan blinds; God illumines. And the spiritual condition of men and women is easily determined by what they love—darkness or light.

"Men loved darkness instead of light because their deeds were evil. . . . But whoever lives by the truth comes into the light" (John 3:19, 21).

Make Wesley's hymn *your* prayer as you walk in a world that needs to hear there is Sonlight for the soul.

*W*orship from the Heart

Reflect on the heavenly city that is described in Revelation 21:23-24: "The city does not need the sun or the moon to shine on it, for the glory of God gives it light, and the Lamb is its lamp. The nations will walk by its light." Praise God for that glimpse of heavenly glory.

*W*alk Thru the Word

New Testament Reading
John 8:1-30
Old Testament Reading
Isaiah 60:19-20

Freedom—living as we ought

"If the Son sets you free, you will be free indeed" (John 8:36).

A short century ago, many nations, races, and individuals only dared to dream of liberation. But since then, freedom has become a reality for millions of men and women worldwide.

Yet, for all the world's accomplishments in the name of political, social, economic, and educational freedom, true liberty remains beyond the reach of humanity. For that you need something more—the freedom from sin's bondage that comes only through Jesus Christ, the divine Liberator.

A. W. Pink defines true liberty.

Walk with A. W. Pink

"There are three chief things concerning which people in general greatly err: misery and happiness, folly and wisdom, bondage and liberty.

"The world counts none miserable but the afflicted, and none happy but the prosperous. The world is pleased with a false show of wisdom, neglecting that which makes wise unto salvation.

"As to liberty, people suppose that true liberty is to be under the control of none above themselves, living according to their heart's desire. But this is a bondage of the worst kind.

"True liberty is not the power to live as we please, but to live as we ought!

"The only One who has ever trod this earth since Adam's fall and enjoyed perfect freedom was the Man, Christ Jesus."

Walk Closer to God

God has given each individual the freedom to choose what he or she will be enslaved to. But only in Christ does slavery become liberty. The world will freely offer you the shackles of license and lawlessness, but only the Son can truly set you free! Freedom from sin, freedom from fear, freedom from the past, and freedom to serve God out of a childlike love and willing mind.

That's your heritage—the birthright of every child of the King—and the greatest liberating force in the world.

Worship from the Heart

Freedom is a precious commodity both in the spiritual and physical realms. Meeting with God's people without fear of government interference or retribution is a liberty enjoyed by only a few. Thank God for the privilege of worshiping freely, and pray for believers elsewhere who are forced to worship secretly.

Walk Thru the Word

New Testament Reading
John 8:31-59
Old Testament Reading
Isaiah 61:1

114

"Neither this man nor his parents sinned," said Jesus, "but this happened so that the work of God might be displayed in his life" (John 9:3).

*T*ragic circumstances leave people groping for explanations. But *why* is a question that has no easy answers.

In chapter 9, John records an incident involving a man born blind. Many believed the blindness was punishment for sin—either his or his parents'.

Albert Barnes elaborates on Jesus' reply to the all-important *why* behind the man's affliction.

Walk with Albert Barnes

"This thing happened that it might appear how great and wonderful are the works of God. It has all happened, not by the fault of his parents or of himself, but by the wise arrangement of God that it might be seen in what way calamities come, and in what way God meets and relieves them.

"From this we may learn that all suffering in this world is not the effect of sin. There may be many modes of suffering that cannot be traced to any particular transgression. We should be cautious, therefore, in saying that there can be no calamity but by transgression.

"It is a part of God's great plan to adapt His mercies to the woes of mankind. Often calamity, poverty, and sickness are permitted so that He may show the provisions of His mercy, that He may teach us to prize His blessings, and that deep-felt gratitude may bind us to Him."

Walk Closer to God

Why is there so much bad news in the world today? The partial answer is clear: This is a fallen world, corrupted by sin and dominated by Satan.

But don't stop! Also ask why there is good news in the world today. God has intervened by sending His Son to break the power of sin and to "purify for himself a people that are his very own" (Titus 2:14).

Through these special people, God wants to demonstrate His power and glory in good times and in bad. Will you volunteer to be that kind of object lesson to your world today?

*T*hat the mercies of God should be revealed

*W*orship from the Heart

Sometimes Christians are as blind as the Pharisees who refused to see the Light of the world. Pray that any spiritual blindness in your life will be healed as you apply this remedy for blindness: "Turn your eyes upon Jesus; look full in His wonderful face. And the things of earth will grow strangely dim in the light of His glory and grace."

*W*alk Thru the Word

New Testament Reading
John 9:1-12
Old Testament Reading
Psalm 107:10-21

115

Matthew Henry (1662-1714) Mining the Truths of God's Word

*T*he Preacher in Ecclesiastes was right when he said, "Of making many books there is no end" (12:12). Countless volumes roll off the presses each year, many destined only to gather dust after brief use. Not many attain the status of a classic—one that endures for generations.

One "classic" which has stood the test of time is, of course, the Book of books, the Bible. Another is a volume which students of Scripture have used for centuries to dig deeply into God's Word. That book —*Matthew Henry's Commentary on the Whole Bible*— remains one of the most popular commentaries today, more than 270 years after it was first published.

Who is Matthew Henry? And what qualities have made his commentary such an enduring treasure? Answering the first question provides a clue to the second.

Born in 1662 during a time of political unrest in England, Henry's childhood was marked by frequent

ailments. His mind, however, was as sharp as his body was weak. Always a thinker and notetaker, he could read and comment on the Bible at the age of three, and responded to the claims of Christ at the age of eleven.

Singleminded and serious, young Henry never wavered from his intention to follow in his father's footsteps. But the instability of the times made it impossible for him to enter the ministry just then. Instead, he switched to a study of law — for which others thought him well suited — until the door to ministry should open.

When Henry was about twenty-five conditions were right for him to resume his original course. He examined his motives for wanting to become a minister by asking these six questions: (1) What am I? (2) What have I done? (3) From what principles do I act in this undertaking? (4) What are the ends I aim at in it? (5) What do I want? (6) What are my purposes and resolutions for the future?" One biographer describes the answers these questions evoked as displaying "the utmost seriousness, humility, and conscientious regard to truth and duty."

Henry began to serve as minister of a church in Chester, where he remained for the next twenty-five years.

The final two years of his life were spent at a church in London, though he often found time to preach in other pulpits as well. He died at the age of fifty-one while on a preaching tour. His dying words form a fitting epitaph to his life: "A life spent in the service of God is the most comfortable and pleasant life that one can live in the present world."

Matthew Henry left behind more than a legacy of faithful church ministry; he also left his commentary on the entire Bible. Notable for its rich devotional insights, Henry's commentary is the product of one mind and heart devoted to mining the truths of God's Word.

Perhaps this month would be a good time to add his commentary to your own library of Bible-study tools. Along with other godly people you will meet this month, he can be your guide in discovering new riches from the pages of Scripture. All it takes is a teachable heart . . . and a few minutes each day.

A Lesson from the life of Matthew Henry

I can have a close relationship with God as I study His Word.

All the reason in the world to worship

Then the man said, "Lord, I believe," and he worshiped him (John 9:38).

John 9 describes a story of front-page significance. A man born blind received his sight—a
miracle duplicated nowhere in the Old
Testament. And this the Pharisees found disturb-
ing. For the more they investigated, the more
they were faced with a decision regarding the
Sight-giver.

They were unwilling to admit in their unbelief
what the man born blind was only too willing to
acknowledge, as Matthew Henry describes.

Walk with Matthew Henry

"Believing with the heart, the man professed
his faith in Christ: 'Lord, I believe you to be the
Son of God.'

"He not only gave Him the civil respect due to
a great man and the acknowledgments owing to
a kind benefactor, but he gave Him the divine
honor, and worshiped Him as the Son of God
come in the flesh.

"None but God is to be worshiped, and by
worshiping Jesus, the man acknowledged Him to
be God.

"True faith will show itself in humble adoration
of the Lord Jesus. Those who believe in Him will
see all the reason in the world to worship Him."

Walk Closer to God

Who in your opinion is Jesus of Nazareth?

Before you answer, consider the implications of
your response.

If you say He is a man (John 9:11), then how do
you explain His miracles?

If you say He is a prophet (John 9:17), then
where did He get His message?

If you say He is a man of God (John 9:33), then
where did He get His authority?

When a head of state enters a room, everyone
stands. What if Jesus Christ, the Son of God, were
to come into the room? What response would He
deserve?

The man born blind saw clearly how to
respond (John 9:38). Let his example be the
model for your response throughout the day.

Worship from the Heart

*As you cope with the
trials that come your
way, let the account
of this miracle com-
fort you. Let God
know that, though
you may not under-
stand the "why" of
your suffering, you
do rejoice that He
will be glorified by its
outcome. Regardless
of your circum-
stances, He is worthy
of your confidence.*

Walk Thru the Word

New Testament Reading
John 9:13-41
Old Testament Reading
Isaiah 2:3

118

The Savior waits ahead

"When he has brought out all his own, he goes on ahead of them" (John 10:4).

*Y*ou're preparing for a trip to a city you've never visited. You pull out the road map to find out how to get there. Anxiety is replaced by confidence because you know *someone has already gone before you.*

Suppose you've been transferred to a new city. You must leave friends, routines, personal ministries, perhaps even family. Does that thought produce an anxious feeling of launching out unaided into the unknown?

It needn't. Jesus said He's gone before you. And if He has called you to a new environment, then He is already there waiting for you. Frances Havergal examines this comforting thought.

Walk with Frances Havergal

"What gives the Alpine climber confidence in wild, lonely, treacherous passes or ascents when he has not passed that way before? It is that his guide 'goes ahead.'

"It is to Christ's own sheep that this promise applies—simply those who believe and hear His voice.

"Perhaps we have been in a sheltered nook of the fold and we are sent to live where it is windier and wilder. The home-nest is stirred up, and we have to go (it may be only for a few days, it may be for years) into less congenial surroundings to live with new people or in a different position or in a new neighborhood.

"We do not put ourselves forth; we would rather stay. But it has to be.

"But Jesus 'goes ahead.' He prepares the earthly as well as the heavenly places for us. He will be there when we get to the new place.

"He is not sending us away from Him, but only leading us forth with His own gentle hand, saying, 'Rise up, My love, and come away with Me.' "

Walk Closer to God

Wherever you may be, if Jesus has brought you there, then He has prepared the way for you. And He has a purpose for your being there. Ask Him to show you what that purpose is.

Worship from the Heart

"Lord, sometimes I have the feeling that I, only I, have walked this troublesome path. Your Word teaches otherwise. Let me trace Your footprints along the sea of sorrow. Let me be as a child who steps into a father's warm footprints in the wet sand, always aware that the fresh prints indicate Your presence just up ahead."

Walk Thru the Word

New Testament Reading
John 10
Old Testament Reading
Deuteronomy 31:1-8

*R*evival of life and hope

Jesus said, "Did I not tell you that if you believed, you would see the glory of God?" (John 11:40).

*O*ne can only wonder what Lazarus had to say about death . . . after having been dead *four* days.

The grieving Mary and Martha didn't have the modern reports of resuscitated individuals to bolster their hopes for their brother. But they did have Jesus, the Resurrection and the Life, and He was far better.

F. B. Meyer shows how Jesus revived both life in Lazarus and hope in Lazarus's grieving sisters.

Walk with F. B. Meyer

"It seems easy for some to believe. The Marys who sit at Jesus' feet, feeding on His words, find the life and light of faith in His beloved presence.

"But others, like Martha, are distracted with so many things that faith seems impossible. And this is the very point where this story is so abundantly helpful.

"In educating Martha to this stupendous act of faith, the Lord gave her a distinct promise: 'Your brother will rise again.' He drew her attention from His words to Himself: 'I am the resurrection and the life.' He forced her to confess her faith. To express it would confirm and increase it: 'Do you believe this?' And He compelled her to act on the faith He had created by allowing the bystanders to remove the stone.

"All her soul woke up as she observed these preparations for her brother's resurrection. She believed, and in her faith she gave the Lord the pivot on which His leverage might rest."

Walk Closer to God

For many, the thought of death can lead only to despair. But for Martha, death became an opportunity for her faith to be stretched and supported by seeing the Master's dominion over death.

When death seems dark and frightening, you too can look to the One death could not master.

For Martha, seeing was believing.

But remember what Jesus said: "Blessed are those who have not seen and yet have believed" (John 20:29).

*W*orship from the Heart

"The whole history of the Christian life is a series of resurrections. . . . Every time a man finds his heart is troubled, that he is not rejoicing in God, a resurrection must follow; a resurrection out of the night of troubled thought into the gladness of the truth."

—*George MacDonald*

*W*alk Thru the Word

New Testament Reading
John 11
Old Testament Reading
Isaiah 26:19

The loving heart of the Father revealed

Then Mary took about a pint of pure nard, an expensive perfume; she poured it on Jesus' feet and wiped his feet with her hair (John 12:3).

Redemption. Propitiation. Justification. Reconciliation. Four big words that describe the work of Christ on the cross. Four big concepts that help to answer the question, "*What* did the death of Christ accomplish?"

The *why* is equally significant. Why did Jesus allow His enemies to cruelly kill Him? The attitude of Mary in John 12 provides a clue, and A. B. Bruce draws upon her example to probe the question.

Walk with A. B. Bruce

"Just such a love as that of Mary, only far deeper and stronger, moved Jesus to sacrifice Himself for us. The simple account of Christ's whole conduct in becoming man and undergoing what is recorded of Him is this: He loved sinners.

"Jesus loved sinners enough to lay down His life for them. Like Mary, He must procure an alabaster box—a human body—fill it with the fine essence of a human soul, and pour out His soul unto death on the cross for our salvation.

"In effect Jesus says to us, 'Do not be afraid to regard My death as an act of the same kind as that of Mary: an act of pure, devoted love. Let the aroma of her ointment circulate about the neighborhood of My cross and help you to discern the sweet savor of *My* sacrifice. Amid all your speculations on the grand theme of redemption, do not fail to see in My death My loving heart, and the loving heart of My Father, revealed.' "

Walk Closer to God

"God demonstrates his own love for us in this: While we were still sinners, Christ died for us" (Romans 5:8).

In the greatest story ever told, the grandest theme of all is found in one four-letter word: love. All else flows from the love of God—His free gift of life for those who did nothing to deserve it.

God expressed His love for us in the precious gift of His Son. How can you, like Mary, express your love for Him in a precious gift in return?

Worship from the Heart

"Look how the whole world has gone after him!" So spoke the Pharisees as they saw the crowds following Jesus in that first Palm Sunday procession. Many today do not follow Him. Are you, as a Christian, living in a way that demonstrates His love? Give thanks that by God's grace you have recognized His voice and that He has given you a part in drawing others to Him.

Walk Thru the Word

New Testament Reading
John 12:1-19
Old Testament Reading
Psalm 18:1

Standing for the unpopular

Yet at the same time many even among the leaders believed in him. But because of the Pharisees they would not confess their faith . . . for they loved praise from men more than praise from God (John 12:42-43).

Who would remember the names of Copernicus and Luther if these men had heeded the attacks of others?

Many ridiculed and attacked them for holding "radical" beliefs. But these two considered truth more important than the approval of others.

In John 12, the beliefs of the rulers were swayed by the opinions of men. Albert Barnes discusses the shortcomings of intellectual assent when compared to true faith.

Walk with Albert Barnes

"It does not appear that the rulers had a living, active faith, but that they were convinced in their mind that He was the Messiah.

"They had that kind of faith which is so common —a speculative acknowledgment that religion is true, but which leads to no self-denial or piety, and fears man more than God. True faith is active. It overcomes the fear of man.

"Nevertheless, it was no unimportant proof that any part of the great council of the Jews were even speculatively convinced of it; and it shows that the evidence could not have been slight when it overcame their prejudices and pride. It forced them to admit that the lowly and poor man of Nazareth was the long-expected Messiah of their nation."

Walk Closer to God

Copernicus and Luther. Neither saw many "converts" to their views at first. Months and years were needed to convince others of what they knew to be true.

But if these two had not stood firm from the start, the accomplishments for which they became famous would have gone to others. They chose to be *right* rather than *popular*.

You may hesitate to believe and proclaim something that is unpopular with those around you.

But ask yourself which is more important—the applause of people, or the praise of God?

Worship from the Heart

Compromise is easy. Standing firm is the stuff of heroes. God's immortal Hall of Fame in Hebrews 11 is a roster of believers through the ages who refused to budge in their faith or godly principles. Praise the Lord that we have such a legacy. Ask His help as you confront the pressure to compromise.

Walk Thru the Word

New Testament Reading
John 12:20-50
Old Testament Reading
1 Samuel 15:1-23

A willingness to serve

"Now that you know these things, you will be blessed if you do them" (John 13:17).

*I*t's relatively easy to find someone to preach, teach, sing, organize, or take charge. But try to find someone willing to wash feet, and you'll discover a "servant shortage" of crisis proportions.

Perhaps one reason servant-leaders are so rare is because people have overlooked the benefits of obedient service:

- happiness (13:17)
- fellowship (13:8)
- Christlikeness (13:15).

Oswald Chambers suggests one more benefit—discovering what God is like and what He is about.

Walk with Oswald Chambers

"If you believe in Jesus, you are not to spend all your time in smooth waters just inside the harbor, full of delight but always moored. You have to get out into the great deeps of God and begin to know for yourself, begin to have spiritual discernment.

"The counterfeit of obedience is a state of mind in which you work up occasions to sacrifice yourself; ardor is mistaken for discernment.

"It is easier to sacrifice yourself than to fulfill your spiritual destiny stated in Romans 12:1-2.

"It is a great deal better to fulfill the purpose of God in your life by discerning His will than to perform great acts of self-sacrifice. 'To obey is better than sacrifice.'

"Beware of harking back to what you were once when God wants you to be something you've never been."

Walk Closer to God

Servant-leaders don't stay in sheltered harbors. They are willing to launch out into the unknown in obedience to God. They are people who are continually being transformed into the likeness of the greatest Servant-Leader of all time.

Combine a servant's heart with an obedient will, and you too will become something you may never have been before: a need-oriented, servant-hearted, Christlike leader. And there's always room for more of those!

*W*orship from the Heart

The Marines are not the only ones who are looking for "a few good men." Your church is sure to need some short- or long-term volunteer help. Could your schedule be tightened up a bit or an unnecessary project dropped in order to lend a hand? Honor God by your willingness to serve others as they have given to you.

*W*alk Thru the Word

New Testament Reading
John 13
Old Testament Reading
Nehemiah 5

*C*omfort from the great Comforter

"But the Counselor, the Holy Spirit, whom the Father will send in my name, will teach you all things" (John 14:26).

*E*leven worried and fearful men eat their last meal with the Master. Their thoughts move as one: *What does this talk of betrayal really mean? Is Jesus going to leave us? What will happen after He departs?*

Anticipating the disciples' questions, Jesus calms their fears by introducing them to the divine Comforter, the Holy Spirit, the One who will become their Teacher, Counselor, and ever-present Friend.

If your heart is troubled today, let the words of John 14 and the insights of R. A. Torrey point the way to true comfort.

*W*orship from the Heart

"Where can I go from your Spirit? Where can I flee from your presence? If I go up to the heavens, you are there; if I make my bed in the depths, you are there. If I rise on the wings of the dawn, if I settle on the far side of the sea, even there your hand will guide me, your right hand will hold me fast" (Psalm 139:7-10).

Walk with R. A. Torrey

"While we await Christ's return from the throne of the Father, we have another Person just as divine as He, just as wise, just as strong, just as able to help, just as loving, always by our side, ready at any moment that we look to Him to counsel us, to teach us, to give us victory, to take control of our lives.

"This is one of the most comforting thoughts in the New Testament. It is a cure for loneliness, for the breaking hearts of those separated from loved ones, for fear of darkness and danger.

"But it is in our service for Christ that this thought of the Holy Spirit comes to us with greatest helpfulness. We need not be robbed of joy and liberty in our service because fear hampers us.

"We need only remember that this responsibility is not really upon us but upon another, the Holy Spirit. If He is permitted to do the work, our fears and cares will vanish."

Walk Closer to God

When you allow the Holy Spirit to minister to your deepest need, you will experience a fresh love for Christ and His Word.

Invite the Comforting Helper to exercise His unique ministry in your life today.

He's right there with you this very moment!

*W*alk Thru the Word

New Testament Reading
John 14
Old Testament Reading
Psalm 139:7-12

Coping in a hostile world

"I have chosen you out of the world. That is why the world hates you" (John 15:19).

I have good news . . . and bad news!" Jesus' final instructions to His disciples just hours before the cross of Calvary contained both.

The good news: Abiding in Him produces lasting fruit; continuing in His love speaks volumes to the world; believing prayer is the path to divine provision. And . . .

The bad news: The world hated Christ and will treat His followers no differently. We can expect hostility from those who do not honor Christ.

But, by knowing the bad news in advance, there is no excuse for allowing persecution and opposition to take you by surprise, as J. C. Ryle points out.

Walk with J. C. Ryle

"Let it be a settled principle in our minds that the true Christian must always enter the kingdom of God through much tribulation.

"His best things are yet to come. This world is not our home.

"If we are faithful servants of Christ, the world will hate us, as it hated Him. In one way or another grace will always be persecuted.

"No consistency of conduct, however faultless, no kindness and amiability of character, however striking, will exempt a believer from the world's dislike.

"It is foolish to be surprised at this. It is a mere waste of time to murmur at it. It is a part of the cross, and we must bear it patiently."

Walk Closer to God

Hostility and antagonism from the world and Satan's forces shouldn't surprise you when you recall that "our struggle is not against flesh and blood, but against the rulers, against the authorities, against the powers of this dark world and against the spiritual forces of evil in the heavenly realms" (Ephesians 6:12).

For that kind of warfare, you can't afford to be unprepared or caught off guard in any way. Anticipation—not alarm—is the proper response when good news becomes bad news for you.

Worship from the Heart

Make a quick mental check to be sure it is your Christian faith that brings the hostility you may experience from others and not some personal habit. We may find that persecution attributed to our faith is actually a result of a hypocritical or annoying characteristic in our humanity. Then, rejoice that our great God is able to change us from the inside out.

Walk Thru the Word

New Testament Reading
John 15:1–16:4
Old Testament Reading
Jeremiah 20:7-9

Tender care from above

"When he, the Spirit of truth, comes, he will guide you into all truth. . . . taking from what is mine and making it known to you" (John 16:13-14).

When a newborn child is hungry, it is not enough to point the way to the refrigerator for a bottle. A baby needs constant parental care to provide for its every need.

A new Christian may feel at times that he has been left on his own. But Charles Spurgeon reminds us that the Holy Spirit is the Christian's tender "nursemaid."

Walk with Charles Spurgeon

"There are times when all the promises and doctrines of the Bible are of no avail, unless a gracious hand shall apply them to us.

"When a soldier is wounded in battle, it is of little use for him to know that there are those at the hospital who can bind his wounds, and medicines there to ease all the pains which he now suffers. What he needs is to be taken there and the remedies applied.

"It is thus with our souls. To meet this need there is one, the Spirit of truth, who takes of the things of Jesus and applies them to us.

"The good Samaritan did not say, 'Here is the wine, and here is the oil'; he actually poured in the oil and the wine. So Jesus not only gives you the sweet wine of the promise, but holds the golden chalice to your lips and pours life into your mouth. The wayworn pilgrim is not merely strengthened to walk, but he is borne up on an eagle's wings.

"Glorious gospel, which provides everything for the helpless, which draws nigh to us when we cannot reach after it, which brings us grace before we seek for grace!"

Walk Closer to God

Like a parent tending the needs of an infant, the Holy Spirit cares for you. But unlike the child who outgrows his need for a parent's care, you will never outgrow your need for the Holy Spirit —His nurture, His cleansing, His empowering.

Such care is an eternal gift of the Father to His children.

Worship from the Heart

Believers well grounded in the faith can be a solid source of strength for new-born Christians. Allow the Holy Spirit to use you to disciple or encourage a new-born. A Bible study before work . . . a few minutes of prayer over the telephone— there are dozens of ways to undergird the growth of a young Christian. Ask God today to make you a one-on-one reflection of His love.

Walk Thru the Word

New Testament Reading
John 16:5-33
Old Testament Reading
Jeremiah 17:5-8

"Now this is eternal life: that they may know you, the only true God, and Jesus Christ, whom you have sent" (John 17:3).

A mother stood on the English coast watching her missionary son sail for China. As the boat pulled away from the shore, a "cry of anguish . . . was wrung from the mother's heart as she felt that he was gone."

At that emotional moment, wrote Hudson Taylor, he experienced as never before the truth that "God so loved the world."

Years earlier that mother had knelt in prayer for her son many miles away . . . at the very moment he became a Christian. Read thoughtfully as Hudson Taylor describes from firsthand experience what it means to know God.

Walk with Hudson Taylor

"There is a far closer connection than we sometimes realize between the knowledge of God and the practical use of that knowledge.

"We cannot separate these things. If we want to know the power of His resurrection, we must also know the fellowship of His sufferings, being made conformable to His death (Philippians 3:10). There must be the living out of the life of God in order that we may learn to know Him more fully and perfectly.

"It is in carrying this gospel through the world, in manifesting it at home and abroad, that we shall realize and learn to know God. As we become like Him, we shall understand Him.

"O friends! When we are brought into the position of having practical fellowship with God in trial and sorrow and suffering, we learn a lesson that is not to be learned amidst the ease and comfort of ordinary life. This is why God so often brings us through trying experiences."

Walk Closer to God

To be like Christ, to truly know Him, to follow Him in obedience, one must forsake "ease and comfort" and share some of the sufferings He experienced.

The path of Christlikeness may be an uphill journey . . . but it's worth every step!

*K*nowing the only true God

*W*orship from the Heart

Discouragement can loom heavily when we contemplate our personal suffering for Christ's sake. Martin Luther suggests we look at it differently. "When I consider my crosses [to be] tribulations, and temptations, I shame myself almost to death, thinking what are they in comparison to the sufferings of my blessed Savior, Jesus Christ."

*W*alk Thru the Word

New Testament Reading
John 17
Old Testament Reading
Zechariah 13:7-9

127

A zeal approved by God

Then Simon Peter, who had a sword, drew it and struck the high priest's servant, cutting off his right ear (John 18:10).

*P*eter, seldom held up as a "model of moderation," overzealously cut off another's ear in the heat of the moment, and was rebuked by his Master for doing so.

John Calvin points out that zeal without obedience is not what Christ expects from His followers.

Walk with John Calvin

"John describes the foolish zeal of Peter, who attempted to defend his Master in an unlawful manner. Courageously indeed, he incurs great risk on Christ's account. But as he does not consider what his calling demands, and what God permits, his action is severely blamed by Christ.

"In the person of Peter, Christ condemns everything people dare to attempt out of their own fancy. Nothing is more common than to defend, under the cloak of zeal, everything we do, as if it were of no importance whether God approved or not.

"It was thoughtless of Peter to attempt to prove his faith by his sword while he could not do so by his tongue. When he is called to confess, he denies his Master; now, without his Master's authority, he raises a tumult.

"Warned by so striking an example, let us learn to keep our zeal within proper bounds; and as the flesh is always eager to attempt more than God commands, let us learn that our zeal will succeed ill whenever we venture to undertake anything contrary to the Bible. Let obedience, therefore, be the foundation of all we undertake."

Walk Closer to God

Peter needed to heed the words of James: "Everyone should be quick to listen, slow to speak and slow to become angry, for man's anger does not bring about the righteous life that God desires" (James 1:19-20).

When the urge strikes, don't *you* strike . . . until first God's Word has had a chance to guide your response. Rather than striking someone's ear, use your own to hear and obey God!

Worship from the Heart

"Holy Father, may I be impassioned with a holy zeal so not to sidestep the responsibility of obedience to Your Word. Teach me the difference between self-serving passion and a godly enthusiasm for truth."

Walk Thru the Word

New Testament Reading
John 18
Old Testament Reading
Proverbs 30:32-33

128

No neutral ground at Calvary

But they shouted, "Take him away! Take him away! Crucify him!" (John 19:15).

The cross brings out the best and worst in people. Its shadow is a dividing line between those who would receive God and those who would blatantly refuse Him.

If we are truly to appreciate the depth of divine grace, then we must remember that we too were enemies of Christ. We were, in the words of the apostle Paul, no better than the rest (Romans 3:9). But now, because of His sacrifice, we have stepped from that mob to stand under the cross.

Jessie Penn-Lewis conveys the dividing force of the cross when she points out that we must now see ourselves as crucified with Christ.

Walk with Jessie Penn-Lewis

"Soldiers and thieves, chief priests, elders and scribes, with all the multitude, were of one mind that awful day. All forgot the barriers that separated them, and joined together at Calvary.

"So it is today. All the elements of this evil world become united at Calvary. The fleshly element, the wise element, the criminal classes, and the traditional religionists join with the special forces of the evil one in the great revolt against the cross. And once again they who stand by the cross of Jesus are a little band, the very preaching of the cross marking them as 'crucified to the world.' The cross becomes the instrument of their crucifixion as of His. There is no neutral ground at Calvary."

Walk Closer to God

Self-image is an important concept to most of us. We don't want to appear too holy, too eccentric, or too fanatic in our convictions. We'd prefer to present ourselves as sophisticated diplomats, quiet ambassadors for the cause of Christ. But if sophistication dilutes our identification with Christ, then we betray the cross of Christ.

Jessie Penn-Lewis stated it well: "There is no neutral ground at Calvary." We, who once stood in the circles of the profane screaming, "Crucify Him!" should now stand in the circle of the redeemed shouting, "He is Lord!"

Worship from the Heart

Let the words of this hymn by Isaac Watts be your meditation today: "Forbid it, Lord, that I should boast / Save in the death of Christ, my God. / All the vain things that charm me most, / I sacrifice them to His blood. / Were the whole realm of nature mine, / That were a present far too small; / Love so amazing, so divine, / Demands my soul, my life, my all."

Walk Thru the Word

New Testament Reading
John 19:1-27
Old Testament Reading
Joshua 24:14-15

No need for additions

Jesus said, "It is finished." With that, he bowed his head and gave up his spirit (John 19:30).

*M*ost Christians begin well; but finishing well—or even at all—is another matter entirely.

Jesus was a finisher. He completed the work of redemption that He came to accomplish. He left nothing undone.

In the closing hours of His life he could pray to His Father, "I have brought you glory on earth by completing the work you gave me to do" (John 17:4).

John Flavel shares this thought on the completed work of Christ.

Worship from the Heart

For a moment, imagine that you are Pilate trying to maintain control in a country seething with religious and political rivalries. Where on earth could you look for guidance? Ask God to give you insight into the spiritual reality behind the contemporary political and social events that you see. Praise Him that He won the victory over the evil forces of this world.

Walk with John Flavel

"Did Christ finish His work? How dangerous it is to join anything of our own to the righteousness of Christ in pursuit of justification before God! Jesus Christ will never endure this; it reflects upon His work dishonorably. He will be all, or none, in our justification.

"If He has finished the work, what need is there of our additions? And if not, to what purpose are they? Can we finish that which Christ Himself could not complete?

"Did He finish the work, and will He ever divide the glory and praise of it with us? No, no; Christ is no half-Savior.

"It is a hard thing to bring proud hearts to rest upon Christ for righteousness. God humbles the proud by calling sinners wholly from their own righteousness to Christ for their justification."

Walk Closer to God

If these thoughts from the apostle Paul are the expression of your heart, pray them back to God:

"I want to know Christ and the power of his resurrection and the fellowship of sharing in his sufferings, becoming like him in his death . . . Brothers, I do not consider myself yet to have taken hold of it. But one thing I do: Forgetting what is behind and straining toward what is ahead, I press on toward the goal to win the prize for which God has called me heavenward in Christ Jesus" (Philippians 3:10, 13-14).

Walk Thru the Word

New Testament Reading
John 19:28-42
Old Testament Reading
Genesis 3:14-15

130

Submit your doubt to faith

[Thomas] said to them, "Unless I see the nail marks in his hands, . . . and put my hand into his side, I will not believe it" (John 20:25).

*T*he Beloved." "The Rock." "Sons of Thunder."
It seems each of Jesus' men carried a nickname!

But history has reserved one of the most curious for the disciple named Didymus (11:16). Perhaps you know him better as "Doubting Thomas."

But his doubts and questions never excluded him from the circle of disciples.

It's a reminder that Jesus welcomes *your* questions and understands *your* doubts.

But avoid Thomas's mistake of trying to dictate terms to God, as Joseph Parker observes.

Walk with Joseph Parker

"The mistake which Thomas made was to lay down the one and only way in which Christ should come to him: 'Unless . . . I will not believe.'

"That is to say, I must have it my way, not God's way. I must appoint the gate through which the Lord must come into my life, and if He attempts to come by any other way, I will not receive Him.

"This is the mistake of the world: to say the Bible ought to consist of so many books, written at such and such times, by such and such men, and all the pieces should dovetail in such and such a way, or we will not believe. And what does our not believing amount to? We are really saying, 'Unless every comma and semicolon written in the Bible agrees with me, I will give up the whole thing.' And what will happen if he gives up the whole thing? Nothing good!"

Walk Closer to God

Saving faith does not require that you be an eyewitness of the resurrected Lord. Jesus told Thomas, "Blessed are those who have not seen and yet have believed" (John 20:29).

All the historical proof you will ever need has already been supplied in the Bible. Proof that Jesus lived . . . died . . . rose again . . . and lives today to be your Savior.

The next step is not a "leap in the dark," but an intelligent step of *faith* in the *facts* of the gospel.

Worship from the Heart

C. S. Lewis, commenting on his conversion, said he had to be dragged to the door of faith, kicking and screaming. But he did pass through and became a formidable foe to Satan. Thomas, too, passed skeptically through the door to become a fiery proclaimer of the gospel. Can you think of at least one atheistic or agnostic friend with whom you can share the gospel of Christ this week? You never can tell what our great God will do!

Walk Thru the Word

New Testament Reading
John 20
Old Testament Reading
Judges 6:1-24

*H*eart of the loving Shepherd

"Simon, son of John, do you truly love me?" He answered, "Yes, Lord, you know that I love you." Jesus said, "Take care of my sheep" (John 21:16).

*O*ne of the truest tests of your devotion to Christ is your devotion to the *body of Christ.*

Jesus demonstrated a shepherd's heart throughout His earthly ministry. And in His absence He knew His followers would need undershepherds to care for them.

Peter may have misunderstood the Lord's questions in John 21, but his ministry shows that he grasped the principle: *Every shepherd must be willing to lay down his life for the sheep.*

Oswald Chambers explains.

*W*orship from the Heart

Linger for a few minutes over the words of Psalm 23. Note the ways our Lord is the Good Shepherd. He offers rest, restoration, direction, comfort—to name just a few. Rejoice that the Good Shepherd is your Shepherd.

Walk with Oswald Chambers

"Jesus did not say, 'Make converts to your way of thinking,' but 'Look after My sheep; see that they get nourished in the knowledge of Me.'

"We count as service what we do in the way of Christian work; Jesus Christ calls service what we are to Him, not what we *do* for Him.

"Discipleship is based on devotion to Jesus Christ. There is no argument and no compulsion, but simply, 'If you would be My disciple, you must be devoted to Me.'

"People do not want to be devoted to Jesus, but only to the cause He started. Jesus Christ is a source of deep offense to the educated mind of today that does not want Him in any other way than as a comrade.

"If I am devoted to the cause of humanity only, I will soon be exhausted and come to the place where my love will falter; but if I love Jesus Christ personally and passionately, I can serve humanity even though treated with contempt."

Walk Closer to God

This month you've met the Good Shepherd "up close and personal." You have learned that life must be nurtured to become healthy, mature, and capable of reproduction.

"Feed my lambs. . . . Take care of my sheep. . . . Feed my sheep." That's a threefold reminder that Peter badly needed. Do *you* need to heed those challenging words as well?

*W*alk Thru the Word

New Testament Reading
John 21
Old Testament Reading
Ezekiel 34:11-31

Life and Death in the Arena of Faith

The book of Acts has all the makings of a best-selling novel. Plenty of action. Tense confrontation. Martyrdom. Controversy. Gripping dialogue. Travel. Courtroom drama. Even humorous situations. And undergirding all is a sense that in the end everything will turn out as the Author intended.

The main character in Acts is not Peter, Paul, nor any figure, but rather the Holy Spirit. In the opening verses, Jesus commands His followers to wait in Jerusalem until "the Holy Spirit comes on you; and you will be my witnesses in Jerusalem, and in all Judea and Samaria, and to the ends of the earth" (Acts 1:8). The rest of the book recounts how those words of Jesus began to be fulfilled.

Acts 1–7 presents the early days of the New Testament church in Jerusalem. Peter preaches Spirit-inspired sermons that pierce the hearts of thousands. Others begin to speak out as the influence of the gospel multiplies, until Stephen's martyrdom ushers in a period of intense persecution. Acts 8–12 chronicles the spread of the gospel into the regions surrounding Jerusalem. Paul's transformation from antagonist to apostle of Christ and the conversion of the Roman centurion Cornelius set the stage for the good news to be carried to "the ends of the earth." Acts 13–28 begins in Antioch, the first great missionary center of the church, and ends in Rome, the capital of the then-known world. Paul and his various companions spread the good news of the resurrected Christ everywhere they travel.

The main character in Acts is not Peter, Paul, nor any human figure, but rather the Holy Spirit.

The book of Acts closes with chapter 28, but the story of Acts continues today as disciples of Jesus Christ take the gospel to their Jerusalem, Judea, Samaria, and the ends of the earth. Think of Acts as your training manual on "How to Be an Effective Witness." Jesus Christ has provided the plan; the Holy Spirit provides the power. All that is needed is a person through whom God can work. God wants you to take the good news of salvation to your neighborhood, your school, and your office. It's an exciting assignment!

The secret will of God

He said to them, "It is not for you to know the times or dates the Father has set by his own authority" (Acts 1:7).

The "right of the public to know" is often invoked in defense of leaking vital information. Governments may not be able to keep their secrets, but God can surely keep His. There are things He knows that are best left unrevealed, and He reserves the right to do precisely that.

The disciples wanted to know if it was time to restore the kingdom to Israel. But as Martin Luther points out, God has His reasons for keeping this—and many of His plans—TOP SECRET.

Walk with Martin Luther

"What God does not want to reveal, you are not to know. What He has not revealed, it is impossible to understand.

"Therefore guard against the temptation of wanting to know: Why does God do this anyway? When the Devil tempts and says, 'Why?', determine whether you are told to know; if not, be silent.

"It was not enough for Adam to have all the trees in Paradise, but the Devil revealed the hidden will of God to him, saying 'Why?' The apple is still sticking in all our throats; for people are still so constituted that they are not always pleased by what God does. The forbidden fruit brought Adam and all of us death, for what God did not want to reveal is not proper for me to know.

"Adam might have said: 'What business of yours is this? Why God has done this, I do not want to know.'

"Be silent about the secret will of God. Listen instead to God's revealed Word."

Walk Closer to God

The disciples asked about the future of a nation; Jesus responded with a worldwide commission. Though the disciples were hardly prepared for the answer they got, in their obedience they received far more than merely the answer they sought.

What does God want from you—*questions* or unquestioning *obedience?* The answer to that is NO SECRET.

Worship from the Heart

Jesus promised to return but gave no timetable. The disciples hoped for His return in their lifetimes. For 2,000 years believers have looked for His coming. What an opportunity for you to live each day as if it were the promised day. Make your heart ready to greet Him. He may return today.

Walk Thru the Word

New Testament Reading
Acts 1
Old Testament Reading
Deuteronomy 29:29

"Men of Israel, listen to this: . . . God has raised this Jesus to life, and we are all witnesses of the fact" (Acts 2:22, 32).

The scene resembled Babel in reverse. Never before had so many people from so many places heard the wonderful works of God proclaimed in their own languages at the same time!

But there were perplexing questions to be answered. How could these unlearned Galileans be speaking so many different languages? Just what was happening?

The multitude needed guidance, so Peter opened the Scriptures and used the occasion to share God's wonderful plan of salvation with the multinational audience. Listen as F. B. Meyer examines the power behind Peter's proclamation.

Walk with F. B. Meyer

"A while ago he trembled like an aspen leaf before the question of a maid; but when that day breaks he stands like a lion, able to charge men with their sin. No hesitancy in speech, no cringing in demeanor, no quailing of the fearless eye.

" 'This man was handed over to you by God's set purpose and foreknowledge; and you, with the help of wicked men, put him to death . . . [on] the cross' (2:23)—such is our challenge.

" 'God exalted him to his own right hand as Prince and Savior' (5:31)—such is our unhesitating announcement.

"Have you reached this stage of holy boldness so that at your rebuke the wicked man is arrested, the attention of the careless compelled, and the ungodly pricked to the heart? If it be otherwise, your 'day of Pentecost' has not fully come."

Walk Closer to God

Peter's message on the Day of Pentecost is both *timeless* and *timely*. He shows that the death and resurrection of Christ have historical roots and contemporary relevance (2:22-32), that "everyone who calls on the name of the Lord will be saved" (2:21). Put these together and you have a compelling witness for the gospel. A witness you can proclaim boldly to individuals from your "tribe and tongue and people and nation."

*F*laming hearts produce fearless tongues

*W*orship from the Heart

"Holy Father, set my heart afire with Your truth and give me Your boldness to share Christ with co-workers, neighbors, and friends. Make me realize that it is Satan's intention to keep them in the dark and it is Your intention to bring them into the light. May I hold the light of Christ high in all my actions, attitudes, and words. Amen."

*W*alk Thru the Word

New Testament Reading
Acts 2
Old Testament Reading
Psalm 16

Walking, jumping, praising His name

He jumped to his feet and began to walk. Then he went with them into the temple courts, walking and jumping, and praising God (Acts 3:8).

"And leap, ye lame, for joy!" With those words, Charles Wesley closes his hymn of praise, "O for a Thousand Tongues to Sing." And it wouldn't be surprising to think that Wesley had the lame man of Acts 3 in mind.

The man, who had been crippled since birth, had plenty of reason to begin "jumping for joy." Albert Barnes offers this instructive commentary on the man's exuberant response to God's work in his life.

Walk with Albert Barnes

" 'He jumped to his feet. . . ' This was a natural expression of joy, a striking fulfillment of prophecy in Isaiah 35:6: 'Then will the lame leap like a deer.'

"The man had been lame since childhood; he had never walked. And there was more in the miracle than merely giving strength.

"The art of walking is one that is acquired by long practice. Children learn slowly. When, therefore, this man was able to walk at once, it was clear proof of a miracle.

" 'Praising God.' This was the natural and appropriate expression of his feelings on this occasion. It is remarkable that he praised God without being taught or entreated to do so. It was instinctive—the natural feeling of the heart.

"Likewise a sinner's first feelings, when he is converted, will be to ascribe the praise to God. He needs no prompter; he knows that no power on earth is equal to the work of converting the soul."

Walk Closer to God

Perhaps the words of Wesley's hymn express your thoughts:

O for a thousand tongues to sing
My great Redeemer's praise,
The glories of my God and King,
The triumphs of His grace!
He breaks the power of cancelled sin,
He sets the prisoner free;
His blood can make the foulest clean,
His blood availed for me.

Worship from the Heart

"I will exalt you, my God, the King; I will praise your name for ever and ever. Every day I will praise you and extol your name for ever and ever. Great is the Lord and most worthy of praise; his greatness no one can fathom"
(Psalm 145:1-3).

Walk Thru the Word

New Testament Reading
Acts 3
Old Testament Reading
Isaiah 35:1-10

When they saw the courage of Peter and John and realized that they were unschooled, ordinary men, they were astonished and they took note that these men had been with Jesus (Acts 4:13).

A life brimming with God

*G*ive your life to *learning,* and you will appear learned. Give your life to *Christ,* and you will grow increasingly *Christlike.*

From the perspective of an educator, Peter and John were unlearned and ignorant. But their boldness and faith caused onlookers to take a second look. Being with Jesus transformed them from ordinary men into extraordinary disciples.

Take note as Gipsy Smith explains how your life can become an irresistible sermon.

Walk with Gipsy Smith

"Let your life be in harmony with your profession. That is what it means to seek those things that are above.

"Live a life in harmony with the law of God, that shall glorify God, that shall be God-honoring, that shall be a witness to the world in which you live, that shall be saying quietly, though you never say a word, 'My life is what God has made it, and He can do the same for you.'

"Beautifully lived, beautifully clean, full of music, full of God—that life will be a sermon unanswerable. And many will listen to a sermon like that who would never listen to one from the pulpit.

"Though they will not read Matthew, Mark, Luke, John, or Acts, they will search your life, and they will see that you have been with Jesus.

"What the world wants more of today is the faithful sermon lived in the workshop, marketplace, warehouse, bank, and store—the life which is Christlike."

Walk Closer to God

You may at times feel unlearned, ignorant, or lacking in accomplishments when compared to others. You may even feel that you have no special skills or talents. But take it from Peter and John. As the divine music of your life flows into the lives of those around you, they will sense that you have been with Jesus.

Worship from the Heart

As you prepare to worship with other believers, meditate on these words by Ernest Southcott: "The holiest moment of the church service is the moment when God's people— strengthened by preaching and sacrament—go out of the church door into the world to be the church. We don't go to church; we are the church."

Walk Thru the Word

New Testament Reading
Acts 4
Old Testament Reading
Isaiah 33:14-16

The precious fellowship of His suffering

The apostles left the Sanhedrin, rejoicing because they had been counted worthy of suffering disgrace for the Name (Acts 5:41).

Imprisonment, beating, stoning, martyrdom. Words the first-century Christians knew first-hand! For them, *following* the Savior often meant experiencing the *fellowship* of His sufferings—personally and painfully.

Think about the early Christians' tenacity as you read A. W. Tozer's cogent words.

Walk with A. W. Tozer

"Those first believers turned to Christ with the full understanding that they were espousing an unpopular cause that could cost them everything. Shortly after Pentecost some were jailed, many lost all their earthly goods, a few were slain, hundreds were 'scattered abroad.'

"They could have escaped all this by the simple expedient of denying their faith and turning back to the world. This they steadfastly refused to do.

"To make converts, we are tempted to play down the difficulties and play up the peace of mind and worldly success enjoyed by those who accept Christ.

"We will never be completely honest with our hearers until we tell them the blunt truth that, as members of a race of moral rebels, they are in a serious jam, one they will not get out of easily.

"If they refuse to repent and believe on Christ, they will most surely perish. If they do turn to Him, the same enemies that crucified Him will try to crucify them."

Walk Closer to God

How would you feel after receiving a beating for attending church, or a jail sentence for sharing your faith?

Luke records the apostles' startling reaction to their abusive treatment. They left the council *rejoicing* over the privilege of being "counted worthy of suffering disgrace for the Name."

You may never be physically persecuted, but if the reception you're receiving in your role as ambassador for Christ sometimes seems rocky, take heart! You're in good company.

Worship from the Heart

Most persecution today comes in a more subtle form. Our message is taken lightly, our lives considered a bit odd or quirky. We're encouraged to tone down our message. But the intent is the same as those who silenced early Christians with stones and swords. Consider what you can do to make your words and life still stand out in the crowd.

Walk Thru the Word

New Testament Reading
Acts 5
Old Testament Reading
Jeremiah 26:8-16

Now Stephen, a man full of God's grace and power, did great wonders and miraculous signs among the people (Acts 6:8).

The message of power in a manner of meekness

*A*cts 6 introduces you to Stephen, a man "full of grace and power." A man with an irresistible message. And yet, when called on to defend the faith with his life, Stephen responded with Christlike humility.

Though his message was full of power, his demeanor was full of meekness—a contrast that Jonathan Edwards helps to explain.

Walk with Jonathan Edwards

"The truly humble Christian is clothed with lowliness, mildness, meekness, gentleness of spirit and behavior. These things are just like garments to him.

"Christian humility has no such thing as roughness, or contempt, or fierceness, or bitterness in its nature. It makes a person like a little child, harmless and innocent, that no one needs to fear; or like a lamb, free of all bitterness, wrath, anger, and clamor.

"Yet in searching and awakening the conscience, he should be a son of thunder. He should do it without judging individuals, leaving it to conscience and the Spirit of God to make the particular application.

"But all his conversation should reflect lowliness and good will, love and pity to all mankind.

"He should be like a lion to guilty consciences, but like a lamb to men and women."

Walk Closer to God

Gentle as a lamb and powerful as a lion. That seems to be a contradiction—until you know the Lamb of God who is also the Lion of Judah. Jesus Christ, the One who possesses all power, yet dealt tenderly with those He came to serve, points the way to a witness that is more powerful than words alone.

A witness that is both tender and tough. That speaks the truth in love, and clothes strength in humility.

A witness that others around you need to hear and experience today.

Worship from the Heart

"Choose seven men from among you. . . ."
As you think about your church, praise God for the godly men and women who serve in various positions of leadership. Ask that God will bless in their service, their families, and their personal needs.

Walk Thru the Word

New Testament Reading
Acts 6
Old Testament Reading
Proverbs 29:23

Looking up while others look around

But Stephen, full of the Holy Spirit, looked up to heaven and saw the glory of God, and Jesus standing at the right hand of God (Acts 7:55).

*P*ower is something many desire, but few possess. But power has a price, whether it's units of personal sacrifice, increased fuel consumption, higher payroll, or skewed relationships.

The Holy Spirit is the Power Source for the Christian. A high price was paid to make that possible—nothing less than the sacrifice of a perfect life on the cross. But what benefits accrued because of it!

F. B. Meyer examines that power at work in the life of Stephen, and indeed, in any child of God.

Walk with F. B. Meyer

"The blessed characteristic of Stephen lay in his being perpetually full of the Holy Spirit. Those who are full of the Holy Spirit are always looking steadfastly upwards. They look not at the things which are seen, but at those which are not seen. To them heaven stands always open.

"Those who are full of the Holy Spirit see and are transfigured by the glory of God. The Council beheld Stephen's face, as if it were the face of an angel. Here the glory of God shone from the open door of heaven.

"Those who are full of the Holy Spirit see Jesus, in His glory, as their Priest. It is the special work of the Holy Spirit to direct their gaze to Jesus. The Spirit takes the things of Jesus and reveals them to the loving and obedient; especially those that concern His priestly work on the cross and in heaven."

Walk Closer to God

Stephen, in the power of the Holy Spirit, preached to the people of Jerusalem about the One who could give them power as well.

Consider the power *you* have received through your relationship with Christ: power over death, power over sin, power to live pleasing to God.

And the price of this power? That's the best news of all! It has been paid in full already by your loving Lord. Look to Jesus for your power, and receive all you need.

Worship from the Heart

When a disinfectant stings your wound, you do not smash the bottle it came in. Truth can sting too, and Stephen was stoned for speaking it. When someone's words sting you, ask God to help you see if there is truth in them. Thank Him for the creative ways and the supportive friends He has used to get His message across to you.

Walk Thru the Word

New Testament Reading
Acts 7:1–8:3
Old Testament Reading
2 Chronicles 24:17-22

Prayer as a means of study

Then Philip ran up to the chariot and heard the man reading Isaiah the prophet. "Do you understand what you are reading?" Philip asked (Acts 8:30).

The difference between spiritual life and spiritual death hinges on a proper understanding of and response to God's Word.

Apart from Philip's insight and explanation, the Ethiopian eunuch may never have understood the good news of the Messiah come to earth.

But how do you master the Word of the Master? Listen as a master student of the Scriptures— Charles Spurgeon—comments.

Walk with Charles Spurgeon

"We would be abler teachers of others, and less liable to be carried about by every wind of doctrine, if we sought to have a more intelligent understanding of the Word of God.

"As the Holy Spirit, the Author of the Scriptures, alone can enlighten us rightly to understand them, we should constantly ask His teaching and His guidance unto all truth.

"When the prophet Daniel sought to interpret Nebuchadnezzar's dream, what did he do? He set himself to earnest prayer that God would open up the vision. Therefore if, for your own and others' profiting, you desire to be 'fill[ed] . . . with the knowledge of his will through all spiritual wisdom and understanding,' remember that prayer is your best means of study. Like Daniel, you shall understand the dream, and its interpretation, when you have sought God.

"You may force your way through many barriers to understanding with the leverage of prayer.

"Thoughts and reasonings are like the steel wedges which give a hold on truth, but prayer is the lever which forces open the treasure hidden within."

Walk Closer to God

In journalism, going to the "primary source" is a cardinal rule. Daniel knew well where to go first for his information. When you think about it, asking the Author to explain the contents of His own Book is a logical step to take.

Worship from the Heart

Prayer is our faith on wing. And faith is the key to understanding God's Word. Consider St. Augustine's thoughts on the relationship of faith and understanding: "Understanding is the reward of faith. Therefore seek not to understand that thou mayest believe, but believe that thou mayest understand."

Walk Thru the Word

New Testament Reading
Acts 8:4-40
Old Testament Reading
Daniel 2:16-19
Ezra 7:10

The power that deepens our lives

"Now get up and go into the city, and you will be told what you must do" (Acts 9:6).

Even in the blinding moment of his conversion, Saul wanted to know what the Lord had for him to *do!*

Like many new Christians, Saul needed to learn the importance of *becoming*, not simply the feverish activity of *doing*.

Activity is no guarantee of *productivity* in the Christian life.

For Saul, waiting to discern the Lord's will was part of his preparation for ministry. Phillips Brooks stresses the need for "deepening times" in your walk with God.

Walk with Phillips Brooks

"There is so little rest! There is such an unreasoning passion for activity! And so we skim the surface of all things.

"We know no more of the real depth of our own lives than a child who crosses a frozen lake knows how deep the lake is. He does not even know that it has a depth. But before our life can get depth into it, it must get God into it. God is the only power that deepens our lives.

"A life with no intention of God in it must be shallow. And there is no life so hard and crusted that God cannot enter into it, break its crust, and deepen it to untold richness."

Walk Closer to God

If you want to build the habit of frequent meditation, begin by acknowledging your need for quiet reflection.

- Time for prayer and confession.
- Time for reading and savoring God's Word phrase by phrase.
- Time to enjoy God's presence.

As you sow seeds of quiet meditation, it may surprise you to see what "germinates": insight and discernment . . . maturity and stability . . . a growing, deepening love for God . . . a ministry to others you never before imagined.

But only you can choose to leave the shallowness of busyness for the depths of becoming all that He created you to be.

Worship from the Heart

Let the experience of Thomas Moore be yours as you seek to maintain an attitude of constant prayer and praise today: "As down in the sunless retreats of the ocean,/ Sweet flowers are springing no mortal can see, / So deep in my soul the still prayer of devotion/ Unheard by the world, rises silent to Thee."

Walk Thru the Word

New Testament Reading
Acts 9
Old Testament Reading
Joshua 1:8

142

The angel answered, "Your prayers and gifts to the poor have come up as a memorial offering before God" (Acts 10:4).

/n the case of Cornelius, his prayers smelled sweet to God even before the centurion professed his faith in Christ. Luke describes him as "devout and God-fearing; he gave generously to those in need and prayed to God regularly" (Acts 10:2).

A. B. Simpson analyzes the kind of prayer that has an aroma God finds irresistible.

Walk with A. B. Simpson

"What a beautiful expression the angel used with Cornelius: 'Your prayers and gifts to the poor have come up as a memorial offering.'

"It would almost seem as if the supplications of the years had accumulated before the Throne, and at last the answer broke in blessing over Cornelius, even as the accumulated evaporation of months will burst at last in floods of rain.

"So God is represented as treasuring the prayers of His saints in vials; they are described as sweet odors. They are placed like fragrant flowers in the chambers of the King, and kept in sweet remembrance before Him. And later they are represented as poured out upon the earth. There are voices, and thunderings, and great providential movements fulfilling God's purposes.

"We are commanded to give the Lord no rest, day or night, but to crowd the heavens with our petitions. In due time the answer will come with its accumulated blessings.

"No breath of true prayer is lost. The longer it waits, the larger it becomes."

Walk Closer to God

Cornelius's fervent prayers resulted in salvation for him and his household. And as one of the first Gentile converts to the faith, he helped to open the door for the expansion of the gospel to "the ends of the earth" (1:8).

Persistent prayer will reap fragrant blessings for both the pray-er and the object of his prayer. That's a lesson you'll want to do more than merely sniff at!

Treasured fragrances of the King

Worship from the Heart

Our prayers are not so much a battering ram to heaven's door as they are a sweet fragrance drifting heavenward. Praise the King of Glory that He finds pleasantness, even in our feeble attempts to communicate. And raise before Him the sweetest offerings you can find: words of praise for His character, His attributes, and the love He manifests through His Son.

Walk Thru the Word

New Testament Reading
Acts 10
Old Testament Reading
Lamentations 3:24-26

Respectful of the name you bear

The disciples were called Christians first at Antioch (Acts 11:26).

Organize a club, and the first order of business is to select a name—a name that somehow reflects the functions or history of the group.

For some time the believers in the New Testament church were nameless. But eventually they are given a title, meant in derision, but saturated with significance: Christians, "little Christs."

What's in a name? Matthew Henry comments on what it means to represent the Lord.

Worship from the Heart

The Judean disciples were horrified that Peter sanctioned the baptism of Gentiles. But their dismay soon turned to rejoicing. Their God was bigger than even they thought. Look for signs of spiritual life where you least expect it. You'll rejoice to see there is evidence everywhere that God is bigger than you thought, too.

Walk with Matthew Henry

"Those who first claimed the name 'Christian' laid upon themselves, and all that should ever profess that name, a lasting obligation to submit to the laws of Christ, to follow the example of Christ, and to be devoted to the honor of Christ.

"We ought to do nothing to reproach that name. May it not be said of us what Alexander the Great said to a soldier named Alexander who was noted for being a coward: 'Either change your name or mend your manners.'

"As we must look upon ourselves as Christians and conduct ourselves accordingly, so we must look upon others as Christians and treat them accordingly. A Christian brother, though not agreeing with us in everything, should be loved and respected for whose name he bears."

Walk Closer to God

The disciples made an impact in Antioch—and were promptly labeled with the name of their Lord. But in the rest of the New Testament, no follower of Christ ever called himself a "Christian." Perhaps none thought himself deserving of the title.

What would it take for someone to compare you to Christ? A turnaround in your business ethics? A change in your personal, family, or church relationships? A new outlook on unforeseen circumstances?

When you carry the name of Jesus Christ, don't be surprised if others seemingly fail to share your enthusiasm. And don't be satisfied until the name of your Lord is magnified for all to see.

Walk Thru the Word

New Testament Reading
Acts 11
Old Testament Reading
Exodus 20:7

Peter was kept in prison, but the church was earnestly praying to God for him (Acts 12:5).

*I*f the opponents of the church had known better, they would have left it alone.

Persecution only pours oil on the fire, spreading the gospel all the more. Killing James and imprisoning Peter drove the church to its knees —not in submission, but in prayer.

Yet even the church was surprised by God's miraculous power! A. B. Simpson reflects on the awesome power of prayer.

Walk with A. B. Simpson

"Prayer is the link that connects us with God. It is the bridge that spans every gulf and bears us over every abyss of danger or need.

"How significant is this picture of the New Testament church: Peter in prison, the Jews triumphant, Herod supreme, the arena of martyrdom awaiting the dawning of the morning.

" 'But the church was earnestly praying to God for him.'

"And what is the sequel?

"The prison open, the apostle free, the Jews baffled, the wicked king divinely smitten, and the Word of God rolling on in greater victory.

"Do we know the power of our supernatural weapon? Do we dare to use it with the authority of a faith that commands as well as asks? God grant us holy audacity and divine confidence.

"He is not wanting great men and women, but He is wanting people who will dare to prove the greatness of their God."

Walk Closer to God

Which motto summarizes your habits in prayer?
"When all else fails, pray."
"Before doing anything, pray."

The first epigram views prayer as the place of last resort when human abilities have run out. The second realizes that unless God Himself empowers and directs, human strength and wisdom will never suffice.

Are you tired of trying to stand on your own?

Dropping to your knees gives God the opportunity to prove His greatness in your life.

Seeing is not always believing

Worship from the Heart

"Are not all angels ministering spirits sent to serve those who will inherit salvation?" (Hebrews 1:14). Meditate on the various duties and functions that angels perform. Though you may never recognize an angel in this life, they work day and night on behalf of believers. Praise God for this unseen army of protectors and defenders.

Walk Thru the Word

New Testament Reading
Acts 12
Old Testament Reading
Psalm 66:18-19

The high mission of every believer

"We tell you the good news" (Acts 13:32).

Chapter 13 opens with Paul and Barnabas being set apart "for the work to which I have called them."

And it closes with this summary: "The word of the Lord spread through the whole region" (v. 49). As missionaries, Paul and Barnabas obviously hit the ground running!

"Good for *them*," you may be thinking, "but I'*m* no missionary."

Perhaps not. Your church may never officially set you apart, then send you out. But the mission of *all* believers is to "publish glad tidings," as Mary Thomson reminds us.

Worship from the Heart

Let the words of this verse by Grace E. Uhler touch your heart with gratitude that you have heard the gospel and inspire you to consider what you can do to share God's love. "For God so loved the world, not just a few, / The wise and great, the noble and the true, / Or those of favored class or rank or hue. / God loved the world. Do you?"

Walk with Mary Thomson

O Zion, haste, your mission high fulfilling,
   To tell to all the world that God is light;
That He who made all nations is not willing
   One soul should perish, lost in shades of night.

Behold how many thousands still are lying,
   Bound in the darksome prison-house of sin,
With none to tell them of the Savior's dying,
   Or of the life He died for them to win.

Proclaim to every people, tongue, and nation
   That God, in whom they live and move, is love:
Tell how He stooped to save His lost creation,
   And died on earth that man might live above.

Publish glad tidings, tidings of peace;
   Tidings of Jesus, redemption, and release.

Walk Closer to God

Though that hymn was written well over a century ago, the need is no less urgent today.

Believer, your assignment is to declare glad tidings—good news. That task may take you across the street or across the globe. It may take your assets, time, and dedication. It may take your wholehearted support of others who go where you cannot. It surely takes your full commitment and much prayer.

The Lord waits to guide and empower you to accomplish that assignment.

Walk Thru the Word

New Testament Reading
Acts 13
Old Testament Reading
Habakkuk 1:5

146

*L*imiting spiritual injury with wise leadership

Paul and Barnabas appointed elders for them in each church and . . . committed them to the Lord, in whom they had put their trust (Acts 14:23).

*U*nattended infants have a remarkable knack for inflicting injury on themselves and others. In a similar way, the chances of spiritual injury in the church are increased when there is inadequate supervision by those who are more mature in the faith.

Johann Peter Lange underscores from Acts 14 two keys to nurturing a young church.

Walk with Johann Peter Lange

"We can here perceive the happy combination, and the genuine and reciprocal influence, of teaching and ruling—of the action of man and the action of divine grace.

"It is the firm conviction of the apostles that the congregations which had recently been planted could be protected and strengthened solely by the presence and grace of Christ. They commend these congregations, with genuine earnestness of spirit, and with fasting and prayer, to the care of the Lord. But far from assuming a fanatical character, they labor personally, by word and deed, to strengthen and establish those newly formed congregations.

"They do not primarily resort to human arrangements or plans, as if these constituted a guarantee of success, but by exhortation and instruction—all founded on the Word of God.

"The apostles do not agree with those who assign no value whatever to forms, rites, and ordinances of the church, and who dispense with them entirely. On the contrary, they invest certain persons in every congregation with the office of elders."

Walk Closer to God

• A wise leader will look to the Word for guidance in shepherding others.

• God's Word makes clear the importance of wise leaders.

One without the other leads to misplaced *trust* or misguided *standards*. But put them together in your church, and watch for commendable results!

*W*orship from the Heart

Think about these words of C. S. Lewis: "There are no ordinary people. You have never talked to a mere mortal. . . . It is immortals whom we joke with, work with, marry, snub, and exploit—immortal horrors or everlasting splendors." (From The Weight of Glory.*) Today treat the people around you like the immortal creatures they are. Pray for them with eternity in mind.*

*W*alk Thru the Word

New Testament Reading
Acts 14
Old Testament Reading
Malachi 2:7

Standing fast for our freedom in Christ

Then some of the believers who belonged to the party of the Pharisees stood up and said, "The Gentiles must be circumcised and required to obey the law of Moses" (Acts 15:5).

*P*rejudice is a dirty word. But prejudice is not limited to race. The first church council was called because of the prejudice of one group of Christians. The newly converted Pharisees wanted the Gentiles to participate in ceremonies that foreshadowed the sacrifice of Christ.

But Paul stood firm. Once Jesus shed His blood, God required no more blood to be shed. And if God no longer required it, how could the Pharisees? Paul's thought is echoed by Charles Hodge.

Walk with Charles Hodge

"It is a great error in morals, and a great practical evil, to make that sinful which is in fact innocent. Christian love never requires this or any other sacrifice of truth. Paul would not consent, even to avoid giving offense, that eating food offered to idols should be made a sin. In fact, he sees those who thought differently as weak in faith, as being under an error from which more knowledge and piety would free them.

"We should stand fast in the freedom from which Christ has set us free, and not be burdened by a yoke of slavery to human opinions. There is a strong tendency to treat as matters of conscience things which God has never enjoined.

"It is often necessary to assert our Christian liberty at the expense of incurring censure in order to preserve right principles. Our Savior consented to be regarded as a Sabbath-breaker, a drunkard, and a friend of tax collectors and 'sinners'; but wisdom was proved right by her actions."

Walk Closer to God

Judgment by the standard of the Bible is required (2 Timothy 3:16). But judgment by an arbitrary standard is forbidden (Matthew 7:1). As you examine your personal traditions and opinions for judging others, praise God that in His Word we have a trustworthy standard to distinguish duty from freedom.

Worship from the Heart

Long ago King Solomon observed that "there is . . . joy for those who promote peace" (Proverbs 12:20). Today, ask God to show you the difference between opinion and truth. Pray that He will guide you through His Word toward the highway of peace so that you may avoid strife with fellow believers and thus bring glory to Him.

Walk Thru the Word

New Testament Reading
Acts 15:1-21
Old Testament Reading
Proverbs 20:5

148

So we all agreed. . . . It seemed good to the Holy Spirit and to us not to burden you with anything beyond the following requirements (Acts 15:25, 28).

*C*ontroversy in the church is nothing new. Where two or three are gathered together, there you'll find a difference of opinion. But woe to the church that spends more time in *debate* than in *prayer* . . . that has more people trying to fix the *blame* than are trying to fix the *problem.*

G. Campbell Morgan points to the example of the New Testament church in reaching agreement on complex questions.

Walk with G. Campbell Morgan

"Consider the method of the findings: 'It seemed good to the Holy Spirit and to us.' Communion with Christ by the Holy Spirit lies at the very root of that expression. Also, an outcome of this is the unity of the church by the Spirit. And finally there is the unanimity of the Spirit and the church.

"The picture of the council in Jerusalem is that of a company of men and women, sharing the life of Christ, desiring only to know the mind of the Lord, having no selfish views for which to contend. These are the conditions upon which it is possible for any such assembly to say, 'It seemed good to the Holy Spirit and to us.'

"The church does not seem able to say that today, either locally or in great councils. We shall come to unanimity when we are prepared to discuss our absolute differences freely and frankly, on the basis of a common desire to know the mind of the Lord."

Walk Closer to God

It's not the color of the curtains but the quality of the commitment to Christ that makes a church effective.

While unanimity is always a desirable goal in the church decision making process, there is a more important consideration than "Did everyone vote *my* way?" And that is "Did everyone search his or her heart and vote *God's* way?"

When the outcome "seems good" to Him, it can't help but be good for you!

*T*he unanimity that is based on unity

*W*orship from the Heart

When Moses needed help to carry out his work of intercession, Aaron and Hur brought him a rock to sit on and added their strength to his. Together with Joshua and his men, they defeated the enemy. As you thank God for the spiritual leaders in your life, be sensitive to their needs and uphold them in prayer.

*W*alk Thru the Word

New Testament Reading
Acts 15:22-41
Old Testament Reading
Exodus 17:8-14

G. Campbell Morgan
(1863-1945)
Preacher on the Move

One hundred years ago, a young English preacher lost faith in the Book he claimed to believe. Confusing theories about the Bible caused him to question the truth of God's Word. But rather than continue to question, this searching twenty-one-year-old minister locked away all his books about the Bible. He sat down with only the Bible to discover for himself what it had to say.

His own study convinced him of the truth of Scripture, and for the next sixty years George Campbell Morgan—regarded by many as the "prince of expositors"—taught the Bible to all who would listen.

Born in a small English village on December 9, 1863, Morgan lived in an environment of Christian preaching and practice. His father was a minister, and young Morgan would emulate him by preaching to a mock congregation of his sister's dolls.

At the age of thirteen, Morgan preached his first "real" sermon; by age fifteen he was preaching on a regular basis.

Though by trade he was a schoolteacher, Morgan's passion to preach and teach God's Word never waned.

He married, accepted the pastorate of a small church, and was ordained in 1890. From this

point on, tracing Morgan's ministry step by step is
nearly impossible. Like the apostle Paul, he traveled
constantly—crossing the Atlantic fifty-four times to
teach God's Word in England and America.

From Los Angeles to London, Morgan never
tired of explaining and applying the Bible to hungry
hearts. More than sixty books resulted from his
teaching.

The culmination of his sixty years of ministry
occurred at the prestigious Westminster Chapel in
London, England, during the difficult days of
World War II. Morgan served there until his death
in 1945 at the age of eighty-one.

Morgan's teaching ministry had strategic
impact. In the late 19th and early 20th centuries,
God had used evangelists such as Charles Finney,
Dwight L. Moody, Gipsy Smith, and Billy Sunday
to lead thousands to faith in Jesus Christ.

But the arrival of so many new converts into the
churches signaled the need for preachers who
could explain the Scriptures—a need Morgan was
uniquely equipped by God to meet.

His life stands as an eloquent reminder that
after the milk of the gospel must come the meat of
the Word.

As you read insights from the pen of G.
Campbell Morgan, perhaps you will agree with the
evaluation of one commentator who noted that
Morgan "will not attempt to overpower you with
rhetoric, or entertain you with ancient anecdotes . . .
or dazzle you with brilliant quotations. . . . But he
will . . . build up a solid, sustained, carefully thought
out and apparently unanswerable argument . . . .

"Wherever he goes people quickly discover him
. . . and crowd to listen to him, although he does
little except to expound the Book which clever crit-
ics tell us is no longer read!"

If spiritual nourishment is your goal whenever
you read the Word of God, then servants of God
such as G. Campbell Morgan can teach you much
about feeding upon the truths of Scripture.

As you continue to read this devotional guide,
thank God for the privilege of coming
to His Word for strength and direction.
There's food for thought—and growth
—every day.

A Lesson from the life of G. Campbell Morgan

I can have confidence in God's Word and can be assured that He will reveal Himself to me as I study it.

Dealing gently with the sheep

Paul wanted to take him [Timothy] along on the journey, so he circumcised him because of the Jews who lived in that area, for they all knew that his father was a Greek (Acts 16:3).

*I*f a wolf is causing havoc with the sheep, one way to get rid of the wolf is to blow up the sheep. But that's a harmful solution.

Timothy's Gentile background was a stumbling block to the Jews of Lycaonia. Paul could have berated the Jews for their bigotry; instead he dealt with the situation in a sensitive manner.

Martin Luther offers this perspective on solving problems in the family of God without causing bigger ones in the process.

Walk with Martin Luther

"Consider this analogy: If an enemy had tied a rope about your brother's neck and you pulled the rope toward you with all your energy or lunged at it with a knife, you might do your brother more harm than good. If you really want to help, this is what you must do: The enemy you may punish as he deserves; but you must handle the rope gently until you get it off of your brother's neck, or you might strangle him.

"In the same way you may be harsh in dealing with the liars and tyrants, and their works, for they are not willing to listen to you. But the simple people, whom they have bound with their teachings and whose lives they have endangered, you must treat altogether differently.

"You see, you must treat wolves and lions differently from the way you treat the weak sheep. With the wolves you cannot be too severe; with the weak sheep you cannot be too gentle."

Walk Closer to God

The *right* way to correct a wrong leads to healing; the *wrong* way inflicts pain. The right way deals severely with "wolves" and tenderly with "sheep." The right way removes old stumbling blocks; the wrong way erects new stumbling blocks. The right way results in the church being "strengthened . . . and [growing] daily in numbers" (Acts 16:5).

What is *your* way?

Worship from the Heart

Paul and Silas reached out not only to other prisoners, but to those who had imprisoned them as well. God's love for you enables you to stretch forth a hand of loving-kindness to those who have abused you. Praise God that not only has He forgiven you, but that He has given you the ability to bring healing and restoration through the power of forgiveness.

Walk Thru the Word

New Testament Reading
Acts 16:1-15
Old Testament Reading
Proverbs 16:20-25

152

"Sirs, what must I do to be saved?" They replied, "Believe in the Lord Jesus, and you will be saved" (Acts 16:30-31).

*T*wo notorious "outlaws" in the prison at Philippi . . . locked in solitary confinement . . . singing hymns at midnight. Suddenly, without warning, a violent earthquake . . . every prisoner's chains loosed . . . every door opened.

Imagine the dismay of the Philippian jailer. For a man in his position the escape of even one prisoner meant certain death. Yet in his midnight moment of crisis, the jailer discovered someone who specializes in giving life. J. Wilbur Chapman provides this timely comment on the jailer's newfound life.

Walk with J. Wilbur Chapman

"God makes it clear that there can be no real life until there is a step taken first of all by faith.

"To make it very clear, the best answer is the one given to the Philippian jailer: 'Believe in the Lord Jesus, and you will be saved.'

"There is something very significant in the way the names of Jesus Christ are used. When He is called Lord, it is to emphasize His kingly office, His reigning power; and what can the meaning be but this, when we are told to believe on Him as Lord?

"We must reach the place where we are willing to let Him rule and reign in our lives.

"Can you submit to this? He will never make a failure of it.

"Give Him absolute control; never take a step without His guidance—this is the secret of grace and joy."

Walk Closer to God

The Philippian jailer didn't need a lecture on theology. He just needed a simple, one-sentence sermon: "Believe in the Lord Jesus, and you will be saved—you and your household."

When the heart is prepared, the odds are good you won't need oratory or arguments to lead another to the Savior.

So keep it short. Clear. Sincere. And when the door swings ajar, be ready to enter!

*K*eeping the simple truth simple

*W*orship from the Heart

Praise God for the simplicity of the gospel message. Although it is a complex theological truth, the depth of which is inexhaustible, it is simple enough to be understood by a small child. Thank Him that the kingdom road is as simple and straight as "Believe in the Lord Jesus, and you will be saved."

*W*alk Thru the Word

New Testament Reading
Acts 16:16-40
Old Testament Reading
Ezekiel 18:23, 29-32

In Him we have our being

Worship from the Heart

As you seek God in the pages of His Word, let Psalm 143:6, 8 echo your thoughts, "My soul thirsts for you like a parched land. Let the morning bring me word of your unfailing love, for I have put my trust in you. Show me the way I should go, for to you I lift up my soul."

Walk Thru the Word

New Testament Reading
Acts 17
Old Testament Reading
Genesis 28:10-17

" . . . *that men would seek [the Lord] and perhaps reach out for him and find him, though he is not far from each one of us. 'For in him we live and move and have our being'* " (*Acts 17:27-28*).

The Athenians "spent their time doing nothing but talking about and listening to the latest ideas" (17:21). But when it came to the Good News, some listened politely, while most laughed in derision.

When Paul saw the misguided thinking and living of cosmopolitan Athens, he preached a sermon filled with truth which people of all ages need to consider—truth that John Calvin highlights for those willing to listen today.

Walk with John Calvin

"It is a person's duty to seek God, who comes to meet us in such a way that we can have no excuse for our ignorance.

"Surely nothing is more absurd than that people should be ignorant of their Author, especially people who have been given understanding principally for this use. And we must also note the goodness of God, in that He so familiarly introduces Himself, that even the blind may grope after Him.

"Because of this fact, the blindness of people, who are touched with no feeling of God's presence, is even more shameful and intolerable.

"For God has not darkly shadowed His glory in the creation of the world, but He has everywhere engraven such marks that even the blind may know them.

"Therefore we see that people are not only blind but blockheaded, when, being helped by such excellent testimonies, they profit nothing."

Walk Closer to God

The world around you offers ample evidence of the Creator's glorious handiwork (Romans 1:20; Psalm 19:1), and proof for His existence is always as close as the nearest window.

With such proof before your eyes, can there be any good excuse for ignoring the good news about the One in whom "we live and move and have our being"?

154

The danger is real

While Gallio was proconsul of Achaia, the Jews made a united attack on Paul . . . But Gallio showed no concern whatever (Acts 18:12, 17).

*A*pathy suffocates the church of Jesus Christ and paralyzes the work of truth. All that is necessary for evil to prevail is for good people to do nothing. And nothing is precisely what indifference breeds.

What happens when unconcerned listeners encounter uncompromising truth? The apathetic person comes out the loser every time. H. A. Ironside elaborates.

Walk with H. A. Ironside

"Gallio the Indifferent! History tells us that he was the brother of Seneca the philosopher, who exclaimed, 'Few men are so agreeable about anything as my brother Gallio is about everything!'

"Yet this amiable man lost a marvelous opportunity to hear the gospel from the lips of Paul, and perhaps lost his soul as well, just because he did not consider eternal things worthy of his attention.

"To him the whole matter was beneath contempt, consisting only, as he supposed, of a quarrel about words and names and Jewish ceremonial observances. So he turned scornfully away without hearing that glad message that God was sending out in grace to a needy world.

"His attitude stands out as a warning to others not to treat lightly the privileges God gives, lest the day of doom find them still in their sins."

Walk Closer to God

If someone announced excitedly, "The building is on fire!" would you respond with a yawn and a shrug? Of course not! Life-threatening situations demand life-saving steps. If the warning is true, then the danger is real. And only prompt action can avert certain disaster.

Think of the gospel as just such a call to action. The danger is real; the penalty for sin is sure; but the lifeboat is standing by in the person of Jesus Christ, the Savior. Good news indeed for all who take shelter in Him. But not for those who—like Gallio—greet Him with a yawn and a shrug.

Worship from the Heart

"Lord, forgive me for the times I have been more concerned with proving my point to others than with showing Your love. As I interact with others, help me to reason rather than argue, to listen instead of lashing out, and to always respond with sensitivity. Use me as You will. Amen."

Walk Thru the Word

New Testament Reading
Acts 18
Old Testament Reading
Psalm 53

Burning books and bridges

Worship from the Heart

The Ephesian Christians bravely stepped up to the fiery pyre and tossed their sinful past into the flames. Their obedience to God crowded out thoughts of compromise. In your time alone with God, ask Him to help you in the areas where you face the greatest temptation to compromise.

A number who had practiced sorcery brought their scrolls together and burned them publicly (Acts 19:19).

*W*ould you build a bonfire using $350,000 worth of kindling?

That's approximately what "fifty thousand pieces of silver" in Roman times would be worth in today's currency!

The book burning in Ephesus was an expensive demonstration, and Luke records how the gospel brought about economic disruption in the idolatrous city. But such changes are often necessary when God is at work, as Albert Barnes explains.

Walk with Albert Barnes

"The Word of God had power in this wicked city, and the power must have been mighty which would make them willing to destroy their property.

"From this instructive passage we may learn that:

1. True religion has the power to break the hold of sinners on unjust and dishonest means of living.
2. Those who have been engaged in an unchristian and dishonorable practice will abandon it when they become Christians.
3. Their abhorrence of their former course ought to be expressed as publicly as was the offense.
4. The evil practice will be abandoned at any sacrifice, however great. The question is, 'What is right?' Not 'What will it cost?'

"If what they did when they were converted was right—and who can doubt it?—it sets forth a great principle on which new converts should act."

Walk Closer to God

Cherished dreams. Ingrained habits. Goals for advancement in a career. Previously unquestioned ethics. Sorcery in its many subtle forms. Each may take on a new appearance when seen in the light of God's Word.

Albert Barnes's remarks provide helpful guidelines to show believers how the Word of God prevails in our daily life to replace un-Christlike conduct with Christian convictions.

Walk Thru the Word

New Testament Reading
Acts 19:1-22
Old Testament Reading
Psalm 32:1-11

156

"Men, you know we receive a good income from this business. And you see and hear how this fellow Paul has convinced and led astray large numbers of people here in Ephesus and in practically the whole province of Asia. He says that man-made gods are no gods at all" (Acts 19:25-26).

*C*hristianity is just a crutch." Has anyone ever summarily dismissed your faith with those words?

To such a critic, Christianity is made foolish because the Christian has a vested interest in believing in God. The believer is accused of being emotionally weak, psychologically troubled, or simply covering all the bases in case there really is an afterlife. But according to Matthew Henry, Christians are not the only ones bringing vested interests to the claims of Christ.

Walk with Matthew Henry

"It is natural for men to jealously guard, whether right or wrong, the means by which they get their wealth. Many have, for this reason alone, set themselves against the gospel of Christ, because it calls men off from those crafts which are unlawful, however much wealth is to be obtained by them.

"There are those who will haggle for that which is most grossly absurd and unreasonable, and which carries along with it its own conviction of falsehood, if it has but human laws and worldly interests on its side."

Walk Closer to God

Is our critic's complaint legitimate? In a word, no. A "vested interest" critic is wielding a two-edged sword. His own decision not to believe is not without its motives. Since he rejects Christ because of his own vested interest, his criticism of us is hypocrisy.

God commands us to "answer a fool according to his folly, or he will be wise in his own eyes" (Proverbs 26:5). Be prepared to give an answer for the hope that you have and "do your best to present yourself to God as one approved. . . who correctly handles the word of truth" (2 Timothy 2:15).

*W*e take every thought captive

*W*orship from the Heart

As you pray for your lost friends today, ask God to give you insight into the real reasons behind the arguments they make against Christianity. He will glorify Himself by showing you exactly how to pray for them. You have only to ask.

*W*alk Thru the Word

New Testament Reading
Acts 19:23-41
Old Testament Reading
Exodus 20:1-6

A service commission from Jesus Christ

"I consider my life worth nothing to me, if only I may finish the race and complete the task the Lord Jesus has given me" (Acts 20:24).

*W*hich is easier to say: "I want to do this for God" or "God wants to do this through me"? For those who truly desire to serve God, letting Him decide what is best is the proper choice.

When Paul received divine orders to preach the gospel, he subordinated his own ambitions in order to fulfill his calling.

Oswald Chambers examines the importance of God's calling.

Walk with Oswald Chambers

"It is easier to serve God without a vision, easier to work for God without a call, because then you are not bothered by what God requires; common sense is your guide, veneered over with Christian sentiment.

"It is even possible to be more prosperous and successful, more leisure-hearted, if you never realize the call of God.

"But if once you receive a commission from Jesus Christ, the memory of *what God wants* will always come like a goad.

"What do I really count dear? If I have not been gripped by Jesus Christ, I will count service dear, time given to God dear, my life dear unto myself.

"Paul says he counted his life dear only in order that he might fulfill the ministry he had received. He refused to use his energy for any other thing.

"Never consider whether you are of use, but ever consider that you are not your own but His."

Walk Closer to God

Some Christians are affected by tunnel vision—unable to see God's purpose because they are preoccupied with their own interests. But God's calling is specific—and often demanding.

Paul's words of encouragement to the elders at Ephesus are words you too can draw upon with confidence: "I commit you to God and to the word of his grace, which can build you up and give you an inheritance among all those who are sanctified" (20:32).

*W*orship from the Heart

"Father, Your purpose in my life is sometimes obscured by my own interests. Strip away the superfluous nonsense that keeps me from taking seriously my service to You. Prod me on, ever reminding me that I am an ambassador in Your service. Let Your vision for the world become my vision today."

*W*alk Thru the Word

New Testament Reading
Acts 20
Old Testament Reading
Amos 7:14-15

158

*T*he privilege of paying a debt

"I am ready not only to be bound, but also to die in Jerusalem for the name of the Lord Jesus" (Acts 21:13).

*I*n spite of rumors to the contrary, missionaries are only human. They aren't ten feet physically . . . or spiritually.

Like other Christians, they struggle with illness, attitudes, and rebellious children. And their "job description" is basically the same as that of every other Christian: to proclaim the gospel.

David Livingstone describes the attitude that is essential for successful service for the Lord— whether at home or abroad.

Walk with David Livingstone

"People talk of the sacrifice I have made in spending so much of my life in Africa.

"Can that be called a sacrifice which is simply acknowledging a great debt we owe to our God, which we can never repay?

"Is that a sacrifice which brings its own reward in healthful activity, the consciousness of doing good, peace of mind, and a bright hope of a glorious destiny? It is emphatically no sacrifice. Rather it is a privilege.

"Anxiety, sickness, suffering, danger, foregoing the common conveniences of life—these may make us pause, and cause the spirit to waver, and the soul to sink; but let this only be for a moment.

"All these are nothing compared with the glory which shall later be revealed in and through us.

"I never made a sacrifice. Of this we ought not to talk, when we remember the great sacrifice which He made who left His Father's throne on high to give Himself for us."

Walk Closer to God

Christ gave His life gladly, not considering it too great a sacrifice to die for sinners.

Why then should it be too great a sacrifice to invest your life in spreading His love today? You don't have to cross an ocean to do that. Your mission field may be as near as your neighbor.

A neighbor who needs to hear the news that God has only one Son. A Son He sent as a missionary to all the world.

*W*orship from the Heart

"Father, I praise You for how faithfully You've preserved both Your people and Your Word through the centuries. My prayer for both myself and those I worship with is that we, like the psalmist, will say, 'My heart is set on keeping your decrees to the very end' (Psalm 119:112)."

*W*alk Thru the Word

New Testament Reading
Acts 21:1-36
Old Testament Reading
Ruth 2:10-12

When His enemies become our enemies

"I . . . heard a voice say to me, 'Saul! Saul! Why do you persecute me?' "(Acts 22:7).

*I*f the enemies of Christ could get their hands on Him today, as they did 2,000 years ago, perhaps they would leave His followers alone.

But the world is unable to persecute Christ Himself, so it persecutes His followers.

Martin Luther offers this advice when the hatred of the world flares into open hostility toward the soldiers of the Cross.

Worship from the Heart

Pray for the enemies of the Cross. God's grace can still reach down to touch the Sauls of this world. Perhaps there are enemies at your work or in your neighborhood; you can regularly pray for their salvation. May your Sauls soon become Pauls!

Walk with Martin Luther

"Observe this for your comfort: These enemies are never called our enemies, or those of Christendom, but enemies of the Lord Jesus. For Christ, who sits above at the right hand of the Father, cannot be attacked; they cannot hurt one hair on His head, much less drag Him down from His throne.

"They attack Him, but Christians must suffer and be plagued by these enemies. Still they are properly called His enemies, not ours.

"For the world and the Devil do not attack and plague us because we have merited it or caused it. The only reason for it is that we believe this Lord and confess His Word. Otherwise they would be in agreement with us, and we would be at peace with them.

"Everything that happens to the individual Christian, whether it comes from the Devil or from the world—such as the terrors of sin, anxiety, and grief of the heart, torture, or death—He regards as though it happens to Him. Thus He also says through the prophet Zechariah, 'Whoever touches you touches the apple of [My] eye.' "

Walk Closer to God

"Whatever you did for one of the least of these brothers of mine, you did for me" (Matthew 25:40). What comforting words for Christians under attack! Christ has promised to be with His children always (Matthew 28:20). So when persecution comes your way, remember this thought: *The fact that you're attacked means that you resemble your Savior!*

Walk Thru the Word

New Testament Reading
Acts 21:37–22:29
Old Testament Reading
Zechariah 2:8-13

A conscience touched by God

Paul . . . said, "My brothers, I have fulfilled my duty to God in all good conscience to this day" (Acts 23:1).

The conscience tells you when you have done right or wrong. It may not keep you out of trouble, but at least it lets you know when you are in trouble, so you can deal with the problem.

Everyone has a conscience. But not everyone has a clear conscience. Thomas à Kempis shares these thoughts on how to keep a good conscience toward God.

Walk with Thomas à Kempis

"The glory of a good person is the testimony of a good conscience. A good conscience is able to bear very much and is very cheerful in adversities. An evil conscience is always fearful and unquiet. Never rejoice except when you have done well. You shall rest sweetly if your heart does not accuse you.

"Sinners never have true joy or feel inward peace, because 'there is no peace, says my God, for the wicked' (Isaiah 57:21). The glory of the good is in their consciences, and not in the tongues of others. The gladness of the just is of God, and in God; and their joy is of the truth.

"A person will easily be content and pacified whose conscience is pure. If you consider what you are within, you will not care what others say concerning you. People consider the deeds, but God weighs the intentions.

"To be always doing well and to esteem little of one's self is the sign of a humble soul.

" 'For it is not the one who commends himself who is approved, but the one whom the Lord commends,' says Paul (2 Corinthians 10:18).

"To walk inwardly with God, and not to be kept abroad by any outward affection, is the state of a spiritual person."

Walk Closer to God

All it takes to maintain a bad conscience is to do nothing; ignore the tugging of the Spirit and the still, small voice of God. By contrast, a good conscience is a Christ-cleansed conscience, one that is sensitive to the Spirit's promptings. And that is only a heartfelt prayer away!

Worship from the Heart

Read the story of Joseph in Genesis 39:7-12 and ask God for a conscience as sharp as Joseph's, as well as the realization that sin is sin not only against some other person but against God as well. May the desire of your heart always be to please God in all you do and say.

Walk Thru the Word

New Testament Reading
Acts 22:30–23:35
Old Testament Reading
Genesis 39:7-12

Focusing the eye of the soul

"I strive always to keep my conscience clear before God and man" (Acts 24:16).

Preschool children have a disarming way of putting into practice the old saying, "Confession is good for the soul." They tug on mommy's skirt or daddy's trouser leg and confess to such hideous crimes as spilling their milk or marking on the wall. Then, with their slate wiped clean, they skip merrily off to play.

Contrast that with the adult conscience, trained through long experience to *ignore guilt* rather than *confess wrongdoing.*

Listen as Oswald Chambers discusses the importance of your maintaining a clear conscience.

Walk with Oswald Chambers

"Conscience is that faculty in me which attaches itself to the highest that I know, and tells me what the highest I know demands that I do.

"It is the eye of the soul which looks out either toward God or toward what it regards as the highest authority.

"If I am in the habit of steadily facing toward God, my conscience will always introduce God's perfect law and indicate what I should do.

"The point is, will I obey? I have to make an effort to keep my conscience so sensitive that I walk without offense. I should be living in such perfect sympathy with God's Son that in every circumstance the spirit of my mind is renewed.

"The one thing that keeps the conscience sensitive to Him is the habit of being open to God on the inside.

"When there is any debate, quit. There is no debate possible when conscience speaks."

Walk Closer to God

If you could shine a light into the spiritual recesses of your life, what would that light disclose?

Would it be a life free from "secret sin," resulting in clear spiritual vision? Or would it be a life clouded with unconfessed offenses against God and against others resulting in a dim and unfocused spiritual vision?

Worship from the Heart

Is the need of your heart today a clear conscience before God? Approach Him in childlike innocence. Be quick to confess rather than conceal your sin. With the psalmist, ask God to "Create in me a pure heart, O God, and renew a steadfast spirit within me" (Psalm 51:10).

Walk Thru the Word

New Testament Reading
Acts 24
Old Testament Reading
Psalm 51:1-10

162

The miracle of long-suffering

"If, however, I am guilty of doing anything deserving death, I do not refuse to die" (Acts 25:11).

If anyone had cause to wallow in self-pity, it was the apostle Paul. Yet, in the midst of the mockery and malice of his enemies, he radiated integrity and strength.

Meditate on the words of Joseph Parker as he points out the striking spiritual qualities exhibited in the life of this great saint.

Walk with Joseph Parker

"When he appears before Festus we mark in him the same quietness, the same dignity, the same defense that is Christianity. If it were a fight in words, the battle might sometimes go wrong, because there are men against us, skilled in sentences and arguments; but it is an affair of the sweetness of the soul. Long-suffering is eloquence. This is a Christian miracle.

"There are three remarkable things to notice about Paul here. He represents, first of all, the spiritual influence which follows society, coloring its questions, lifting up its wonder, troubling its conscience.

"Second, he demonstrates spiritual confidence. He would rather be fighting, but the Lord had appointed him to waiting.

"Third, he embodies the highest aspect of spiritual culture. From the human side, Paul was being punished; from the Divine side, he was being rested and trained.

"There are two sides in all human events. If we take the lower aspect of our life we shall groan and fret; but if we look down upon it from God's point we shall see all things work together for good."

Walk Closer to God

Paul's suffering served as an international platform for the gospel, and he took advantage of every audience—even kings.

We are to do the same. Instead of groaning and fretting about our troubles, God is glorified when we stand erect in unwavering confidence and dignity. And whether we realize it or not, we, like Paul, are on that same platform testifying to the world our faith in God through Jesus Christ.

Worship from the Heart

"Father God, may I be so identified with Christ that wherever You take me or whatever suffering I experience, His life will flow through me to others. Let me say with martyrs of old, 'What does it matter if I am put in prison? I will preach to prisoners.' Turn my suffering into spiritual achievement and victory.

Walk Thru the Word

New Testament Reading
Acts 25
Old Testament Reading
Psalm 94:16-19

163

When close is not close enough

Paul replied, " . . . I pray God that not only you, but all who are listening to me today may become what I am, except for these chains" (Acts 26:29).

*C*lose is never close enough when the issues are life and death. Tottering on the verge of belief, Agrippa was unwilling to take the final step toward salvation. His heart was moved by Paul's message; intellectually he agreed. But in the final analysis, all he could say was "almost . . ."

By contrast Adam Clarke defines Christianity as the life of God in the soul of man—with no "almosts" allowed.

Worship from the Heart

Salvation is indeed all of God, none of us. Rejoice that this plan of the ages was initiated in heaven, executed on earth, and completed with Christ's cry at Golgotha. Rejoice that an empty tomb stands as a monument that, as He conquered sin and death, so shall we.

Walk with Adam Clarke

"It is with extreme difficulty that any person can be persuaded that he needs a work of grace on his heart. And such a salvation from bondage the gospel of Christ offers to a lost world.

"If Christianity implies the life of God in the soul of an individual—the remission of sins, the thorough purification of the heart, producing that holiness without which none can see the Lord—then it is evident that God alone can do this work, and that neither birth nor education can bestow it.

"By birth, everyone is sinful; by practice, everyone is a transgressor, for all have sinned. God alone, by faith in Christ, can save sinners from their sins.

"Reader, has God saved you from this state of wretchedness and brought you into the glorious liberty of His children? Let your conscience answer for itself."

Walk Closer to God

"Lord, Your Word has convinced me that You are the Son of God—the Savior of the world.

"Today, as best I know how, I receive You into my heart by faith, asking You to forgive my sins and become my Guide through life.

"I realize from Agrippa's words that an 'almost' faith is really no faith at all. And so I hold nothing back from You.

"Lord, I am persuaded. Thank You that my life has been invaded by Your loving presence. Amen."

Walk Thru the Word

New Testament Reading
Acts 26
Old Testament Reading
Deuteronomy 30:15-20

The God who can be touched

"Keep up your courage, men, for I have faith in God that it will happen just as he told me" (Acts 27:25).

*E*ven as the winds and waves lashed his vessel, Paul heard the angel of the Lord assure him that he would complete his journey. And with a faith in God that was unsinkable, Paul carried that angelic announcement to his skeptical shipmates and gave them hope.

Is your spiritual "hearing" that attuned? If not, A. W. Tozer describes how the Holy Spirit can awaken your spiritual senses.

Walk with A. W. Tozer

"The Bible assumes as a self-evident fact that men and women can know God with at least the same degree of immediacy as they know any other person.

"The same terms are used to express the knowledge of God as are used to express knowledge of physical things:

" 'TASTE and see that the Lord is good' (Psalm 34:8).

" 'My sheep HEAR my voice' (John 10:27 KJV).

" 'Blessed are the pure in heart, for they will SEE God' (Matthew 5:8).

"We apprehend the physical world by exercising the faculties given us for the purpose; we possess spiritual faculties by means of which we can know God and the spiritual world if we will obey the Spirit's urge and begin to use them. But the spiritual faculties of the unregenerate person lie asleep in his nature; they may be quickened to active life by the operation of the Holy Spirit in the new birth!"

Walk Closer to God

The saints of old were skilled in the use of their spiritual senses.

- They had 20/20 vision to see God at work in their day.
- They had ears to hear the urgings of the Spirit.
- They had tastebuds to enjoy the goodness of God in His every provision.

For them, walking with God was not a mysterious "leap in the dark," but a touchable, seeable, hearable experience.

Worship from the Heart

As you read Acts 27, note the details: the geography, the individual names, the descriptive story of the shipwreck. This is a real-life encounter without the telltale signs of myth. In the midst of it all, God's personal message to Paul affects reality. Just think, the God who invaded human history, who really spoke to Paul, is our God, our Savior, our Friend.

Walk Thru the Word

New Testament Reading
Acts 27
Old Testament Reading
Ezekiel 33:30-32

*T*he sweet spirit of friendships

The brothers there had heard that we were coming, and they traveled . . . to meet us. At the sight of these men Paul thanked God and was encouraged (Acts 28:15).

*T*he apostle Paul had traveled hundreds of miles to Rome to be tried before Caesar's tribunal. But he was not alone. The Christians in Rome assembled to greet him and assure him that he had friends in the city. The work of preaching the gospel had been carried by others to Rome before him.

John Calvin shares a comforting reminder when spreading the Good News seems like a solo assignment.

*W*orship from the Heart

Supportive fellowship was of great comfort to Paul. Think of believers you know who are facing difficult decisions . . . serious surgery . . . financial hardship. Those experiencing loneliness . . . frustration . . . weakness. Thank God for their lives, both for the many ways they have touched you and for the privilege of upholding them before Him now.

Walk with John Calvin

"God comforted Paul with the brethren who came out to meet him that he might more quickly and joyfully defend the gospel.

"At that time it was not only an odious thing to profess the Christian faith, but it might also have resulted in hazard to their lives. Neither was it merely a private danger, for the Jews' envy might have affected the whole church.

"But nothing was more dear to them than their duty; they could not be negligent, lest they be counted sluggish and unthankful.

"Therefore, the brethren, by their dutifulness, testified of their godliness toward Christ, and Paul's resolve was strengthened. For though he might have been endowed with invincible strength, God gave to him new strength by means of the brethren.

"As often as God shows to His servants any fruit of their labor, He pricks them forward with a goad, that they may proceed more courageously in their work."

Walk Closer to God

"Father, telling others about the good news of Your Son at times seems a hard and lonely task.

"Yet I know You are at work in my city, just as Paul saw You at work in the city of Rome.

"Thank You that I too can be a spokesperson for Your mercy—a part of Your invincible team. In Jesus' name I pray. Amen."

*W*alk Thru the Word

New Testament Reading
Acts 28
Old Testament Reading
Psalm 133

Mining the Unsearchable Treasures of the Gospel

For generations Christians have regarded the book of Romans as one of the meatiest books of the Bible, brimming with rich theological truths. Augustine, Luther, Wesley and many other "movers and shakers" of the church trace their conversions back to a personal encounter with this "manifesto of the Christian faith." Luther went so far as to claim that Romans should become the subject of the believer's daily meditation, while Calvin maintained that someone who understood this letter would be able to understand the entire Scriptures.

But don't assume that because Romans is significant, reading it will be a simple task. Perhaps Peter was thinking of Romans when he said that some of Paul's writings were hard to understand (2 Peter 3:15-16). Think of your task in reading the book of Romans as that of a prospector mining the pages of God's Word. There is gold for you to discover each day this month.

But be sure never to forget this: Romans was not too difficult or too theological for the Holy Spirit to instruct Paul to send to Christians in Rome, many of whom were from the lower classes of Roman society and could neither read nor write. But they could, and did, study this letter sent to them by Paul. With God's help, therefore, you can understand Paul's message in Romans.

The book of Romans overflows with good news for Paul's day and for ours, describing "the gospel, . . . the power of God for the salvation of everyone who believes" (Romans 1:16). You will be reminded of our human predicament (Romans 1–2), God's provision (Romans 3–5), God's power (Romans 6–8), God's plan (Romans 9–11), and the practical applications of your faith in Christ (Romans 12–16). Couple that with the seasoned insights of godly men and women from the past, and you are in for an inspirational month indeed! Begin mining those golden truths of Romans, guaranteed to enrich your life.

Think of your task in reading the book of Romans as that of a prospector mining the pages of God's Word.

Satisfied claims of God's holy law

For in the gospel a righteousness from God is revealed, a righteousness that is by faith from first to last, just as it is written: "The righteous will live by faith" (Romans 1:17).

*W*ords with more than one meaning can make communication challenging one minute and comical the next. Often you cannot be sure of a meaning without a close look at the context.

F. B. Meyer examines two sides of a key term in Paul's letter to the Romans.

Worship from the Heart

If you are surrounded by scoffing unbelievers, rejoice that your Savior endured the shame of the cross in order to reconcile fallen humanity to God. Meditate on what He relinquished in heaven and the shame He endured on earth; then ask God to take away your fear of rejection and give you a spirit of boldness to witness to those who need Him.

Walk with F. B. Meyer

"In the deepest sense, *righteousness* stands for two things: first, our standing before God; and next, our personal character—what we are in Jesus, and what we are in ourselves by the Holy Spirit. The term righteousness, therefore, covers justification and sanctification, of which the former is discussed in the first five chapters of this epistle.

"Justification is our position through the wonderful grace of God, and by virtue of the finished work of Christ, which is imputed to (put to the account of) all who believe. All that He is, is reckoned to us who are in Him. We are not merely forgiven, great and wonderful as that act of love and grace would be; but we are dealt with as though we had never sinned.

"Instead of the law being against us, as we deserve, it is on our side, defending and protecting us. Our salvation actually rests on law. We may claim it as an absolute right. And all this because of God's infinite grace: because, in the person of Jesus, He has perfectly met, and satisfied, the claims of His holy but broken law."

Walk Closer to God

Righteousness. On the one hand, it's a legal declaration. On the other hand, it's a way of life. And both aspects are essential for the Christian. Take one or the other away, and you have frustration and futility. Put them together, and you have the full-orbed picture of new life in Christ.

The Christian knows that righteousness was never intended to be an "either/or" proposition; it's strictly "both/and" in the family of God!

Walk Thru the Word

New Testament Reading
Romans 1:1-17
Old Testament Reading
Psalm 118:5-14

*R*ighteous wrath of a holy God

The wrath of God is being revealed from heaven against all godlessness and wickedness of men who suppress the truth by their wickedness (Romans 1:18).

*H*uman anger is an emotion that is seldom productive, and often destructive. (Ask the parent of any tantrum-throwing two-year-old.) But there are times when anger is an appropriate response. Paul himself speaks of the wrath of God.

Unlike human rage, God's wrath is righteous and He often expresses it in beneficial ways, as Albert Barnes explains.

Walk with Albert Barnes

"It is clear that when we think of the word *wrath* as applicable to God, it must be divested of everything that is like human passion, and especially the passion of revenge. It is one of the most obvious rules of interpretation that we are not to apply to God passions and feelings which, among us, have their origin in evil.

"[God's wrath] is the opposition of the divine character against sin; and the determination of the divine mind to express that opposition in a proper way, by excluding the offender from the favors which He bestows on the righteous.

"We admire the character of a father who is opposed to disorder, vice, and disobedience in his family, and who expresses his opposition in a proper way. We admire the character of a ruler who is opposed to all crime in the community, and who expresses those feelings in the law.

"Why shall we not be equally pleased with God, who is opposed to all crime in all parts of the universe, and who determines to express His opposition in the proper way for the sake of preserving order and promoting peace?"

Walk Closer to God

The parent who expresses righteous anger when a child throws a tantrum demonstrates a godly concern for the child and a desire to promote order and peace. How much more so does God, who patiently endures the rebellions of the human race.

Why wait for His wrath when you can respond today to His love!

*W*orship from the Heart

Human behavior hasn't changed much in the almost 2,000 years since Romans was written, but the redemptive power of God is as active now as it was then. As you ponder the darkness around you, don't despair. Honor God by letting the light of Christ shine through you—in prayer, in worship, and in witness.

*W*alk Thru the Word

New Testament Reading
Romans 1:18-32
Old Testament Reading
Joshua 23:16

The blinding power of pride

So when you, a mere man, pass judgment on them and yet do the same things, do you think you will escape God's judgment? (Romans 2:3).

Would you feel sympathy for a man who ruined his health with alcohol? Or a woman who forsook her husband for another man? Or a couple who lost their savings at the roulette table?

Broken health, home, or finances would normally be cause for sympathy. But when the *recipients* of disaster actually are the *cause* of the disaster, the final blame must rest on their shoulders.

The Jews found great fault in the Gentiles, but they failed to look at themselves. Robert Haldane discusses the shortsightedness of the Jews.

Walk with Robert Haldane

"We may here observe how prone human beings are to abuse, to their own destruction, those advantages which God bestows on them.

"God had separated the Jews from the Gentiles, to manifest Himself unto them. By doing so, He had exalted them above the rest of the world. The proper use of this superiority would have been to distinguish themselves by a holy life.

"But instead of this, they committed the same sins as the Gentiles and plunged into the same excesses. In fact, what they considered as an advantage became a snare to them; for wherein they judged others, they condemned themselves.

"We should observe, therefore, how much self-love can blind people into making false judgments. The Jews judged correctly concerning the Gentiles; but when it concerned themselves, although they were equal in guilt, they would not admit that they were equally the subjects of condemnation."

Walk Closer to God

The Jews squandered their favored position with God. But instead of wandering in darkness like the Gentiles, they had the light of God's Word—the same Word you hold in your hand today.

The warning is clear: Take care lest you, like they, be blinded—rather than guided—by the light.

Worship from the Heart

"Father, I thank You for Your law. Forgive me for the many times I have heard and yet not heeded it. Engrave Your law on my heart, so that by Your grace I may follow with gladness in the steps of Your Son, doing Your will in all I undertake. Amen."

Walk Thru the Word

New Testament Reading
Romans 2:1-16
Old Testament Reading
Micah 3:9-12

*A*voiding the error of self-deception

A man is a Jew, if he is one inwardly; . . . Such a man's praise is not from men but from God (Romans 2:29).

*I*ncredible but true, in California entire cities exist today in which no one lives!

Old West stagecoach towns . . . quaint villages from the turn of the century . . . busy metropolises. But no one lives there. They are sets used for producing films—make-believe worlds designed to imitate the real world. Appearance is not always reality. True in Hollywood, it can also be true of those who take the name "Christian."

Paul warned the Romans of the consequences of such self-deception. Listen as H. C. G. Moule reminds us that when it comes to faith, God only settles for the genuine item.

Walk with H. C. G. Moule

"Here the apostle warns us against the fatal but easy error of perverting privilege into pride. More explicitly, he warns us against that subtle tendency of the human heart to substitute the outward for the inward, the mechanical for the spiritual.

"It was the temptation of Israel to put circumcision in the place of faith and holiness. It is the temptation of some Christians now to put the church and its sacraments in the place of spiritual regeneration and communion, rather than in their rightful places as divine seals.

"Let it be ours to reverence, to prize, to use the ordinances of our Master with a devotion such as we might feel if we saw Him stretch His hand out to break the bread and hallow it and give it at the table. Sacred indeed are the God-given externals of Christian order and ordinance."

Walk Closer to God

A freshly painted car may look like a good buy—but don't forget to check under the hood. Without an engine, a car is useless.

Without God's powerful presence in your life, trying to live the Christian life is as impossible as driving an engine-less car. But with Him comes the *will* and the *wherewithal* to live a life that is praiseworthy to Him—a life of inner beauty and reality. A life that can begin today!

*W*orship from the Heart

Love God. This is the central function of a believer's life. Loving God enables us to love others more deeply, and it gives us a new compassion for those who are suffering and lost. Consider ways that you can reach out with God's love to someone who needs your help or comfort today.

*W*alk Thru the Word

New Testament Reading
Romans 2:17-29
Old Testament Reading
Deuteronomy 10:12-22

171

Spiritual heredity and the effects of sin

We have already made the charge that Jews and Gentiles alike are all under sin. As it is written: "There is no one righteous, not even one" (Romans 3:9-10).

Not all things that "run in the family" are as harmless as red hair or big feet. Many men of royal families in 19th-century Europe inherited hemophilia, an often fatal disease.

In the case of the human race, spiritual heredity has brought the disease of sin into the life of every man and woman, boy and girl. No one escapes from the sickness called sin, as Paul points out in Romans 3. Charles Hodge probes the inner workings of this fatal and universal disease.

Walk with Charles Hodge

"If the permanent moral dispositions of a human being are evil, it follows that his acts of transgression will be beyond counting. Every hour there is some work of evil, some wrong thought, some wicked act, some improper word, to add to the number of his offenses.

"The evil exercise of an evil heart is like the ceaseless swinging of the pendulum. While conscience sleeps, or our attention is directed to other subjects, the number of our transgressions grows like the unnoticed pulsations of our heart. It is not until we pause and call ourselves to an account that we see how great is the distance at which we habitually live from God and how constantly we lack conformity to His will. "

Walk Closer to God

Fortunately, this fatal disease has a cure. It requires nothing less than a "transfusion" of blood from the one Man whose heredity differs from all others.

Jesus, the sinless Son of God, never yielded to the power of sin. And His blood, when applied to your life, counteracts sin's deadly course. In the words of the apostle Paul, "We have redemption through his blood, the forgiveness of sins" (Ephesians 1:7).

Because sin is a part of your human heredity, the only cure is a perfect pedigree—the one you receive by becoming a part of God's family of faith.

Worship from the Heart

Skeptics may scoff that the words of Jesus are not practical in the real world, but are what Marx called "the opiate of the people." But praise God that when His Word is put into practice it does change the real world, and the hearts of sinful men and women. Celebrate Paul's cry: "Let God be true, and every man a liar."

Walk Thru the Word

New Testament Reading
Romans 3:1-20
Old Testament Reading
Psalm 14:1-3

172

The cost of satisfying divine justice

God presented him [Christ Jesus] as a sacrifice of atonement, through faith in his blood. He did this to demonstrate his justice, because in his forbearance he had left the sins committed beforehand unpunished (Romans 3:25).

*F*inished products often disguise the hard work that made the end result possible. For instance, a beautiful sculpture conceals to all but the trained eye the sculptor's weeks of tireless labor. But without his labor and sacrifice, the work would not exist.

To admire the finished work of Christ without acknowledging His sacrificial toil on your behalf limits your appreciation of the final "product."

Martin Luther reminds you of the price paid by the Son of God.

Walk with Martin Luther

"Because Christ has become a King and Priest for you and has bestowed this great blessing on you, you dare not imagine that it cost little or comes to you because of your merit. Sin and death were overcome for you in Him and through Him.

"Grace and life were given you, but meant bitter work for Him. He earned it at the greatest expense with His own blood, body, and life. For to put down God's wrath, judgment, hell, death, and everything evil, and to gain everything good, could not be done without satisfying divine justice.

"This is why Paul is in the habit of touching also on Christ's suffering and blood whenever he preaches God's grace in Christ, in order to note that all our blessings are given to us through Christ, but not without His unspeakable merit and cost."

Walk Closer to God

"Dear Father, there is such irony in the salvation I enjoy: a free gift, yet purchased at great price; a new life, made possible by a cruel death; the right to call myself Your child, all because You were willing to turn Your back on Jesus as He bore my sins on the cross. Keep me mindful, Lord, of all my Savior endured in order to shout triumphantly from Calvary, 'It is finished!'

"In the name of my Sin Bearer I pray. Amen."

Worship from the Heart

As you meditate on the words of Psalm 22, allow the true cost of Christ's sacrifice to touch your heart—and drive you to your knees—in thanksgiving, praise, and wonder.

Walk Thru the Word

New Testament Reading
Romans 3:21-31
Old Testament Reading
Psalm 22

*F*aith, works, and the fruit of a holy life

What does the Scripture say? "Abraham believed God, and it was credited to him as righteousness" (Romans 4:3).

*F*or it is by grace you have been saved, through faith . . . not by works" (Ephesians 2:8-9). "Faith without deeds is useless" (James 2:20). Which does the Bible teach? Which do you believe?

If your answer was anything except "Both!", it may be time for a refresher course on the basics of the faith. What Paul and James have said about faith and works can at first appear to be contradictory, rather than complementary.

Philip Schaff shows how the two passages are descriptive of one grand walk of faith.

Walk with Philip Schaff

"Paul presents Abraham as a man of faith in order to confirm that the foundation of salvation lies not in us, but outside of us, in the free grace of God, and that this must be grasped first by faith, before we can do any good works. James, on the other hand, represents Abraham as a man of holy obedience who proved his faith by his works.

"Both views are right. Paul goes to the root of the matter, the vital principle, that animated Abraham; James looks at the fruit produced thereby.

"Faith and works, righteousness and holiness, are as inseparable as light and heat, as cause and effect. Paul himself, after laying the only true foundation, insists upon a holy life as strongly as James does. But the essential element in both is unconditional confidence and trust in God's truth and mercy."

Walk Closer to God

Only one verse after declaring that salvation is not of works, Paul goes on to say that you were "created in Christ Jesus to do good works" (Ephesians 2:10). James opens his epistle by emphasizing the faith which provides the foundation for all good works (James 1:3, 6).

Focusing on one side of the faith/works "equation" in no way denies the importance of the other. Both are vital to a healthy walk with the Lord. Are both in balance in *your* walk of faith?

*W*orship from the Heart

When you were a child, if you had faith in your parents' love, you delighted to do those things that pleased them. You were not trying to earn their favor; you didn't have to. Your relationship with your heavenly Father is no different. Those works that please Him are the outpoured offerings of your thankful heart.

*W*alk Thru the Word

New Testament Reading
Romans 4:1-12
Old Testament Reading
1 Samuel 14:6-14

174

He [Abraham] did not waver through unbelief regarding the promise of God, but was strengthened in his faith and gave glory to God (Romans 4:20).

No, it's not a 20th-century A.D. episode on "That's Incredible," but a 20th-century B.C. account of a faithful man and his wife. Year after year, Abraham and Sarah had waited, but the hoped-for baby never came. Yet Abraham was "fully persuaded that God had power to do what he had promised" (4:21).

In a skeptical age, such faith is the real story. Charles Spurgeon challenges the Christian to remain strong in faith, for God is as trustworthy as His Word.

Walk with Charles Spurgeon

"If we want blessings from God, nothing can pull them down but faith. Prayer cannot draw down answers from God's throne unless it is the earnest prayer of the one who believes.

"Faith is the angelic messenger between the soul and the Lord Jesus in glory. If that messenger is withdrawn, we can neither send up prayer nor receive the answers.

"Take faith away, and in vain I call to God. There is no road between my soul and heaven. Faith links me with divinity. Faith insures every attribute of God in my defense. It helps me defy the hosts of hell. It makes me march triumphant over the necks of my enemies. Without faith how can I receive anything of the Lord?"

Walk Closer to God

Abel . . . Enoch . . . Noah . . . Abraham . . . Sarah . . . Moses . . . Gideon . . . Samson . . . David— their physical eyes could not always see the answer on the horizon. But that scarcely mattered, because with the eyes of faith they stared intently into the face of their Lord, and there found that "many promises God has made . . . are 'Yes' in Christ. And so through him the 'Amen' is spoken by us" (2 Corinthians 1:20).

Take a look and what do you see? If the prospects for the future leave you frowning, maybe you need a "faith lift."

The road between my soul and heaven

Worship from the Heart

"Faith of our fathers! We will love / Both friend and foe in all our strife: / And preach Thee, too, as love knows how, / By kindly words and virtuous life. / Faith of our fathers, holy faith! / We shall be true to thee till death."
—Frederick W. Faber

Walk Thru the Word

New Testament Reading
Romans 4:13-25
Old Testament Reading
Isaiah 26:3-4

The basis of salvation

For . . . when we were God's enemies, we were reconciled to him through the death of his Son (Romans 5:10).

*W*hat good is a worship service if there is no God to worship? What good is placing your faith in Christ if He has done nothing to deserve such trust? Without a cause, there can be no effect.

Without a risen Savior, there is no hope for salvation. "If Christ has not been raised," the apostle states, "your faith is futile; you are still in your sins." (1 Corinthians 15:17). The work of Christ is the irreplaceable heart of the Christian faith.

Oswald Chambers clarifies the all-important distinction between what Christ has done, and what our faith in Him accomplishes.

Walk with Oswald Chambers

"It is not repentance that saves me; repentance is the sign that I realize what God has done in Christ Jesus. The danger is to put the emphasis on the effect instead of on the cause.

"Is it my obedience that puts me right with God? Never! I am put right with God because prior to all else, Christ died. When I turn to God and by belief accept what God reveals, instantly the stupendous atonement of Jesus Christ rushes me into a right relationship with God. By the miracle of God's grace I stand justified, not because of anything I have done, but because of what Jesus has done.

"The salvation of God does not stand on human logic; it stands on the sacrificial death of Jesus. Sinful men and women can be changed into new creatures by the marvelous work of God in Christ Jesus, which is prior to all experience."

Walk Closer to God

Dwight L. Moody was once asked, "Sir, what must I do to be saved?" His reply startled the questioner: "I'm sorry, it's too late."

"Too late to be saved?"

"No, too late to do something."

Jesus Christ did all that needed to be done 2,000 years ago on Calvary. All that remains is to make His provision your supply. A simple "Thank you, Lord" is a wonderful place to begin.

Worship from the Heart

Paul says that he can rejoice in his sufferings—not after God has delivered him, but in the midst of them. When you are suffering, begin praising your Lord, who has known all the depths of human suffering. As soon as you begin to rejoice in Him, His presence will strengthen your heart.

Walk Thru the Word

New Testament Reading
Romans 5:1-11
Old Testament Reading
Exodus 14:10-14

We must go to Jesus Christ

Grace . . . reign[s] through righteousness to bring eternal life through Jesus Christ our Lord (Romans 5:21).

*T*he church is packed. The organist plays reverently. The smiling groom awaits his bride.

And here she comes down the aisle—dress tattered and torn, face streaked with grime—anything but the picture of beauty.

Yet the groom lovingly cleans her up and then receives her. That's the picture of Christ—who is both groom and groomer—and His church.

The same gift of grace that saves is a gift of righteousness that purifies, as Anne Ross Cousins explains.

Walk with Anne Ross Cousins

Oh! I am my Beloved's,
    And my Beloved is mine!
He brings a poor vile sinner
    Into His "House of wine."
I stand upon His merit,
    I know no other stand
Not e'en where glory dwelleth
    In Immanuel's land.

The Bride eyes not her garment,
    But her dear Bridegroom's face;
I will not gaze at glory,
    But on my King of Grace—
Not at the crown He giveth,
    But on His pierced hand:
The Lamb is all the glory
    Of Immanuel's land.

Walk Closer to God

The church is the bride of Christ who "gave himself up for her to make her holy" (see Ephesians 5:25-32). In Christ the bride becomes beautiful with a purity acceptable to God. The dirt of sin and the curse of death cannot be removed in any other way.

Christ is preparing for Himself a bride that is cleansed, spotless, holy, and without blemish.

Grace leading to righteousness. Unmerited favor leading to upright behavior. They go hand in hand for the one eagerly preparing to meet the Lord.

Worship from the Heart

Our relationship with the heavenly Bridegroom is the most beautiful one we can have. Yet we often fail to give Him proper attention. Ask the Spirit to reveal ways you can deepen your relationship with Jesus.

Walk Thru the Word

New Testament Reading
Romans 5:12-21
Old Testament Reading
Proverbs 20:9

Making Christ the center of life

Since Christ was raised from the dead, he cannot die again; death no longer has mastery over him (Romans 6:9).

O ne by one the mourners file past to pay their last respects to the deceased. One by one they emerge with tears in their eyes—not tears of grief but tears of gladness.

Why? Because the One they had come to mourn turns out to be alive and well. His grave stands empty, bearing silent testimony of resurrection life!

Death vanquished; life vindicated. Matthew Henry probes some of the marvelous implications of Christ's resurrection.

Walk with Matthew Henry

"In two things we must conform to the resurrection of Christ: First, He rose to die no more. We read of others who were raised from the dead, but they rose to die again. Christ rose to die no more. Therefore He left His graveclothes behind. In contrast Lazarus brought them out with him, for he would have occasion to use them again.

"Over Christ, death has no more dominion. He was dead, but He is now alive forever. Thus we must rise from the grave of sin never to return to it, nor to have any more fellowship with the works of darkness, having departed that grave.

"Second, He rose to live unto God, to receive that glory which was set before Him. He rose to intercede and rule, and all to the glory of the Father.

"Thus must we rise to live to God. This is what Paul refers to as newness of life—to live by new principles, with different goals. To live indeed is to live to God, with our eyes ever toward Him, making Him the center of all our actions."

Walk Closer to God

Those who come back from the brink of death are said to have received a new lease on life. How much more those who have discovered life everlasting in the person of the resurrected Savior.

In Christ, what formerly looked like a hopeless end is transformed into an endless hope. That fact should bring a smile to your face and holiness to your life every time you remember the empty tomb.

Worship from the Heart

What sin do you fall into most often? Confess it to God in true repentance and ask His forgiveness. Can you see that sin in you nailed to the cross with Jesus Christ? As you contemplate that sinful disposition in you dying with Christ, give Him heartfelt thanks that He made it possible for you to have a new life in Him.

Walk Thru the Word

New Testament Reading
Romans 6:1-14
Old Testament Reading
Psalm 40:1-3

178

For the wages of sin is death, but the gift of God is eternal life in Christ Jesus our Lord (Romans 6:23).

The poisonous sting of sin

*A*ddictions can have dreadful consequences—especially when the addict refuses to believe that he or she is even being victimized.

Once a cure has been effected, however, the power of the disease becomes evident to the one freed from bondage. The "delivered one" must remain wary lest he slip back into enslaving habits.

Sin is like that: a destructive force enslaving the non-Christian and lying in wait for the unsuspecting Christian. Charles Spurgeon offers wise words for those with ears to hear.

Walk with Charles Spurgeon

"Sin has the same deadly character to both Christians and non-Christians. You, Christian brother, cannot fall into sin without its being poison to you; in fact, to you it is more evidently poison than to those hardened to it.

"If you sin, it destroys your joy, your power in prayer, your confidence toward God. If you have spent evenings in frivolity with worldlings, you have felt the deadening influence of their society.

"What about your prayers? The operation of sin upon your spirit is most injurious to your communion with God. You are like a man who has taken a noxious drug, whose fumes are stupefying the brain and sending the heart into slumber.

"Sin is deadly to everyone, whoever he or she may be; and were it not for the mighty, curative operation which the Spirit of God is always performing upon the believer's nature, not one of us would survive the deadly effects of even those sins of infirmity and ignorance into which we fall."

Walk Closer to God

Sin is not to be treated lightly. The person who toys with a poison-tipped arrow will not live long enough to learn his lesson the hard way.

For the Christian, sin no longer means eternal death. But its poison can still make you miserable. Learn to recognize sin for what it is: attractive in appearance, deadly in consequence, and something to be avoided at all cost!

Worship from the Heart

Ponder these words of William Shakespeare on the quality of mercy: "Though justice be thy pleas, consider this: / That in the course of justice none of us / Would see salvation. We do pray for mercy, / And that same prayer doth teach us all to render / The deeds of mercy."

Walk Thru the Word

New Testament Reading
Romans 6:15-23
Old Testament Reading
Deuteronomy 7:1-6

My heart, Christ's home

For when we were controlled by the sinful nature, the sinful passions aroused by the law were at work in our bodies, so that we bore fruit for death. But now . . . we have been released from the law (Romans 7:5-6).

*A*n Xray reveals a serious break in your leg. Do you blame the Xray for the problem? Or would you blame your doctor for informing you of a life-threatening situation? Of course not!

In the same way, the law was designed by God to diagnose the sinful condition of the human race—to make men and women aware of their need for a Savior.

In *The Pilgrim's Progress,* John Bunyan gives this illustration of the relationship of the law to the gospel of grace, as spoken through the Interpreter.

Walk with John Bunyan

"This parlor is the heart of a man who was never cleansed by the sweet grace of the gospel; that dust is his inward corruption that has defiled the whole man.

"He who began to sweep at first is the law, but she who brought the water and did sprinkle it is the gospel.

"Now, so soon as the first began to sweep, the dust did so fly about that you were almost choked therewith. This is to show you that the law, instead of cleansing the heart from sin, does revive, put strength into, and increase it, for it does not give the power to subdue.

"Again, the damsel sprinkling the room with water is to show you what happens when the gospel comes in.

"As the damsel settled the dust by sprinkling the floor with water, sin is vanquished and subdued, and the soul made clean through faith; and consequently made fit for the King of Glory to inhabit."

Walk Closer to God

The law merely reveals the soiled condition of the human heart.

What the law of God stirs up, only the grace of God can clean up.

It's enough to make even twentieth-century pilgrims respond in grateful praise!

*W*orship from the Heart

"My heart is Christ's home." Meditate on the metaphor of your heart, or inner being, as the dwelling place of Christ. Have you simply tried to "clean up a few rooms for company," or are all the rooms of your life available for His use? In a prayer of commitment, give Him the key to all the rooms of your heart and invite Him to make the changes He feels necessary.

*W*alk Thru the Word

New Testament Reading
Romans 7:1-6
Old Testament Reading
Job 4:8

180

*T*he inward willing of the heart

I do not understand what I do. For what I want to do I do not do, but what I hate I do (Romans 7:15).

*T*oo often the gap between promise and performance is wide, even when intentions and motives are pure.

Christians are not immune to the struggle of matching words with actions. The apostle Paul's words in chapter 7 can be echoed by every person who longs to glorify God.

But is that reason enough to cease hoping that daily victory over sin can be won? Paul didn't think so, and neither did Abraham Kuyper, who adds this perspective.

Walk with Abraham Kuyper

"What Paul has said here is that our ideal always stands above us, and that we ever have to mourn our inability to make it actual in real life.

"When it comes to carrying out the inner intention of your heart against the world, the flesh, and the Devil it constantly happens that, with the best of will, you meet with stubborn resistance. You find no power in yourself, and you leave undone what you honestly purposed in your heart to do.

"This tempts you all too frequently to deny all worth to this inner willing of your heart. What good is it if, when it comes to action, you fail? This, however, must be resisted. Ten times better fail and be punished in your conscience, than in every ordinary way to sin along with the world without knowledge of this conflict with your conscience.

"Moreover, this inward willing in your heart of what God wills is of supreme worth, even though strength fails you to carry it into effect."

Walk Closer to God

Left to your own strength, there is good reason for despair. But, as Paul goes on to explain, you have another power source. The same powerful Spirit who raised Jesus from the dead is at work in your life, bridging the gap between the willing heart you have and the obedient walk you seek.

In His strength, you can know what to do, and can do what you know.

*W*orship from the Heart

Pain warns us that something harmful is happening in our body so that we can seek healing. The pain of a guilty conscience serves as a warning to the havoc that sin can bring to our spirits. Thank God for your conscience, and praise Him that you can turn to Him for cleansing and healing!

*W*alk Thru the Word

New Testament Reading
Romans 7:7-25
Old Testament Reading
Genesis 12:10-20

Firmly focused on things of the Spirit

Those who live according to the sinful nature have their minds set on what that nature desires; but those who live in accordance with the Spirit have their minds set on what the Spirit desires (Romans 8:5).

The game is into sudden-death playoff. The crowd is hushed. The player studies the angle of the shot. He concentrates, lifts his club, begins his swing . . . and someone in the crowd sneezes. He falters slightly on the downswing, and the ball rolls by the cup.

It was only a momentary distraction—but it may have cost him the win.

To focus intently on your task is half the battle in reaching any goal. Let Ruth Paxson explain how to keep your mind set on life's highest objective.

Walk with Ruth Paxson

"Set your mind on things of the Spirit. That doesn't mean once in awhile, or even in a few moments of devotional fellowship with Christ. It means the whole bent of our minds is to be fixed upon Christ, upon the things of the Spirit.

"It means before you go to the kitchen or the office, when you first wake up in the morning, your mind goes to Him. Even while you are dressing, your mind can go to Him. Then you can sit down and have some time over the Book and in prayer with your mind fixed on Him.

"If that takes place, He is in your mind and His Word is in your mind, so that you do not have to go out with your forehead all wrinkled up, saying 'How am I going to get through this day?' You go to your duties with a quiet, assured mind, so that you do your work the way it ought to be done. "

Walk Closer to God

High achievers nearly always have clearly defined goals and definite plans for reaching them. They set their minds on their goals, and by hard work, determination, and concentration, more often than not they reach their goals.

God's goal for believers is to make them like Jesus Christ. And He uses all the circumstances of life to do it. Check your mind-set. Is your goal for your life the same as God's?

Worship from the Heart

Rejoice that God has placed gifted men and women in the body of Christ as teachers and leaders. Thank God for those people who have ministered to you and have nurtured your spiritual growth. Pray that God will keep them unspotted from the world and faithful to Him.

Walk Thru the Word

New Testament Reading
Romans 8:1-11
Old Testament Reading
Psalm 1:1-2

182

A hope that is firm and certain

For in this hope we were saved. But hope that is seen is no hope at all. Who hopes for what he already has? (Romans 8:24).

What do you have to look forward to in the next few minutes . . . the next several days . . . the next few years . . . the rest of eternity? Chances are there's some event on your calendar, some person on your heart, that keeps you looking ahead. Perhaps it's a vacation, a birthday, a reunion with a friend, or even the return of Jesus Christ.

The future can be an incentive in the present. Robert Haldane discusses the motivating power of the Christian's blessed hope.

Walk with Robert Haldane

"If believers were in the full possession of their salvation, faith would no longer be the conviction of things hoped for, since things hoped for are not things enjoyed. When Romans 8:24 says that we are saved in hope, it implies that all the good we can for the present enjoy of that distant and future happiness is obtained by hoping for it.

"The foundation and support of Christian hope is firm and certain. First, we have the immutable promises of God, for heaven and earth shall pass away, but His word shall remain forever. God has promised heaven as the eternal inheritance of His people. Shall we doubt His fidelity?

"We have, second, the blood of the Son of God, with which His promise has been sealed; and Jesus' obedience even unto death, which He has rendered to His Father, for the foundation of this hope. We have, third, the intercession of our great High Priest, who also makes intercession for us. He declares, too, that our hope enters into heaven, where Jesus, our forerunner, has entered for us."

Walk Closer to God

If you are a child of God, then the future is bright with hoped-for but as yet unseen promises. Here is one of the most exciting: "An inheritance that can never perish, spoil or fade— kept in heaven for you" (1 Peter 1:4).

Too good to be true? Take it from Peter and Paul, God's promises are never too much to hope for!

Worship from the Heart

"Lord God, I believe Your promises— every single one of them—with all my being. But You wept over Lazarus. Even Mary was told that a sword would pierce her heart. Thank You for taking human flesh and sharing human pain so that I might find true hope and comfort in You. Amen."

Walk Thru the Word

New Testament Reading
Romans 8:12-39
Old Testament Reading
Job 19:25-27

*O*ne deadline no one can afford to miss

For the Scripture says to Pharaoh: "I raised you up for this very purpose, that I might display my power in you" (Romans 9:17).

*F*inal notice: failure to pay taxes by the deadline will result in immediate prosecution.

If you received such an announcement, chances are you would need no further encouragement to pay promptly. Like paying taxes, dying is an inevitable consequence of being alive. But, curiously, more people worry about their taxes than worry about their eternity.

Perhaps if salvation were only available until April 15, more people would take it seriously. But only God knows when your "final notice" will be given. Jonathan Edwards shares these thoughts about the need to act while there is still time.

Walk with Jonathan Edwards

"God insists that we acknowledge His sovereignty —even in a matter that so closely and infinitely concerns us as our own eternal salvation.

"This is the stumbling block on which thousands fall and perish; and if we go on contending with God about His sovereignty, it will be our eternal ruin. It is absolutely necessary that we should submit to God as our absolute sovereign.

"Do not presume upon the mercy of God and so encourage yourself in sin. Many hear that God's mercy is infinite, and therefore think that if they delay seeking salvation for the present and seek it later, God will bestow His grace upon them.

"But though God's grace is sufficient, He is still sovereign. If you put off salvation until the hereafter, salvation will not be in your power. Seeing, therefore, that in this affair you are so absolutely dependent on God, it is best to follow His direction in seeking it, which is to hear His voice today."

Walk Closer to God

On April 15, thousands of people rush to beat the tax deadline. And what's at stake? Only money.

By contrast, consider what is at stake when God's deadline for responding to the gospel finally arrives. That's one "final notice" you can't afford to ignore.

*W*orship from the Heart

Pray with Adelaide A. Pollard her beautiful words of commitment: "Have Thine own way, Lord! Have Thine own way! / Thou art the Potter. I am the clay. / Mold me and make me / After Thy will, / While I am waiting, / Yielded and still."

*W*alk Thru the Word

New Testament Reading
Romans 9:1-29
Old Testament Reading
Psalm 24

Confess with your mouth "Jesus is Lord." . . . For . . . it is with your mouth that you confess and are saved (Romans 10:9-10).

I never knew you were . . . "
"You never asked."
"I'd never have guessed."

Such conversations reveal the gap that frequently exists between what you know to be true about yourself, and what others know about you.

And it's particularly awkward when the "secret" you've been hiding is that you belong to Christ. Yet confessing Him before others is the prerequisite for His confessing you before the Father (Matthew 10:32-33). Albert Barnes expands on what it means to confess Jesus as Lord of your life.

Walk with Albert Barnes

"He who in all appropriate ways professes his attachment to Christ shall be saved.

"He who declares his belief makes a profession. He who associates with Christian people does it. He who is baptized, and commemorates the death of the Lord Jesus, does it. He who leads an humble, prayerful, spiritual life does it. He shows his regard for the precepts and example of Jesus Christ; his regard for them more than for the pride and pomp and allurements of the world. All these are included in a profession of religion.

"The reason why this is so important is that there can be no true attachment to Christ which will not manifest itself in one's life. A city that is set on a hill cannot be hid. It is impossible that there should be true belief in the heart of a person, unless it should show itself in his life and conversation."

Walk Closer to God

In order to profess Christ before others, you may first need to confess your sins to Him. Then you'll be ready to answer "everyone who asks you to give the reason for the hope that you have" (1 Peter 3:15).

Mr. Barnes offered many suggestions for making clear where you stand. But only you can choose to pledge yourself publicly to Christ. When you do so, it will be one confession you'll never regret.

*M*aking clear where you stand

*W*orship from the Heart

To be in Christ is to live according to the tempo of the universe, not against it. Contemplate the reality that you know as a spiritual being in Christ. Rejoice today that to be in Christ is to be residing in Life, in Light, and in Love.

*W*alk Thru the Word

New Testament Reading
Romans 9:30–10:21
Old Testament Reading
Jonah 3:1-4

Albert Barnes (1798-1870) Student of God's Word

*T*he number of printed editions and copies of the Bible that have been published over the centuries is staggering, making it by far the best of the best sellers.

In addition, the Bible's popularity has caused it to become the subject of countless other books: commentaries, dictionaries, systematic theologies, concordances—all designed to help the reader become a better student of the Scriptures.

Best-selling books have a way of rising like a meteor—and disappearing just as quickly. The same could be said for many books about the Bible.

A few remain, however, guiding each new generation of readers through the truths of God's Word year after year. One such work is Albert Barnes's *Notes on the Old and New Testaments*. For well over a century, students and teachers have benefited from the author's insight into every "jot and tittle" of Scripture, though that author aspired to write about the Bible only during the latter years of his life!

Albert Barnes was born on December 1, 1798, in Rome, New York. Young Barnes learned the trade of his father, who was a canner and small farmer. At the age of 17, Barnes decided to go to school

and study to become a lawyer. Over the next five years he worked his way through college by teaching primary school. He graduated in 1820.

While in school, Barnes seriously committed his life to Jesus Christ. Until that time he had lived an outwardly moral life, although he had not acknowledged the truth of Christianity. In his own words, he admitted his lack of Christian knowledge: "I was entirely ignorant on the subject of religion; had never owned a Bible; and up to the time when my mind was seriously informed, I do not know that I ever read twenty chapters in that Book." Such a background prepared him to deal with the excuses of unbelievers in his later work.

After his graduation from college, Barnes entered Princeton Seminary, where Charles Hodge had just begun to teach. He pastored his first church in 1825 in New Jersey, and moved to a large Presbyterian church in Philadelphia five years later. He remained there until shortly before his death in 1870. As a Christian pastor, Albert Barnes served Christ on several fronts. He is best known for his *Notes on the Old and New Testaments,* which he wrote primarily to help Sunday school teachers with their classes.

Carefully and understandably, he covers the entire Bible, verse by verse, and offers a practical application of the truths contained therein.

But Barnes was far more than just a writer. His writing schedule never extended past 9:00 in the morning, at which time other pastoral duties required his attention.

He was not bashful about addressing the heated issues of his day. He fought against the abuse of alcohol, worked for the abolition of slavery, and sought practical ways to apply the truths of God's Word. Perhaps that helps to explain the enduring value of his commentaries on Scripture.

You may not have the opportunity to write a best-selling set of Bible notes, as Albert Barnes did. But don't let that keep you from making God's Word your noteworthy study project today — and every day. There's wealth to be found in every page!

A Lesson from the life of Albert Barnes

When my entire life is committed to God, it may have far-reaching effects which I cannot even imagine.

Making choices that count for eternity

And David says: "May their table become a snare and . . . a stumbling block . . . May their eyes be darkened so they cannot see, and their backs be bent forever" (Romans 11:9-10).

Some of David's poems were composed while he kept one step ahead of his enemies. As such his words reflect an attitude of revenge and anger.

But David's words also foreshadow what will happen to the enemies of Messiah, predictions which Charles Spurgeon helps us understand.

Worship from the Heart

"Father, I want to denounce the sin of my society, tell those around me of Your love, and warn them of Your wrath. But I tremble and am afraid. Give me a lion's share of boldness to speak the truth, no matter how unpopular it may be. Amen."

Walk with Charles Spurgeon

"Those who choose evil shall have their choice. Men who hate divine mercy shall not have it forced upon them, but (unless sovereign grace interpose) shall be left to themselves to aggravate their guilt and ensure their doom.

"They have loved darkness rather than light, and in darkness they shall abide. Eyes which see no beauty in the Lord Jesus, but flash wrath upon Him, may well grow yet more dim, till death which is spiritual leads to death which is eternal.

"What can be too severe a penalty for those who reject the incarnate God, and refuse to obey the commands of His mercy? They deserve to be flooded with wrath, and they shall be; for upon all who rebel against the Savior, 'the wrath of God has come upon them at last' (1 Thessalonians 2:16).

"God's indignation is no trifle. The anger of a holy, just, omnipotent, and infinite Being, is above all things to be dreaded; even a drop of it consumes, but to have it poured upon us is inconceivably dreadful."

Walk Closer to God

In a nutshell, the hard words of David help us understand that the choices we make in this world have great significance for the next. As Paul said earlier in Romans, "The wrath of God is being revealed. . . against all the godlessness and wickedness of men" (Romans 1:18).

Learning to hate what God hates and to love what God loves makes even the sometimes-hard-to-swallow words of Scripture worthy of your attention and respect.

Walk Thru the Word

New Testament Reading
Romans 11:1-10
Old Testament Reading
Psalm 75

Consider therefore the kindness and sternness of God: sternness to those who fell, but kindness to you, provided that you continue in his kindness (Romans 11:22).

Longevity is no guarantee of legitimacy. Tradition alone is no safeguard of the truth. Over a period of time, what is right and true can easily become perverted and powerless.

It happens in the Christian life with surprising regularity. The revolutionary claims of the gospel become routine; holiness becomes humdrum. And when that happens, it's time for God to snap His children out of their spiritual stupor, as Matthew Henry explains.

Walk with Matthew Henry

"God is most severe toward those who, in their profession, have been nearest to Him, if they rebel against Him. Patience and abused privilege turn to the greatest wrath.

"It is possible for churches that have long stood by faith to fall into such a state of infidelity as to be their ruin. Their unbelief not only provoked God to cut them off, but by this they cut themselves off.

"You do not stand in any strength of your own. You are no more than the grace of God makes you.

"Continue in His goodness, in a dependence upon and compliance with the free grace of God. Be careful to keep up your interest in God's favor by being continually careful to please Him and equally fearful of offending Him. The sum of your duty, the condition of your happiness, is to keep yourself in the love of God. 'Come trembling to the Lord and to his blessings' (Hosea 3:5)."

Walk Closer to God

Serving God should be the pattern of your existence. But in the process, never let it become routine—ordinary, stale, monotonous. Greet each new day as a fresh challenge to display the goodness of God to a waiting world.

Just as there was no stale manna for Israel in the wilderness, so keep your faith fresh through daily feeding on the bread of life. Then you, as Mr. Henry suggests, will be "continually careful to please [God] and equally fearful of offending Him."

Standing by God's grace alone

Worship from the Heart

Saul once persecuted those who proclaimed the risen Christ. Later, blinded by the glory of that same Christ, Paul proclaimed Him the Son of God. As you reflect on the changes the resurrected Lord has made in your life, worship Him for His power and ask Him to give you a renewed vision of His glory.

Walk Thru the Word

New Testament Reading
Romans 11:11-24
Old Testament Reading
Leviticus 10:1-3

*A*lways more than you think He is!

For from him and through him and to him are all things. To him be the glory forever! Amen (Romans 11:36).

E=mc². This simple equation has transformed the world of science in this century, as did the theory of gravity in the 17th century. Yet no one can fully explain either gravity or relativity.

In the same way, Paul's simple words in Romans 11:36 defy easy explanations. F. B. Meyer probes the mystery of God in the simplest of terms.

Walk with F. B. Meyer

"*From Him . . . through Him . . . to Him.* A child just learning to read could easily spell these monosyllables. But who can exhaust their meaning?

"*From Him.* The entire scheme of redemption, the marvelous history of the chosen people, the universe of matter—all have emanated out of God. From this stream of all created things let us climb to Him, who is their source and origin. In Him let us learn to fill our own souls to the very brim.

"*Through Him.* Through Jesus Christ, the Mediator, God has poured the entire grace and wealth of His nature to bless and help us. There is no good thing that does not come to us through the Second Person of the Trinity. Through Him God made the worlds. Through Him we have received reconciliation. Through Him all grace abounds towards us.

"*To Him.* Creation, providence, redemption— all are tending back to God. The tide is moving toward the throne. Glory will result from all that has happened within time."

Walk Closer to God

What do you see in a tree? Shade . . . firewood . . . food . . . shelter? Yet a tree is far more than any of the above. Complex in its makeup, it is also complex in its purpose.

God possesses attributes that defy attempts to understand Him fully. And yet, He rewards those who diligently seek to know Him (Hebrews 11:6).

Consider Paul's simple words as stepping-stones in your quest to understand more about the Most High God. But never forget that God is always more than you think He is.

*W*orship from the Heart

Ponder the words of Frederick W. Faber's hymn as you prepare for worship: "There's a wideness in God's mercy / Like the wideness of the sea; / There's a kindness in His justice / That is more than liberty. / There is welcome for the sinner, / And more graces for the good; / There is mercy with the Savior; / There is healing in His blood."

*W*alk Thru the Word

New Testament Reading
Romans 11:25-36
Old Testament Reading
Exodus 3:13-15

*Just as each of us has one body with many members . . .
so in Christ we who are many form one body, and each
member belongs to all the others (Romans 12:4-5).*

*T*hrombosis. It's a dangerous blood clot that can
mean life-threatening danger. And the prognosis? Often immediate surgery.

Sin. It's a condition that can mean life-threatening danger in the church, endangering not only
the part it attacks, but the health and vitality of
the entire church body.

Again, surgery may be the only remedy, but
clearly prevention is the best medicine. A. B.
Simpson offers this diagnosis and prescription for
a healthy church.

Walk with A. B. Simpson

"Sometimes our communion with God is cut off
or interrupted because of something wrong with
a brother, or some lack of unity in the body of
Christ. We try to break through to the Lord, but
we cannot because we are separated from some
member of the Lord's body, or because there is
not the freedom of His love flowing through
every part.

"Therefore, we must be right with all His children, and meet in the body of Christ in the sweetest, fullest fellowship if we would keep our perfect
communion with Christ Himself. Sometimes we
will find that an altered attitude to one Christian
will bring us into the flood-tides of His fellowship.

"It seems impossible to have faith without love
or to have Christ alone without full fellowship
with all His dear saints."

Walk Closer to God

Sin effectively short-circuits the Christian's personal joy in God. But sin also affects the interrela-
tionship of the members of the body of Christ.

Remember the principle? "Each member
belongs to all the others." When a clot impedes
the flow of blood, the result can be stroke, paralysis, or even death. And so medical personnel are
trained to detect, treat, and prevent that from
happening.

How much more should the body of Christ work
to detect, treat, and prevent the deadly effects of sin.

*M*embers belonging to each other

Worship from the Heart

*Because God is God,
no finite mind can
comprehend Him
completely. But we
can worship Him
because He has
revealed Himself to
us and through
Christ has made us
members of His body.
That's reason enough
for praise—and
adoration.*

Walk Thru the Word

New Testament Reading
Romans 12:1-8
Old Testament Reading
*Proverbs 3:30; 20:3;
26:17*

Overcoming evil with good

Do not be overcome by evil, but overcome evil with good (Romans 12:21).

Being familiar with the book of Romans is one thing. Putting its teaching to work in your life is something else.

Beginning with chapter 12, Paul focuses his thoughts on the practical side of Christian living.

Home and government, church and community—each should reflect the dynamic nature of the doctrine you believe, as John Henry Jowett describes.

Walk with John Henry Jowett

"How can we cast out evil?

"The surgeon cannot cut out the disease if his instruments are defiled; while he removes one ill growth, he sows the seeds of another.

"It must be health which fights disease.

"And therefore I must cultivate a virtue if I would eradicate a vice. If there is some immoral habit in my life, the best way to destroy it would be to cultivate a good one.

"Take the mind away from the Evil One. Deprive it of thought food. Give the thought to the nobler mood, and the ignoble will die.

"And this also applies to the faults and vices of my brother. I must fight them with their opposites. If he is harsh and cruel, I must be considerate and gentle. If he is grasping, I must be generous. If he is acting devilish, I must act Christlike.

"This is the warfare which tells upon the empire of sin. I can overcome evil with good."

Walk Closer to God

As darkness is the absence of light, evil is the absence of good. And all that is necessary for evil to prevail is for good men to do nothing . . . to take their light and hide it under a bushel basket . . . to "leave well enough alone."

Overcome. It's a word that demands an active response if what you believe is truly going to affect how you behave. Don't wait for someone else to take the initiative in fighting the pockets of evil in your community. Get involved on the side of good today.

Worship from the Heart

"Father, I praise You for the instruction of Romans 12:9, 21 and that Jesus set the example for us to follow. Evil is so much a part of our world that sometimes I simply ignore it or overlook it. I pray that You will open my eyes and help me assess my surroundings, my actions, and my attitudes by the standard of Your holiness. Amen."

Walk Thru the Word

New Testament Reading
Romans 12:9-21
Old Testament Reading
Psalm 34:14

The blessing of civil government

Everyone must submit himself to the governing authorities, for there is no authority except that which God has established. The authorities that exist have been established by God (Romans 13:1).

*J*ust as God established marriage, He established civil government. To arbitrarily rebel against what He set up is to rebel against Him. On the other hand, to govern without regard to the One who instituted government is equally rebellious. In one brilliant stroke Paul forbids both anarchy and tyranny.

What does this mean in our time? W. H. Griffith Thomas gives this helpful application.

Walk with W. H. Griffith Thomas

"*1. How beautifully applicable this teaching is to every form of government.* Whatever country may be ours these great principles apply. The institution of civil authority is according to the will and plan of God, but no particular type is necessarily expressive of the divine will.

"*2. How clearly the apostle insists on the Christian's fulfillment of his duties to the state.* They are as truly an obligation as the most spiritual function. Paying taxes is just as Christian as praying at a meeting. Of course, we are not to do at the bidding of the state that which is morally wrong, but, short of this, submission, not resistance, is the Christian law.

"*3. How entirely independent of the moral character of the civil government is this fulfillment of our duty.* Questions as to the state's precise moral character do not touch our duty, so long as the demand does not entrench on the domain of the conscience.

"*4. How agreeable it would be to the progress and welfare of Christianity if such loyalty and submission were always practiced.* If our duties as citizens were fully realized, it would constitute a splendid witness for God."

Walk Closer to God

We have the privilege to play a role in placing our leaders in their positions. Thus we share responsibility for how they lead. Have you considered ways that you can be faithful in this stewardship God has providentially given you?

Worship from the Heart

When your relationship with God is filled with love and adoration, it becomes natural for that love to spill over into other relationships. Ask God to show you ways to demonstrate your love for Him to those you meet in the course of your everyday activities. Praise Him for His demonstration of love in your life.

Walk Thru the Word

New Testament Reading
Romans 13:1-7
Old Testament Reading
Deuteronomy 29:24

193

The debt that has been paid in full

Let no debt remain outstanding except the continuing debt to love one another, for he who loves his fellow-man has fulfilled the law (Romans 13:7-8).

*P*AID IN FULL. When those words are stamped across a promissory note it's cause for rejoicing. You are no longer under obligation to another; financial freedom has been purchased, often at great price.

As a Christian, your debt of sin has been paid in full by the blood of Jesus Christ! Spiritual freedom is yours, purchased at great price.

God's grace leaves only one "debt" outstanding in your life—the debt of gratitude you owe your Redeemer. How should you repay it? As Joseph Parker explains, repay it in units of love.

Worship from the Heart

Love is the characteristic that distinguishes the Christian life. It fulfills the law and covers sin. And where can such a love be found? Only in the person of Jesus Christ. As you draw close to Him in worship today, thank Him that He gives you His love to share with those around you.

Walk with Joseph Parker

"Owe no man anything but love. Love is a debt you can never discharge. When you have paid it, you have only acknowledged it; when you have strained yourself to love some other human creatures, you have only begun to realize the meaning of the divine sovereignty.

"He that loves not, knows not God, for God is love. And His love is not a little surface rain that sprinkles the leaves and stems of things, but a plentiful baptism of the heart that goes down to springs and roots, filling, reviving, and blessing all.

"Nor must this be regarded as mere sentiment. Mere sentiment is never found in the gospel of Christ. A religion founded on a cross soon puts an end to all mere sentiment. It is the cross that determines the quality of all that follows."

Walk Closer to God

Through His love God made it possible for the sin debt to be retired forever! Clearly, human effort can never repay such love. Yet, those who have been freed from sin can express gratitude in loving actions and attitudes.

The early Christians celebrated by spreading the news of God's grace. More significant than burning a mortgage marked "Paid in Full," they burned with desire to tell others of their freedom.

They owed everything to the One who owed them nothing. Do you owe any less?

Walk Thru the Word

New Testament Reading
Romans 13:8-14
Old Testament Reading
Proverbs 15:17

194

For this very reason, Christ died and returned to life so that he might be the Lord of both the dead and the living . . . So then, each of us will give an account of himself to God (Romans 14:9, 12).

Under the scrutiny of the Lord

Aspiring politicians dread the thought of skeletons in the closet coming to light. But even the most anonymous John or Jane Doe will one day stand before the light of God's judgment. And then, no secrets will be safe.

"Everything is uncovered and laid bare before the eyes of him to whom we must give account" (Hebrews 4:13). The God who knows even the thoughts and intentions of the heart will one day judge all.

Donald Barnhouse advises the Christian how to live in the light of that knowledge.

Walk with Donald Barnhouse

"We must understand that 'whatever a man sows' must be taken in its widest meaning, and that every thought and intent of the heart will come under the scrutiny of our Lord at His coming.

"We can be sure that at the judgment seat of Christ there will be a marked difference between the Christian who has lived his life before the Lord, clearly discerning what was for the glory of God, and another Christian who was saved in a rescue mission at the tag end of a depraved and vicious life, or a nominal Christian saved on his deathbed after a life of self-pride, self-righteousness, self-love, and self-sufficiency.

"All will be in heaven, but the differences will be eternal. The consequences of our character will survive the grave and that we shall face those consequences at the judgment seat of Christ."

Walk Closer to God

Although the penalty of sin is removed for the Christian, the consequences of sin continue to operate in a fallen world. Murder always means the loss of life; adultery, the destruction of a home; lying, the loss of integrity—for Christian and non-Christian alike.

This is ample reason to keep on your toes and stay on your knees in your walk with the Lord.

Worship from the Heart

Meditate on the great truth of Romans 14:17. Ask God to reveal any areas in which you have become intolerant or judgmental. Open the eyes of your heart to see your fellow believers through the eyes of the Spirit.

Walk Thru the Word

New Testament Reading
Romans 14:1-12
Old Testament Reading
Jeremiah 17:10-11

*D*aily delighting in our Savior

For the kingdom of God is not a matter of eating and drinking, but of righteousness, peace and joy in the Holy Spirit (Romans 14:17).

*W*hich would be easier to housebreak: a mechanical dog or the real thing?

If the expectation of the right conduct is your only reason for owning a pet, then the mechanical dog is your logical choice.

But if you'd like an affectionate lick and the wag of a happy tail, the flesh-and-blood dog is for you.

The mechanical dog can provide *obedience,* but not *affection.* And therein lies a parable. For the Christian's relationship to his Master holds the potential to be more than mechanical obedience. Andrew Murray explains.

*W*orship from the Heart

"Heavenly Father, may I daily delight You with a love-driven obedience to Your Word. Help me to say 'I love You' with my life. I ask this in the sweet name of my Beloved. Amen."

Walk with Andrew Murray

"The deep significance of joy in the Christian life is often regarded as something secondary, whereas its presence is essential—the proof that God does indeed satisfy us.

"In our domestic life we do not feel satisfied if only the correct behavior is observed and each does his duty to the other. True love makes us happy in each other; as love gives out its warmth of affection, gladness is the sunshine that fills the home with its brightness.

"Even in poverty, the members of a loving family are a joy to each other. Without this gladness, especially, there is no true obedience on the part of the children. It is not the mere fulfillment of a command, or performance of a service, that a parent looks to; it is the willing, joyful, prompt response."

Walk Closer to God

A general orders his troops to march cross-country with little rest. The soldiers obey his command, grumbling every step of the way. But when the general gets out of his jeep and begins to walk with his troops, the mood lightens. The reason? The general has established a relationship with his soldiers that goes beyond the verbal commands and their visible compliance.

Do you enjoy a relationship like that with your heavenly Leader?

*W*alk Thru the Word

New Testament Reading
Romans 14:13-23
Old Testament Reading
Isaiah 61:10-11

May the God of hope fill you with all joy and peace as you trust in him (Romans 15:13).

*N*ever has the search for world peace been more vigorous than in the 20th century. But political peace is illusive and fragile. However, there is a spiritual peace that "passes all understanding"— peace that comes from knowing and loving God.

The peace treaty between God and humanity was sealed by Jesus Christ. Martin Luther explains what that peace means in your daily life.

Walk with Martin Luther

"Those who rejoice in God are satisfied with their peace in Him. They bravely endure tribulation and do not desire the peace which reason calls for: removal of the evil. They stand firm and await internal strength through faith.

"Neither do they think and worry what the end will be but always place that matter in the hands of God. They are not fretting to know when, how, or where their trouble will be ended. This is why God, in turn, grants them grace and prepares for an end for their evil—an end which shows benefits so great as to exceed all expectations and desires.

"Behold, this is the peace of the Cross, the peace of God, the peace of conscience, Christian peace.

"Reason cannot comprehend how we can have peace in the midst of strife. Nor can reason accomplish this. It is a work of God that is known only to the person who has experienced it."

Walk Closer to God

In a day when fortifications are built and forces are rushed in to "keep the peace," the peace that is found in Christ operates by entirely different means.

"For [Christ] himself is our peace, who has made the two one and has destroyed the barrier, the dividing wall of hostility. . . . His purpose was to create in himself one new man out of the two, thus making peace. . . . He came and preached peace to you who were far away and peace to those who were near" (Ephesians 2:14-15, 17).

Isn't it about time your world learned what peace is all about?

*F*inding peace in the midst of strife

*W*orship from the Heart

Many people experience futility, despair, and hopelessness in their daily lives. They have no joy. But there is a door out of emptiness, and that door is Jesus Christ. Fly through that door into the open arms of the Father, who is waiting to receive you. In His embrace you will find the place of salvation —and of peace.

*W*alk Thru the Word

New Testament Reading
Romans 15:1-13
Old Testament Reading
Psalm 85:8-13

Life with an exclamation point

Therefore I glory in Christ Jesus in my service to God (Romans 15:17).

For some people, the mere mention of the word Christian conjures up images of straight-laced, somber figures.

After reading Romans, you may disagree with that image of the Christian life. As W. H. Griffith Thomas describes, the abundant life is the proper focus for the Christian.

Walk with W. H. Griffith Thomas

"A Christian on his deathbed spoke these words: 'I shall be satisfied if I can but creep into heaven on my hands and knees.' We can easily understand the spirit which prompted those words; he felt his service was as nothing compared with his need for God's mercy. At the same time there is another sense in which the words are not rightly applicable to the Christian, for Peter speaks of our having an abundant entrance given us in the everlasting kingdom (2 Peter 1:11).

"In keeping with this, Paul constantly emphasized the Christian life with words such as *wealth, riches, abundance,* and he prayed that Christians might be 'filled to the measure of all the fullness of God' (Ephesians 3:19).

"He was not satisfied with a bare entrance into heaven. Paul's desire was that both he and his converts would have the fullest possible Christian life here below, and then enter fully into the joy of the Lord above. This is the true Christian life—the life of fullness, power, depth, and reality."

Walk Closer to God

As you continue to read the New Testament, keep both eyes open and alert for words Griffith Thomas lists above:

- "the incomparable riches of his grace" (Ephesians 2:7)
- "overflowing joy" (2 Corinthians 8:2)
- "the fullness of him who fills everything" (Ephesians 1:23)

Your salvation in Jesus Christ brings you wealth the world could never imagine.

Worship from the Heart

Praise God that the Christian life is punctuated with an exclamation point and not a question mark. We can delete "wincing" and "groveling" from our vocabularies. Consider the words David uttered in hiding as Saul sought to hunt him down: "Taste and see that the Lord is good; blessed is the man who takes refuge in him" (Psalm 34:8).

Walk Thru the Word

New Testament Reading
Romans 15:14-33
Old Testament Reading
Exodus 34:5-8

I want you to be wise about what is good, and innocent about what is evil (Romans 16:19).

A clear sense of God's ideal

*W*ithout a clear sense of purpose, it's difficult to know which direction to turn when confronted with a choice. And without a clear sense of God's purpose for *your* life, you'll never understand the pressures He uses to shape you into the likeness of Jesus Christ.

"For those God foreknew he also predestined to be conformed to the likeness of his Son" (Romans 8:29). Donald Barnhouse challenges you to think through your goals as a disciple of Jesus Christ.

Walk with Donald Barnhouse

"God will begin with you as you are at this moment. What is your ideal? Consider this carefully. Think of what you would really like to be.

"If God would give you the tools to make yourself into the ideal person, in what direction would you go? If you think deeply enough, you will discover that all you have thought about in your concept of the ideal has been fulfilled in Jesus Christ.

"Now after you have drawn your picture of what is good, what is ideal, what is Christlike, then draw another picture of what you are in yourself.

"How far have you grown? What level have you reached in spiritual development? What victories have you won? From what evils have you turned away? What good have you achieved?

"When you have made a frank measure of yourself, then compare what you are with what you previously set forth as your ideal. The difference between what you are and what you desire to be is the measure of your present opportunity."

Walk Closer to God

"Holy Father, You have taken me from a pit of miry clay, and set my feet upon a Rock. May I never be satisfied until my entire life radiates the reality of that new position of privilege and power.

"You have set before me the goal of Christlikeness; help me to set aside pursuits and guard against detours that would sidetrack me from achieving Your purpose for my life. In the name of the One whose life is my ideal. Amen."

*W*orship from the Heart

Daniel set his heart on keeping himself pure before the Lord and obeying His commands. Though he probably never imagined the far-reaching results, his testimony influenced an entire nation. As you complete your reading of Romans, let 12:1-2 challenge you anew to make the same commitment Daniel did.

*W*alk Thru the Word

New Testament Reading
Romans 16
Old Testament Reading
Daniel 1:8-21

*C*hristian Living at the Practical Level

*P*aul's two letters to the Corinthians deal with growing pains in the Christian life.

*A*ll roads lead to Rome." If that saying was true in Paul's day, then it was equally true that most of those roads led through Corinth. A crossroads of commerce and trade, Corinth was a prosperous, bustling city whose influence—both good and bad—stretched far beyond the city limits. It became a key center for the ministry of the apostle Paul. Chased out of Thessalonica and Berea by Jewish troublemakers and confronted by indifference in Athens, Paul probably arrived in Corinth in low spirits. There he stayed for the next eighteen months, preaching the good news in a city like Corinth!

Paul's two letters to the Corinthians deal with growing pains in the Christian life. Living in the center of a corrupt society, the Corinthian church had mighty potential . . . and many problems. Paul's first letter responds to questions raised by the Corinthians on a variety of topics, both personal and corporate. He expresses concern over divisions and factions, immorality, abuse of Christian liberty, misunderstandings about the resurrection, disorderly church worship, and improper use of spiritual gifts.

In his second letter, the apostle opens his heart to show his fatherly concern for those who have come to Christ through his ministry. It resembles a miniature autobiography in which he sets forth his calling, credentials, message, and struggles on behalf of the Corinthian believers. He seeks to silence any who question his motives and his authority as an apostle of Christ.

From time to time you may find that Paul's words produce an uncomfortable "pinching" sensation in your Christian life. That's God's way of showing you where you need to grow in Him or where you need to work on your relationships with others. With the guidance of God's Word and the insight of godly people, you can do just that this month. So take a trip to Corinth. With the influence of the Scriptures and through the Spirit, you'll come back a changed person.

Freely you have received, freely give

God, who has called you into fellowship with his Son Jesus Christ our Lord, is faithful (1 Corinthians 1:9).

*W*hen toddlers play together, territorial disputes are inevitable. Youngsters jealously—even savagely—guard the "right of private property."

In Corinth Paul confronted a church filled with spiritual toddlers who protected their own interests and lacked a true understanding of what biblical fellowship is all about.

G. Campbell Morgan offers this insightful look at what Christians share in common.

Walk with G. Campbell Morgan

"This word *fellowship* is rich in connotations. The simple idea is that of having all things in common. It is the word that marks the most perfect realization of unity in every way—in possessions, in purpose, and in effort.

"Those who are in fellowship have resources and responsibilities in common. Here, then, is the truth about the relationship existing between all Christian souls and the Lord. All His resources are at their disposal; all their resources are at His disposal. They are committed to His responsibilities; He is committed to their responsibilities. That covers the whole fact of Christian life and service.

"If there is any failure in this relationship of resource and responsibility, it is in us, and not in Him. Are all our resources at His disposal? Are we availing ourselves of His resources? Are we facing His responsibilities? Are we trusting Him to undertake our responsibilities?"

Walk Closer to God

Childish squabbles are easily resolved—*if* both sides compromise. But the impasse between holy God and sinful man was not solved by compromise. It was only bridged when God's Son endured the humiliation and horror of the cross.

God "shared" His Son with selfish men and women that they might learn to freely give away the new life they had received. Don't be stingy with your Savior; share Him with others—as only grown-up children in Christ can!

Worship from the Heart

"No one is indispensable." Paul is reminding the church of this truism. When a beloved and influential spiritual leader leaves a church—or, worse, reveals a serious moral failing—the members grieve, and rightly so. But we have One who will never leave us or fail us. Rejoice in Him today.

Walk Thru the Word

New Testament Reading
1 Corinthians 1
Old Testament Reading
Malachi 3:16

Not for eyes or ears

"No eye has seen, no ear has heard, no mind has conceived what God has prepared for those who love him" (1 Corinthians 2:9).

*J*udas went and hanged himself."
"Go and do likewise."
"What you do, do quickly."
If you flip through your Bible randomly, you might discover a series of passages just as bizarre as these.

The Bible has been used—and abused—for many purposes. People with their own ideas of truth have often tried to gain support for their views by appealing to Scripture. Instead of seeking the one true God, they have sought to justify their own self-serving notions. Martin Luther explains the problem of such a self-centered approach.

Walk with Martin Luther

"They are truly very odious folk who try first to devise something that agrees with reason and then try to confirm it with passages from Scripture.

"The articles of faith are, in truth, statements about things that no eye has seen, that no ear has heard, and that have not entered into the heart of man; they are learned and understood only through the Word and the Holy Spirit.

"This is the nature of all the articles of faith, that reason always abhors them. For they cannot be understood without the Holy Spirit; they are the depths of wisdom divine, in which reason is entirely submerged.

"Therefore he who would be a Christian must ignore his reason and hear only what God says, must give himself captive to God and say: 'Although the things I hear are incomprehensible and incredible to me, yet, because God has spoken them, I do believe them.' "

Walk Closer to God

More than 1,500 years ago, Augustine said, "I believe, in order that I may understand."

Eyes and ears may uncover many of earth's mysteries, but only the Word of God can lead to a knowledge of the mysteries of God.

Search the Scriptures, for therein is Life itself.

Worship from the Heart

Men have not heard nor has the eye seen the true majesty and unfathomable power of our God. Until the end of time we shall see His glory through His creation, His Word, and His Son. Are you gazing daily on His glory?

Walk Thru the Word

New Testament Reading
1 Corinthians 2
Old Testament Reading
Isaiah 64:1-4

Being built into God's foundation

Each one should be careful how he builds. For no one can lay any foundation other than the one already laid, which is Jesus Christ (1 Corinthians 3:10-11).

The innovative cooling system of the new building was the talk of the town. There was just one problem: the builder hadn't figured out a way to keep his creation—made completely out of ice cubes—from melting in the warm Florida sun!

Innovative, but totally impractical is also an apt description of Christians who try to build a solid life of godliness with the flimsiest of materials.

The gold of godliness . . . the silver of sanctification . . . the precious stones of practical obedience—F. B. Meyer elaborates on the proper construction of the Christian life.

Walk with F. B. Meyer

"We are all builders, whether we choose to be or not! Each heart, each life, each character, can become a temple of the Holy Spirit.

"Every act we do, every word we utter, the way we spend any moment of time, is either a fragment of gold, silver, and precious stones, or of wood, hay, and stubble, built into the structure of the edifice entrusted to our skill and pains.

"It does not so much matter *what* we do, but *how* we do it. Every time we perform any action with the best motives and spirit, we deposit a tiny grain of gold dust; whenever we do something in a careless manner, we weave into the structure a material that will inevitably show itself as wood, hay, and stubble before a flame.

"We shall not be saved by our works. The only thing that can secure salvation is being built into God's foundation, the Rock Jesus Christ. But we shall be rewarded according to the manner in which we have built upon that foundation."

Walk Closer to God

What if you had to pass a building inspection? Would the foundation you are building upon and the materials you are building with satisfy the Architect and Finisher of your faith?

That's a question you won't want to postpone until Inspection Day!

Worship from the Heart

"Father, the world around me puts so much emphasis on the end product. Keep me aware that in my walk with You, it is the process—the walk itself—that matters. Allow me to relax in the knowledge that the end product will be beautiful, because You will have shaped it."

Walk Thru the Word

New Testament Reading
1 Corinthians 3
Old Testament Reading
Isaiah 28:16-17

203

Star without equal

For who makes you different from anyone else? What do you have that you did not receive? (1 Corinthians 4:7).

*H*e can do it all!"

Those words usually mean one of two things: (1) That individual is a jack-of-all-trades, capable of doing everything, or (2) No one else is willing to help, so he will have to do everything!

Both attitudes are extreme, and neither is appropriate in the church of Jesus Christ. All the members of Christ's body have been given spiritual gifts that when exercised serve to develop a healthy church. John Calvin explains that when "shared ministry" is absent, imbalance results.

Walk with John Calvin

"The Lord has appointed order in His church— that the members of Christ's body may be united together, and that each one may be satisfied with his own place, his own office, and his own honor.

"If one member desires to leap over into the place of another, what will become of the entire body? Let us know, then, that the Lord has so placed us in the church that, being under one Head, we may be mutually helpful to each other.

"We have been given diverse gifts so that we may serve the Lord with modesty and humility and promote *His* glory. This is the best remedy for correcting the ambition of those who desire distinction—to call them back to God, so that they might acknowledge that it was not according to anyone's pleasure that they were placed in a high or low station, but by God alone.

"God does not confer so much upon anyone as to elevate him to the place of the Head, but distributes His gifts in such a manner that He alone is glorified in all things."

Walk Closer to God

Janitors, judges, and just ordinary people— Jesus is Lord of all. The ground is truly level at the cross.

Self-interest has no place in a community gathered to serve the Savior of the universe. The world may spend vast amounts of time and money catering to celebrities. But the church has only one Superstar—and He will never lose His brilliance.

Worship from the Heart

The great medieval cathedrals, with their soaring designs, their glorious stained glass, and intricate carvings, were created by artists who deliberately remained anonymous. They worked for the glory of the Creator who had given them their talents. Praise God for the talents He has given you and purpose to use them for His glory today.

Walk Thru the Word

New Testament Reading
1 Corinthians 4
Old Testament Reading
Deuteronomy 8:11-20

A truly unleavened lump

Don't you know that a little yeast works through the whole batch of dough? Get rid of the old yeast that you may be a new batch without yeast—as you really are (1 Corinthians 5:6-7).

*T*he Corinthian church was suffering from a serious condition . . . and didn't realize it.

Moral laxness, like yeast in a batch of dough, was threatening to permeate the entire assembly—a radical condition calling for an equally radical solution, as G. Campbell Morgan explains.

Walk with G. Campbell Morgan

"The whole body of Christ is affected by the sin of one member.

"The church's life is weaker if one in the fellowship continues in sin. The church's testimony to those outside is weakened by that fact.

"Thus, we have no right to refuse to exercise the discipline of love in the case of anyone who, to our knowledge, has flagrantly sinned.

"The law which the apostle states here is that the leaven [yeast] is to be purged. Leaven communicates itself, spreads its own corrupting force wherever it goes.

"A little leaven—one man sinning and permitted to remain within the fellowship of the church—will spread, first unconsciously and insidiously, but most surely throughout the whole church.

"There is no more difficult or delicate thing awaiting us in our church fellowship than the matter of discipline.

"May God give us of His Spirit that we may dare to deal with sin and refuse to give it harbor or refuge within our fellowship."

Walk Closer to God

Surgery is never pleasant.

But when the choice is between difficult, delicate discipline and a body whose strength is sapped by sin, which course would you choose?

Better yet, don't wait until surgery is called for. Deal with sin promptly . . . personally . . . biblically (Matthew 18:15-17). Confession and repentance are much less painful than surgery for all involved.

*W*orship from the Heart

"Holy Father, teach me to tend the garden of my heart so that no corrupt seed can sprout and no unworthy weed will be there to offend when I stand before You. I praise You today for being the Master Gardener and for pruning the 'dead branches' from my life. Even though it sometimes hurts, I know it is for my good."

*W*alk Thru the Word

New Testament Reading
1 Corinthians 5
Old Testament Reading
Proverbs 4:14-19

In the safe hands of a loving Father

Do you not know that your body is a temple of the Holy Spirit, who is in you, whom you have received from God? You are not your own (1 Corinthians 6:19).

"Y ou're in good hands with . . ."

Such advertising slogans have a comfortable ring to them. After all, who doesn't want to be in good hands—especially when the circumstances of life seem to be out of hand.

But if the hands you put yourself in are human, don't be surprised if they prove unreliable.

By contrast, what if you could take a care or worry out of your own hands and place it into the strong hands of someone who never makes a mistake, never drops the ball? If you are a child of God, you are invited to do precisely that!

A. B. Simpson reflects on the Savior's care.

Walk with A. B. Simpson

"What rest lies hidden in the words, 'Not my own.' I am not burdened by my cares, not obliged to live for my interests, but altogether His; redeemed, owned, saved, loved, kept in the strong, unchanging arms of His everlasting love.

"Oh, the rest from sin, self, and care which true consecration brings! To be able to give Him our poor life, with its awful possibilities and its utter helplessness, and know that He will accept it, and take a joy and pride in making out of it the utmost possibilities of blessing, power, and use-fulness; to give all, and find in so doing we have gained all; to be so yielded to Him in entire self-surrender that He is bound to care for us as for Himself.

"We are putting ourselves in the hands of a lov-ing Father, more solicitous for our good than we can be, and only wanting us to be fully submitted to Him that He may be more free to bless us."

Walk Closer to God

Whose hands are you in? If you are growing weary of trying to hold on to your cares, consider handing them over to the only One strong enough to bear them. He never tires, never loses His grip, never disappoints His precious ones.

Of Him—and Him alone—can be said, "You're in God's hands with the Savior!"

Worship from the Heart

"Your will be done on earth as it is in heaven." Look at your hands the next time you pray those words. If your body is truly a temple of the Holy Spirit, it is your hands that enable God's will to be done on earth. Offer them to Him.

Walk Thru the Word

New Testament Reading
1 Corinthians 6
Old Testament Reading
Numbers 3:11-13

The witness of your walk

How do you know, wife, whether you will save your husband? Or, how do you know, husband, whether you will save your wife? (1 Corinthians 7:16).

It's ironic the number of partners who are married in a church, buried in a church, but in the intervening years when queried about the church, respond, "It's okay for my spouse, but don't expect me to go there."

When only one spouse is a Christian, *tension* rather than *tenderness* often marks the marriage relationship.

How does one go about encouraging an unsaved spouse to make a life commitment to Christ? Albert Barnes offers this perspective.

Walk with Albert Barnes

"It is not by a harsh, fretful, complaining temper; it is by kindness, tenderness, and love. It is by demonstrating the excellency of religion; by patience when provoked, meekness when injured, love when despised, forbearance when words of harshness and irritation are used; by kind and affectionate conversation when alone, when the heart is tender, when calamities visit the family.

"When a husband will not hear, God can hear; when he is angry, morose, or unkind, God is gentle, tender, and kind; and when a husband or wife turns away from the voice, God's ear is open, and God is ready to hear and to bless.

"We are never to cease setting a Christian example; never to cease living as a Christian should live; never to cease praying fervently to the God of grace, that the partner of our lives may be brought under the full influence of Christian truth, and so may enjoy heaven with us."

Walk Closer to God

Beating your beloved with the Bible is not the best way to lead an unsaved spouse to the Lord. The intense desire for the spouse's salvation can provoke a zeal that offends rather than attracts. The challenge is not so much to declare the message as it is to demonstrate the character of Christ.

And remarkable but true, you can do that without saying a word!

Worship from the Heart

In an earnest desire to provide spiritual nurture for families, Christians sometimes forget that God does not call everyone into marriage. Praise God that whether single or married, you have opportunity to glorify Him by your godly life.

Walk Thru the Word

New Testament Reading
1 Corinthians 7
Old Testament Reading
Esther 9:23-28

Someone is looking up to you

When you sin against your brothers in this way and wound their weak conscience, you sin against Christ (1 Corinthians 8:12).

*L*ittle brothers who tag along after big brothers sooner or later find themselves in trouble. They are simply too small, too slow, too weak, or too immature to keep up. The result? A frustrated, disheartened "younger set."

The family of God is no different. Old and young, babe in Christ and "spiritual man"—all must live together in the household of faith.

Charles Hodge examines how big brothers in Christ need to watch out for their little brothers.

Worship from the Heart

Meditate on the sweet words of this hymn: "I would be true, for there are those who trust me; / I would be pure, for there are those who care; / I would be humble, for I know my weakness; / I would be brave, for there is much to dare."

Walk with Charles Hodge

"We sin against our brother when we wound his weak conscience. When we bring on him a wrong sense of guilt, we inflict the greatest evil in our power, because a sense of guilt alienates us from God and brings us under the power of Satan. He who thus sins against his brother, sins against Christ.

"An injury done to a child is an injury to the parent because parent and child are so united that the injury of the one is the injury of the other.

"So also it is a manifestation of lack of love for Christ, an insult and injury to Him, to injure His people. He and they are so united that whatever of good or evil is done to them is done also to Him.

"If we believed this, we would be careful not to wound our fellow Christians, and would feel it an honor to relieve their wants."

Walk Closer to God

What is it that makes big brothers get involved in the lives of little brothers whose immaturity might otherwise label them as nuisances?

Family love—the link that prompts us to respond, "He's not heavy; he's my brother."

Tempering your liberty in the Lord for the sake of a young brother in the Lord works the same way. What outsiders might call a sacrifice is nothing more than acting as a responsible, loving family member.

Say, brother, how's it going?

Walk Thru the Word

New Testament Reading
1 Corinthians 8
Old Testament Reading
Malachi 2:1-9

I have become all things to all men so that by all possible means I might save some. I do all this for the sake of the gospel (1 Corinthians 9:22-23).

*W*ould you ever volunteer for a job where occupational hazards include imprisonment, beatings, shipwreck, poverty, and death? Of course you would! It's called being a disciple, and the living illustration of its costly demands can be seen in the life of Paul.

Paul was ever prepared to preach the Good News—and ever ready for the painful consequences of being faithful to his calling. Oswald Chambers explores the requirements of the job.

Walk with Oswald Chambers

"Paul's whole heart and mind and soul were taken up with the great matter of what Jesus Christ came to do; Paul never lost sight of that one thing.

"We have to face ourselves with the one central fact—Jesus Christ and Him crucified.

" 'I have chosen you.' It is not that you have got God but that He has got you. He is at work, bending, breaking, molding, doing just as He chooses. Why He is doing it, we do not know; He is doing it for one purpose only—that He may be able to say, 'This is My man, My woman.'

"When God has put His call on you, woe be to you if you turn to the right hand or to the left. He will do with you what He never did with you before the call came; He will do with you what He is not doing with other people. Let Him have His way."

Walk Closer to God

"Ready to go, ready to stay"—those words summarize Paul's attitude toward the call of God upon his life.

Ready to go to Asia and Bithynia . . . and willing to alter plans if God directs instead to Macedonia.

Ready to start churches in Thessalonica, Philippi, Berea, and Corinth . . . and willing to stay in jail while others nurtured those churches into fruitful congregations.

Ready to follow where the Master leads. Can that be said of you?

*W*ithout knowing what lies ahead

*W*orship from the Heart

Paul as a young man must have planned his future, but he could not have foreseen his real vocation. Mary did not plan to be Jesus' mother. Peter thought he would spend his life catching fish. Keep your spiritual eyes and ears open. Our God is a God of wonderful surprises!

*W*alk Thru the Word

New Testament Reading
1 Corinthians 9
Old Testament Reading
Ruth 1:6-18

Showing delicate shades of Christian love

"Everything is permissible"—but not everything is beneficial. "Everything is permissible"—but not everything is constructive (1 Corinthians 10:23).

Worship from the Heart

Jeremiah 32:38-41 reveals God's power to change insensitive and inflexible human hearts into hearts that have a passion for Him and for His laws. Celebrate the freedom that you have in Christ to keep God's laws, not out of duty, but out of love.

*W*hich driver would you choose to transport your infant son or daughter across a lofty mountain range? (a) The one who boasts of how fast he can drive and how close to the edge he can steer, or (b) The one who stays as far away from the edge as possible, even if it means driving more slowly?

Out of love, you would choose the second driver. And if baby believers mean anything to you, you'll steer clear of the world and not try to see how close to the edge *you* can come.

A. B. Simpson elaborates on the Christian view of defensive driving.

Walk with A. B. Simpson

"I may be free to do many things, the doing of which might wound my brother's conscience, and love will gladly surrender the little indulgence so that she may save her brother from temptation.

"There are many forms of recreation which in themselves might be harmless, but they have become associated with worldliness and godlessness and have proved to be snares to many a young heart. The law of love leads me to avoid them and in no way encourage others to participate in them.

"It is in these activities that are not required of us by absolute rules, but are the impulses of a thoughtful love, that the highest qualities of Christian character show themselves, and the most delicate shades of Christian love are manifested."

Walk Closer to God

You cannot cultivate a close walk with God by doing a tightrope walk with the world.

You cannot follow the law of love by ignoring the impulse of love and thereby lead others into temptation through your use of liberty.

In the Christian life, playing fast and loose with questionable activities may seem exhilarating—for a time. But rest assured that when God says in His Word to "watch your step," a genuine danger exists . . . and it's a long way to the bottom for you and for those who might follow your example.

Walk Thru the Word

New Testament Reading
1 Corinthians 10:1–11:1
Old Testament Reading
Jeremiah 32:38-41

Celebrate His death till He comes

For whenever you eat this bread and drink this cup, you proclaim the Lord's death until he comes (1 Corinthians 11:26).

Try answering a few questions about the Lord's Supper as described in 1 Corinthians 11:
1. What do the bread and the cup represent?
2. How often should the church celebrate communion?
3. What event does communion look back on?
4. What does it look ahead to?
Johann Peter Lange provides a quick refresher on this meaningful part of church life.

Walk with Johann Peter Lange

"The Lord's Supper is a memorial to our Lord's death. The bread signifies the body that was broken on our behalf; the wine calls to mind the blood that was shed for the forgiveness of our sins and by which the covenant that ensures to us eternal life was sealed.

"But while it is a memorial, the Lord's Supper is at the same time a feast to the soul. Our Lord therein presents Himself to the church as the true bread from heaven which gives life unto the world, and by means of which we are to eat His flesh and drink His blood, so that He shall dwell in us and we in Him.

"It is, moreover, a proclamation of our Lord's death, a significant exhibition to the world of what He has done, and is still ready to do, in behalf of all believing sinners. In celebrating it the church sends forth its invitation to the world bidding everyone who hungers and thirsts to come and eat without money and without price.

"It is a pledge of the Lord's return. As it points backward to His death, so does it also point forward to that marriage supper where He, the returning Bridegroom, will entertain His bride clothed in white array."

Walk Closer to God

The next time you take the bread and the cup, ponder the price that Christ paid to enable you to eat that most significant supper "in remembrance of Him." Celebrate His life, remember His death, look forward to His return!

Worship from the Heart

Your church probably has never been the scene of the kind of behavior Paul describes at communion services held in Corinth. But your church manners may need attention. For the honor of the Lord you worship, reach out to newcomers and visitors and do all you can to make your worship service true worship.

Walk Thru the Word

New Testament Reading
1 Corinthians 11:2-34
Old Testament Reading
Exodus 12:21-27

The free flow of God's Spirit

There are different kinds of gifts, but the same Spirit. Now to each one the manifestation of the Spirit is given for the common good (1 Corinthians 12:4, 7).

A football team has a diversity of talented players, all united in the common purpose of beating the opposition. A company has a diversity of employees, united to reach maximum profitability and productivity for the company.

Diverse . . . yet united. That's a picture of the church of Jesus Christ as well. Spirit-gifted men and women, with differing functions, responsibilities, and roles, united in the task of glorifying God.

But it doesn't happen by accident, and Alexander Maclaren will show you how to do it.

Walk with Alexander Maclaren

"I have said that the only condition of possessing the fullness of God's Spirit is faith in Jesus Christ.

"It is the old story—the miraculous flow of the oil stopped when the widow had no more pots and vessels to bring. The reason why some of us experience so little of that divine Spirit is because we have not held out our vessels to be filled.

"You can diminish the flow by ignoring it, by neglecting to use the little that you have for the purpose for which it was given.

"The manifestation of the power of the Spirit is given to you. If you shut it up and never do an atom of good with it, either to yourself or to anybody else, you will one day find that your vessels are empty."

Walk Closer to God

A concert pianist once remarked, "If I fail to practice for one day, I can tell. If I skip two days, my family can tell. If I miss three days, my friends can tell. More than that, and everybody can tell."

Like the dedicated pianist, the Christian needs to "practice the presence of the Spirit" every day—appropriating the power of God, cultivating spiritual gifts from God, being equipped for service in the church of God.

And the goal of it all? "The common good" of the family of God. Who is profiting from *your* spiritual life today?

Worship from the Heart

Just as each part of the physical body serves in its own way, so each member of Christ's body, the church, has a unique service to offer. Rejoice today in the people and gifts God has placed in the church. Thank Him for the many ways they enrich your life and your worship.

Walk Thru the Word

New Testament Reading
1 Corinthians 12:1-31a
Old Testament Reading
Nehemiah 3

If I give all I possess to the poor . . . but have not love, I gain nothing (1 Corinthians 13:3).

*T*he root and spring of all virtue

C ompassion.
Compulsion.

Only two letters separate these words in the dictionary, but they are miles apart in meaning.

Compassion is motivated by love, compulsion by fear. Compassion is others-oriented; compulsion focuses on I, me, and mine. Both may result in an apparent good deed, but only one is the genuine item as set forth in God's love chapter, 1 Corinthians 13.

Jonathan Edwards expands on the kind of compassion which only godlike love can produce.

Walk with Jonathan Edwards

"Love will dispose people to all acts of mercy toward their neighbors when they are under any affliction, for we are naturally disposed to pity those that we love when they are afflicted.

"It will dispose individuals to give to the poor and to bear one another's burdens. It will dispose a people toward the duties they owe to their rulers. And it will dispose rulers to rule their people justly, seeking their subjects' good and not their own personal gain.

"Love will dispose children to honor their parents, servants to be obedient to their masters, and masters to exercise gentleness and goodness toward their servants.

"Thus love would dispose to all duties both toward God, and toward mankind. And if it will thus dispose to all duties, then it follows that it is the root and spring of all virtues. It is a principle, which if it be implanted in the heart, is alone sufficient to produce all good practice."

Walk Closer to God

"Father, my obedience to You does not always spring from the purest of motives. Purify my heart, Lord, and reveal any hardness. Make me long to serve You and my fellow man, not simply because it is a command, but because I long to cultivate Christlike love. In the name of Jesus, who demonstrated heavenly compassion on my behalf. Amen."

Worship from the Heart

The love Paul describes here is beyond purely human capability. But look at the cross: "See from His head, His hands, His feet, / Sorrow and love flow mingled down." This is Christ's love for you. Open your heart to receive it with thanksgiving and joy.

Walk Thru the Word

New Testament Reading
*1 Corinthians
12:31b–13:13*
Old Testament Reading
Numbers 14:11-19

Putting away childish things

Brothers, stop thinking like children. In regard to evil be infants, but in your thinking be adults (1 Corinthians 14:20).

*D*olls and toys are the playthings of the young, and rightly so. But if those same toys are still the focus of the child's life ten years later, there's genuine reason for concern.

The same is true of the "growing up" process in God's family. Childish patterns of thinking and behavior give way to full-grown understanding and discernment. Jonathan Edwards examines the problem of immaturity in the Corinthian church.

Walk with Jonathan Edwards

"Do not behave like little children. They admire and are astonished at what is novel. They are pleased with anything that will amuse them.

"It is sometimes well to appeal to Christians in this manner, and to show them that what they are engaged in is unfit to occupy their attention.

"Much, alas, very much of that which engages the attention of Christians is just as unworthy of the dignity of the mind as were the aims and desires which Paul rebuked among the Christians at Corinth.

"Much that pertains to dress, to accomplishment, to living, to employment, to amusement, to conversation, will appear, when we come to die, to have been like the playthings of children. We shall feel that time has been wasted and strength exhausted by that which was foolish and childish."

Walk Closer to God

As a child grows, play gives way to the real world of adulthood. Toy guns are replaced by the issues of war and peace; dolls and dollhouses are transformed into the challenges of marriage and parenting.

Maturity thus becomes a measure of one's ability to forsake the childish and embrace the "grown-up" in attitudes and actions. Our generation has been described as one that "worships its work, works at its play, and plays at its worship." Christian, if you are to become an exception to the status quo, how will you approach your responsibilities in the household of faith?

Worship from the Heart

On Resurrection Day Christ burst from the tomb, evidence that His sacrifice for sin had been accepted and God's justice was satisfied. Greet this day with the ancient cry of triumph: "The Lord is risen!"

Walk Thru the Word

New Testament Reading
1 Corinthians 14:1-25
Old Testament Reading
Proverbs 2:1-9

For God is not a God of disorder but of peace
(1 Corinthians 14:33).

*T*he pastor was leading a group of young children from his church in a spelling bee. "All
right," he turned to the next child, "your word to
spell is worship."

"Warship. W-A-R-S-H-I-P. Warship. Am I
right?" the child asked. With a deep sigh, the
pastor replied, "Yes, unfortunately, much of the
time you are!"

In the Corinthian church, confusion and strife
were marking the worship services. John Calvin
points to the importance of peace and order as
priorities in corporate worship.

Walk with John Calvin

"We do not serve God unless we are in any
case lovers of peace and are eager to promote it.
Whenever there is a disposition to quarrel, there
you can be certain God does not reign.

"Yet many people fly into a rage about nothing, or they trouble the church from a desire that
they may somehow ride into view and seem to
be someone.

"Let us therefore bear in mind that, as servants
of Christ, this mark must be kept in view—to aim
at peace and concord, conduct ourselves peace-
ably, and avoid contentions to the utmost of our
power.

"For if we are called to contend against wicked
doctrines, we must persevere in the contest. We
must make it our aim that the truth of God may
maintain its ground without contention."

Walk Closer to God

Interruptions and distractions, disorder and
discord—it's not a pretty scene under any circumstances but it's particularly inappropriate in
the family of God.

Why? Because God has called His people to
worship Him in a way that draws attention to the
object of worship, not the worshipers themselves.
Worship that is in spirit . . . in truth . . . in peace
. . . in order.

As John Calvin has commented, "How easy it
is to say this!" But what will you do about it?

*P*eace: A priority for worship

*W*orship from the Heart

*"Heavenly Father,
peaceful relationships
with others begin
with a pleasing rela-
tionship with You.
Please keep me from
wandering off the
path of righteousness
and into the jungle of
strife. In the name of
the One who is the
Author of Peace.
Amen."*

*W*alk Thru the Word

New Testament Reading
1 Corinthians 14:26-40
Old Testament Reading
Proverbs 16:7

The wonder of victory

For what I received I passed on to you as of first importance: that Christ died for our sins according to the Scriptures (1 Corinthians 15:3).

The power of death is all too frequently and painfully demonstrated. Every day brings the passing of relatives . . . friends . . . acquaintances.

Only Jesus Christ has ever demonstrated power over death. And that one demonstration has proved a source of power and comfort ever since.

Without Christ's victory over death, all the rest of His words and works on your behalf cannot accomplish salvation.

How well do you understand the significance of the Resurrection? Allow Andrew Murray to offer his keen insight.

Walk with Andrew Murray

"Let us take this one thought, this one aim, this one joy home to our hearts: Christ lived and died and reigns; I live and die and in His power I shall reign; only for this one thing, 'that God may be all in all.' Let it possess our whole heart and life.

"How can we do this? I wish to give a simple answer. Foremost of all: Allow God to take His place in your heart and life. As Luther often said, 'Do let God be God.'

"Give God His place. And what is that place? 'That God may be all in all.' Let God be all in all every day, from morning to evening. God to rule and I to obey. Ah, the blessedness of saying, 'God and me!' What a privilege that I have such a partner! God first, and then me!"

Walk Closer to God

When the Son of God confronted the ultimate enemy—death—who won? " 'Death has been swallowed up in victory.' 'Where, O death, is your victory? Where, O death, is your sting?' The sting of death is sin, and the power of sin is the law. But thanks be to God! He gives us the victory through our Lord Jesus Christ" (1 Corinthians 15:54-57).

Paul could not exhaust the wonder of that victory in fifty-eight verses! Think of it, resurrection power is available to you as a spoil of the victory which Jesus won over sin and death.

Worship from the Heart

It is a natural thing to grieve when someone you love dies. Tears are a God-given release for pain. They are a gift from Him. But Christian realism requires you to recognize that you weep for yourself, not for your loved one. Those who die in the Lord have never been better off!

Walk Thru the Word

New Testament Reading
1 Corinthians 15:1-34
Old Testament Reading
Habukkuk 3:16-19

But thanks be to God! He gives us the victory through our Lord Jesus Christ (1 Corinthians 15:57).

For more than 200 years, America has celebrated her national birthday. Similar times of national festivity dot the calendars of nations around the world.

For the church, Easter Sunday is a victory celebration of infinitely greater proportions. On that day, Jesus' resurrection won the victory over sin and death—Independence Day for captive sinners.

An anonymous Latin author has provided these stirring words to help celebrate the greatest victory of all time.

Walk with an Anonymous Poet
The strife is o'er, the battle done;
The victory of life is won;
The song of triumph has begun. Alleluia!

The powers of death have done their worst,
But Christ their legions hath dispersed:
Let shouts of holy joy outburst. Alleluia!

The three sad days have quickly sped;
He rises glorious from the dead:
All glory to our risen Head! Alleluia!

He closed the yawning gates of hell;
The bars from heaven's high portals fell;
Let hymns of praise His triumphs tell. Alleluia!

Lord, by the stripes which wounded Thee,
From death's dread sting Thy servants free,
That we may live and sing to Thee. Alleluia!

Walk Closer to God
Singing triumphant hymns at Easter is a good way to celebrate Christ's victory over death. But what will you do to celebrate during the other 364 days?

Paul has a timely suggestion: "Therefore, my dear brothers . . . give yourselves fully to the work of the Lord, because you know that your labor in the Lord is not in vain" (v. 58).

Where there is no fear of *losing*, there should be no fear of *serving*.

*L*et the redeemed of the Lord say so!

*W*orship from the Heart
In heaven you will glance with joy at the faces of your loved ones and will even look with wonder at the streets of gold. But as you gaze into the beautiful face of Jesus Christ your Redeemer, you will fall at His feet in adoration, wondering why you did not love Him more. Worship Him now.

*W*alk Thru the Word
New Testament Reading
1 Corinthians 15:35-58
Old Testament Reading
Psalm 107

The power of love

Be on your guard; stand firm in the faith; be men of courage; be strong. Do everything in love (1 Corinthians 16:13-14).

*M*ost of us know a person whom we might call a "gentle giant"—someone who possesses great physical power, but chooses not to use it, or to use it only for the most tender of purposes.

Christians have the power of God at their disposal. But they also possess the love of God. How do the two work in tandem? Alexander Maclaren explains.

Walk with Alexander Maclaren

"If you will take love in its widest sense, it is the sum of all commandments of the Christian life. If we love God, consciously having our affection engaged with Him, do you think that any evil or temptation would have power over us?

"In the proportion to which I love God, I conquer all sin. I see through all the hollowness and the shams, and detect the ugliness and the filth of the things that otherwise would be temptations.

"How beautifully the apostle states the great truth that the strongest type of human character is the gentlest and most loving. The mighty man is not the man of intellectual or physical force but the man who is much because he loves much.

"If we would come to supreme beauty of Christian character, there must be inseparably manifested in our lives, and lived in our hearts, strength and love, might and gentleness. That is the perfect man, and that was the union set before us, in the highest form, in the One we call our Savior, and whom we are bound to follow."

Walk Closer to God

The military might of the Roman Empire ruled the first-century world with an iron hand. But another power was also at work—a force so great that no emperor on earth could stand against it.

That power, of course, was the love of God—a love that nailed Jesus to the cross and three days later raised Him from the tomb. Put that power to work in your life, and you too can become a giant in the sight of God.

Worship from the Heart

"Father, as I go about this day, may all people that I meet be recipients of Your love flowing through me. Let all my attitudes and actions be governed and controlled by love. In the name of the One whose love is unlimited. Amen."

Walk Thru the Word

New Testament Reading
1 Corinthians 16
Old Testament Reading
1 Kings 2:1-7, 26-27

218

For just as the sufferings of Christ flow over into our lives, so also through Christ our comfort overflows (2 Corinthians 1:5).

Comfort that only Christ can bring

Starting a business is easy. All you need is experience in manufacturing, advertising, marketing, accounting, and customer service. Perhaps that's why partnerships are so popular—two or more individuals pooling their strengths can compensate for each other's weaknesses.

The Christian shares a similar partnership with Jesus Christ, with one important difference. Jesus has no hidden weaknesses! Where you are weak, He is always strong. Johann Peter Lange explores this spiritual partnership.

Walk with Johann Peter Lange

"Christians enjoy a threefold fellowship: in suffering, in consolation, and in prayer. Their life is derived from what Christ has suffered for them. This is the source of all their peace and strength, and this brings them into affectionate communion with Him, so that His cause becomes their own.

"Just as He took on Himself their guilt, they appropriate the cause of righteousness, of God and of His kingdom for which He suffered, and share in all His struggles and sufferings.

"As this fellowship and unity with Him is common to them all, the suffering of any one of them for the common cause is shared also by each: They all wrestle in prayer for that one, and they all become sharers in his consolation and joy.

"There is a wonderful power in this fellowship. It is not merely the highest and brightest realization of God's great scheme of mercy, but it also glorifies His power by binding heaven and earth in one great communion."

Walk Closer to God

When you suffer as a Christian, you suffer with Christ. Losing a job, burying a loved one, or feeling the sting of persecution—none of these is pleasant. But all can become occasions to experience the consolation which only Christ can bring.

It is true that misery loves company—especially when the company is that of your Comforter.

Worship from the Heart

Jesus is the Yes to all the promises of God. There are thousands of promises in God's Word, and to each of them Jesus has written Yes in His own blood. Rejoice that being in Christ means that you receive the benefits of those promises.

Walk Thru the Word

New Testament Reading
2 Corinthians 1:1–2:11
Old Testament Reading
Psalm 13

$\mathcal{A}$ heart that is occupied with Christ

And we, who with unveiled faces all reflect the Lord's glory, are being transformed into his likeness with ever-increasing glory, which comes from the Lord, who is the Spirit (2 Corinthians 3:18).

What would life be like without mirrors—those shiny reflectors that help us transform *dirty* into *clean . . . rumpled* into *well-groomed*. Take away the mirror, and you take away the objective picture of what you really look like.

Some transformations can be effected with cosmetics and a comb. But others go far beyond skin deep and require the inner change that only Jesus Christ can bring. H. A. Ironside explains.

Walk with H. A. Ironside

"The secret of holiness is heart-occupation with Christ. As we gaze upon Him, we become more and more like Him.

"Do you want to be holy? Spend much time in His presence. Let the loveliness of the risen Lord so fill the vision of your soul that all else is shut out. Then the things of the flesh will shrivel up and disappear and the things of the Spirit will become supreme in your life.

"We do not become holy by looking into our own hearts. There we find only corruption. But as we look away from self altogether, and as we contemplate Jesus' holiness, purity, love, and compassion, His devotion to the Father's will, we shall be transformed into His blessed image.

"There is no other way by which we may be delivered from the power of the flesh and of the principles of the world."

Walk Closer to God

Paul is not the only New Testament author to describe the Christian life in terms of a mirror. James comments on the same illustration:

"Anyone who listens to the word but does not do what it says is like a man who looks at his face in the mirror and, after looking at himself, goes away and immediately forgets what he looks like. But the man who looks intently into the perfect law that gives freedom, and continues to do this, not forgetting what he has heard, but doing it—he will be blessed in what he does" (James 1:23-25).

Worship from the Heart

Meditate on verses 14-17 of chapter 2. How is fragrance spread? Some flowers seem to fill the air with their fragrance, even those as small as the lily of the valley. Others, though showy, have little if any scent. What is the aroma of Christ? Does your life in Christ spread His fragrance?

Walk Thru the Word

New Testament Reading
2 Corinthians 2:12–3:18
Old Testament Reading
Genesis 6:22

220

Daily renewal for spiritual growth

All this is for your benefit. . . .Therefore we do not lose heart. Though outwardly we are wasting away, yet inwardly we are being renewed day by day (2 Corinthians 4:15-16).

*T*he circumstances surrounding the death were bizarre. The man had died of thirst—in a houseboat on a freshwater lake.

Water, water everywhere, but not a drop was drunk. And the result was the same as if the man had been stranded in a desert.

In the Christian life, it's easy to surround yourself with the things essential for spiritual vitality: God's Word, God's people, God's house. And like the man on the houseboat, your spiritual life can still shrivel and die.

Andrew Murray suggests what is lacking.

Walk with Andrew Murray

"All young Christians should learn the absolute necessity of fellowship with Jesus each day. Each one should realize that the grace he has received of forgiveness of sins, of acceptance as God's child, of joy in the Spirit, can only be enjoyed by the daily renewal in fellowship with Jesus Christ Himself.

"Many Christians are unable to stand against the temptations of the world or of their old nature. They strive to do their best to fight against sin and to serve God, but they have no strength.

"They have never grasped the secret: The Lord will every day from heaven continue His work in them. But on one condition—the soul must give Him time each day to impart His love and grace. Time alone with the Lord Jesus every day is the indispensable condition for growth and power.

"For Christ's sake, and in order to please Him, I will learn to spend time each day—without exception—in fellowship with my Lord. So will the inner man be renewed from day to day."

Walk Closer to God

Just as daily food and water are vital to your physical life, daily communion with God is vital to your spiritual life. Don't wait for desert times to come before you discover the difference a daily drenching in the Water of Life can make!

Worship from the Heart

Being in Christ means being changed into His likeness. There is no goal in life greater than that. It is the believer's destiny; it is the eternal purpose of God. How exciting it is to know that the process has already begun: "Though outwardly we are wasting away, yet inwardly we are being renewed" (v. 16).

Walk Thru the Word

New Testament Reading
2 Corinthians 4
Old Testament Reading
Exodus 34:29-35

Bringing delight to the heart of God

For we must all appear before the judgment seat of Christ, that each one may receive what is due him for the things done while in the body, whether good or bad (2 Corinthians 5:10).

People want approval and acceptance and will do any number of things to achieve it.

It is one thing to seek the fleeting approval of a parent, spouse, or employer. It is something infinitely more significant to seek—and experience—the approval of almighty God, as C. S. Lewis explains.

Walk with C. S. Lewis

"How God thinks of us is infinitely more important than how we think of God. Indeed, how we think of Him is only of importance in so far as it is related to how He thinks of us.

"In the end that face which is the delight or terror of the universe must be turned upon each of us either with one expression or the other, either conferring glory inexpressible or inflicting shame that can never be cured or disguised.

"It is written that we shall 'stand before' Him, shall appear, shall be inspected. The promise of glory is the promise—only possible by the work of Christ—that some of us shall find approval with God.

"To please God, to be a real ingredient in the divine happiness, to be loved by God, not merely pitied, but delighted in as an artist delights in his work or a father in his son—it seems impossible, a weight or burden of glory which our thoughts can hardly sustain. But so it is."

Walk Closer to God

Perhaps without knowing it, you have been bringing delight to the heart of God. In your life He has the satisfaction of an artist gazing at his masterpiece, the joy of a father well pleased with his child.

Put the two together, and they spell "approval" —approval that will one day be expressed and rewarded at the judgment seat of Christ.

It's an "eternal glory" (2 Corinthians 4:17) that can lift your thoughts in praise to the One who made it possible.

Worship from the Heart

Prepare to worship with a group of believers this week, by meditating on the fact that the church itself is a new creation in Christ. As His bride, believers also live a collective life before the unbelieving world. Praise God for your fellow believers and for what they mean to you. Pray for those who are hurting. Rejoice with those who are rejoicing.

Walk Thru the Word

New Testament Reading
2 Corinthians 5:1-10
Old Testament Reading
Malachi 3:3

Therefore, if anyone is in Christ, he is a new creation; the old has gone, the new has come! (2 Corinthians 5:17).

*G*iven a choice between a new or a used item, people almost always choose new. Newness indicates life and vitality. It's a fresh, hope-filled concept—and one that touches the life of every child of God.

When you became a Christian, you became a curious mixture of new and used; new nature, used reputation. New character; old habit patterns. Yet God is working to effect a transformation, as Oswald Chambers describes.

Walk with Oswald Chambers

"There is only one thing God wants of us, and that is our unconditional surrender. When we are born again, the Holy Spirit begins to work in us, and there will come a time when there is not a bit of the old order left. The old attitude to things goes, and 'the new has come.'

"How are we going to demonstrate the life that has no lust, no self-interest, the love that is not provoked, that thinks no evil, that is always kind?

"The only way is by allowing not a bit of the old life to be left; but only simple, perfect trust in God.

"Have we come to the place where God can withdraw His blessings and it does not affect our trust in Him? When once we see God at work, we will never bother our heads about things that happen, because we are actually trusting in our Father in heaven, whom the world cannot see."

Walk Closer to God

Before you came to Christ, you were dressed in used rags of self-righteousness, pride, and self-sufficiency. Now, clothed in the righteousness of Christ, it's time to put on new garments.

Paul describes the process this way: "Put off your old self, which is being corrupted by its deceitful desires . . . and . . . put on the new self, created to be like God in true righteousness and holiness" (Ephesians 4:22-24).

Child of God, your new wardrobe of righteousness has been provided. Now try it on.

*F*rom rags to riches in Christ

*W*orship from the Heart

Today's Old Testament reading reminds us that when God raised the bones, He did not leave them with no covering. He added flesh. Praise God that He has replaced the dead skin of your old life with eternal life, a fresh new life in Christ.

*W*alk Thru the Word

New Testament Reading
2 Corinthians 5:11–6:2
Old Testament Reading
Ezekiel 37:1-10

A dwelling in which God lives

We are the temple of the living God. As God has said: "I will live with them and walk among them, and I will be their God, and they will be my people" (2 Corinthians 6:16).

Temples don't mean much to 20th-century Christians. Most of us worship God in places that have little in common with the temples of antiquity.

But to understand more fully what Paul's temple metaphor means, we need to be "time-travelers"—we need to put ourselves in the historical context of Paul and his audience.

Travel back in time with Alfred Edersheim as he shows us how one old temple ceremony perfectly pictured the new temple made up of Christ and those on whom He has poured living water.

Walk with Alfred Edersheim

"One year, on the last day of the feast (after the priest had poured out the water and the interest of the worshipers was at its highest pitch), a voice resounded through the temple from amidst the mass of people chanting and shaking a forest of leafy branches. It was Jesus, who stood and cried, 'If anyone is thirsty, let him come to me and drink. . . . Streams of living water will flow from within him.'

"Suddenly roused by being face to face with Him in whom every type and prophecy is fulfilled, many people said, 'Surely this man is the Prophet.'

"When the crowd from Jerusalem took palm branches and went out to meet him shouting, 'Hosanna to the Son of David,' they applied to Christ one of the chief ceremonies of the feast. They were praying that God through the Son of David would now send the salvation which was symbolized by the pouring out of water."

Walk Closer to God

In the Old Testament, the glory of the Lord filled the temple through the cloud. In the New Testament, God the Son fills the church—the new temple—through God the Holy Spirit. Paul expects that to energize the Corinthians to greater holiness. Wouldn't he expect it to do the same for us?

Worship from the Heart

Healthy, flowing streams are a source of life in their environment. Streams blocked by debris or mud stagnate, stifling the life within them. Ponder the stream of your life for a moment. Ask God to reveal and remove any debris that keeps the life of Christ from flowing through you to others.

Walk Thru the Word

New Testament Reading
2 Corinthians 6:3–7:1
Old Testament Reading
Ezekiel 37:26-28

*T*ime for sorrow, time for turning

See what this godly sorrow has produced in you: . . .
what eagerness to clear yourselves (2 Corinthians
7:11).

*S*top! Don't take another step."
"Why? Is something wrong?"
"You don't know? You're walking through a
mine field."
"Well, it doesn't look dangerous to me. How
can I be sure I'm really in a mine field?"
"Take my word for it. If you wait to discover
the truth 'firsthand,' it may cost you your life."
It's difficult to protect a person who doesn't
know he's in imminent danger. But unless there
is a willingness to move in a new direction,
death—though preventable—is inevitable.
The Bible calls this process of changing directions *repentance*. Charles Spurgeon explores the
meaning of godly repentance.

Walk with Charles Spurgeon
"True repentance has a distinct reference to the
Savior. When we repent, we must have one eye
upon sin and another upon the cross; or it will be
better still if we fix both our eyes upon Christ and
see our transgressions only in the light of His love.
"No one can truly say he hates sin if he lives in it.
Repentance makes us see the evil of sin, not merely
as a theory, but experientially—as a burnt child
dreads fire. We shall be much afraid of it, and we
shall shun it in everything—both great and little.
"True mourning for sin will make us careful lest
in anything we offend. Each night we shall close
the day with confessions of shortcoming, and each
morning awaken with prayers that God would
hold us up so that we will not sin against Him."

Walk Closer to God
If you saw a sign that said "Mine Field, Keep
Out!" would you keep out? Of course you would.
If you saw a group of picnickers who had
ignored the sign and whose lives were in jeopardy,
would you warn them? Of course you would.
Now apply that parable to the Christian friend
in your life who is continuing unrepentantly in
sin. Has God put it in your heart to warn that
person?

*W*orship from the Heart
Hosea 14 shows what
happens when a
straying child of God
turns back to the
Father. "He will
blossom like a lily
. . . like the grain . . .
like a vine." Praise
God that the restora-
tion that follows
repentance is real,
and that it can be
obtained when a
believer practices
1 John 1:9.

*W*alk Thru the Word
New Testament Reading
2 Corinthians 7:2-16
Old Testament Reading
Hosea 14

*O*bedience is an affair of the heart

I am not commanding you, but I want to test the sincerity of your love by comparing it with the earnestness of others (2 Corinthians 8:8).

*S*ervice with a smile—a motto that speaks of pleasant people eager to help.

Service with a sneer—a motto that is unlikely to attract many customers eager to be served.

In the case of the Corinthians, Paul wanted the believers to understand the force—external or internal—that motivated them to give to the needs of others. Charles Hodge explains Paul's challenge to the church.

Walk with Charles Hodge

"It was not obedience, but spontaneous liberality, that Paul desired. Alms-giving in obedience to a command or to satisfy conscience is not an act of liberality. What is not spontaneous is not liberal.

"Paul, therefore, would not coerce them by a command. His object was to put the genuineness of their love to the test.

"The real test of the genuineness of any inward affection is not so much the character of the feeling it reveals in our consciousness, as the course of action to which it leads. Many persons, if they judged themselves by their feelings, would regard themselves as truly compassionate; but a judgment founded on their actions might lead to the opposite conclusion.

"Thus many suppose that they really love God because they are conscious of feelings which they dignify with that name, yet they do not obey Him. It is therefore by the fruits of obedience that we must judge love's genuineness both in ourselves and in others."

Walk Closer to God

Paul's challenge to the Corinthians may have left some gritting their teeth. But it also pointed out how far they had to go in making obedience an "affair of the heart."

The question Paul would have for you is simply this: "Do you obey God with a joyful spirit?"

Answer correctly, and you will bring a smile to God's face.

*W*orship from the Heart

"Praise God from whom all blessings flow." ALL blessings: your family, your friends, the talent to earn a living, the never-ending care and love of God. As you ponder your blessings, let your heart fill with gratitude and love for the Giver of every good and perfect gift.

*W*alk Thru the Word

New Testament Reading
2 Corinthians 8
Old Testament Reading
Psalm 31:23-24

God's work done in God's way

And God is able to make all grace abound to you, so that in all things at all times, having all that you need, you will abound in every good work (2 Corinthians 9:8).

Leading a group discussion with new believers about priorities, a missionary asked, "What is a missionary's number-one priority?" Expecting to hear, "God . . . the Bible . . . reaching the lost," he was shocked to hear them respond, "Money!"

Where had they gotten that idea? From the missionaries' discussions among themselves about their limited funds. Unintentionally—but unmistakably—their *gold* spoke louder than their *God.*

Hudson Taylor shares his perspective on both the potential and the pitfalls of money in the ministry.

Walk with Hudson Taylor

"In every case we had recourse—I say it reverently—to our Great Treasurer, the Lord Himself. He has not failed us, and never will fail us, though the expense of living is increasing considerably, and the number to be supplied is increasing also.

"The great resources of our great God are undiminished, and we rest upon them with a full assurance that His Word is as true now as it ever has been. Our business is to 'seek first his kingdom and his righteousness, and all these things will be given to [us] as well.'

"Time would fail me to dwell upon the instances when God has given of His faithfulness. I still encourage you to trust in the faithful God.

"I like to think of Him who sent three million Israelites to bed without a crumb in the cupboard for breakfast the next morning, and to remember they never got up in the morning and found no breakfast ready to be gathered."

Walk Closer to God

When the missionary asked the group what they gave priority in their own lives, they replied, "Money." Instead of hearing the missionaries' words about the one true God, the believers had embraced their leaders' attitude toward money.

Funny thing about people. They seem to hear whatever our lives shout the loudest.

Worship from the Heart

In 2 Kings 4:1-7 we see that God takes care of His own. Even with the death of the family's provider, the needs of the widow and her sons were met. If we are doing God's work in God's way, we will never lack God's provision. Our God controls the gold and owns the cattle on a thousand hills.

Walk Thru the Word

New Testament Reading
2 Corinthians 9
Old Testament Reading
2 Kings 4:1-7

Hudson Taylor (1832-1905) Faithful Servant of God in China

During the 19th century concern grew phenomenally for the spread of the gospel to the uttermost parts of the earth. The mighty revivals that swept Great Britain and America sparked renewed interest in sharing the Good News of Christ with those who had never heard it.

William Carey in India . . . David Livingstone in Africa . . . Adoniram Judson in Burma . . . J. Hudson Taylor in China—all were pioneers of mission enterprises that continue today.

The life of Hudson Taylor is a familiar one in missionary circles, but his story deserves a far wider audience. Besides being a pioneer in taking the gospel to China, Taylor also pioneered a way of life that challenges every Christian to reevaluate his or her commitment to the calling of Christ.

Living by faith. Trusting God to provide in every situation. Making each need known to Him in daily prayer. Hudson Taylor's life shines as a testimony to the faithfulness of God.

Born in 1832 to godly parents, Hudson grew up telling others, "When I am a man, I plan to be a missionary and go to China." Discussions of Christianity around the family table nurtured this early ambition. Taylor's interest in medicine seemed a natural outlet for his desire to minister to others.

But first he had to come face to face with his own need of a Savior. One day in his seventeenth year, Taylor was reading in his father's library when he was struck by

the phrase, "the finished work of Christ." That same day — a hundred miles away — his mother was on her knees praying for her son's salvation.

Taylor's mind and heart seized upon the importance of that phrase in his own life. He fell to his knees, expressing his faith in the finished work of Christ on his behalf. As he did, his mother miles away sensed the calm assurance that her prayers had been answered.

The next years of his life were spent in preparation for planting the gospel in China.

It was during this time that he first began to trust God to provide for his material needs. The frequent miracles of God's faithfulness in small matters gave Taylor confidence that God could — and would — provide, even many miles away from Taylor's native England.

Taylor sailed for China in 1853. From the outset, his methods differed from those of his fellow missionaries. He preferred to imitate the Chinese in dress and lifestyle rather than live by his Western cultural patterns, reasoning that Christ was Lord over all cultures.

He concentrated extensively on the interior of China rather than the more accessible coastal regions. Twelve years later he began his own mission organization, the China Inland Mission.

In addition to his ministry in China, Taylor traveled widely in Great Britain and America, encouraging others to take up the challenge of missions.

The struggles and victories of this tender man of vision gave him a platform from which to speak of the faithfulness of God on behalf of His servants. And he never called others to undertake what he had not first experienced.

By the time of his death in China in 1905, Hudson Taylor's China Inland Mission had sent out more than 800 missionaries and had seen more than 125,000 Chinese come to Christ.

But God's faithfulness is not limited only to missionaries in faraway places. "God, who has called you into fellowship with His Son Jesus Christ our Lord, is faithful" (1 Corinthians 1:9).

Perhaps you are troubled by nagging concerns or worries that would best be left in the hands of your faithful God. Take the time to talk to Him about it right now. He is the One worthy to be trusted!

A Lesson from the life of Hudson Taylor

I can count on God to supply what I need to accomplish the work He has given me to do.

Winning the battle for the mind

We demolish arguments and every pretension that sets itself up against the knowledge of God, and we take captive every thought to make it obedient to Christ (2 Corinthians 10:5).

A mind is a terrible thing to waste. Or manipulate. Or neglect.

"As he thinketh in his heart," Solomon reminds us, "so is he" (Proverbs 23:7 KJV). This means you cannot afford to let the input of the world replace the input of the Word.

F. B. Meyer challenges you to let God guard the door of your mind.

Walk with F. B. Meyer

"Christ counts evil thoughts as traitors not only to us, but also to Him. Like the psalmist, you may say, 'I hate vain thoughts; not only because of the curse they bring to my heart, but for the grief they give to my King.' Their intrusion is forbidden by the double barrier of our own choice and the keeping power of Jesus.

"Let the peace of God keep the door of your heart and mind, scrutinizing each intruder and turning back the unfit. Let the Holy Spirit bring every thought into captivity to the obedience of Christ.

"Let the faithful Savior have the keeping of the soul entrusted to Him, that He may watch every menacing thought which lurks in the shadow or steals up the glen. He is well able to keep what is committed to Him. He will not fail the suppliant whose lips are familiar with the prayer: 'Cleanse the thoughts of our hearts by the inspiration of Your Holy Spirit, that we may perfectly love You and worthily magnify Your holy name.' "

Walk Closer to God

Any thought that infiltrates your mind from Satan's camp must be taken prisoner immediately. There can be no exceptions, no delay. Why? Because wherever your thoughts lead, your actions will almost certainly follow.

Let that captivating thought be your call to battle today—a battle you can win as you march in obedience to Christ.

Worship from the Heart

Jot down the words of Psalm 19:14 on an index card and carry it with you. Throughout the day, try to remain aware of your thoughts, and evaluate them continually in the light of this verse. Praise the Lord that "He is well able to keep what is committed to Him."

Walk Thru the Word

New Testament Reading
2 Corinthians 10
Old Testament Reading
Psalm 19:14

Standing firm against Satan's schemes

And no wonder, for Satan himself masquerades as an angel of light (2 Corinthians 11:14).

*I*f you had the task of devising clever schemes to deceive people about the person and program of God, what dirty tricks would you suggest?

Perhaps you would start a "God Can't Be Trusted" campaign . . . or you'd encourage people to procrastinate with their souls . . . or you'd spread the lie that Christians don't enjoy life. Sadly, all of these schemes—and countless others—have been used by the father of lies and his demons.

The need has never been greater for Christians who can stand tall against Satan's deceitful attacks, as Martin Luther points out.

Walk with Martin Luther

"The person who takes to heart the lesson that Christ hurts when the heart of a Christian is sad or frightened has won half the battle. For when I get to know the Enemy who wants to frighten and depress me, I already have solid ground on which I can stand against him.

"The Devil disguises himself as an angel of light. But this is a sign by which we may recognize him: He creates a timid, frightened, troubled conscience.

"False teachers cannot comfort or make happy a timid conscience; they only make hearts confused, sad, and melancholy so that people are gloomy and act sad. This, however, is nothing but the deception of the Devil, who delights to make hearts fearful, cowardly, and timid.

"To be sure, a Christian leads a life that has much suffering and many temptations on the outside. Nevertheless, he can have a confident, happy heart toward God and can expect the best from Him."

Walk Closer to God

For the first half of his life, Luther lived like the very people he describes: afraid of God, dismayed by life. But once he understood the grace of God, Luther's fears gave way to a contagious exuberance that God would use to transform a continent.

Don't be deceived by an angel of light. Instead, fall at the feet of the Light of the world, and discover anew that life is worth the living.

Worship from the Heart

"Father, Your Word is a light to my path. Help me to hide it in my heart that I might not sin against You. Use it to open my eyes to recognize the Enemy's attacks. And as I read and ponder Your Word, may the Holy Spirit help me see beyond the words to the Living Word. Amen."

Walk Thru the Word

New Testament Reading
2 Corinthians 11:1-15
Old Testament Reading
Proverbs 3:5-6

231

The mystery of the thorn

Worship from the Heart

Ponder these words by John Greenleaf Whittier as you worship with others this weekend: "All things are Thine; no gift have we, Lord of all gifts to offer Thee; And hence, with grateful hearts, today Thine own before Thy feet we lay."

To keep me from being conceited. . . , there was given me a thorn in my flesh, a messenger of Satan, to torment me (2 Corinthians 12:7).

The hero is suspended in a wooden cage ten feet above the ground, his hands and feet bound with vines. He can escape—if only he can free his hands. As he struggles, the vines only tighten.

Suddenly a flaming arrow whizzes toward his cage. Surely our hero will be burned alive!

But wait. The fiery darts may be his means of escape. If he can stand the heat long enough, the vines will burn away. It's worth a try . . .

Just as our fictitious hero used adversity to his advantage, Amy Carmichael shows what God can do with the trials in your life.

Walk with Amy Carmichael

"As a child I puzzled over the fact that, though all Christian people spoke of pain as sent from God, they usually did all that they could to avoid it—or if it came—to get rid of it. Doctors who helped them to do so were prayed for as very special servants of God. And yet the doctors were working against the very thing that God had sent.

"It was very puzzling, and I can remember the delight of finding the words, 'An enemy did this' (Matthew 13:28), and feeling that these words must apply to all who hurt or are wounded either in spirit or body. Yet there was a mystery somewhere. And it was not explained.

"I think now that it never will be explained until we stand in the light of God; but these words from Paul help us to understand—the thorn was a gift.

"The Spirit of God takes care to let us know that it was Satan's hand, not the Father's, that hurt Job. Yet that cruel hand was turned into a crucible, and the fire refined the gold. The power of darkness crucified the Lord of glory. But Love won on Calvary."

Walk Closer to God

No believer has to be held captive by circumstances. As you begin to recognize God's hand in the trials of your life, you'll be able to turn Satan's attacks around so that they bring glory to God.

Walk Thru the Word

New Testament Reading
2 Corinthians 11:16–12:10
Old Testament Reading
Job 1

May the grace of the Lord Jesus Christ, and the love of God, and the fellowship of the Holy Spirit be with you all (2 Corinthians 13:14).

*I*t's the glue that holds the family together." The "it" of that oft-voiced sentiment may be a place, a person, or even a tradition. But whatever the "glue," it's certain to be something that the whole family shares in common.

Christians too are members of a family. And the glue that holds this diverse family together is the Holy Spirit. The glue that welds the family of God together is at work in each individual member as F. B. Meyer explains.

Walk with F. B. Meyer

"The word *communion* signifies 'having in common.' It is used of our fellowship with one another and with God. The bond of such fellowship is always through the Holy Spirit. The blessed Spirit unites the Persons of the Trinity to each other, and us to them, and secures that oneness for which our Savior prayed.

"How wonderful it is to have the privilege of this divine fellowship! That we need never be alone again; that we can at any moment turn to Him for direction; that we may draw on His resources for every need; that it is impossible to exhaust His willingness to counsel and sustain; that there is no service or suffering into which He is not prepared to enter with us! Surely, if we would but give ourselves time to realize these marvelous privileges, there would be no room for the despondency which at times threatens to deprive us of hope.

"Such divine union as lies within our reach certainly demands on our part watchfulness, a tender conscience, a yielded will, and a heart which has no other love—nothing that is inconsistent with the Spirit's fellowship."

Walk Closer to God

In close families, disgracing the family name would be unthinkable. How much more should you guard your conduct and conversation, as befitting the heavenly family—and the heavenly Father—whose name you share!

*I*t's all in the family

*W*orship from the Heart

Your Christian community is essential to your spiritual growth. Its members guide, correct, comfort, and forgive you. God designed it that way. Think about your "immediate family" in Christ, those you worship and fellowship with. Thank God for the ministry that each individual has in your life.

*W*alk Thru the Word

New Testament Reading
2 Corinthians 12:11–13:14
Old Testament Reading
Zechariah 4:6

The Believer's Lifelong Challenge

Jesus Christ is the focal point of Galatians, Ephesians, Philippians, and Colossians. In these four letters, Paul explains who Christ is, what He is like, and what He has done.

Galatia. Ephesus. Philippi. Colosse. You won't find them on a modern map. Once important religious and commercial centers, all that remain now are archaeological ruins and historical records. But though nineteen centuries have swept over their memory, they are still vitally important to you today because of four letters written in the first century by Paul.

Many books written today offer struggling Christians the "secret" to living the Christian life. But the best way to confront that issue is to focus on what the apostle writes in these books: "I have been crucified with Christ, and I no longer live, but Christ lives in me. The life I live in the body, I live by faith in the Son of God, who loved me and gave himself for me" (Galatians 2:20); "so Christ may dwell in your hearts through faith . . . that you may be filled to the measure of all the fullness of God" (Ephesians 3:17, 19); "filled with the fruit of righteousness that comes through Jesus Christ—to the glory and praise of God" (Philippians 1:11); "So then, just as you received Christ Jesus as Lord, continue to live in him" (Colossians 2:6). In other words, the Christian life is life in Christ. You cannot study it or live it without Him.

Christ is the focal point of these four letters. In them, Paul explains who Christ is, what He is like and what He has done. In Galatians, Paul reminds forgetful Christians of the wonderful salvation they enjoy. In Ephesians, he breaks forth in praise for the riches of life that God's children enjoy through Jesus Christ. In Philippians, the apostle writes to encourage a church to improve in Christlikeness. And in Colossians, Paul addresses a congregation he has never met face to face, reminding them of the incomparable greatness of Christ as Lord and Savior.

There is no greater challenge—or privilege—for the one who has "received Christ Jesus as Lord" than to "live in Him." At the end of this month, you should be many steps closer to resembling the One you call "Lord."

Sounds in the desert

Nor did I go up to Jerusalem to see those who were apostles before I was, but I went immediately into Arabia and later returned to Damascus (Galatians 1:17).

A newcomer in any group often goes through a process called "paying one's dues" before the novice finds his niche.

For much of his life Paul was a violent opposer of the gospel. But overnight all that changed as he became a zealous proclaimer of the gospel. With good reason, other believers were wary to take his profession at face value!

Clarence Macartney explains the importance of the "desert years" in Paul's Christian experience.

Walk with Clarence Macartney

"Greatly called of God and converted to Christ from his persecution of the church, Paul, no doubt, was impatient to begin his work as an apostle and proclaim the grace of God that had delivered him from sin and the power of darkness.

"Instead, he was sent into Arabia, far from Tarsus, Antioch, Damascus, Jerusalem, and the pulsing tides of the world's stir. And there he apparently stayed for three years—a long time of seclusion and waiting. But that was where God wanted him to be, and there God spoke to his soul.

"Think of Arabia as the place of silence, when God breaks up the fixed order of our lives and speaks a message to us which we could not hear elsewhere. The experience of Paul was one through which many of God's servants are called to pass.

"In these 'Arabia' periods of withdrawal and retirement, we have time to be alone. What seems at first to be only a lonely desert place and experience, with our spirits chafing to get free of it, turns out to be a place that draws us nearer to God."

Walk Closer to God

In the loneliness of being the new kid on the block or the isolation of a desert experience, God doesn't leave His children to fend for themselves. Paul had the best "big Brother" possible when things got tough or days got lonely. And that same older Brother is the one you have today—none other than the Lord Jesus Himself.

Worship from the Heart

Like Elijah of old, Paul discovered that the still, small voice of God can be easily lost in the commotion of daily living—and easily heard in the quiet of daily devotion. Thank God for the freedom to sit in His presence each day. If you take time to meet God each day, you'll be delighted with what you hear.

Walk Thru the Word

New Testament Reading
Galatians 1
Old Testament Reading
1 Kings 19:9-18

235

Under the stroke of justice

[We] know that a man is not justified by observing the law, but by faith in Jesus Christ. So we, too, have put our faith in Christ Jesus (Galatians 2:16).

*P*ardon . . . parole . . . reprieve—no sweeter words exist for a prisoner. They symbolize to the convict hope of being set free before the full sentence has been served.

The entire human race stands convicted of breaking the law of God. But there is no parole to lighten the sentence of sin. The penalty must be paid in full.

Bad news? On the contrary! It's good news for those who discover that their sentence has already been served. Listen as Albert Barnes explains.

Walk with Albert Barnes

"What is justification? It is the declared purpose of God to regard and treat those sinners who believe in Jesus Christ as if they had not sinned, on the ground of the merits of the Savior.

"It is not mere pardon. Pardon is a free forgiveness of past offenses. It has reference to those sins as forgiven and blotted out.

"Justification has respect to the law, and to God's future dealings with the sinner. It is an act by which God determines to treat him hereafter as righteous—as if he had not sinned. The basis for this is the merit of the Lord Jesus Christ, merit that we can plead as if it were our own.

"He has taken our place and died in our stead; He has met the descending stroke of justice, which would have fallen on our own heads if He had not interposed."

Walk Closer to God

Every pardon carries with it the hope that the criminal has been truly reformed—that he will commit no more crimes.

But the justification which Christ's death accomplishes is no mere wishful thinking. The result is nothing less than a new creation (2 Corinthians 5:17)—a sinner-turned-saint, a reclaimed convict for Christ.

Has that verdict been handed down in your life? The Judge stands ready to hear your plea.

Worship from the Heart

"Lord, I do not like to be criticized. But if a committed Christian offers criticism, as Paul offered it to Peter, open my heart to hear it. This, too, may be Your voice, checking and redirecting me. I thank You for the friends who keep me accountable."

Walk Thru the Word

New Testament Reading
Galatians 2
Old Testament Reading
Jeremiah 2:22

*T*he remedy of the Cross

All who rely on observing the law are under a curse, for it is written: "Cursed is everyone who does not continue to do everything written in the Book of the Law" (Galatians 3:10).

*F*or the human race, there is no statute of limitations on sin. When confronted by a holy God, a sinner cannot excuse his behavior by saying, "That was long ago." Or by pleading, "I'll try to do better next time." Or by pointing to his good deeds and arguing, "Won't that tip the scales in my favor?"

No, never. There is nothing the sinner can do.

The pervasive power of sin demands that drastic measures be taken. These words of H. A. Ironside focus on the futility of human efforts to solve the problem of sin.

Walk with H. A. Ironside

"Can we not deliver ourselves? Though we have broken the law in the past, can we not decide that from this moment on we will be very careful to observe every precept of the moral law of God?

"In the first place, we could not do that. It is impossible for people with fallen natures to fully keep the law of God. Take the commandment, 'You shall not covet'; you cannot help but covet, even though you know it is wrong. You look at something your neighbor has and involuntarily your heart says, 'I wish that were mine.' On second thought, you say, 'I should really rejoice for my neighbor' but still, have you not coveted?

"Suppose you were able to keep the law from this very day until the last day of your life, would that not undo and make up for all the wrongdoing of the past? Not at all. The past failure still stands on God's record. 'God will call the past to account' (Ecclesiastes 3:15)."

Walk Closer to God

The curse of sin finds its only remedy in the cross of Christ. Paul explains: "Christ redeemed us from the curse of the law by becoming a curse for us, for it is written: 'Cursed is everyone who is hung on a tree' " (Galatians 3:13).

It's too late to turn over a new leaf. But it's not too late to respond to the old, old story of Jesus and His love!

*W*orship from the Heart

Visualize yourself standing before a mirror that reflects every thought, word, and deed that is in violation of God's law. Notice each wrinkle, each ugly growth. How do you look? Now turn in faith to Christ. See His perfect righteousness reflected in you, and thank Him with all your heart.

*W*alk Thru the Word

New Testament Reading
Galatians 3:1-14
Old Testament Reading
Deuteronomy 27:11-26

Living by faith in the Son

So the law was put in charge to lead us to Christ that we might be justified by faith (Galatians 3:24).

Although the Galatians had graduated from "law school," they were living like ungraduates. But the law's work as their schoolmaster was finished. Since they had received salvation through faith in Christ, they didn't need to return to their "alma mater." Paul reminds them how the law's chief purpose was to point men and women to faith in Christ.

Now, as followers of Christ, the Galatians were guilty of making the law's demands their path to perfection. As John Calvin relates, the Christian life is walking in the light of God's revealed Word.

Walk with John Calvin

"Faith denotes the full revelation of those things which, during the darkness of the shadows of the law, were dimly seen; for Paul does not intend to say that the fathers, who lived under the law, did not possess faith. Those who were under the law were partakers of the same faith as New Testament believers.

"The Old Testament might be said to foreshadow Christ, but to us He is represented as actually being present. They had only the mirror; we have the substance.

"Whatever might be the amount of darkness under the law, the fathers were not ignorant of the road in which they ought to walk. Though the dawn is not equal to the splendor of noon, yet, as far as a trip is concerned, travelers do not wait till the sun is fully risen. Their portion of light resembled the dawn, which was enough to preserve them from all error and guide them to everlasting blessedness."

Walk Closer to God

If the Old Testament saints' portion of light resembled the dawn, you enjoy the full blaze of the noontime sun.

If they were able to live by faith with only a glimpse of the coming Savior, you can surely live by faith, thanks to the full portrait of His appearing, which you possess in the Word of God.

Worship from the Heart

The Old Testament reminds us that Christ is the source of perfect peace and sufficient strength to battle the onslaughts of life (Isaiah 26:3-4). Praise Him that His perfect peace and strength are appropriated by faith and not by our wills or efforts.

Walk Thru the Word

New Testament Reading
Galatians 3:15-25
Old Testament Reading
Deuteronomy 30:11-14

*P*rivileged heirs to a vast estate

What I am saying is that as long as the heir is a child, he is no different from a slave, although he owns the whole estate. He is subject to guardians and trustees until the time set by his father (Galatians 4:1-2).

*A*nd to my son, I leave the entirety of my estate and all assets to be held in trust until he reaches the age of twenty-one . . . "

Many a young heir has chafed under such words. For before that time, he can anticipate, but not experience, the full riches of his inheritance.

In Galatians 4, Paul compares the inheritance of an estate to the blessings of salvation. In both cases, wealth is received through the plan of a benevolent father. Johann Peter Lange explores the analogy.

Walk with Johann Peter Lange

"The Christian is heir in full possession of the Father's estate. For thus an older son is distinguished from a younger son.

"For a younger son, the inheritance is administered by others, and from time to time receives out of it what is necessary for him.

"So it is with man under the law; as he first sees in God one who commands and strictly regulates life, so also he sees in Him one who bestows good only according to merit, and who just as certainly inflicts punishment where punishment is deserved.

"It is otherwise with the son of full age and with the Christian. He is heir, in possession and full enjoyment of the paternal estate. As the older son freely disposes of the paternal estate, so also the Christian in faith freely applies himself, as it were, as often as he will, to his Father's treasure, and takes from it whatever he needs."

Walk Closer to God

As Christians, we possess "every spiritual blessing in Christ" (Ephesians 1:3). Through Christ we are members of God's family, with all the privileges and responsibilities pertaining to that heavenly household.

Christians are "heirs of God and co-heirs with Christ" (Romans 8:17). Sound too good to be true? Not if we have learned firsthand about the giving character of our heavenly Father.

*W*orship from the Heart

A beggar was found dead in a filthy alley. His emaciated body was wrapped in layers of rags and grime. Later he was identified as the heir to a great fortune. Your inheritance as a child of God far surpasses his. Praise God that you can know who you are in Christ and can claim your inheritance now. You don't have to live like a beggar.

*W*alk Thru the Word

New Testament Reading
Galatians 3:26–4:20
Old Testament Reading
Genesis 22:18

Freedom to serve the Savior

It is for freedom that Christ has set us free. Stand firm, then (Galatians 5:1).

Everyone likes the word *free;* everyone uses it freely. But many place upon it a definition it was never intended to carry.

Some people think *free* means free to do as they please—even at another's expense. But freedom that is merely license is actually bondage of the worst kind—no commitments, no responsibilities.

What does Paul mean when he speaks of freedom in the Christian life? John Calvin offers this timely perspective on the freedom that Christ's death accomplished.

Walk with John Calvin

"Freedom of faith is one of the most important doctrines connected with salvation. The liberty of which Paul speaks is exemption from the ceremonies of the law that were demanded by false apostles. But let us remember that such liberty is only a part of what Christ has procured for us; for how small a matter would it be if He had only freed us from ceremonies. Rather, He has rescued us from the tyranny of sin, Satan, and death.

"This liberty was obtained for us by Christ on the cross. Thus Paul warns the Galatians not to allow a snare to be laid for their consciences. If men lay an unjust burden upon us, it may be borne; but if they endeavor to bring our consciences into bondage, we must resist valiantly.

"If men be permitted to bind our consciences, we shall be deprived of an invaluable blessing, and at the same time an insult will be offered to Christ, the Author of our freedom."

Walk Closer to God

A stop sign at a dangerous intersection may at first appear to restrict your driving freedom, but in fact it guards you from potential tragedy and frees you to enjoy the highway.

Christian liberty is no different. Only when you have been freed from "the tyranny of sin, Satan, and death" will you discover the surpassing joy of freedom to serve your Savior. "Free from . . . " "Free to . . . " Inseparable halves of your liberty in Christ.

Worship from the Heart

"Faith of our fathers! God's great power / Shall win all nations unto Thee; / And through the truth that comes from God / Mankind shall then indeed be free. / Faith of our fathers, holy faith, / We will be true to thee till death." As you worship with others, make this hymn your own commitment.

Walk Thru the Word

New Testament Reading
Galatians 4:21–5:15
Old Testament Reading
Genesis 2:15-17

240

Since we live by the Spirit, let us keep in step with the Spirit (Galatians 5:25).

*B*lack and white. Hot and cold. High and low. Faith and works. In the minds of many, these pairs are examples of opposites. Yet the last pair—faith and works—deserves a second look.

In Galatians Paul contrasts the faith in Christ that saves with the works of the law that enslave. In chapter 5, Paul points to the kind of works that saving faith produces in the believer's life.

Charles Spurgeon explains how faith and works—like two oars on a rowboat—go together to make a life that is pleasing to God.

Walk with Charles Spurgeon

"You will never find true faith unattended by true godliness; nor will you ever discover a truly holy life which does not have at its root a living faith based upon the righteousness of Christ. Woe to those who seek one without the other!

"There are some who cultivate faith and forget holiness. These may be very high in orthodoxy, but they shall be very deep in condemnation, for they hold the truth in unrighteousness. There are others who have strained after holiness of life, but have denied the faith, like the Pharisees whom the Master said were 'whitewashed tombs.'

"We must have faith, for this is the foundation; we must have holiness of life, for this is the superstructure. We need the superstructure of spiritual life if we would have comfort in the day of doubt. But do not seek a holy life without faith, for that would be to erect a house which can afford nopermanent shelter, because it is not founded on a rock."

Walk Closer to God

When applying for a job, if you lack either education or experience your chances of employment may be hindered.

So too in the Christian life, faith and works are in tandem. Neglect one or the other, and your life will turn as aimlessly as a one-oared rowboat makes circles in a pond.

After all, Christianity—like rowing—was never intended to be an "either/oar" proposition.

*T*win truths of a living faith

*W*orship from the Heart

Survival of the fittest: a law of nature. "Love your neighbor as yourself": the law of God. Meditate on Galatians 5:15. Paul warns that those who bite each other will ultimately consume each other. Your privilege is to pray for fellow believers and to speak words of encouragement and edification. Thank God for those who do that for you.

*W*alk Thru the Word

New Testament Reading
Galatians 5:16-26
Old Testament Reading
1 Samuel 15:19-22

Energy for a life of service

May I never boast except in the cross of our Lord Jesus Christ, through which the world has been crucified to me, and I to the world (Galatians 6:14).

During Passion Week, not much is made of the day Christ died; life continues much as usual. But on Easter Sunday—resurrection day—nearly everyone seems to be wearing new clothes!

Coincidence? Or an unconscious effort to forget the sacrifice so as not to spoil the celebration?

The cross is as much a part of Christianity as the empty tomb, uncomfortable though it may be to gaze upon Golgotha. The benefits of Christianity can sometimes overshadow the blood that was spilled to obtain them. Oswald Chambers puts the work of Christ into proper perspective.

Walk with Oswald Chambers

"To know the energy of God, you must brood on the tragedy of God. 'Look to Me,' Jesus said. Pay attention to the objective Source, and the subjective energy will be there. We lose power if we do not concentrate on the right thing. The effect of the Cross is salvation, sanctification, healing, but we are not to preach any of these. We are to preach Jesus Christ and Him crucified.

"The proclaiming of Jesus will do its own work. Concentrate on God in your preaching, and though your crowd may apparently pay no attention, they can never be the same. We have to concentrate on the great point of spiritual energy, the Cross, to keep in contact with that Center where all the power lies—and the energy will be let loose.

"The feebleness of churches is being criticized today, and one reason for the feebleness is that there has not been this concentration of spiritual energy; we have not brooded enough on the tragedy of Calvary or on the meaning of redemption."

Walk Closer to God

In Christianity—as in the culinary arts—all sugar and no substance is an unhealthy diet. But as you make Christ's sacrifice part of your daily meditation, don't be surprised to discover new reservoirs of strength to walk with Him in sacrificial service.

Worship from the Heart

Jesus is Lord of all. Having suffered the utmost agony, both physical and spiritual, He stands ready to meet your needs in times of testing or pain. You have a High Priest who knows what you go through. He's been there—and emerged victoriously. And so can you.

Walk Thru the Word

New Testament Reading
Galatians 6
Old Testament Reading
Psalm 116

Grace and peace to you from God our Father and the Lord Jesus Christ (Ephesians 1:2).

Most people today encounter the word *lord* only when it is a part of a bigger word, such as *landlord* or *warlord*. But when *Lord* is applied to the Son of God, Jesus Christ, it takes on no such limitations. He is not confined to any geographical location or restricted to any sphere of influence. His lordship extends as far as the universe.

Listen as Charles Hodge paints a word picture describing the greatness of your Lord and Savior.

Walk with Charles Hodge

"The Greek word for *lord* is indeed used in Scripture in the sense of master, and as a mere honorary title as in the English Sir. But, on the other hand, it is the translation of *Adonai*, supreme Lord, an incomparable name of God, and the substitute for *Jehovah*, a name the Jews would not pronounce. It is in this sense that Christ is 'the Lord, the Lord of lords, the Lord God'; Lord in that sense in which God alone can be Lord—having a dominion of which divine perfection is the only adequate or possible foundation.

" 'No one can say, "Jesus is Lord," except by the Holy Spirit' (1 Corinthians 12:3). It is a confession which implies the apprehension of the glory of God as it shines on Him. It is an acknowledgement that He is God manifested in the flesh.

"Blessed are all who make this acknowledgement with sincerity; for flesh and blood cannot reveal the truth therein confessed, but only the Father who is in heaven."

Walk Closer to God

Lord may be an easy word to say. But how well do you heed this warning of the One you call *Lord?* "Thus, by their fruit you will recognize them. Not everyone who says to me 'Lord, Lord,' will enter the kingdom of heaven, but only he who does the will of my Father who is in heaven" (Matthew 7:20-21).

It's not what you say about your Lord that counts, so much as what you do in obedience to His Word.

Not only what you say, but what you do

Worship from the Heart

"My Lord and my God, open my eyes to catch the vision of Daniel and Paul of 'when the times will have reached their fulfillment.' Often I see only the obstacle, hear only the discourager, feel only the transient pleasures and pains of daily living. As I meditate on Ephesians 1:10, may I become aware of a world far greater than I yet know."

Walk Thru the Word

New Testament Reading
Ephesians 1:1-14
Old Testament Reading
Daniel 7:13-14

243

Taking time for prayer

For this reason, ever since I heard about your faith in the Lord Jesus and your love for all the saints, I have not stopped giving thanks for you, remembering you in my prayers (Ephesians 1:15-16).

I can't believe it. I absolutely promised myself (more important, I promised God!) that I would pray at least thirty minutes this morning. Instead, I pushed the snooze button so many times that I didn't have enough time to pray at all. Still worse, I haven't had a decent quiet time now for four days in a row! What in the world is wrong with me?"

Sound familiar? Many of us have feeble prayer lives. Our world is a busy world, and God understands that. Yet Scripture instructs us to pray constantly.

Alexander Whyte encourages us to work at prayer (rather than just pray at work).

Walk with Alexander Whyte

"I am certain that the secret of much mischief to our own souls and to the souls of others lies in the way we starve our prayers by hurrying over them. Prayer that God will call true prayer takes far more time than one-in-a-thousand thinks. After all that the Holy Spirit has done to make true prayer independent of times, and of places, and of an unspiritual and undevotional world— we shall not succeed in prayer without such times, and places, and other assistances.

"Take good care lest you take your salvation far too cheaply. If you find your life of prayer to always be so short, and so easy, and so spiritual, as to be without strain and sweat to you, you may depend upon it, you have not yet begun to pray. As sure as you sit there, it is just in this matter of time in prayer that so many of us are making shipwreck of our souls and of the souls of others."

Walk Closer to God

"The Spirit helps us in our weakness. We do not know what we ought to pray for, but the Spirit himself intercedes for us with groans that words cannot express" (Romans 8:26). Keep that in mind and you will struggle in prayer rather than with prayer.

Worship from the Heart

"Father, I ask Your forgiveness when I fail to meet You on a regular basis in prayer. Make my soul desire so much to be in communion with You that I cannot resist. Show me, Father, again, my need to make my relationship with You my highest priority."

Walk Thru the Word

New Testament Reading
Ephesians 1:15-23
Old Testament Reading
Psalm 68:19-20

Seated with Christ on high

God . . . made us alive with Christ. . . . And God raised us up with Christ and seated us with him in the heavenly realms in Christ Jesus (Ephesians 2:4-6).

*T*wo men visit the same town. One stands on a busy corner, only inches away from whizzing traffic. The colors are bright, the noise deafening, the action nonstop. The other man goes to the top of the town's tallest building. Now the traffic is only a blur; the noise is muted, the colors subdued.

What a difference perspective can make! Albert Simpson explains the perspective of the Christian who sees life from the vantage point of being seated with Christ.

Walk with Albert Simpson

"Ascension is more than resurrection. Much is said of it in the New Testament. Christ rises above all things. We see Him in the very act of ascending, though we do not in the actual resurrection. With hands and lips engaged in blessing, He gently parts from the disciples, so simply, with so little imposing ceremony as to make heaven so near to our common life that we can fairly touch it.

"We, too, must ascend, even here on earth. We must learn to live on the heaven side and look at things from above. How it overcomes sin, defies Satan, lifts us above trials, separates us from the world, and conquers the fear of death to contemplate all things as God sees them, as Christ beholds them, as if we were now really seated with Him.

"Let us arise with His resurrection, and in fellowship with His glorious ascension learn henceforth to live above."

Walk Closer to God

Problems that loom large on your horizon are no problem for the God whom Isaiah describes this way: "He sits enthroned above the circle of the earth. . . . He stretches out the heavens like a canopy. . . . He brings princes to naught" (Isaiah 40:22-23).

Take your seat with Christ in the heavenlies, and gain a new perspective on your problems—one in which the peace of God rules within your heart (Philippians 4:6-7).

Worship from the Heart

"Crown Him the Lord of heaven, enthroned in world above; / Crown Him the King to whom is given the wondrous name of Love. / Crown Him with many crowns as thrones before Him fall; / Crown Him, ye kings, with many crowns, for He is King of all."

Walk Thru the Word

New Testament Reading
Ephesians 2:1-10
Old Testament Reading
Psalm 110

*O*ne in the Son

For [Christ] is our peace, who has made the two one and has destroyed the barrier, the dividing wall of hostility (Ephesians 2:14).

*S*eldom in history have there been so many voices crying for fairness and equality—and so much hatred based on religion, race, and nationality.

Prejudice is not a new problem. In New Testament times, Jews, Gentiles, and Samaritans all had problems seeing eye to eye. But once these feuding groups shifted their focus to the same Savior, their hatred for one another melted away, as Alexander Maclaren elaborates.

Walk with Alexander Maclaren

"The old distinction between Jew and Gentile, which often led to bitter hatred on both sides, was swept away in that strange new community of believers drawn together in Jesus Christ.

"The Jewish Christian and the Gentile Christian became brothers because they had received one new life. They who shared common feelings of faith and loved the same Savior together with a common character drawn from Him could never cherish the old emotions of racial hate.

"When we, in this day, try to picture the love that bound the early Christians together, we may well ask why it is that the ugly chinks in the foundation seem to remain between those who profess a common faith in one Lord, who all assert that Jesus Christ is for them the chief cornerstone."

Walk Closer to God

Make these healing words of Francis of Assisi your prayer today:

Lord, make me an instrument of Thy peace: where there is hatred, let me sow love; where there is injury, pardon; where there is doubt, faith; where there is despair, hope; where there is darkness, light; where there is sadness, joy.

O divine Master, grant that I may not so much seek to be consoled as to console, to be understood as to understand, to be loved as to love; for it is in giving that we receive; it is in pardoning that we are pardoned; it is in dying that we are born to eternal life.

*W*orship from the Heart

Think of Christian churches in your city or county: rich, poor, American, Hispanic, African—denominations of every sort. Thank God for the tremendous variety, and pray that you will never have a "some-Christians-are-more-equal-than-others" mentality.

*W*alk Thru the Word

New Testament Reading
Ephesians 2:11-22
Old Testament Reading
Jeremiah 50:4

That you, being rooted and established in love, may have power, together with all the saints, to grasp how wide and long and high and deep is the love of Christ, and to know this love that surpasses knowledge (Ephesians 3:17-19).

*C*an you calculate the capacity of a box with the following dimensions?

Length: Infinite. Width: Infinite. Height: Infinite. Infinity times infinity times infinity equals . . . infinity! That's the capacity of God's love.

Since no one can comprehend infinity, you'll never reach the limits of His love. But like William Cowper, you can plumb its depths in praise.

Walk with William Cowper

Hark, my soul, it is the Lord!
'Tis thy Savior, hear His word;
Jesus speaks, and speaks to thee,
"Say, poor sinner, lovest thou Me?

"I delivered thee when bound,
And when bleeding, healed thy wound,
Sought thee wandering, set thee right,
Turned thy darkness into light.

"Mine is an unchanging love,
Higher than the heights above,
Deeper than the depths beneath,
Free and faithful, strong as death."

Lord, it is my chief complaint
That my love is weak and faint;
Yet I love Thee, and adore:
O for grace to love Thee more!

Walk Closer to God

"I am convinced that neither death nor life, neither angels nor demons, neither the present nor the future, nor any powers, neither height nor depth, nor anything else in all creation, will be able to separate us from the love of God that is in Christ Jesus our Lord" (Romans 8:38-39).

Whether you sing it or say it, be sure you communicate it: "Lord, thank You for Your limitless, unchanging love."

*N*o limits to God's love

*W*orship from the Heart

Visualize the person you have loved more than anyone else on earth. God loves you far more than you love that dear person. Now think of the person you have disliked most, perhaps even scorned or hated. God's love for that person is as great as His love for you. Make this exercise a regular part of your prayer life, and see what happens.

*W*alk Thru the Word

New Testament Reading
Ephesians 3
Old Testament Reading
Psalm 136

Coping in the long run

Be completely humble and gentle; be patient, bearing with one another in love (Ephesians 4:2).

If life were a 100-yard dash, speed—not stamina—would be of prime importance. But in reality, life is more akin to a marathon, complete with the mental anguish and physical exhaustion that only those who have run twenty-six miles nonstop can appreciate fully.

"Our present sufferings," Paul told the church of Rome, "are not worth comparing with the glory that will be revealed in us" (Romans 8:18). But those sufferings demand long-suffering if you are to cope over the long haul of life. Albert Barnes provides this timely word.

Walk with Albert Barnes

"Long-suffering is that which is to be manifested in our manner of receiving the provocations of our brothers. No virtue, perhaps, is more frequently demanded in our relationships with others.

"We do not go far with any fellow traveler on the journey of life before we find there is great occasion for its exercise. He has a temperament different from our own. He has peculiarities of taste and habits and disposition which differ much from ours. He has his own plans, and his own way and time of doing things.

"Neighbors have occasion to observe this in their neighbors; friends in their friends; kindred in their kindred; one church member in another.

"Hence we must learn to bear and forbear. It is by the daily and quiet virtues of life—the Christian temper, the meek forbearance, the spirit of forgiveness—that good is to be done."

Walk Closer to God

"Father, I confess that my 'irritation quotient' is often high, and my ability to cope is often low. I quickly lose patience with my family and friends over even the smallest aggravation.

"Remind me often that my impatience only requires others to be long-suffering. Help me to become the cause of peace and not strife in my world today. In the name of the One who endured the cross for me. Amen."

Worship from the Heart

God's own Son is our best example of a long-suffering spirit. In spite of despicable treatment, He endured it so that we might have eternal life. May we always remember to look to Jesus as our example when impatience and temper threaten our relationships.

Walk Thru the Word

New Testament Reading
Ephesians 4:1-16
Old Testament Reading
Isaiah 53:7

248

Therefore each of you must put off falsehood and speak truthfully to his neighbor, for we are all members of one body (Ephesians 4:25).

*T*he search for truth is a familiar aspect of court-room drama. Evidence . . . testimony . . . verdict . . . sentence—all hinge on the discovery of truth.

The issue is not trivial, for lives hang in the balance. But truth is not confined to the courtroom. All of life requires people to be truthful, or life would be a hopeless search for solid ground.

Johann Peter Lange dissects truth from falsehood and underscores its importance.

Walk with Johann Peter Lange

"The lie is a fundamental vice. It is the loveless misuse of language with the design of deceiving our neighbor.

"The untruth is intentional; it is not merely 'not true,' an error not amounting to a lie. The deception is premeditated. Drama, irony, satire, joke— all are not lies; for in these it is presupposed that our neighbor understands this language.

"A lie is an act of lovelessness against our neighbor, even when not intended to injure him, perhaps only to help or assure ourselves or others. The word itself may not make the lie; it may be consummated in silence, in countenance, in gesture or act; but at all events it is an abuse of God's gift for the manifestation of our thoughts and perceptions. Its opposite is truthfulness, love of truth."

Walk Closer to God

Think back to a time when you knowingly told a lie. Do you remember how you lived in dread of the day when your lie would be found out?

Those who traffic in untruth are miserable people. They fear being found out and live bitterly once their lie is unmasked. Like Peter, who struggled with guilt and remorse after denying his Master (Luke 22:54-62), they shed bitter tears— but after the damage has been done.

Courtroom drama may thrive on the search for truth, but for a child of God there is a simpler way: Always tell the truth. Then you don't have to worry about remembering what you said!

*T*ruth is not a trivial issue

*W*orship from the Heart

Paul urges believers to put on the new nature—a conscious act of will. Ponder what the process of "getting dressed" spiritually means for you as you prepare to face each new day.

*W*alk Thru the Word

New Testament Reading
Ephesians 4:17-32
Old Testament Reading
Proverbs 12:17-22

*S*hun the darkness; stand for the light

*W*orship from the Heart

Paul exhorts the Christians at Ephesus to make the most of every opportunity surrounded as they were by evil (v. 16). We think of our time as our own and feel virtuous when we "donate" some of it to God. But God gives us every minute of our lives! As you praise Him for the gift of life and time, acknowledge that all of your time belongs to Him, and ask Him to work through you as He would like.

*W*alk Thru the Word

New Testament Reading
Ephesians 5:1-21
Old Testament Reading
Psalm 141:1-5

Have nothing to do with the fruitless deeds of darkness, but rather expose them (Ephesians 5:11).

*B*ad company corrupts good morals. Where good and evil are found in close proximity, trouble is sure to follow.

In chapter 5 of Ephesians, Paul cautions the children of God to beware of the dark, even as they stand for the light. Charles Hodge explains.

Walk with Charles Hodge

"The duty of Christians in reference to the works of darkness is twofold; first, to have no communion with them, and second, to expose them. The former is expressed by the words 'have nothing to do with.' Those who have things in common, who are congenial, who have the same views, feelings, and interests, are said to be in fellowship.

"So we are said to have fellowship in anything that we delight in and partake of. To have fellowship with the works of darkness, therefore, is to delight in them and to participate in them. All such association is forbidden as inconsistent with the character of the children of light.

"Our second duty is to 'reprove' [expose] them. It is not simply admonishing or rebuking. It means to convince by evidence.

"When the Spirit is said to reprove people of sin, it means that He sheds such light upon their sins as to reveal their true character, and to produce the consciousness of guilt. The duty here enjoined is to shed light on these works of darkness, to exhibit them in their true nature as vile and destructive. By this method they are corrected."

Walk Closer to God

Those who have grown accustomed to the dark shy away from the light—not because they do not need it, but because they do not want it to unmask their wickedness.

Your task as the light of the world is to remove yourself from the fellowship of the wicked and expose their deeds of darkness. Only then will you be an influence for good—rather than a casualty—"in a crooked and depraved generation" (Philippians 2:15).

Chosen above all others

"For this reason a man will leave his father and mother and be united to his wife, and the two will become one flesh." This is a profound mystery—but I am talking about Christ and the church (Ephesians 5:31-32).

*A*fter a brief ceremony, and an exchange of vows and rings, a man and woman are united in marriage. Two become one.

Joyous? Indeed! Mysterious? To be sure. How can 1 + 1 = 1?

It's a question well worth pondering, for the marriage relationship pictures another mystery of infinitely greater scope.

Jonathan Edwards probes this mystery of Christ and His bride, the church.

Walk with Jonathan Edwards

"The mutual joy of Christ and His church is like that of bridegroom and bride, in that they rejoice in each other for their nearest, most intimate, everlasting friends and companions.

"The church is Christ's chosen. He has chosen her, not to be mere servants, but friends. As the bridegroom chooses the bride above all others in the world, so Christ has chosen His church for a particular nearness to Him, as His flesh and His bone, and the high honor and dignity of betrothal above all others, even the angels.

"On the other hand, the church chooses Christ above all others: He is in her eyes the chief among ten thousand, fairer than the sons of men; she rejects the suit of all His rivals, for His sake; her heart relinquishes the whole world; He is her pearl of great price, for which she parts with all, and rejoices in Him, as the choice of her soul.

"All things are Christ's, but He has a special interest in His church."

Walk Closer to God

Two twenty-three-year-olds making a fifty-year commitment to each other—that's a mystery!

The Savior of mankind pledging His loyal love to those deserving only His wrath—that's a mystery!

And your response of gratitude in the face of such selfless devotion—that should be no mystery at all!

Worship from the Heart

You are not likely to be anyone's legal slave. But you do have to obey authority—employer, government, church. Rather than doing your duty grudgingly with inward feelings of resentment and rebellion, rejoice that each duty can be an act of worship. Offer your time, energy, and possessions wholeheartedly in God's service today.

Walk Thru the Word

New Testament Reading
Ephesians 5:22-33
Old Testament Reading
Genesis 2:22-24

Family life at its finest

Children, obey your parents in the Lord, for this is right. "Honor your father and mother"—which is the first commandment with a promise (Ephesians 6:1-2).

*P*aul quotes the words of Moses to show that obedient children enjoy life "well . . . and . . . long . . . on the earth" (Ephesians 6:3). And obedient children develop best when rooted "in the training and instruction of the Lord" (Ephesians 6:4).

John and Charles Wesley, great 18th-century revival leaders in England, were taught to obey as Jesus did. Their mother, Susannah Wesley, gave this description of their upbringing.

Walk with Susannah Wesley

"I insisted on conquering a child's will, for when this is thoroughly done a child can be governed by the reason and piety of his parents until its own understanding comes into maturity, and the principles of religion have taken root in its mind.

"Self-will is the root of all sin and misery. Whatever promotes this in children ensures their wretchedness; whatever checks it increases their future happiness. The parent who indulges the child's self-will does the Devil's work: makes religion impracticable, salvation unattainable, and is working to damn his child's soul forever.

"Without renouncing the world no one can follow my method. Very few would devote more than twenty years of their life to save the souls of their children which they think may be saved without so much ado. Yet that was my intention, however unskillfully and unsuccessfully managed."

Walk Closer to God

Young person, if God's own Son willingly submitted to earthly parents, is He asking too much for you to do the same?

Parents, if your children see you as "standing in the place of God," what needs to change in order for the picture to communicate accurately and consistently?

Obedient children . . . honored parents . . . God-honoring lives. That's family life at its finest—in the family of God!

Worship from the Heart

"My heavenly Father, how gracious You have been to me. I sometimes wandered far from my true home, but You drew me to Your side, not only saving me, but even adopting me as Your child. I take Your Son as my example in all matters of obedience and submission, for my desire is to be a child that gives You joy."

Walk Thru the Word

New Testament Reading
Ephesians 6:1-9
Old Testament Reading
Proverbs 6:20-22

Therefore put on the full armor of God, so that when the day of evil comes, you may be able to stand your ground, and after you have done everything, to stand (Ephesians 6:13).

A tortoise's shell is so strong that very few natural predators can kill one as long as the shell is intact. But should his shell become cracked or weakened, the tortoise is susceptible both to disease and attack and will rarely survive.

Just as God designed protective plating for the tortoise, He has provided believers with unseen, but vitally important, armor. Jessie Penn-Lewis explains the importance of our God-given armor.

Walk with Jessie Penn-Lewis

"The objective in the cited passage is clearly not victory over sin—this is assumed—but victory over Satan. The armor in detail, as set forth here, is provided that the child of God should be "able to stand" against the wiles of the Devil.

"It is a real armor, provided for meeting a real foe, and it must demand a real knowledge on the part of the believer—to whom the fact of the provision, the fact of the foe, and the fact of the fight, must be as real as any other facts declared in the Scriptures.

"The believer who takes up the whole armor of God as a covering and protection against the foe must walk in victory over the Enemy.

"He must have (1) his spirit indwelt by the Holy Spirit, so that he is strengthened with the might of God to stand unshaken; (2) his mind renewed (Romans 12:2) so that he has his understanding filled with the light of truth (Ephesians 1:18), displacing Satan's lies, and destroying the veil with which Satan once held it; (3) his body subservient to the Spirit (1 Corinthians 9:25) and obedient to the will of God in life and service."

Walk Closer to God

The tortoise may lose its armor through no fault of its own; but you Christian, are responsible for your own armor. After you receive the helmet of salvation, you must go on to acquire the other pieces. The whole armor is top priority for warfare!

*R*eal armor for facing a real foe

*W*orship from the Heart

If Paul needed the continual prayers of other Christians, we certainly do. "Pray . . . on all occasions . . . keep on praying for all the saints." Are you grateful for the privilege of interceding for other believers? Begin today to do your part. You might start a chain reaction.

*W*alk Thru the Word

New Testament Reading
Ephesians 6:10-24
Old Testament Reading
2 Chronicles 16:1-9

253

Martin Luther (1483-1546) Champion of Salvation

On October 31, 1517, a professor in the German town of Wittenberg nailed several sheets of paper, covered with his Latin handwriting, to the door of the town church.

His purpose was simply to open debate on some theological problems he had with official church positions. Yet within a few years he would become the best-known figure in the European church.

Anyone claiming to be a Protestant can trace his roots back to this one man—Martin Luther—often considered to be larger than life because of his many gifts, his powerful personality, his commitment to Jesus Christ, and his impact on society.

Born in 1483 at Eisleben, Germany, Luther's early education prepared him to become a lawyer. But a terrifying experience in a thunderstorm at the age of twenty-two caused him to seek spiritual comfort.

Possessed of an acute sense of his own unworthiness before God, Luther felt that becoming a priest offered the best way to deal with the problem.

As the young priest received formal

theological training, he began to lecture on the Bible, all the while wrestling with his own spiritual condition. How could he be saved? The answer came with ringing clarity from the pages of Scripture: God saves those who look to Christ alone for their salvation and trust in nothing else.

Centuries of tradition and misunderstanding had allowed an unscriptural idea—that a person's works were the means of salvation—to creep into church doctrine. But Luther realized that salvation is the gift of God, not of works (Ephesians 2:8-9).

Not long after his conversion, Luther nailed his ninety-five theses to the Wittenberg church door. What he said challenged the traditions that had caused him so much soul-searching and grief.

The storm of debate about salvation eventually raged through all Europe. Luther was called to stand trial for his beliefs before church and secular courts. His reply was strong and sure—"Here I stand; I can do no other."

Luther was concerned that the message of salvation would continue to pierce hearts, so he translated the Bible into German—the language of the common people—and wrote pamphlets that were widely distributed. He wrote hymns (including "A Mighty Fortress Is Our God"), developed worship services, and preached the Word of God.

The Protestant Reformation, which was largely spawned by his godly commitment, did more than form new Christian denominations. It affected family life, politics, the arts, and education. And all because one man boldly declared the true meaning of salvation in Jesus Christ. By the time of his death in 1546, Luther's impact could be neither denied nor ignored.

Every generation needs more Martin Luthers—Christians of commitment and courage who know what they believe and can defend those beliefs.

In fact, men and women like Martin Luther are in short supply today. But you can help change that.

Determining to believe and obey God's Word and walk closer to Him—regardless of popular opinion—is the place to begin.

A Lesson from the life of Martin Luther

When I am sure of what I believe, I will have the courage to stand against error.

255

Enemies no more

It is true that some preach Christ out of envy and rivalry, . . . out of selfish ambition, not sincerely, supposing that they can stir up trouble for me while I am in chains (Philippians 1:15, 17).

"Don't get mad, just get even." "Do not be over-come by evil, but overcome evil with good."

Which philosophy do you embrace—reciprocal revenge or turn-the-other-cheek tolerance? For the Christian, enemies should receive the same treatment as friends. But it's a difficult attitude to adopt—and maintain—when so many would rather fight than forgive.

Paul's attitude toward such people was to look for the good in their actions. Martin Luther draws this application from Paul's example.

Walk with Martin Luther

"We must live among ungrateful people, but we should not take offense or cease to do good on that account. Instead, we should continually do good and pay no attention to the poor thanks we reap.

"For if you do good in order to earn the grati-tude and applause of the world, you will find the very opposite. And your lot is just and fair. If you grow very angry, want to pull down mountains, and are determined to do no more good, you harm yourself and accomplish nothing.

"Can you not see that you are living in a world that is bound to be full of vice and ingratitude? The Proverbs speak of those who return evil for good. The man who does not want to learn this may run out of the world, for it requires no skill to live with the pious only and to do good to them; but it does require ability to associate with the wicked without becoming wicked yourself."

Walk Closer to God

Paul didn't let hatred infect him; rather, he looked for good to come out of his mistreatment. In spite of wrong motives, the preaching of the gospel was bringing others to Christ. While human preachers thought they were getting even with Paul, God was getting glory from Paul's predicament.

Righteousness, not revenge—is that the way you strive to "settle the score"?

Worship from the Heart

Imprisoned and threatened with death, Paul rejoiced. He had learned from his Lord that inno-cent suffering, offered for God's glory, is redemptive. As you worship, thank God that when you are unjustly treated, you, like Paul, have an opportunity to show forth the love of Christ.

Walk Thru the Word

New Testament Reading
Philippians 1
Old Testament Reading
Numbers 22:1-31

Your attitude should be the same as that of Christ Jesus (Philippians 2:5).

*T*he border between two countries can represent an immense contrast. A citizen who is a
pauper by one nation's standards may vastly
improve his living standard simply by crossing
the border.

By contrast, Jesus Christ left the home of His
Father in heaven and entered the domain of sinful humanity. He exchanged the rights of a King
for the poverty of an earthling. F. B. Meyer elaborates on history's most distinguished "emigrant."

Walk with F .B. Meyer

"In all Scripture there is no passage that com-
bines such extraordinary extremes as this. The
apostle opens the golden compasses of his faith,
placing one jeweled point on the throne of divine
glory and the other at the edge of the pit, where the
cross stood. Then he asks us to measure the vast
descent of the Son of God as He came to help us.

"Mark the seven steps: He was in the form of
God, that is, as much God as He was afterward a
servant. He did not grasp at equality with God,
for it was already His. He emptied Himself; that
is, refused to avail Himself of the use of His
divine attributes, that He might teach the meaning of absolute dependence on the Father.

"He obeyed as a servant the laws that had their
source in Himself. He became man—a humble
man, a dying man, a crucified man. He lay in the
grave. But the meaning of His descent was that of
His ascent, and to all His illustrious names is
now added that of 'Jesus—Savior.' "

Walk Closer to God

Christ came to earth, not only to pave the way
for men and women to go to heaven, but to bring
"foreign aid"—the riches of heaven—to earth.

First and foremost in this "development program" is the implanting of His mind-set in the
lives of those who desire to follow Him—a mind
that humbles itself before the Father, allowing
Him to work His will "on earth as it is in heaven."

That same mind can be at work in you right
now as you kneel before your Lord Christ.

*B*uilding bridges, crossing borders

*W*orship from the Heart

*"All hail the power
of Jesus' name! Let
angels prostrate
fall;/Bring forth the
royal diadem,/And
crown Him Lord of
all/Sinners whose
love can ne'er for-
get/The wormwood
and the gall,/Go,
spread your trophies
at His feet,/And
crown Him Lord
of all!"*

*W*alk Thru the Word

New Testament Reading
Philippians 2:1-11
Old Testament Reading
Psalm 138:1-6

Set safely at the right hand of God

Worship from the Heart

"Do not fret because of evil men," says the psalmist. Come into God's presence today with quiet confidence that He is in control —of world affairs as well as your personal circumstances. Rejoice that though the wicked may prosper, God's care for His children never ceases.

Walk Thru the Word

New Testament Reading
Philippians 2:12-18
Old Testament Reading
Psalm 37:1-7

Therefore, my dear friends, as you have always obeyed, . . . work out your salvation with fear and trembling (Philippians 2:12).

What's in a word?
If the word is *run*, the answer is plenty! Its dozens of meanings demonstrate a richness and variety of meaning out of all proportion to its size.

The same could be said for the word *work*. Context becomes all-important in sifting through its many connotations. In chapter 2, before you "run" to a false conclusion about Paul's use of the word *work*, allow Alexander Maclaren to guide you to the proper interpretation.

Walk with Alexander Maclaren

"If this injunction is addressed to those who are looking only to the perfect work of Christ for their salvation, how can they work it out themselves?

"To answer this question, we have to remember that the Scriptural expression *salvation* is used several ways. It sometimes means the whole of the process, from the beginning to the end, by which we are delivered from sin in all its aspects, and are set safely at the right hand of God.

"It sometimes means one or the other of three different parts of that process—either deliverance from the guilt, punishment, and condemnation of sin; or second, the gradual process of deliverance from sin's power in our own hearts; or third, the completion of that process by the final and perfect deliverance from sin, sorrow, and death.

"Salvation, in one aspect, is a thing *past* to the Christian; in another, it is a thing *present;* in a third, it is a thing *future*. But all three are one; all are elements of the one deliverance—the one mighty and perfect act which includes them all. These three all come equally from Christ Himself."

Walk Closer to God

Regardless of its context, *salvation* is a word with deep significance. It is our deliverance from the past, our anchor for the present, our hope for the future—all wrapped up in the person of our Savior (John 4:42).

Because of Jesus, salvation is indeed the faith that works!

258

For everyone looks out for his own interests, not those of Jesus Christ (Philippians 2:21).

*W*ANTED: Understudy for well-traveled, soon-to-retire missionary. Must be able to suffer hardship; to teach and be taught; to interact with all types of people; to evangelize, organize and perform a variety of vital church functions. Low pay, long hours, intense opposition. Interested applicants contact Paul the apostle.

That ad is fictitious, but the position was real. It was filled by a young man named Timothy.

Timothy was like a spiritual son to Paul, so when Paul needed someone to check on the Philippians' growth, he knew he could count on Timothy. Albert Barnes discusses Timothy's commitment to Paul and to the ministry of Christ at Philippi.

Walk with Albert Barnes

"How many professing Christians in our cities and towns are there now who would be willing to leave their comfortable homes and go on embassy duty to Philippi as Timothy did?

"How many are there who would not seek some excuse, and thus show that they 'looked out for their own interests' rather than the things which pertained to the kingdom of Jesus Christ?

"Paul implies here that it is the duty of those who profess faith to seek the things which pertain to the kingdom of the Redeemer, to make that the great and leading object of their lives.

"There are few Christians who deny themselves much to promote the kingdom of the Redeemer. People live for their own ease, for their families, for their businesses—as if a Christian could have anything which he has a right to pursue, and without regard to God's will and glory."

Walk Closer to God

The foremost qualification for the job of disciple in Timothy's day—and yours—is willingness. Willingness to learn, to obey, to serve. Timothy demonstrated this willingness to do God's will at the sacrifice of his own will. You can do the same today.

So what will you do?

*G*od's will: your willingness

*W*orship from the Heart

Timothy exemplifies a spirit of humility combined with fear of the Lord. Those two attitudes together produce willingness. And that leads to true riches and honor—abundant life. Timothy experienced it. Ask God to give you the same.

*W*alk Thru the Word

New Testament Reading
Philippians 2:19-30
Old Testament Reading
Proverbs 22:4

The choice that shapes your destiny

What is more, I consider everything a loss compared to the surpassing greatness of knowing Christ Jesus my Lord, for whose sake I have lost all things (Philippians 3:8).

When Jesus Christ confronts an individual, choices are inevitable. The rich young man of Mark 10:17-23 chose to keep his possessions rather than follow Jesus. Centuries later, another rich young man, Francis of Assisi, renounced his inheritance to spend his life serving Christ.

The rich young man of Jesus' day was never heard from again. Francis of Assisi is still remembered for his devotion to Christ. The choice of each man helped shape his destiny. Let this old Irish hymn guide you into the choice of a lifetime.

Worship from the Heart

Truth. Door. Messiah. Lamb. Light. Life. Teacher. Master. Friend. Savior. Lord. Judge. As you meditate on what each of these names or titles for Jesus means to you, praise Him for the real and personal ways He works in your life. Thank Him for specific ways He has shown His love by being each of those things to you.

Walk with an Irish Hymnwriter

Be Thou my Vision, / O Lord of my heart;
Nought be all else to me, / Save that Thou art—
Thou my best thought, / By day or by night,
Waking or sleeping, / Thy presence my light.

Be Thou My Wisdom, / And Thou my true Word;
I ever with Thee / And Thou with me, Lord;
Thou my great Father, / I Thy true son;
Thou in me dwelling, / And I with Thee one.

Riches I heed not, / Nor man's empty praise,
Thou mine inheritance, / No and always:
Thou and Thou only, / First in my heart,
High King of heaven, / My treasure Thou art.

High King of heaven, / My victory won,
May I reach heaven's joys, / O bright heaven's Sun!
Heart of my own heart, / Whatever befall,
Still be my Vision, / O Ruler of all.

Walk Closer to God

Two rich young men wrestled with life-changing decisions. One concluded, "I will follow gold." The other, "I will follow God."

One thought he had gained the world. The other knew he had lost much from the world's perspective, yet gained far more. What will be the end result of your decision?

Walk Thru the Word

New Testament Reading
Philippians 3:1-11
Old Testament Reading
1 Chronicles 29:1-9

One thing I do: . . . I press on toward the goal to win the prize for which God has called me heavenward in Christ Jesus (Philippians 3:13-14).

A speeding train fails to negotiate a curve. An investigation uncovers the cause of the resulting wreck: a distracted engineer.

The Christian life has its own subtle—yet dangerous—distractions, which can keep us from "pressing toward the goal . . . in Christ Jesus." A. B. Simpson shows what happens when focus is lost in the Christian life.

Walk with A. B. Simpson

"One of Satan's favorite employees is the switchman. He likes nothing better than to sidetrack one of God's express trains sent on a blessed mission.

"Something will come up in the pathway of the earnest soul to attract its attention and occupy its strength and thought.

"Sometimes it is a little irritation or provocation. Sometimes it is a petty grievance. Sometimes it is somebody else's business in which we become interested and which we feel bound to rectify.

"And before we know it, we are absorbed in distracting cares that turn us aside from the great purpose of our life.

"Leave all these things alone. Let grievances come and go, but press forward steadily and irresistibly, crying as you hasten to the goal, 'One thing I do.' "

Walk Closer to God

Which statement better describes your life: "One thing I do and do well"? Or . . . "Forty things I dabble at?"

If you answer is the latter, it may be time to refocus with these spiritual "vision correctors":

"Seek ye first the kingdom of God, and His righteousness" (Matthew 6:33 KJV).

"One thing . . . I seek: that I may dwell in the house of the Lord all the days of my life" (Psalm 27:4).

When your focus is on the things of God and your heart is attuned to His, you'll be delighted to see how much easier it is to "stay on track" in your pursuit of Christlikeness.

Staying on track in the Christian life

Worship from the Heart

"Father, my goal is to be a Christlike person, to be like Your Son. But the world has many attractions. Deaden the attraction I feel for the world with its gadgets and glamour. All day today, Lord, prod me to awareness if my gaze shifts to anything other than Jesus Christ."

Walk Thru the Word

New Testament Reading
Philippians 3:12–4:1
Old Testament Reading
Joshua 1:6-8

In Him there is true victory

I can do everything through him who gives me strength (Philippians 4:13).

What parent would give a child a toy shovel and a pail, then ask him to move a mountain? What mayor would expect an entire city to be lighted by the power of one flashlight battery?

In each case, the power is inadequate for the task. A toy shovel works well in a sandbox; batteries are excellent for flashlights. But cities and mountains require more.

The Christian life also requires more power than one person can muster. A life that pleases God is only possible with God's help. That's where Jesus Christ comes in, as John Henry Jowett explains.

Walk with John Henry Jowett

"The tragedy in so many professedly Christian lives is here—they have no adequate power supply. When they are confronted with a supremely difficult task, they fail to cope with it and are disastrously overwhelmed. They draw their power from ideals and philosophies, and to do so is as precarious as depending upon the electricity that we can entice from the clouds.

"What we need is a living personality who will pour the floods of His own vitality into our impoverished souls. It is only 'in Him' that there is 'bread enough to spare.'

"If we are to live a vigorous and triumphant life, we need a mighty dynamic, and we can find it only in the risen and glorified Lord. 'In Him' we can do all things, even the apparently impossible. 'In Him'—that is where the victory lies."

Walk Closer to God

Moving a mountain a cupful at a time is an impossible endeavor. Yet many Christians attempt to live a heavenly life using only earthly power, which is just as foolish. "If at first you don't succeed, try, try again" may help you climb a mountain, but don't expect to move one that way.

Read again Paul's description of the power available to the person who is "in Him." Christ is the only dynamic you will ever find—or need—to turn spiritual mountains into molehills.

Worship from the Heart

Whatever is true, honorable, just, pure, lovely, gracious, excellent—such are the ingredients of the spiritual food that Paul prescribes for those who would realize the presence of God. Your physical health suffers on a diet of junk food. So does your spiritual health. Feast with thanksgiving on the meat of God's Word and the richness of His presence.

Walk Thru the Word

New Testament Reading
Philippians 4:2-23
Old Testament Reading
2 Samuel 22

We always thank God, the Father of our Lord Jesus Christ, when we pray for you, because we have heard of your faith in Christ Jesus (Colossians 1:3-4).

*Y*ou are standing in the reception line after a wedding, waiting to greet the newlyweds. Will you say, "Congratulations!" or "Thank you!"?

Weddings are traditionally times of celebration, not gratitude. Yet, celebration should leave room for gratitude, as Paul teaches in Colossians 1, and as John Calvin reminds us in this comment.

Walk with John Calvin

"Notice that Paul makes use of thanksgiving in place of congratulation, teaching us that in all our joys we must readily remember the goodness of God, for everything that is pleasant and agreeable to us is a kindness conferred by Him.

"He also admonishes us, by his example, to acknowledge with gratitude not merely those things which the Lord confers upon us, but also those things which He confers upon others.

"But for what does Paul give thanks to the Lord? For the faith and love of the Colossians. He acknowledges, therefore, that both are conferred by God; otherwise the gratitude would be false. And what do we have other than that which comes through His liberality? If, however, even the smallest favors come to us from that source, how much more ought this same acknowledgment be made in reference to those two gifts in which the entire sum of our excellence consists?

"Let us therefore bear in mind that we must rejoice in the favors that we have already received, and give thanks to God for them in such a manner as to seek at the same time from Him perseverance and advancement."

Walk Closer to God

When you offer congratulations to others, don't forget to offer thanks to God. Why? Because His goodness is the reason behind all true celebration. Rather than be caught up in the joy of the moment, let each opportunity for celebration tune your heart anew to thank the Giver of every good and perfect gift.

The source of all joy is God Himself. So celebrate!

*C*ome before His presence with singing

*W*orship from the Heart

Even in harsh circumstances Paul maintained exuberant vitality and inexhaustible hope. You'll see why when you notice the stream of praise that runs through his letters. When you become discouraged, or if you are feeling depressed today, sing aloud: "Praise Him, praise Him, all ye little children! God is love, God is love."

*W*alk Thru the Word

New Testament Reading
Colossians 1:1-14
Old Testament Reading
Psalm 100

*H*is ways are past finding out

That they may know the mystery of God, namely Christ, in whom are hidden all the treasures of wisdom and knowledge (Colossians 2:2-3).

*T*hose who enjoy mystery stories often go back through the twists and turns of the plot to see where their guesses went wrong. Clues are essential to the unraveling of mysteries. And the mysterious parts of the Christian faith have their own clues for the diligent "detective."

Martin Luther, whose careful investigation uncovered the long-lost meaning of salvation by faith, offers this sage advice.

Walk with Martin Luther

"If you wish to act rightly, you can do no better than to be interested in God's Word and works.

"This is the work of your redemption, in which you may apprehend God with certainty and perceive that, if you believe, He will not condemn you because of your sins but will give you eternal life, as Christ told Nicodemus.

"Paul says, 'In Christ are hidden all the treasures of wisdom and knowledge.' This will give you more than enough to study. You will marvel at this sublime revelation of God and will learn to delight in God and love Him. It is a work that can never be exhausted by study in this life.

"And, as Peter says, even the angels cannot see enough of it but find endless joy and delight in contemplating it (1 Peter 1:12)."

Walk Closer to God

Some readers of mysteries enjoy the challenge of independent investigation. Others like the plot clearly laid out.

Christianity provides plenty of both. For those who like to investigate, there is "the depth of the riches of the wisdom and knowledge of God! How unsearchable his judgments, and his paths beyond tracing out!" (Romans 11:33).

And Paul reminds those who like to keep things simple that he was determined to "know nothing while I was with you except Jesus Christ and him crucified" (1 Corinthians 2:2).

Either way, the place to uncover the plot is in the pages of God's Word!

*W*orship from the Heart

If you become impatient with the mystery in your walk with Christ, stop and think. If you, one small part of His creation, could fully understand Him, how could He be truly God? Meditate on the mystery of what God is doing. Concentrate on Christ, where all the treasures of wisdom and knowledge are hidden. You'll grow richer day by day.

*W*alk Thru the Word

New Testament Reading
Colossians 1:15–2:5
Old Testament Reading
Isaiah 11:1-2

*H*aving the habit of holiness

Just as you received Christ Jesus as Lord, continue to live in him, rooted and built up in him, strengthened in the faith (Colossians 2:6-7).

*H*abits are like cork or lead. They tend to keep you up . . . or drag you down. There are good habits and bad habits, and it's easy to tell the difference. Good habits are difficult to start and easy to break; bad habits are easy to start and difficult to break.

Walking with God is a habit only careful cultivation will produce. A. B. Simpson explains why.

Walk with A. B. Simpson

"It is much easier to keep the fire burning than to rekindle it after it has gone out. Let us abide in Christ. Let us not have to remove the ashes from our hearthstones every day and kindle a new flame, but let us keep it burning and never let it expire.

"It takes a lot less effort to maintain a good habit than to form it. A true spiritual habit once formed becomes a spontaneous tendency of our being, and we grow into delightful freedom in following it. 'Let us . . . go on to maturity, not laying again the foundation of repentance from acts that lead to death' (Hebrews 6:1).

"Every spiritual habit begins with difficulty and effort and watchfulness. But if we will only let it get thoroughly established, it will become a channel along which currents of life will flow with divine spontaneity and freedom."

Walk Closer to God

"[Our] most deadly enemy is not cancer or heart disease, but habit—all the routines of thinking, feeling, and doing that enable humans to get through life without living it."

And yet, some routine is essential: No one questions the importance of clean teeth, employment, and knowing current events.

What about the "routine" of walking with Christ? A healthy spiritual walk requires good habits of holiness: time with God, Bible study, prayer, fellowship with believers.

Difficult habits to start? To be sure. But delightful to maintain!

*W*orship from the Heart

After King Darius had signed the decree that would send Daniel to the lions, Daniel did not wait to see the outcome before giving thanks. It was enough that he had put himself in God's hands. Give thanks today that the God of Daniel is your God and that you can pray with the same confident faith that Daniel prayed.

*W*alk Thru the Word

New Testament Reading
Colossians 2:6-23
Old Testament Reading
Daniel 6:4-23

265

Essentials for life in Christ

For you died, and your life is now hidden with Christ in God (Colossians 3:3).

Before a team of astronauts blasts off on a mission, they check and double-check for vital supplies: oxygen to breathe, fuel to burn, food and water for sustenance. They know that space is hostile and unforgiving to those who take survival for granted.

The hostile environment of the world is no more forgiving for Christians. Like astronauts, we dare not take supplies for granted: the milk and meat of the Word, the power of the Spirit, the refreshment of forgiveness—in a word, the Bread of Life!

Oswald Chambers explores the significance of life in Christ.

Walk with Oswald Chambers

"We talk as if it were the most precarious thing to live the sanctified life; it is the most secure thing, because it has almighty God in and behind it.

"If we are born again, it is the easiest thing to live in right relationship to God and the most difficult thing to go wrong, if only we will heed God's warnings and keep in the light.

"When we think of being delivered from sin, of being filled with the Spirit, and of walking in the light, we picture a great, high mountain, and we say—'Oh, but I never could live up there!' But when we do get there by God's grace, we find it is not a mountain peak, but a plateau where there is ample room to live and to grow.

"When you really see Jesus, I defy you to doubt Him. 'Your life is hidden with Christ in God,' and the peace of Jesus Christ is imparted to you."

Walk Closer to God

Food for the hungry. Energy for the weak. Water for the thirsty. All are found in the "life [that] is now hidden with Christ in God"—the life that is Christ Himself. Paul says, "When Christ, who is your life, appears, then you also will appear with him in glory" (Colossians 3:4).

And where He is, you can be sure there will be no lack of the essentials needed to live life as He intended.

Worship from the Heart

Her job was dull, and she worked automatically with one eye on the clock. Her heart was not in her tasks, but she performed adequately. Wasn't that enough? Paul's answer is revealing: "Whatever you do, work at it with all your heart, as working for the Lord, not for men." Thank your Lord that regardless of where you are, your life is hidden with Christ in God—even in a dull, thankless job.

Walk Thru the Word

New Testament Reading
Colossians 3:1–4:1
Old Testament Reading
Genesis 5:24

266

Epaphras, who is one of you and a servant of Christ Jesus, sends greetings. He is always wrestling in prayer for you (Colossians 4:12).

*P*aul closes his letter to the Colossians with both an exhortation and an example.

The exhortation? "Devote yourselves to prayer, being watchful and thankful. And pray for us, too" (4:2-3).

The example? "Epaphras, . . . a servant of Christ, . . . is always wrestling in prayer for you" (4:12).

Put them together, and you have a powerful stimulus to prayerfulness, as F. B. Meyer notes.

Walk with F. B. Meyer

"This is a very beautiful epitaph on a good man's life. Amid all the crowding interests of Epaphras's visit to Rome, his heart was with his friends. He strove for them in prayer.

"It was no passing thought that he voiced; no light breathing of desire; no formal mention of their names. It seemed as though he were a wrestler, whose muscles strained as he agonized for the prize. He labored.

"We shall never know, till we stand in the clear light of heaven, how much has been wrought in the world by prayer. Here, at least, there is mention of a man's labors. Probably the work on the results of which we are inclined to pride ourselves is due less to us than we suppose, and more to unrecognized fellow laborers.

"Let us be careful to mingle much intercession with all our prayers, especially on behalf of Christian workers, that they may realize we are actually working and laboring beside them."

Walk Closer to God

"Father, I confess that my prayers have too often been only shallow phrases rather than heartfelt wrestlings.

"Help me learn from Epaphras's example and see the eternal value of laboring in prayer.

"I lift up my friends and co-laborers in Christ. I pray, as Epaphras did, that they might 'stand firm in all the will of God.' In the name of the One who taught us to pray. Amen."

*W*orking in prayer

*W*orship from the Heart

Despite his mother's pleas, Augustine remained a pagan. Then his mother stopped pleading and began fervent, secret intercession for his conversion. Soon a chain of events began that brought Augustine to the Lord. Prayer is not a glamorous task, but it is the work God calls His children to do—without ceasing. As you obey, thank Him for the privilege.

*W*alk Thru the Word

New Testament Reading
Colossians 4:2-18
Old Testament Reading
1 Samuel 12:23

267

Your Manual for Growing Relationships

Paul's letters to the Thessalonians and to Timothy, Titus and Philemon help the church set priorities for relationships and ministry in light of Christ's return.

*L*etters are probably the most intimate form of written communication. They can present information, communicate emotion, and provide inspiration. Paul's letters portray the depth of the relationships he enjoyed with his readers. Far from being mere "people in the pews," Paul addresses them as "brothers," "fellow workers," "son in the faith," "dear friend," and "those who love us in the faith"—all terms of endearment and affection.

Paul's two letters to the church in Thessalonica demonstrate a parent's love and concern; he compares himself both to a caring mother and an encouraging father (1 Thessalonians 2:7, 11). The church was Paul's spiritual family, and like any family it required nurture, discipline, instruction, and exhortation.

In his letters to Timothy and Titus, Paul shows the depth of his relationship with two of his coworkers. These young men were pastoral trainees of the apostle. The two letters to Timothy contain personal advice on the conduct of the minister and provide guidelines by which the young pastor could evaluate faithful men for church leadership. Titus emphasizes "our great God and Savior, Jesus Christ" (Titus 2:13), as the One who enables us to live a God-pleasing life, redeemed by God's grace and zealous to serve.

Philemon, Paul's postcard-size letter, deals with the specific case of a runaway slave named Onesimus. After escaping from his Christian master, Onesimus encountered Paul and found a new master—Jesus Christ. Paul, sensing the need to reconcile the slave with his human master, writes a brief letter to accompany Onesimus as he returns to Philemon.

One thing is certain as you begin your journey through these letters: You will encounter people. That's why Paul's letters remain so timely! Let him share with you each day this month how you can better relate to others. At the same time, you'll find your own relationship with the Lord deepening, for as you get to know other Christians, you get to know the Lord who lives in them.

Choosing to obey

We continually remember before our God and Father your work produced by faith, your labor prompted by love, and your endurance inspired by hope in our Lord Jesus Christ. For we know, brothers loved by God, that he has chosen you (1 Thessalonians 1:3-4).

*F*or the Christian, the future is as bright as the promises of God. But fascination with the future—a longing for knowledge before the fact—can be dangerous. When preoccupation with the future causes you to neglect the lessons of the past and the urgencies of the present, be careful!

What has God done? What is He doing? What will He do? All three answers find resolution in a personal relationship with Jesus Christ, as Charles Spurgeon explains.

Walk with Charles Spurgeon

"Many people want to know their election [choosing] before they look to Christ. But they cannot learn it thus; it is only to be discovered by 'looking unto Jesus.'

"Look to Jesus, believe on Him, and you shall make proof of your election directly, for as surely as you believe, you are elect. If you will give yourself wholly up to Christ and trust Him, then you are one of God's chosen ones. Go to Jesus just as you are. Go straight to Christ, hide in His wounds, and you shall know your election.

"Christ was at the everlasting council. He can tell you whether you were chosen or not; you cannot find out any other way. Go and put your trust in Him. There will be no doubt about His having chosen you, when *you* have chosen Him."

Walk Closer to God

When it comes to Jesus Christ, focusing on the past or pondering the future means little until first you have chosen Him in the present.

The question to ask is not "What does He think of me?" ("God demonstrates his own love for us in this: While we were still sinners, Christ died for us" Romans 5:8.) Rather, the question to ask is "What do I think of Him?" ("Anyone who trusts in him will never be put to shame" Romans 10:11.)

How will you answer today?

Worship from the Heart

Today's Old Testament reading reveals that when God first called Abraham, He did not reveal the destination. Abraham's response is instructive: He went. When God reveals His will on a matter, your joy is simply to follow, not to hold an internal debate about whether or not you like the assignment. Ask God to give you the obedience and flexibility of Abraham.

Walk Thru the Word

New Testament Reading
1 Thessalonians 1
Old Testament Reading
Genesis 12:1-4

Truth that stands through time and trials

We also thank God continually because, when you received the word of God, which you heard from us, you accepted it not as the word of men, but as it actually is, the word of God (1 Thessalonians 2:13).

*P*oliticians square off for an election-year debate, drawing upon statistics and projections, opinion polls and expert testimony. And what is their goal? To sway you to their point of view.

But what if all the candidates offer convincing arguments? Then if you haven't considered the issues and come to your own conclusions, you may find yourself vacillating.

The same could be said of your Christian beliefs. Where you got them will often determine how strongly you hold them. The Thessalonians not only knew *what* they believed, they also knew *why*. Their well-considered convictions are an example for modern Christians, as Albert Barnes explains.

Walk with Albert Barnes

"The word they received was not of human origin, but a divine revelation. You were not led to embrace it by human persuasion, but by your conviction that it was a revelation from God.

"It is only when the gospel is embraced in this way that religion will show itself sufficient to abide the fiery trials to which Christians may be exposed.

"He who is convinced by mere human reasoning or eloquence may have his faith shaken by opposite artful reasoning. He who embraces religion from mere respect for a pastor, parent, or friend, may abandon it when the popular current turns in a different direction; but he who embraces religion as the truth of God, and from the love of the truth, will have a faith, like that of the Thessalonians, that will abide every trial."

Walk Closer to God

Satan, the father of all lies, is skillful at planting seeds of doubt about God's truth into the minds of men and women who aren't sure what they believe or why.

The Thessalonians knew where they stood. Will you stand with them?

Worship from the Heart

As you hear the Word of God, sitting safely in among other believers, give thanks. Rejoice that the truth of the Word is so strong that it has survived innumerable attempts to eradicate it. Rejoice that across 2,000 years the words of Jesus now come to you.

Walk Thru the Word

New Testament Reading
1 Thessalonians 2:1-16
Old Testament Reading
Proverbs 18:15

Caught up for His purpose

We sent Timothy, who is our brother and God's fellow worker in spreading the gospel of Christ, to strengthen . . . you (1 Thessalonians 3:2).

*A*ll great actors are known for their ability to change their personality at will. Without losing their own individuality, they learn to make the character they are portraying come to life.

The Christian life calls for a similar decrease of self and increase of Christ's character. Oswald Chambers describes the proper attitude for a Christian intent on portraying Christ to a waiting world.

Walk with Oswald Chambers

"God has taken you up into His purpose by the Holy Ghost. He is using you now for His purposes throughout the world as He used His Son for the purpose of our salvation.

"If you seek great things for yourself, you put up a barrier to God's use of you. As long as you have a personal interest in your own character, or any set ambition, you cannot get through into identification with God's interests. You can only get there by losing forever any idea of yourself and by letting God take you out into His purpose for the world.

"I have to learn that the aim in life is God's, not mine. God is using me from His great personal standpoint; all He asks of me is that I trust Him.

"When I stop telling God what I want, He can catch me up for what He wants without hindrance. He can crumple me up or exalt me; He can do anything He chooses. He simply asks me to have implicit faith in Him and in His goodness."

Walk Closer to God

The ambitions of fame and fortune often work at cross purposes to the need for great acting—the kind that makes the characters better remembered than the actors who portrayed them.

God is looking for men and women who want to portray Christ in word and deed—who long to bring fame to the name of their Savior. There is room in the spotlight for only one. Christian, which will it be—you, or your Lord?

Worship from the Heart

When separated from family and friends, we are often concerned about their health, safety, happiness. But our primary concern should be that their relationship with the Lord remain strong. Praise God for family members and close friends who are walking with the Lord. Pray specifically for those you know who are still unsaved.

Walk Thru the Word

New Testament Reading
1 Thessalonians 2:17–3:13
Old Testament Reading
Malachi 1:11

Simply staying where you're put

Finally, brothers, we instructed you how to live in order to please God, as in fact you are living. Now we ask you and urge you in the Lord Jesus to do this more and more (1 Thessalonians 4:1).

*T*he "greener grass" syndrome affects everyone occasionally, but for some it's a chronic ailment.

The symptoms? A longing gaze over the fence. A tendency to see grass that is greener when it is not under one's own feet. Constant expressions of discontent at present circumstances. A tendency to wander in search of more fulfilling pastures.

And even Christians are not immune, as A. B. Simpson explains.

Walk with A. B. Simpson

"How many dear Christians are in the place that the Lord has appointed them, and yet the Devil is harassing their lives with a sense that they are not quite pleasing the Lord.

"If they could just settle down in the place that God has assigned them and fill it sweetly and lovingly, there would be more joy in their hearts and more power in their lives. The secret of accomplishing the most for Him is to recognize our place from Him and our service in it as pleasing Him.

"In the greatest factory and machine there is a place for the smallest screw and rivet as well as the great driving wheel and piston. So God has His little screws whose business is simply to stay where He puts them and to believe that He wants them there and is making the most of their lives in the little spaces that they fill for Him."

Walk Closer to God

"Father, I confess that I too suffer from the 'greener grass' syndrome. Too often I have looked at what others are doing and wished that I were doing the same, forgetting that You have gifted me in ways that serve You best.

"Forgive me for my tendency to neglect the good for the glamorous; the true for the convenient; Your will for my will. Make me content with what You have for me.

"In the name of the One who never swerved from doing Your will. Amen."

Worship from the Heart

"The old laws of morality are yesterday's news. Times have changed." Have you heard that view recently? Yes, times have changed, but the God who created you has not. He who loves you more than any human being ever could, can enable you to be all that He made you to be. How exciting to know that "He who began a good work in you will carry it on to completion until the day of Christ Jesus" (Philippians 1:6).

Walk Thru the Word

New Testament Reading
1 Thessalonians 4:1-12
Old Testament Reading
Genesis 13:1-15

To gaze on His face forever

After that, we who are still alive and are left will be caught up together with them in the clouds to meet the Lord in the air. And so we will be with the Lord forever (1 Thessalonians 4:17).

*C*lose families separated by long distances know the bittersweetness of reunions; they long for an extended time together.

It's the same with the family of God; times of fellowship now are nothing compared to the joy eternity will bring. And the time spent with the Head of the family will be the most enjoyable of all. Charles Spurgeon elaborates.

Walk with Charles Spurgeon

"Even the sweetest visits from Christ, how short they are! One moment our eyes see Him and we rejoice; but again a little time and we do not see Him, for our Beloved withdraws Himself from us.

"Oh, how sweet the prospect of the time when we shall not behold Him at a distance but shall see Him face to face! In heaven there shall be no interruptions caused by care or sin; no weeping shall dim our eyes; no earthly business shall distract our happy thoughts; nothing shall hinder us from gazing forever on the Sun of Righteousness with unwearied eyes.

"Oh, if it is sweet to see Him now and then, how sweet to gaze on that blessed face forever and never have to turn one's eyes away to look on a world of weariness and woe. If to die is but to enter into uninterrupted communion with Jesus; then death is indeed gain, and the black drop is swallowed up in a sea of victory."

Walk Closer to God

When family and friends reunite for a visit, they quickly catch up on the past and look ahead to the future. There's hardly a moment of silence among those who care about each other.

When you come into the presence of your Lord Jesus, come with a heart full of gratitude for His companionship in the past . . . His comforting promises for the present . . . His guidance for the future. You should have plenty to share with One so near and dear!

Worship from the Heart

A family friend came to the funeral home where the boy's body lay—16 when he died in a car crash. "How tragic! All that bright promise lost." "No!" his Christian mother replied. "Mourn for us, but not for him. All that promise will be fulfilled." Praise God that when death strikes our loved ones and grief comes our way, our confidence is in the Lord.

Walk Thru the Word

New Testament Reading
1 Thessalonians 4:13-18
Old Testament Reading
2 Samuel 12:23

When His life lights my life

You are all sons of the light and sons of the day.
We do not belong to the night or to the darkness
(1 Thessalonians 5:5).

*F*or the Christian, light and darkness represent the conflict between the ways of God and the ways of the world.

As John describes in his gospel: "In him [Christ] was life, and that life was the light of men. The light shines in the darkness, but the darkness has not understood it" (John 1:4-5). You will learn more about living in the light by reading Charles Hodge's helpful description.

Walk with Charles Hodge

"Christians should live as children of the light. Light stands for knowledge, holiness, and happiness. Darkness stands for ignorance, sin, and misery.

"The exhortation therefore, is in its negative form, not to sink back into the world, which belongs to the kingdom of darkness. That is, not to give yourself up to the opinions and practice of the world, and thus involve yourself in the ruin in which the kingdom of darkness must ultimately issue.

"It is an exhortation to act as becomes those who are members of the kingdom of Christ. An exhortation to exhibit the knowledge and holiness, especially in faith, hope, and charity, which characterize those who belong to that kingdom.

"The motive by which this exhortation is enforced is that we are destined not to wrath but to salvation (1 Thessalonians 5:9). And this salvation is secured by Christ who died, that whether we live or die, we should live together with Him."

Walk Closer to God

As a Christian, you no longer live in the darkness. Because Christ has become your light, you can see where you are going. You can avoid life's pitfalls; you can follow the paths of holiness.

Jesus said it best: "I am the light of the world. Whoever follows me will never walk in darkness, but will have the light of life" (John 8:12). Invite Him to do what light does best in your life . . . right now.

Worship from the Heart

Consider Jesus, whose speech is described as "lips . . . anointed with grace" (Psalm 45:2). As you strive to encourage and build each other up, thank Him for setting the perfect example of tactfulness, encouragement, and wise counsel in all relationships.

Walk Thru the Word

New Testament Reading
1 Thessalonians 5:1-11
Old Testament Reading
Ecclesiastes 8:1

274

*T*inted with a glory and a glow

Be joyful always; pray continually; give thanks in all circumstances, for this is God's will for you in Christ Jesus (1 Thessalonians 5:16-18).

*F*or the Christian, moments of suffering or confusion—when viewed with 20/20 hindsight—often become the cause for rejoicing. Why? Because time frequently reveals the previously unknown purposes of God.

In this passage, Paul adds to the thought contained in Romans 8:28 to show why rejoicing is always appropriate, even when circumstances aren't particularly joyful. Alexander Maclaren adds these timely words.

Walk with Alexander Maclaren

"The look of things in this world depends very largely on the color of the spectacles through which you behold them. If a person in communion with God looks at the events of his life as he might put on a pair of colored glasses to look at a landscape, it will be tinted with a glory and a glow as he looks.

"As we look back, we see the meaning of the former days, and their possible blessings, and the loving purposes which sent them, a great deal more clearly than we did while we were passing through them. If we, from our vantage point in God, will look back on our lives, losses will disclose themselves as gains, sorrows as harbingers of joy, conflict as a means of peace; and we can give thanks for everything in the past.

"But, that is possible only when we 'pray continually' and dwell beside God all the days of our lives, and all the hours of every day. Then, and only then, shall we be able to thank Him for all the ways by which He has led us these many years in the wilderness."

Walk Closer to God

Are there events and circumstances beyond your understanding today? Stop right now and tell God: "Thank you, Father, for all that this will mean to me when I see it from the same perspective You have seen it from all along. Make me truly grateful for all that is past, and for all that is yet ahead."

*W*orship from the Heart

"The one who calls you is faithful" (v. 24). You can trust God to keep His promises. Abraham and Sarah had their long-hoped-for son. The ancient Hebrews did reach the Promised Land. The exile in Babylon came to an end. Christ rose from the dead. And He promises those who believe on Him redemption and eternal life. Hallelujah!

*W*alk Thru the Word

New Testament Reading
1 Thessalonians 5:12-28
Old Testament Reading
Psalm 92

*T*apping into the power supply

. . . that the name of our Lord Jesus may be glorified in you, and you in him (2 Thessalonians 1:12).

*T*urning on the light in a dark room may appear as easy as flipping a switch. But moving the switch makes no difference unless there is a power source attached to it.

You have been called to be the light of the world. You must decide to take that assignment seriously, but it's not your power that enables you to succeed. Rather, the Holy Spirit supplies the power. Without Him, your attempts to bring glory to God are doomed from the start.

F. B. Meyer examines the importance of tapping the right power source.

Walk with F. B. Meyer

"Will you, dear Christian, enter into a solemn agreement with the Holy Spirit that you will live to glorify the name of the Lord Jesus? This is His purpose and aim throughout the present age.

"He seeks the glory of Jesus with the same persistent patience as Jesus sought the glory of His Father, and longs for our fellowship and cooperation. Nothing gratifies the Holy Spirit more than to welcome into partnership those who love the Lord Jesus with a consuming passion and are prepared to glorify Him, at whatever cost to themselves.

"Does this seem too high an aim? Then ponder the gracious assurance that the Lord will fulfill every desire of goodness. He first instills the desire, and then realizes it. Take your desires for goodness to Him; then trust Him, in all faithfulness, to realize and fulfill them.

"He who prompts the desire is well able to fulfill it."

Walk Closer to God

Like the desire to turn on a light, the desire to glorify God means nothing without the necessary power to transform desire into commitment, and commitment into conduct.

"Apart from me," Jesus said, "you can do nothing" (John 15:5).

But with Him? "I can do everything through him [Christ] who gives me strength" (Philippians 4:13).

*W*orship from the Heart

Ponder the solemn words of verse 9: "They will be . . . shut out from the presence of the Lord." Think what such exclusion would mean here and now. No One to stand beside you in grief and pain. No One to entrust your loved ones to in life and in death. No One to whom you could say, "Thank you, Lord." Rejoice that Jesus has made it possible for you to be in the presence of God throughout eternity.

*W*alk Thru the Word

New Testament Reading
2 Thessalonians 1
Old Testament Reading
Isaiah 25:1

276

Living in the light of Christ's return

Concerning the coming of our Lord Jesus Christ . . . we ask you, brothers, not to become easily unsettled (2 Thessalonians 2:1-2).

Preoccupation with the *date* of Christ's return often obscures the *what* and *why* of that "blessed hope." It's more exciting to speculate on the unknown than to live in the purifying light of what is known about Christ's return.

The thought of that future prompted poet John Milton to compose this psalm of meditation.

Walk with John Milton

The Lord will come and not be slow,
  His footsteps cannot err;
Before Him righteousness shall go,
  His royal harbinger.
Truth from the earth, like to a flower,
  Shall bud and blossom then;
And justice, from her heavenly bower,
  Look down on mortal men.

Rise, God, judge Thou the earth in might,
  This wicked earth redress;
And Thou art He who shall by right
  The nations all possess.
For great Thou art, and wonders great
  By Thy strong hand are done;
Thou in Thy everlasting seat
  Remainest God alone.

Walk Closer to God

You may not know when Christ is coming back, but Scripture sheds plenty of light on what will happen when He does. Milton's poem is a helpful summary: righteousness, truth, justice, judgment, retribution.

Christ will come to set things right. How should you live in light of that knowledge?

Be prepared (Matthew 24:44).
Be faithful (Luke 19:13).
Be blameless (1 Thessalonians 5:23).
Be obedient (1 Timothy 6:14).
Be expectant (Titus 2:13).

That's enough to keep you busy until He returns!

Worship from the Heart

At Christ's return the unrighteous will "perish because they . . . have not believed the truth" (vv. 10, 12). Take a moment to examine your life. Does commitment to truth permeate all your relationships, business, service? Allow the God of Truth to shine His cleansing light deep into your heart that you may worship and serve Him—in truth.

Walk Thru the Word

New Testament Reading
2 Thessalonians 2:1-12
Old Testament Reading
Proverbs 13:12

Receiving power from the Spirit

May our Lord Jesus Christ himself and God our Father . . . encourage your hearts and strengthen you in every good deed and word (2 Thessalonians 2:16-17).

What would you think of a neighbor who was willing to loan you a lawnmower (but no gas), a flashlight (but no batteries), or a barbeque grill (but no charcoal)?

Chances are you would look elsewhere for the source of supply. Why? Because in each case, the tool without the fuel is useless.

In chapter 2, Paul underscores some of the obligations of the Christian life. But he doesn't stop there, for he knows that without God's empowering, those obligations become mere wishful thinking. John Calvin provides this powerful insight.

Walk with John Calvin

"When Paul ascribes to Christ a work altogether divine and represents Him, in common with the Father, as the Author of the choicest blessings, we are admonished that we cannot obtain anything from God unless we seek it in Christ Himself.

"Unquestionably there will be but an empty sound striking upon the ear if doctrine does not receive power from the Spirit.

"But how does Paul bolster their confidence in asking? By showing that they are dear to God, who has already conferred upon them distinguished favors, and has bound Himself to them for the time to come.

"And what does Paul pray? That God will sustain their hearts by His consolation, keeping them from giving way through anxiety or distrust, and that He will give them perseverance, both in holy lives and in sound doctrine."

Walk Closer to God

Another of Paul's letters speaks of the same apparent paradox:

"Therefore, my dear friends, . . . work out your salvation with fear and trembling, for it is God who works in you to will and to act according to his good purpose" (Philippians 2:12-13).

God will never ask *of* you that which He is not capable of doing *through* you.

Worship from the Heart

Imagine your church filled with first-century Christians. Paul stands in the pulpit exhorting, "Stand firm and hold to the teachings we passed on to you" Imagine the congregation as the centuries pass—different faces, different clothing, different leaders. But each pastor continues to preach the same truths Paul preached. When you attend worship, you hold to those God-inspired traditions.

Walk Thru the Word

New Testament Reading
2 Thessalonians 2:13–3:5
Old Testament Reading
Exodus 4:10-17

We hear that some among you are idle. They are not busy; they are busybodies. Such people we command . . . to settle down and earn the bread they eat (2 Thessalonians 3:11-12).

*E*at, drink, and be merry, "for tomorrow we die," was the misguided notion of God's people in Isaiah's day (Isaiah 22:13).

"Eat, drink, and be merry, for tomorrow the Lord returns," was the equally misguided notion of God's people in Paul's day. But Paul had a word of advice for the Thessalonians: "If a man will not work, he shall not eat" (2 Thessalonians 3:10). Martin Luther underscores this point.

Walk with Martin Luther

"To put it briefly, God wants people to work. It is true that God could support you without work, could let food and drink grow on the table for you. But He will not do this. He wants you to work and to use your reason in this matter.

"In everything God acts in such a way that He will provide, but we should work. If God did not bless, not one hair, not a solitary wisp of straw, would grow.

"At the same time God wants me to take this stand: I would have nothing whatever if I did not plow and sow. God does not want to have success come without work, and yet I am not to achieve it by my work.

"He does not want me to sit at home, to loaf and wait till a fried chicken flies into my mouth. That would be tempting God."

Walk Closer to God

God has promised to meet your needs; but as Martin Luther points out, He never promised to deliver your meals!

His responsibility, rather, is to "meet all your needs according to his glorious riches in Christ Jesus" (Philippians 4:19).

Your responsibility is this: "So whether you eat or drink or whatever you do, do it all for the glory of God" (1 Corinthians 10:31).

And the best place for you to be when Christ returns: somewhere hard at work!

*G*od feeds the sparrows, but He doesn't throw them worms

Worship from the Heart

Though we may sometimes grumble about our work, it is a beneficial gift we should enjoy. Take a moment to visualize how your workplace can be a place of both service and worship as you become God's hands, His voice, His character reaching out to those who need Him.

Walk Thru the Word

New Testament Reading
2 Thessalonians 3:6-18
Old Testament Reading
Exodus 23:12

*P*reserving the sound doctrine of the gospel

We also know that law is made not for the righteous but for lawbreakers and rebels, . . . and for whatever else is contrary to the sound doctrine that conforms to the glorious gospel of the blessed God (1 Timothy 1:9-11).

*A*berrant teachings and blatant heresies had already filtered into the church at the time of Paul's first letter to Timothy. Paul wanted to alert the young pastor to them and remind him of the importance of centering the Good News on the sound doctrine spelled out in God's Word.

Not much has changed since then, and Phillips Brooks explains why anchoring our hope on God's truth is so critical.

Walk with Phillips Brooks

"Few are the mistakes which men make when they read the Bible as the law of life. Few are the men able to read the Bible rightly when they fasten their eyes on it for speculation. The soul which goes to the Bible to get the thing for which it was given, gets the thing it goes for.

"When St. Paul writes back from Europe to Asia, he bids Timothy teach the disciples that the law is to be used lawfully. He tells him the same lesson which we need. Let us go to our Bible for our Bible's purpose, inspiration, and a law of life, and the idea of what God would have man to be, and the power to become what it is the purpose of our Father that we should become.

"[Go to] the Bible for the Bible's purpose. Always, spirituality is to go back to morality. The idea that man is to be wise with the wisdom of God is to refresh itself with the idea that man is to be good with the holiness of God."

Walk Closer to God

Today thousands of people are following "a way that seems right . . . , but in the end it leads to death" (Proverbs 16:25). This concerned the apostle Paul and it should concern us as well.

The next time a "missionary" knocks on your door or hands you a tract, take time to lovingly present the sound doctrine of the gospel. In the meantime, pray for those lost sheep who, while seeking truth, have wandered off into darkness.

*W*orship from the Heart

Jesus said, "I am the way and the truth and the life. No one comes to the Father except through me" (John 14:6). Contemplate what it means to you to know the truth about yourself, the truth about this physical world and the spiritual realm, and the truth of salvation. Rejoice in Jesus— Truth revealed.

*W*alk Thru the Word

New Testament Reading
1 Timothy 1:1-11
Old Testament Reading
Psalm 119:129-136

Standing on holy ground

I thank Christ Jesus our Lord, who has given me strength, that he considered me faithful, appointing me to his service . . . .The grace of our Lord was poured out on me abundantly, along with the faith and love that are in Christ Jesus (1 Timothy 1:12, 14).

The apostle Paul's blinding encounter on the road to Damascus has become the descriptive term for any dramatic about-face in attitude. When he left Jerusalem, Paul was "a blasphemer and a persecutor and a violent man" (1:13) to the cause of Christ; by the time he arrived in Damascus, his life had been redirected into the service of Christ.

Inexplicable? Not when you know the One he met on the road to Damascus. John Chrysostom describes the response of those who find themselves suddenly, unexpectedly, on holy ground.

Walk with John Chrysostom

"Let us then love God through Christ. For not only is faith necessary, but love also. There are many who believe that Christ is God, yet love Him not, nor act like those who love Him. For how is it that they prefer everything above Him? When we live in defiance of Him, where is our love?

"Has anyone a warm and affectionate friend? Let him love Christ but equally. So let him love God who gave His Son for us—His enemies— who had no merits of our own; who had committed numberless sins; who had dared Him beyond all daring, all without cause.

"Yet He, after numberless instances of goodness and care, did not cast us off even then. At the very time when we did Him the greatest wrong, He gave His Son for us."

Walk Closer to God

When what Paul actually deserved was eternal punishment, he instead received eternal life and a purpose for living. The chief of sinners became the chief spokesman for the Good News he had formerly sought to silence.

You don't have to visit the Holy Land to walk the "Damascus Road." It's holy ground—as near as the place in your journey through life where you yield to the Lord who made you.

Worship from the Heart

No one can take your faith from you. But Paul warns that you can shipwreck your faith by rejecting your conscience. The still, small voice of your conscience may be God's way now of speaking to you. Thank God for the gift of conscience. Ask Him to make you sensitive to yours.

Walk Thru the Word

New Testament Reading
1 Timothy 1:12-20
Old Testament Reading
Job 40:1-5

Well-placed prayers for a peaceable life

I urge, then, first of all, that requests, prayers, intercession and thanksgiving be made for everyone—for kings and all those in authority, that we may live peaceful and quiet lives in all godliness and holiness (1 Timothy 2:1-2).

*G*ood government is a privilege enjoyed by relatively few nations on earth. Certainly in Paul's day Nero won few friends for his use—and abuse—of power.

But that only serves to underscore the importance of Paul's exhortation. The Christian has a God-given obligation to pray for the leaders God has set in office.

Authority properly exercised makes life better for all as Martin Luther explains.

Worship from the Heart

No doubt there are a few people who have wronged you so deeply that praying for them seems impossible. But those very people may be the ones God bids you to uphold in prayer. Ask God to bring to mind those for whom you should pray; remember that He never asks the impossible.

Walk with Martin Luther

"God created and gave everything for the purpose of help, benefit, and use that people might serve their fellow men with it.

"God did not give power to governors and rulers to have them presume upon it and be arrogant because of it, taxing their subjects at will and oppressing and plaguing them in all sorts of ways. Rather, He grants them power so that their subjects may, under their protection, lead quiet lives in all godliness and honesty.

"For this service we are to give them toil and taxes, to fear and honor them. The fact is that the higher and more honorable the station of life that a leader occupies, the more diligently should he see to it that he may assist and encourage others. For whatever God gives us—whether it be spiritual or temporal gifts, wisdom, understanding, ability, power, riches, or goods—we should use it for the improvement and benefit of our neighbor."

Walk Closer to God

For the Christian, dual citizenship both in heaven and on earth adds the responsibility of praying for God's will to be done "on earth, as it is in heaven."

Good government is a gift from God. Don't forget to thank Him for the opportunity to live a "quiet and peaceable life." And don't neglect to pray for those who labor to guard that privilege.

Walk Thru the Word

New Testament Reading
1 Timothy 2
Old Testament Reading
1 Kings 1:36-40

Not limited to leaders

Here is a trustworthy saying: If anyone sets his heart on being an overseer, he desires a noble task (1 Timothy 3:1).

*I*n the modern-day job market, credentials are often given more attention than character.

Contrast that with Paul's description of the qualifications for a church leader. No mention of diplomas or degrees, awards or achievements. Instead Paul takes an X-ray look at the candidate's heart, scrutinizing his reputation, character, and conduct both inside and outside the family of God.

The call to serve Christ is a call for singular commitment to Christlikeness—a call not limited to church leaders. Jonathan Edwards elaborates.

Walk with Jonathan Edwards

"Christ's ministers should be diligent in their studies and in the work of the ministry to which they are called. They should give themselves wholly to it, taking heed to themselves that their hearts be not engaged, nor their minds swallowed up, nor their time consumed in pursuits after the profits and vain glory of the world.

"They should earnestly seek after the knowledge of Christ, that they may live in the clear view of His glory. For by this means they will be changed into the image of the same glory and brightness, the glory of God in the face of Jesus Christ.

"Ministers, in order that they be shining lights, should walk closely with God and keep near to Christ. They should spend much time in seeking God and conversing with Him in prayer.

"Knowing their own emptiness and helplessness, they should depend on Christ, sit at His feet, and learn from Him."

Walk Closer to God

For those who proclaim Christ, the highest calling is to be an imitator of Christ. Paul's list of qualifications is not so much a catalog of leadership qualities as it is a repertoire of Christlike qualities and virtues.

The call to imitate Christ is not limited to church leaders, for taking on His character is the best way for any servant of God—including you—to tackle the job God has set before him.

Worship from the Heart

If you belong to an active church, you are frequently asked to contribute time and energy as well as money. How often do you thank God for these opportunities of service? Thank Him too that caring for your family is also a form of Christian service.

Walk Thru the Word

New Testament Reading
1 Timothy 3
Old Testament Reading
Isaiah 6:1-8

283

The most profitable thing in the world

Train yourself to be godly. For physical training is of some value, but godliness has value for all things, holding promise for both the present life and the life to come (1 Timothy 4:7-8).

*G*odliness is often associated with individuals past the age of sixty-five. But it may surprise you to learn that Paul talks more about godliness in his letters to two young disciples (Timothy and Titus) than in any of his other correspondence.

Johann Peter Lange comments on the practical importance of making godliness your goal.

Walk with Johann Peter Lange

"That godliness is profitable for all things, and thus the most profitable thing in the world, cannot be too strongly enforced against an abstract idealism on one side, and an irreligious materialism on the other.

"There are many who know that godliness is good for a peaceful death but do not hold it necessary for a happy life. Many others think faith very beautiful for the poor, the weak, the suffering, and the dying, but not for real, able, practical people.

"It must always be remembered that the gospel is a power which grasps the whole person. The true Christian is not only the happiest person, but the bravest citizen, the best patriot, the greatest leader.

"In a word, the Christian is, in all relations, a co-worker with God and an honor to Christ."

Walk Closer to God

"Godliness . . . is great gain" (1 Timothy 6:6). It is also a great challenge—a balance between two equally ungodly extremes.

On the one hand is "abstract idealism," as characterized by Simeon Stylites, a fifth-century ascetic who lived atop a pillar most of his life in an attempt to become "saintly." On the other is "irreligious materialism" leading to a preoccupation with wealth.

Genuine godliness makes "real, able, practical" Christians—men and women who respond to God and government, family and society, as He intended—regardless of their age.

Worship from the Heart

"We have put our hope in the living God" (4:10). Our confidence, or trust, in God is not an unfounded hope or simply a wish based on emotions. Instead, the Christian's hope is a sure expectation. Praise God that regardless of any emotional storm you might suffer, the future is secure. You may not know what the future holds, but you do know who holds the future. He is your hope.

Walk Thru the Word

New Testament Reading
1 Timothy 4:1-10
Old Testament Reading
Psalm 15

Keeping the faith as a family

If a widow has children or grandchildren, these should learn first of all to put their religion into practice by caring for their own family and so repaying their parents and grandparents, for this is pleasing to God (1 Timothy 5:4).

"Respect your elders" is a time-honored exhortation to growing children. And there is more at stake than the well-being of the elders.

Children who take this to heart are in line for a special blessing from God. The Ten Commandments state, "Honor your father and your mother, so that you may live long in the land the Lord your God is giving you" (Exodus 20:12).

One indication of a healthy relationship with your heavenly Father is a loving concern for your earthly parents. Patrick Fairbairn shows how the two actions work hand in hand.

Walk with Patrick Fairbairn

"The expression 'to show piety' points back to the fifth commandment, in which the honoring of parents is placed in immediate connection with the reverence and homage due to God.

"To do this first, therefore, toward their own house, as having a prior claim even in comparison to what is due the house of God, and to do it in the way of substantial ministrations of relief, is acceptable before God. He regards it as done to Himself, and sees in it an indication of future worth.

"The homes in which such reverential feelings are cherished, and such acts of lovingkindness are reciprocated, are the best nurseries of the church—churches, indeed, in embryo because they are homes of Christian tenderness, holy affection, self-denying love, and fruitfulness in well-doing."

Walk Closer to God

Reverence for your earthly parents . . . reverence for your heavenly Father. Attentiveness (or neglect) in one area usually points to attentiveness (or neglect) in the other.

The responsibilities of family life provide a perfect laboratory in which to discover the depth of your commitments in the family of God.

Think of it as "keeping the faith" in the family!

Worship from the Heart

Every Christian has at least one spiritual gift. As you pray, ask God to help you discover what your gift is. Consider how best to use it, no matter how small it may seem to you. Realize that when you thankfully offer up your gift in service to God, it builds up the church and glorifies the Giver. You have no greater privilege.

Walk Thru the Word

New Testament Reading
1 Timothy 4:11–5:8
Old Testament Reading
Leviticus 20:8-9

Eternity is serious business

The sins of some men are obvious, reaching the place of judgment ahead of them; the sins of others trail behind them (1 Timothy 5:24).

*A*sk a rich man, "How much money is enough?" and he will respond, "Just a little bit more."

Ask a dying man, "How much longer do you wish to live?" and he will probably tell you, "Just a little bit longer." But ask the person who has gone Christless into eternity, "How much time did you give to a serious consideration of the things of the Lord?" and he will answer, "Not nearly enough."

C. S. Lewis, a serious student of Scripture, examines the consequences of sin in the light of eternity. Read his words thoughtfully out loud.

Walk with C. S. Lewis

"Christianity asserts that every individual human being is going to live forever. Now there are a good many things which would not be worth bothering about if I were going to live only seventy years, but which I had better bother about very seriously if I am going to live forever.

"Perhaps my bad temper or my jealousy are actually getting worse—so gradually that the increase in seventy years would not be very noticeable. But it might be absolute hell in a million years: In fact, hell is precisely the correct technical term for what it would be.

"Be sure there is something inside you which, unless it is altered, will put it out of God's power to prevent your being eternally miserable. While that something remains, there can be no heaven for you, just as there can be no sweet smells for a man with a cold in the nose, and no music for a man who is deaf.

"It's not merely a question of God sending us to hell. In each of us there is something growing up which will of itself be hell unless it is nipped in the bud. The matter is serious: Let us put ourselves in His hands at once—this very day, this hour."

Walk Closer to God

Eternity is serious business. Misery awaits those without Christ. With Christ, heaven and hope lie just beyond. Which eternity awaits *you?*

Worship from the Heart

It has been said that too many Christians leave Sunday worship, lock the church doors, and think God will stay inside and await their return. Don't be the kind of person who goes about business as usual until the next Sunday. Thank God that He is not locked behind church doors but is interested in even the smallest details of your life.

Walk Thru the Word

New Testament Reading
1 Timothy 5:9–6:2
Old Testament Reading
Ecclesiastes 12:13-14

For the love of money is a root of all kinds of evil (1 Timothy 6:10).

Hoarding, holding, letting go

First Timothy 6:10 certainly would sound more appealing if it read, "The lack of money is the root of all evil." Or "Money is the root of all evil."

But notice the correct rendering of the verse. The problem does not rest in having money but in the attitude you have toward money.

The proper use of your assets begins with the proper attitude, as G. Campbell Morgan explains.

Walk with G. Campbell Morgan

"Love of money. Perhaps the word which best conveys the thought is the word avarice.

" 'Love of money' hoards and holds.

"It is indeed a root of all evil. It dries up the springs of compassion in the soul. It lowers the whole standard of morality. It is the inspiration of all the basest things, even covetousness; for if there may be covetousness without the love of money, there is never love of money without covetousness.

"Avarice is often created by prosperity and the consequent possession of money. It is often powerfully present in the lives of those who are devoid of wealth.

"It is wholly material, the result of a wrong conception of life, due to forgetfulness of the fact that 'a man's life does not consist in the abundance of his possessions' (Luke 12:15)."

Walk Closer to God

There is good news for those with humble means. Regardless of your net worth, God wants you to be rich.

Ah, but rich in assets that time cannot tarnish and inflation cannot destroy. Rich in the assets of "righteousness, godliness, faith, love, endurance and gentleness" (1 Timothy 6:11).

You may possess vast earthly treasures yet live like a pauper by the one standard that counts for eternity—God's standard.

Loving God versus loving gold.

There's a wealth of difference between the two. And you can't afford to make the wrong choice.

Worship from the Heart

Remember that a person's life is made up of much more than his or her material goods. Realize that each person you meet has dignity and worth simply because he or she is made in God's image. Praise God for the variety of temperaments, personalities, talents, and skills He has given the people you know.

Walk Thru the Word

New Testament Reading
1 Timothy 6:3-10
Old Testament Reading
Ecclesiastes 5:10-11

No good thing withheld

Command those who are rich in this present world not to be arrogant nor to put their hope in wealth, which is so uncertain, but to put their hope in God, who richly provides us with everything for our enjoyment (1 Timothy 6:17).

*P*eople tend to judge others by their possessions, but earthly wealth can never bring satisfaction. The more you have, the more you want; and like sand, the harder you grasp it, the faster it slips from your hand.

Elizabeth Stam, a missionary who was executed along with her husband during the communist takeover of China in 1934, had these thoughts about what is important to hold onto.

Walk with Elizabeth Stam

"When God consecrated Aaron and his sons for the priesthood, He literally filled their hands for a whole week (Leviticus 8:33). When we consecrate ourselves to God, we think we are making a great sacrifice, when we really are only letting go some little trinkets we have been grabbing. When our hands are empty, He fills them full of His treasures.

And shall I fear
> *That there is anything that men hold dear*
Thou wouldst deprive me of,
> *And nothing give in place?*
That is not so—
> *For I can see Thy Face / And hear Thee now;*
> *'My child I died for thee,*
And if the gift of love and life / You took from Me
Shall I one precious thing withhold—
> *One beautiful and bright,*
One pure and precious thing withhold?
> *My child, it cannot be.' "*

Walk Closer to God

If a believer's hands are tightly clasping earthly baubles, God cannot fill them with His heavenly treasures. We must leave our hands open so that God may remove whatever He will and then fill our hands with His good gifts.

Every gift of God is secure—it cannot be stolen or lost. Loosen your grip on the things of this earth. Leave your hands open for God to fill them.

Worship from the Heart

Exodus 2 reminds us that Jochebed's hands were so open to God that she took three-month-old Moses and cast him afloat. Instead of letting the baby perish, the good hand of God arranged it so that Jochebed was paid to care for her own child. Rejoice in what God does in your life when you open your hands and leave the choices to Him.

Walk Thru the Word

New Testament Reading
1 Timothy 6:11-21
Old Testament Reading
Exodus 2:1-10

*A*n issue every Christian must settle

Yet I am not ashamed, because I know whom I have believed, and am convinced that he is able to guard what I have entrusted to him for that day (2 Timothy 1:12).

*A*sk to open a savings account in any bank and you will likely receive fast, friendly service. But visit the loan office of that same bank and note the reception you get: skeptical loan officers . . . lots of questions . . . credit checks . . . collateral or cosignatories required.

Without proof of your trustworthiness, no bank would give you a loan—and with good reason. Paul raises the issue of trustworthiness in the first chapter of 2 Timothy. Is God worthy to be trusted? It's an issue every Christian must settle.

Allow John Calvin to supply the answer.

Walk with John Calvin

"How widely faith differs from opinion! When Paul says, 'I know whom I have believed,' he means that it is not enough if you believe, unless you have the testimony of God.

"Faith never leans on the authority of mortals, nor rests on God in such a manner as to hesitate, but must be joined with knowledge; otherwise it would not be sufficiently strong against the innumerable assaults of Satan.

"Amidst every storm and tempest, the Christian can enjoy undisturbed repose if he has a settled conviction that God, who cannot lie or deceive, has spoken and will undoubtedly perform what He has promised.

"This passage expresses admirably the power of faith when it shows that, even in desperate affairs, we ought to give to God such glory so as not to doubt that He will be true and faithful."

Walk Closer to God

Perhaps Paul had this Old Testament verse in mind when he wrote of God's trustworthiness: "God is not a man, that he should lie, nor a son of man, that he should change his mind. Does he speak and then not act? Does he promise and not fulfill?" (Numbers 23:19).

What more "collateral" do you need to put your trust in Him?

*W*orship from the Heart

Over the doorway of a Christian nursing home for severely handicapped children is a large poster: "Lord, I know that nothing will happen today that You and I together can't handle." In this place where fear and timidity might be expected, laughter and love, joy and peace fill the air. Meditate on 2 Timothy 1:7.

*W*alk Thru the Word

New Testament Reading
2 Timothy 1:1-14
Old Testament Reading
Job 42:1-6

John Calvin (1509-1564) Reformer and Theologian

*D*ateline: Switzerland, 1536. A book is published that—400 years later—would be called "one of the ten books that shook the world."

The author is only twenty-seven years old. His book bears the ambitious title, *The Institutes of Christian Religion.*

The author's name? John Calvin.

Along with Martin Luther, John Calvin is closely linked with the Protestant Reformation. Luther set the Protestant controversy in motion; Calvin came years later to guide the young movement through stormy times and provide valuable teaching and scholarship. His *Institutes* was published nearly twenty years after Luther's 95 theses were nailed to the Wittenberg church door.

Born in 1509 in Noyon, France, Calvin received an early education and planned to enter the service of the Roman Catholic Church.

At the age of fourteen John entered the University of Paris, but after the death of his father, he decided to become a scholar rather than a churchman and made plans to study law. Little is known

about Calvin's conversion experience except that it occurred shortly after he published his first book.

Forced to leave Paris because of his collaboration on a speech that sounded too "Protestant" for the established church leaders, Calvin made his way to Basel, Switzerland, where he wrote *The Institutes*.

In this monumental work the young Christian scholar summarized and systematized the Protestant faith, demonstrating how far the church had drifted from the historical roots of Christianity.

Calvin's fine mind and clear articulation of Protestant Christianity soon caught the attention of other reformers—notably, Guillaume Farel, who later invited Calvin to Geneva, Switzerland. There he spent the rest of his life seeking to make Geneva a Christian city.

On his arrival, Calvin found Geneva in political, moral, and spiritual chaos. Riots were common; prostitution was rampant; Christianity was tolerated only as long as it made no personal demands on the people—a situation Calvin found intolerable.

Calvin began to preach virtually every day and became involved in the public affairs of the city. He emphasized the importance of Christian and secular education for minister and layman alike. He also sought to make biblical principles the basis for Geneva's government affairs.

And with what success? One writer notes, "The city which had been one of the most licentious in Europe became the cradle of Protestantism." Many came from all over Europe to learn from this godly man.

Calvin died in 1562 at the age of fifty-four. He had been a major influence in Geneva for nearly twenty-five years because of his commitment to apply the Word of God in every area of life.

Your life can be an influence for God as well. But it takes times in His Word—time to read, study, and meditate on what God has said. And then it takes translating that truth into action.

It's not enough to be a hearer of the Word. God is looking for doers of the Word—men and women like John Calvin.

A Lesson from the life of John Calvin

My Christianity can make a difference in others' lives if I allow it to be the ruling force in my life.

*K*eep your eyes on the prize

*W*orship from the Heart

When your Christian journey seems to be all uphill, ponder this poem by John Bunyan, author of Pilgrim's Progress: "He who would valiant be 'gainst all disaster,/ Let him in constancy follow his master./ There's no discouragement shall make him once relent/ His first avowed intent to be a pilgrim." Keep the eyes of your heart on the Savior.

*W*alk Thru the Word

New Testament Reading
2 Timothy 1:15–2:13
Old Testament Reading
Joshua 23:1-8

A good soldier of Christ Jesus . . . anyone [who] competes as an athlete . . . the hard-working farmer. . . . Reflect on what I am saying, for the Lord will give you insight into all this (2 Timothy 2:3, 5-7).

*T*he victorious politician. The winning quarterback. The outstanding student. What do they have in common?

Answer: They all have stirring victories or notable accomplishments to their credit that have earned them the applause of others.

But while many are eager to win acclaim, only a handful are willing to invest the weeks of hard work necessary to make victory possible. A 19th-century classic commentary, *Exposition of the Bible*, elaborates on the apostle's imagery in chapter 2.

Walk with a 19th-century Writer

"The metaphors of soldier, athlete, and farmer are intended to teach the same lesson. In each of them two things are placed side by side—a prize, and the method to be observed in obtaining it.

"Do you, as a Christian soldier, wish for the approval of Him who has enrolled you? Then you must avoid entanglements which would interfere with your service. Do you, as a Christian athlete, wish for the victory? Then you must not evade the rules of the contest. Do you, as a Christian farmer, wish to be among the first to enjoy the harvest? Then you must toil with great diligence.

"The apostle draws attention to the importance of the lesson of devotion and endurance. Paul has confidence that the disciple will be enabled to draw the right conclusion from these metaphors and will have grace to apply it to his own case."

Walk Closer to God

The enlistee endures boot camp in order to become a seasoned soldier. The athlete trains intensively in order to become a champion. The farmer tends his field daily to insure a bountiful harvest. In the same way, Christ's followers apply themselves to the rigors of discipleship in order to gain a reward for faithful service.

Consider what Paul has said, and the Lord will give you understanding in all things.

If a man cleanses himself from the latter, he will be an instrument for noble purposes, made holy, useful to the Master and prepared to do any good work (2 Timothy 2:21).

*A*rtisans who care about their work take extreme care to avoid shoddy craftsmanship and inferior materials. They know even tiny flaws can diminish their reputation for quality.

In the same way, the work of the gospel has no room for shoddy, half-hearted workers. God is looking for those who will represent Him well.

Is it your desire to be an honor to your heavenly Father? F. B. Meyer suggests this "dialogue in prayer" between a willing worker and his Lord.

Walk with F. B. Meyer

"This I would be, O Lord, clay though I am. Make of me what You can by what process You will, only let me be what You can use."

"Can you drink the cup I drink or be baptized with the baptism that I am baptized with?"

"By Your grace I am able. Let me die with You; lie in the grave of obscurity and neglect—only let me be one whom You use, constantly in Your hand."

"The spirit is willing, but the body is weak."

"I know it, I know it, Lord. But I desire to die to the weakness of the flesh, its ache, its tears, its faintness, that I may live in the Spirit. Is not Your grace sufficient? Is not Your strength perfected in weakness? Heed not my weak cryings, only make me a vessel that You can use."

"Whoever wants to become great . . . must be [a] servant."

"I understand You, Master. You would winnow my heart and rid me of all that is proud and selfish. My only desire is for You, for Your glory, for the magnifying of Your name."

Walk Closer to God

Sanctified . . . useful . . . prepared—words that describe a worker who is cleansed and committed in the service of his Master.

Cleansed and committed—the elements necessary in *your* life if you are to become a worker "prepared for every good work."

*M*ake me a vessel God can use

*W*orship from the Heart

Bound in chains, Paul was not discouraged about the spread of the gospel: "God's Word is not chained." Think of places in the world where, in your lifetime, the gospel has been suppressed for many generations. Now it blazes forth, brighter than ever. Rejoice that God's Word has prevailed and always shall prevail.

*W*alk Thru the Word

New Testament Reading
2 Timothy 2:14-26
Old Testament Reading
Zechariah 3:1-7

Carrots or cabbages, sinners or saints

But mark this: There will be terrible times in the last days. People will be lovers of themselves (2 Timothy 3:1-2).

The farmer was perplexed. He had worked the soil . . . watered the seed . . . fertilized the plot. But in place of the cabbages he expected, he found carrots instead.

A miracle . . . or a mistake? Upon closer inspection, the farmer discovered that he had merely reaped what he unknowingly sowed.

Try as you might, nothing will turn sinners into saints until the seed of sin has been eliminated. Hard work may increase the harvest, but it can't change the crop. C. S. Lewis explains.

Walk with C. S. Lewis

"The terrible thing, the almost impossible thing, is to hand over your whole self—all your wishes and precautions—to Christ.

"But it is far easier than what we are all trying to do instead. For what we are trying to do is to remain what we call 'ourselves,' to keep personal happiness as our great aim in life, and yet at the same time be 'good.' We are all trying to let our mind and heart go their own way—centered on money or pleasure or ambition—and hoping, in spite of this, to behave honestly and humbly.

"And that is exactly what Christ warned [that we] could not do. As He said, a thistle cannot produce figs. If I am a field that contains nothing but grass seed, I cannot produce wheat. Cutting the grass may keep it short, but I shall still produce grass and no wheat. If I want to produce wheat, the change must go deeper than the surface. I must be plowed up and resown."

Walk Closer to God

"Every good tree bears good fruit, but a bad tree bears bad fruit. A good tree cannot bear bad fruit, and a bad tree cannot bear good fruit" (Matthew 7:17-18). All the good works in the world cannot make a Christian, any more than wishful thinking and hard work can make carrots into cabbages. But once Christ is planted in the heart, you need never wonder again what harvest will spring up!

Worship from the Heart

In the Greek tragedy Agamemnon, a faithful servant refuses to enter into the intrigue that might harm his absent master's household. "An ox shall stand on my tongue," he vows. When you find yourself drawn into petty quarrels among the members of the church, let an ox stand on your tongue. Your duty is to do honor to your Master. Rejoice in that privilege as you pray for those you worship with.

Walk Thru the Word

New Testament Reading
2 Timothy 3:1-9
Old Testament Reading
Jeremiah 17:5-8

And how from infancy you have known the holy Scriptures, which are able to make you wise for salvation through faith in Christ Jesus (2 Timothy 3:15).

I wish I had a son like that."
"Where did she learn such a bad attitude?"
"How did I go wrong?"
What do these statements have in common?
They're all sad commentaries on what could have been. But we have no record of Timothy's mother ever making such a statement. Her son was one of those young men everyone admires.
What made the difference? Albert Barnes explores the implications arising from this verse.

Walk with Albert Barnes

"Timothy's mother regarded it as one of her duties to train her son in the careful knowledge of the Word of God. The Jewish writings abound with lessons on this subject: 'The boy of five years of age ought to apply to the study of the sacred Scriptures'; and 'When the boy begins to talk, his father ought to converse with him in the sacred language, and to teach him the law.' So it is certain that Timothy had been taught the Scriptures as soon as he was capable of learning anything.

"We may draw the following conclusions: (1) It is proper to teach the Bible to children as early as possible. (2) There is reason to hope that such instruction will not be forgotten, but will have a salutary influence on their lives. The piety of Timothy is traced by the apostle to the fact that early in life he had been taught to read the Scriptures. (3) It is proper to teach the Old Testament to children—since this was all Timothy had, and this was made the means of his salvation."

Walk Closer to God

There was a time when Bible study was considered the primary purpose for learning to read. God's Word was used as the textbook, and children studied it daily.
What about the children in your life? Do they read God's Word? Do you talk with them about spiritual matters? As the Book says: It's profitable for everybody!

Light for a little child

Worship from the Heart

Nothing is new about the so-called New Age practices that many people are turning to. They are but variations of the same beliefs that Paul called myths. They may offer easy answers—but never redemption. Rejoice that you know the One who rose from the dead and offers you eternal life.

Walk Thru the Word

New Testament Reading
2 Timothy 3:10–4:8
Old Testament Reading
Proverbs 22:6

Fellowship in the family of God

Do your best to come to me quickly, for Demas, because he loved this world, has deserted me and has gone to Thessalonica (2 Timothy 4:9-10).

*I*n the world of athletics, there are two kinds of sports: individual and team. And woe to the person who joins a team but continues to play only as an individual!

Though Paul's life was characterized by spiritual success and personal achievement, he rarely traveled alone; he constantly spoke of the "one another" responsibilities in the body of Christ and he established churches for mutual encouragement and fellowship.

Fellowship is not an option, but an imperative in the Christian life, as William Biederwolf explains.

Walk with William Biederwolf

"I do not believe it is possible to be a good Christian without having godly friends.

"If I could find a man who was filled with the Spirit of Jesus, I would rather know him and get into the secret of his heart, and have the benediction and blessing that necessarily come from fellowship with him, than to have all that ever came to Demas through the decision he made when he quit the fight, quit the faith, quit the race, said 'goodbye' to Paul, and went off to Thessalonica.

"Better to have one Christian friend than anything the world might offer me. And this, in the first place, is what Demas lost."

Walk Closer to God

Paul knew that Christians need each other, so he gave instructions on how to treat one another:

"Nobody should seek his own good, but the good of others" (1 Corinthians 10:24).

"Carry each other's burdens" (Galatians 6:2).

"Be kind and compassionate to one another, forgiving each other" (Ephesians 4:32).

"Love one another" (Romans 13:8).

As part of God's family, you have the Lord. But you have something more: an entire family of brothers and sisters in Christ. Trying to live for Him while ignoring them is a losing proposition.

And the loser is you!

Worship from the Heart

Meditate today on the privilege of being in the royal family of the King of kings. As you look forward to being with other members of your family, pray that all of you will honor your Father by keeping Him at the center of your conversation and conduct while you're together.

Walk Thru the Word

New Testament Reading
2 Timothy 4:9-22
Old Testament Reading
Ecclesiastes 4:9-12

Test for truth in teachers

They claim to know God, but by their actions they deny him. They are detestable, disobedient and unfit for doing anything good (Titus 1:16).

The Old Testament test for a prophet of God left no margin for error. If even one prophecy turned out to be false, the penalty was death. In New Testament times, a teacher's words were placed alongside that teacher's works. If the two were inconsistent, both the teacher and his teaching were rejected.

False teachers today still seek to sway believers from the will of God as revealed in His Word. Paul warned Titus of just such deceivers in his letter. Patrick Fairbairn draws a picture of their spiritual condition and just condemnation.

Walk with Patrick Fairbairn

"Paul's words describe [the teachers'] morally shipwrecked condition. They have come within the sphere of religious truth, have had their minds instructed in its principles and duties, but have formally renounced the profession of godliness. They have all along, from sinister motives, withstood the truth. Indeed, they have become adept in following courses at variance with the great principles of morality and religion.

"It may justly be said of such persons that the very foundation of their moral being is off course; and according to God's ordinary methods of dealing, there is no hope of recovering them to truth and righteousness.

"By calling them reprobate [unfit] in regard to every good work, the apostle means that they are of no worth or account in that respect: When the question is about a good work, such persons may be rejected as having no proper affinity to it."

Walk Closer to God

For the Christian, truth and obedience are two sides of the same coin called "Bible doctrine." This suggests a helpful rule to follow when trying to discern teachers of truth from teachers of error: If their words ring true, examine their works. If their works contradict their words, reject their teaching.

Worship from the Heart

Titus, Timothy, Luke—what comfort Paul draws from his friends! Bring to your mind the names and faces of your Christian friends. Remember the times when each has given you strength and joy. Not only is Christ beside you on your journey. He brings into your orbit other lovers of Himself— the only true friends a Christian knows.

Walk Thru the Word

New Testament Reading
Titus 1
Old Testament Reading
Deuteronomy 13:1-5

Fighting the dreadful grip of sin

It teaches us to say "No" to ungodliness and worldy passions, and to live self-controlled, upright and godly lives in this present age (Titus 2:12).

*I*n Shakespeare's play *Macbeth*, Macbeth is faced with a problem after he murders Duncan. Though his hands have no visible bloodstains, he compulsively continues to wash them, never sure he is cleansed of his crime.

Think of Macbeth as a metaphor of the human condition. Even if all physical evidence of sin could somehow be removed, the mental, emotional, and spiritual scars would remain— indelible marks of sin upon the soul.

Martin Luther understood better than most the horror of man's sinfulness—and the wonder of God's forgiveness. Here he shares the proper approach to dealing with sin in your life.

Walk with Martin Luther

"If ungodliness and worldly lusts were painted on the wall of the house, you might run out of it; or if they were knit to a coat, you might take it off; if they grew in your hair, you might shave your head. But since they stick in your heart and possess you through and through, where will you run without taking yourself along?

"As Paul says here, renunciation is to be practiced so that the evil desires within us are mortified. Then no external enticement can harm us.

"This is the right way to flee. If evil desires are not mortified, fleeing from external enticement will not help. We must remain in the midst of enticements and learn through grace to deny worldly lusts and ungodliness. If we are to win the crown, there must be conflict, not fleeing; labor, not rest."

Walk Closer to God

Running from an epidemic does little good if you are in fact a carrier of the disease. You must stand and deal with the problem.

But you don't have to fight the malignancy of sin alone—nor could you if you tried. "If by the Spirit you put to death the misdeeds of the body, you will live" (Romans 8:13). With the Sin Doctor on your case, the prognosis is always bright.

Worship from the Heart

Being an example to nonbelievers without seeming self-righteous is not possible without God's help. Pray these words of Frances Havergal: "Take my intellect, and use / Every power as Thou shalt choose. / Take my will, and make it Thine; / It shall be no longer mine. / Take myself, and I will be / Ever, only, all for Thee."

Walk Thru the Word

New Testament Reading
Titus 2
Old Testament Reading
Ezekiel 36:25-27

Leaning wholly on Him

The kindness and the love of God our Savior toward man appeared . . . [which] he poured out on us generously through Jesus Christ our Savior (Titus 3:4, 6).

Open any world history book and you will find that scholars treat the Christian faith as just another subject to be studied alongside economics, philosophy, and politics for its influence on humanity. Yet the role of Christianity in the rise and fall of nations is only one aspect of the power of the Christian faith.

The power to change individual lives is just as important—especially when it is your life that is at stake. W. H. Griffith Thomas puts the importance of the Christian faith in perspective.

Walk with W. H. Griffith Thomas

"A missionary, translating the New Testament into a tribal language, could not find in the native language any equivalent for the Bible idea of faith. To them 'hearing' was equivalent to faith, and if anyone told another something which he believed, he would reply, 'I hear.'

"The missionary saw that this would not suffice for the New Testament meaning of faith, and for months he sought in vain to find an exact equivalent in the language of the people.

"One day, while he talked to a native, he lifted his feet off the floor and rested his entire weight on the chair in which he was sitting, and asked the native what he was doing. The native replied: 'You are leaning wholly on the chair.' At once the missionary had the words he needed.

"Since then, hundreds of those natives have been showing in their lives that they are leaning wholly and only on Jesus for salvation and everlasting glory. This is trust: Leaning wholly, leaning only, and leaning always on God."

Walk Closer to God

The Christian faith is not a subject to be catalogued, but a life to be lived—present reality firmly anchored in historical truth.

Faith means having your facts straight, but it is far more than facts. With facts you can fill a notebook, but only genuine faith in God can fill your heart as you lean wholly and only upon Him.

Worship from the Heart

Only Christ can make us whole. When you become impatient with others, remember what you were before you knew Christ. Remember the times you have let Him down even though you knew and loved Him. Yet He has forgiven you time after time. As you sit quietly in His presence, thank Him for His mercy and pray that He will help you extend true forgiveness to others.

Walk Thru the Word

New Testament Reading
Titus 3
Old Testament Reading
Jeremiah 15:15-21

How the shackles of sin are broken

Perhaps the reason he was separated from you for a little while was that you might have him back for good (Philemon 15).

*C*onduct a survey asking the question, "Are you a slave?" Chances are good every respondent will answer, "No!"

But in the final analysis, slavery is not an option. Slavery to sin dominates the human race, even when the enslaved are unwilling to admit it. And the shackles of sin are only broken by becoming enslaved to another.

The story of the runaway slave Onesimus and his reconciliation to his master is a picture of the "bonds of love" God desires to place on every sin-bound man and woman, as H. C. G. Moule so beautifully portrays.

Walk with H. C .G. Moule

" 'We are all the Lord's Onesimi.' So says Luther in his vivid way. Is it not so?

"The slavery of man to man is a condition impossible to reconcile permanently with God's will. The slavery of man to God in Christ, the absolute 'belonging,' the entire surrender, is the condition of man's noblest freedom.

"We have run away. And we have been found again, and have come back to our divine Philemon. And He, blessed be His name, has not upbraided us or consigned us to torture or the scourge.

"He gives us the joy of serving Him forever. How shall we receive it and taste its happiness? By loving everything about His household, and in His service, and the humblest things most, for His sake. By seeking to live and serve every hour, thankful, faithful, perfectly possessed, perfectly free, under the very eyes of our divine Philemon."

Walk Closer to God

The gospel has been called the "Emancipation Proclamation" of eternity. Perhaps Paul said it best: "But now that you have been set free from sin and have become slaves to God, the benefit you reap leads to holiness and the result is eternal life" (Romans 6:22).

Worship from the Heart

"Lord, forgive me. I am so quick to consider what others owe me, and so slow to consider how deeply I am in Your debt. I owe You every good thing, every beloved person that I have ever known. I owe You my life, now and after death. Teach me to love others as You love me."

Walk Thru the Word

New Testament Reading
Philemon
Old Testament Reading
Genesis 39:20-23

300

Knowing and Doing: The Balanced Christian Life

Living what you believe is the message of the books of Hebrews and James.

Tightrope walking and juggling are skills requiring intense concentration, especially when the performer attempts to activate both skills at the same time!

Christians often find themselves in a similar tension. On the one hand, they are called on to learn more about their faith in God: "Be still, and know that I am God" (Psalm 46:10). On the other hand, they are commanded to exercise their faith in God: "Do what [the word] says" (James 1:22). Accomplishing both assignments simultaneously requires careful attention and daily diligence. The two books you read this month will help you understand how to achieve that delicate balance. The letter to the Hebrews informs you about the Christian faith; the letter from James instructs you in proper Christian conduct.

Knowing what you must believe is the thrust of the letter to the Hebrews. In his well-crafted explanation, the anonymous author demonstrates the superiority of Christ and His finished work on the cross to any other supposed "plan of salvation." Over and over he stresses that Christ came not to annul the Old Testament, but to fulfill it. Understanding how the Old Testament patterns are fulfilled in the New Testament person of Christ can't help but deepen your faith in Him!

Living what you believe becomes the focus of the book of James. It is inconsistent to say you believe as you should when you behave as you shouldn't! In pithy, practical statements—similar to Proverbs—James sets forth guidelines regarding how to avoid temptation and favoritism, how to use wealth and the tongue, how to respond to widows and orphans. In short, he gives words of wisdom for your daily walk of faith.

After spending a month in the pages of Hebrews and James, you will find that you are better able to maintain a proper balance between doctrinal input and practical output in the Christian life. Knowing what to do and doing what you know—both are essential to growing in Christ.

Anointed above all others

Therefore God, your God, has set you above your companions by anointing you with the oil of joy (Hebrews 1:9).

*H*ow remarkable it is that even atheists who say there is no God nonetheless recognize the Son of God as the epitome of a good teacher, overlooking completely the claims He made to be God in the flesh.

No mere man could do what Jesus did, because Jesus was no mere man. He was the God-man, unique in human history. Matthew Henry explains Christ's inimitable stature.

Walk with Matthew Henry

"Who are Christ's companions? Has He any equals? Not as God, except the Father and Spirit, but these are not what is meant here.

"As man and even as an anointed person, He has companions; but He is above all of them.

"Above the angels, who may be said to be His fellows, as they are the sons of God by creation. Above all prophets, priests, and kings that ever were anointed to serve God on earth.

"Above all the saints, who are children of the same Father, as He was a partaker with them of flesh and blood. Above all those who were related to Him as man, above all the house of David, all the tribe of Judah, all His kinsmen.

"All God's other anointed ones had only the Spirit in a certain measure; Christ had the Spirit without any limitation. None therefore goes through his work as Christ did, none takes so much pleasure in it as Christ did; for He was anointed with the oil of gladness above His companions."

Walk Closer to God

The atheist sees Christ only as a good teacher and a humanitarian. But Christ's position as God-man means far more. In Him the gap between holy God and sinful man has been successfully spanned. "For there is one God and one mediator between God and men, the man Christ Jesus, who gave himself as a ransom for all" (1 Timothy 2:5-6).

That is good news, for a Christ above His fellows is a Christ who is able to save His fellows.

Worship from the Heart

To the Hebrews who received this letter, the Scripture they had known all their lives had suddenly become alive with meaning. The ancient prophecies were fulfilled: The Messiah had come. Praise God that He has opened your ears, your eyes, your heart to hear His Word as the stunning good news that it surely is.

Walk Thru the Word

New Testament Reading
Hebrews 1
Old Testament Reading
Psalm 45

How shall we escape if we ignore such a great salvation? (Hebrews 2:3).

*J*esus declared, "The kingdom of heaven is like a merchant looking for fine pearls. When he found one of great value, he went away and sold everything he had" (Matthew 13:45-46).

That man knew that salvation is worth far more than anything the world has to offer.

Being reminded of the surpassing value of "such a great salvation" gives believers the right perspective when confronted with the concerns of this world, as Martin Luther explains.

Walk with Martin Luther

"The supreme blessing in which one can truly know the goodness of God is not temporal possessions, but the eternal blessing that God has called us to—His holy gospel.

"In this gospel we hear that God will be gracious to us for the sake of His Son, will forgive and eternally save us, and will protect us in this life against the tyranny of the Devil and the world.

"To someone who properly appreciates this blessing, everything else is a trifle. Though he is poor, sick, despised, and burdened with adversities, he sees that he keeps more than he has lost. If he has no money and goods, he knows nevertheless that he has a gracious God; if his body is sick, he knows that he is called to eternal life.

"His heart has this constant consolation: Only a short time, and everything will be better."

Walk Closer to God

Your "great salvation" carries great benefits:
Eternal life (John 3:16)
Forgiveness (Ephesians 1:7)
Deliverance (Colossians 1:13)
Adoption (Galatians 4:4-7)

Salvation is not simply good news; it's great news! So when you have seen enough of this world, do as one hymnwriter has suggested:

Turn your eyes upon Jesus,
 Look full in His wonderful face;
And the things of earth will grow strangely dim
 In the light of His glory and grace.

*T*he greatest treasure ever offered to the world

*W*orship from the Heart

Jesus, priceless treasure, / Fount of purest pleasure, / Truest friend to me. / Long my heart had panted, / 'Til it well nigh fainted, / Thirsting after Thee. (Johann Franck). To neglect such a treasure is life's greatest folly; to enjoy it, life's greatest joy. Consider the value of knowing Jesus; then tell Him how much He means to you.

*W*alk Thru the Word

New Testament Reading
Hebrews 2:1-4
Old Testament Reading
Amos 6:1

*A*voiding the pain of youthful sin

Since the children have flesh and blood, he too shared in their humanity, . . . Because he himself suffered when he was tempted, he is able to help those who are being tempted (Hebrews 2:14, 18).

*P*arents are apt to shrug off many childish actions with the well-worn phrase, "Kids will be kids." But sin at any age should never be excused with a shrug of the shoulders.

Sin knows no generation gap. As Jesus grew to manhood, He experienced every kind of temptation known to man: ". . . tempted in every way, just as we are—yet was without sin" (Hebrews 4:15).

Charles Spurgeon points out some of the temptations of the youthful Christ.

Walk with Charles Spurgeon

"Every age has its temptations. The young will learn that there are peculiar snares for little ones.

"Christ knew these. It was no small temptation at age twelve, to sit among the teachers, answering their questions. It would have turned the heads of most boys, yet Jesus went back to Nazareth and was subject to His parents.

"It is small peril to grow in knowledge and in favor with God and man, if it were not for the word God put in it; to grow in favor constantly with men would be too much temptation for most youths.

"It is good for a man that he bear the yoke in his youth, for youth, when honored and esteemed, is too apt to grow conceited and vain. When a young man knows that he shall become something great, it is not easy to keep him balanced."

Walk Closer to God

As Spurgeon points out, pride and selfishness know no age limit. They trip up the young as well as the young at heart. Intelligence . . . talents . . . riches—each can cause a youthful heart to harden against the Giver of good and perfect gifts.

The lost son of Luke 15 squandered his entire inheritance. Later he returned home to find a waiting, forgiving father. But why duplicate his folly? With Jesus as your model and motivation, you can avoid such painful lessons from the start.

*W*orship from the Heart

If the fear of death is slavery (v. 15), then ours is surely a society in chains. Look around you. What signs of such slavery do you see? To many people, death is the ultimate disaster. Thank God that because of Jesus Christ you can live without the fear of death. Rejoice that your freedom gives you opportunities to minister to those who are in slavery.

*W*alk Thru the Word

New Testament Reading
Hebrews 2:5-18
Old Testament Reading
Genesis 25:29-34

304

But Christ is faithful as a son over God's house. And we are his house, if we hold on to our courage and the hope of which we boast (Hebrews 3:6).

*C*ourage is a much-admired trait in heroes. But did you know that all successful people are also courageous? The winning coach, the successful job-seeker, the marathon runner . . . each won the mental battle to face fear and take risks long before the physical battle even began.

Courage is a vital ingredient in the spiritual life as well. A. B. Simpson describes the problem of spiritual insecurity.

Walk with A. B. Simpson

"Seldom have we seen a sadder wreck than when the enemy has succeeded in undermining the simple trust of a child of God and gotten him into self-accusation and condemnation.

"It is a fearful place when the soul allows Satan to take the throne and act as God, sitting in judgment on its every thought and act, and keeping it in the darkness of ceaseless condemnation.

"This is Satan's objective point in all his attacks upon you: to destroy your trust. If he can get you to lose your simple confidence [your courage] in God, he knows that he will soon have you at his feet.

"For the soul that has known the sweetness of God's love, to lose its perfect trust in Him is enough to wreck both the reason and the life. Beloved, 'Hold on to . . . courage and . . . hope.' "

Walk Closer to God

In the children's story *The Little Engine That Could*, the little engine climbs a steep incline by puffing, "I think I can, I think I can, I think I can!"

Christians can draw courage from a true story of infinitely greater importance—the story of "The Mighty Savior Who Could . . . and Did!"

And what did the Savior do? He conquered sin and death by climbing the hill of Calvary and declaring, "It is finished."

By looking to Him for courage, you can meet any situation that lies ahead of you. "I can . . . I can . . . I can do everything through him [Christ] who gives me strength" (Philippians 4:13).

*C*onfident hope and spiritual security

*W*orship from the Heart

Rather than let your fears keep you from enjoying God's promises, remember that the God you trust is the same God who parted the waters for the Israelites, fed them manna, and provided water in the desert. In the dry times of your life, thank God for faithful believers of the past who proved the validity of His promises.

*W*alk Thru the Word

New Testament Reading
Hebrews 3:1-6
Old Testament Reading
Joshua 14:6-12

A heart focused on pleasing God

But encourage one another daily, as long as it is called Today, so that none of you may be hardened by sin's deceitfulness (Hebrews 3:13).

*E*ach day has its own challenges, responsibilities, and problems. Each can be faced only one at a time. The author of Hebrews suggests three daily disciplines to help you remain faithful, no matter what day it is.

Today, hear God's voice (Hebrews 3:7).

Today, encourage one another (Hebrews 3:13).

Today, do not harden your hearts (Hebrews 3:8, 15).

Listening to God's voice, encouraging your brothers and sisters in Christ, and refusing to harden your heart—three essentials for enjoying daily victory in Christ.

Today, Alexander Maclaren challenges you to examine and avoid that which tempts you to be unfaithful to God.

Walk with Alexander Maclaren

"We may get the things which tempt our desires; and there will be no illusion at all about the reality of the pleasure. But another question must be asked.

"You have received the thing you wanted; what then? Are you much the better for it? Is it as good as it looked when it was not yours?

"Is it as blessed now that you have stretched your hand and made it your own as it seemed when it danced there on the other side?

"Having attained the desire, do we not find that it fails to satisfy us fully?"

Walk Closer to God

"Father, thank You for Your Word, which teaches me how to avoid sin. Help me to listen carefully whenever You speak to me through its pages. Cause me to encourage my brothers and sisters in Christ and to draw strength from their example and fellowship.

"Above all, Lord, grant me a soft, pliable, teachable heart, one that beats strongly for You, one that will not be enticed by worldly pleasure. In the name of the One who wants to keep my heart focused on pleasing You. Amen."

*W*orship from the Heart

Sin has a subtle way of taking hold. Sometimes it's almost parasitic . . . slowly maturing until it encrusts one's heart with its deadly growth. Pray today that God will create in you a hunger for His Word and a deep desire to please Him. Praise Him for the fellow believers in your life who help you walk in His ways and who keep you from error.

*W*alk Thru the Word

New Testament Reading
Hebrews 3:7-19
Old Testament Reading
Jeremiah 3:21

*C*ause and effect in spiritual matters

Let us, therefore, make every effort to enter that rest, so that no one will fall by following their example of disobedience (Hebrews 4:11).

*S*cientific inquiry always looks for the cause-and-effect relationship between observable phenomena. But what if, like the chicken-or-the-egg dilemma, the effect also happens to be the cause? In that case, a vicious circle may ensue.

For the Christian there is another question that deserves an answer: "Which comes first—faith or obedience, unbelief or disobedience?"

Alexander Maclaren explores how those ideas fit together in either a vicious—or a victorious—circle.

Walk with Alexander Maclaren

"Important lessons are given by this alternation of the two ideas of faith and unbelief, obedience and disobedience.

"Disobedience is the root of unbelief. Unbelief is the mother of further disobedience. Faith is voluntary submission within a person's own power.

"If faith is not exercised, the true cause lies deeper than all intellectual reasons. It lies in the moral aversion of human will and in the pride of independence, which says, 'Who is Lord over us? Why should we have to depend on Jesus Christ?'

"As faith is obedience and submission, so faith breeds obedience, but unbelief leads on to higher-handed rebellion. With dreadful reciprocity of influence, the less one trusts, the more he disobeys; the more he disobeys, the less he trusts."

Walk Closer to God

Which cause/effect relationship is at work in your life: faith and obedience, or unbelief and disobedience? The question is worth careful study, for eternity is at stake.

Perhaps John the Baptist said it best: "Whoever believes in the Son has eternal life, but whoever rejects the Son will not see life, for God's wrath remains on him" (John 3:36).

The chicken/egg controversy may never be resolved to everyone's satisfaction. But don't let that keep you from resolving the most important question in your life: your relationship to the Lord.

*W*orship from the Heart

Your relationship with God, established by faith, is the only basis for peace of mind and satisfaction. Ponder the cause and effect expressed in this verse as you put it into practice today: "Delight yourself in the Lord and he will give you the desires of your heart" (Psalm 37:4).

*W*alk Thru the Word

New Testament Reading
Hebrews 4:1-13
Old Testament Reading
Psalm 37:3-8

Bold entrance to the place of pardon

Let us then approach the throne of grace with confidence, so that we may receive mercy and find grace to help us in our time of need (Hebrews 4:16).

A pauper strides confidently into the palace and demands an audience with the king. To the amazement of onlookers, the king grants his wish. Why? Because the pauper carries with him a letter of introduction from the king's son.

Access to people in high places is a valuable asset. In the case of the Christian, access to the very throne of God is made possible through a right relationship with the King's Son, Jesus Christ.

Albert Barnes explains the basis for—and benefits of—such access.

Walk with Albert Barnes

"The illustration here may have been derived from the temple service. In that service God is represented as seated in the most holy place on the mercy seat. The Jewish high priest approached that seat of the divine majesty with the blood of the atonement to make intercession for the people and to plead for pardon.

"That scene was emblematic of heaven. The great High Priest of the Christian calling, having shed His own blood for a sacrifice, is represented as approaching God and pleading for the pardon of men. To a God willing to show mercy He comes with the merits of a sacrifice sufficient for all, and pleads for their salvation.

"We may, therefore, come with boldness [confidence] and look for pardon. We do not come depending on our own merits, but we come where a sufficient sacrifice has been offered for human guilt and where we are assured that God is merciful. We may, therefore, come without hesitancy or trembling and ask for all the mercy that we need."

Walk Closer to God

No matter who you are, your letter of introduction must be signed in the crimson signature of the Savior. Only then can you approach the throne of grace with confidence. With Jesus Christ as your mediator before the Father, you need not fear the reception you'll receive.

Worship from the Heart

If even Jesus could learn obedience through suffering while He walked the earth, how much more can we! Never take it upon yourself to seek suffering, but when it comes, let it be your teacher. Give glory to God by the way that you meet it, and rejoice that in your pain Christ is your companion, closer than ever before.

Walk Thru the Word

New Testament Reading
Hebrews 4:14–5:10
Old Testament Reading
Exodus 28:31-35

Therefore let us leave the elementary teachings about Christ and go on to maturity (Hebrews 6:1).

Students in each grade have an appropriate body of truth to master. For Christians it is equally important to know when to graduate to deeper things of Christ and when to "get back to basics."

Without a foundation, the building collapses. Without a building, the foundation means little. Matthew Henry seeks a balance for the proper construction of the Christian life.

Walk with Matthew Henry

"In order to keep growing, Christians must leave the principles of the doctrine of Christ. They must not despise them or forget them. They must lay them up as the foundation of all their profession. But they must not stay in them. They must build upon the foundation.

"There must be a superstructure, for the foundation is laid on purpose to support the building.

"Then why did the author resolve to set strong meat before the Hebrews, when he knew they were only babes? Though some of them were weak, others had gained more strength, and they must be provided for suitably.

"As those who are more mature Christians must be willing to hear the plainest truths preached for the sake of the weak, so the weak must be willing to hear the more difficult truths preached for the sake of those who are strong. He hoped they would be growing in their spiritual strength and stature, and thus be able to digest stronger meat."

Walk Closer to God

A strong foundation and a growing superstructure are both essential components for a well-built Christian life.

Examine the foundation of your life. Do you find shifting sand or the Rock of Ages?

Inspect what is being built upon that foundation. Do you find gold, silver, and precious stones . . . or wood, hay, and stubble?

If you're not pleased with what you find, talk to the Architect and Builder who holds the blueprint for your life (Hebrews 11:10).

*P*roper building of the Christian life

*W*orship from the Heart

Proverbs 4:18 is a beautiful illustration of God's guidance. We may begin a journey by the light of early dawn, but the full sunlight of noon soon will provide all the light necessary for traveling rougher terrain. In the same way, a deeper study of God's Word will yield the light you need to make right decisions as you face the complex choices of life. Praise God that He never leaves us without guidance.

*W*alk Thru the Word

New Testament Reading
Hebrews 5:11–6:12
Old Testament Reading
Proverbs 4:18

An anchor in the storms of life

We have this hope as an anchor for the soul, firm and secure. It enters the inner sanctuary behind the curtain (Hebrews 6:19).

*W*ould you put money in a bank that advertised, "Your money is as safe with us as a wave tossed back and forth"? Or would you be more comfortable at a bank whose slogan read, "Anchor yourself here. We have your interest at heart."

The Christian concept of hope is not a wishful "I-hope-so" attitude, but a confident expectation. John Calvin unfolds the imagery of hope found in the letter to the Hebrews.

Walk with John Calvin

"It is a striking likeness when the author compares faith, leaning on God's Word, to an anchor.

"In this world, we do not stand on firm ground but are tossed about as if we were on the sea. Satan incessantly stirs up innumerable storms that would sink our vessel if we did not cast our anchor fast in the deep.

"Waves arise and threaten us. But as the anchor is cast through the waters into a dark and unseen place and keeps the vessel from being overwhelmed, so must our hope be fixed on the invisible God. But with this difference—the anchor is cast down into the sea with the earth at its bottom; but our hope soars aloft, for in the world it finds no created things on which it can stand. It rests on God alone.

"As the anchor joins the vessel with the earth, so the truth of God is a bond that connects us with Him. Thus when united to God, though we must struggle with continual storms, we are still beyond the peril of shipwreck."

Walk Closer to God

Faith in God has been likened to a leap in the dark. In reality, it is a leap from the dark into the light of truth. God's Word is a spotlight for those yearning to follow God's will. "Your word is a lamp to my feet and a light for my path" (Psalm 119:105).

Those are comforting words when the storms of life make shipwreck seem imminent.

Worship from the Heart

An 18th-century hymn reminds us of a significant truth: "How firm a foundation, ye saints of the Lord, is laid for your faith in His excellent Word! What more can He say than to you He has said . . . ?" When the Scripture is read in church, give it your full attention and silently thank God that it is available in your language and is applicable to your life.

Walk Thru the Word

New Testament Reading
Hebrews 6:13-20
Old Testament Reading
Psalm 125:1-2

310

This Melchizedek was king of Salem and priest of God Most High (Hebrews 7:1).

Scripture records that Melchizedek was "without father or mother, without genealogy, without beginning of days or end of life, like the Son of God" (Hebrews 7:3).

And, like Melchizedek, Christ is "King of righteousness" and "King of peace" (Hebrews 7:2).

But what does all this mean for the believer? Alexander Maclaren explains Jesus' role as the righteous King.

Walk with Alexander Maclaren

"The very heart of the Christian doctrine is this: As soon as a person puts his trembling trust in Jesus Christ as his Savior, then he receives not merely pardon and the uninterrupted flow of the divine love in spite of his sin, but an imparting to him of that new life, which, after God, is created in righteousness and true holiness.

"Do not suppose that the great message of the gospel is merely forgiveness. Do not suppose that its blessed gift is only that one is acquitted because Christ died.

"All that is true. But there is something more. By faith in Jesus Christ, I am so knit to Him that there passes into me, by His gift, a life which is created after His life, and is in fact kindred with it.

"He is first of all King of righteousness. Let that which is first in all His gifts be first in all your efforts too; and do not seek so much for comfort as for grace to know and to do your duty, and strength to put aside the deeds of darkness and put on the armor of light (Romans 13:12)."

Walk Closer to God

Because Jesus is righteous, you are forgiven, and God sees you as righteous. Because Jesus is righteous, you can live a righteous life—through the power of His life in you.

Abraham gave to Melchizedek a tenth part of all the spoil as a sign of his subjection to one greater than he. Is it too much to ask that you, being made righteous by the King of righteousness, give Him your life in return?

Made new in righteousness and true holiness

Worship from the Heart

Imagine the throne room of God and consider what it represents to you because Jesus died for you. Praise Him for the sacrifice that allows you to go boldly into God's presence. Rejoice that you are anchored forever to Jesus Christ who will bring you safely to the Holy City.

Walk Thru the Word

New Testament Reading
Hebrews 7:1-10
Old Testament Reading
Genesis 14:17-20

Frederick B. Meyer (1847-1929) He Practiced What He Preached

*C*heck the card catalog in your church library and chances are good you will find not one but several listings under "Meyer, Frederick Brotherton."

Yes, anyone familiar with his life may wonder how F. B. Meyer ever found time to write in the first place!

Preacher. Pastor. Social reformer. Commentator. Meyer indeed wore many hats during his long and illustrious life of service for God and mankind.

Yet his busyness for God never crowded out his time to cultivate his relationship with God.

Born in 1847 to a prosperous London family, Meyer grew up in a home where his spiritual as well as physical needs were amply met.

He began to learn the Bible at an early age and saw biblical principles applied in the crucible of home life.

As a youngster, Meyer would "preach" to an appreciative audience of his brothers and sisters. One of the family maids, overhearing the young boy, became a Christian as a result.

Showing such promise as a preacher, it is not surprising that Meyer decided to enter the ministry. He followed the advice of his own pastor by working two years in the business world before commencing his studies.

That experience provided a base for reaching businessmen in his later years. Meyer

himself would one day echo the same advice:

"By all means let [theological students] graduate in the college of city life and study attentively the great books of human nature. It is impossible to preach to young men unless you know young men and possess some knowledge of their peril and temptation."

Upon graduation, Meyer entered the pastorate. In 1874 Dwight L. Moody, the prominent American evangelist, preached a series of messages in Meyer's church. The event transformed the young preacher's life and redirected the course of his ministry:

- He started a prison ministry to inmates.
- He began job brigades for those out of work.
- He organized opposition to prostitution.
- He formed groups to help unwed mothers, and to improve working conditions of the poor.

On top of this already demanding schedule, Meyer found time to preach widely and write prolifically. More than fifty volumes of sermons, commentaries, and treatises resulted.

One of the reasons he could accomplish so much was that he practiced the "equipping of the saints for the work of the ministry, for the edifying of the body of Christ." Involving others in these many ministries freed him up to uncover still other needs that had to be met.

After his death in 1929 at eighty-two, one fellow worker summarized the quality of Meyer's life this way: "The devotion and unworldliness of his nature; his fearless championship of great religious, moral, and social causes; and his deep human sympathy made his services of unspeakable value to all the interest of the kingdom of God."

All this from a man who never experienced personally the hardships and physical suffering he labored so tirelessly to alleviate in the lives of others!

Meyer knew that Jesus Christ is the Source of all help and strength. A Source adequate to meet the needs of every hurting individual, both physically and spiritually.

A Source adequate for your needs— and the needs of the people you will encounter today.

A Lesson from the life of Frederick B. Meyer

Even though I am busy, my relationship with God deserves top priority above all other demands on my time.

*T*he power of an endless life

Another priest . . . appears, one who has become a priest not on the basis of a regulation as to his ancestry but on the basis of the power of an indestructible life (Hebrews 7:15-16).

*P*ersistence in the face of adversity is a praiseworthy virtue, but death is the final adversity that no amount of persistence can overcome.

Jesus, by the power of His perfect life, conquered death. In so doing, He made it possible for others to overcome death as well.

F. B. Meyer explains what happened three days after Jesus' death and burial.

Walk with F. B. Meyer

"This chapter overflows with the message of Easter morning. Its verses witness that He lives by the power of an indissoluble life.

"Remember all that was done to dissolve and loose it. Satan tried to hold the prisoner fast. The Sanhedrin affixed their seal, set the watch, and made the grave as secure as possible.

"But it was all in vain. His body could not see corruption. His life defied death. And what is more, that life can be communicated to us by the Holy Spirit. Because He lives, and as He lives, we shall live also.

"In the first creation God breathed into Adam the breath of life, and he became a living soul. In the second creation Christ breathes into us the spirit of His life.

"See to it that you deny your own life, so that His life will become ever more triumphant within you."

Walk Closer to God

By His encounter with death on the cross, Jesus made it possible for others to conquer death by that same resurrection power.

Nothing else will do. "(For the law made nothing perfect), and a better hope is introduced, by which we draw near to God" (Hebrews 7:19).

Isn't it about time you did exactly that?

> *Was it for sins that I have done*
> *He suffered on the tree?*
> *Amazing pity! Grace unknown!*
> *And love beyond degree!*

*W*orship from the Heart

"I praise You, Lord Jesus, because You're not just a high priest for a lifetime, but forever. You are the only One who has ever been truly worthy of ministering before the Most High God. Thank You for doing this on my behalf."

*W*alk Thru the Word

New Testament Reading
Hebrews 7:11-28
Old Testament Reading
Psalm 110:4

314

A contract that will last for eternity

"The time is coming, declares the Lord, when I will make a new covenant with the house of Israel and with the house of Judah" (Hebrews 8:8).

*R*enegotiating one's contract is a common occurrence in professional sports today. The contract that called for a five-figure salary last year is suddenly inadequate and must be replaced before the next season.

It may surprise you to learn that God has promised to renegotiate a contract of His own, not by arbitrarily changing the terms because of human merit, but by showing His loyal love in the face of human demerit.

Johann Peter Lange explains this new contract.

Walk with Johann Peter Lange

"The new covenant has institutions and arrangements whose foundations are laid in the messianic prophecies of the Old Testament.

"The all-holy God, in His righteousness, does away with the old relation to the covenant-breaking people; but in His grace will institute a system of salvation by a new covenant, for which He already lays the foundation of better promises.

"The superiority of these promises consists in the fact that the divine will is no longer a bare command to come into mere outward contact with the people, but is to live and work within their hearts.

"In consequence of this, a living knowledge of God is to be the common blessing of all members of the covenant, and the distinction between priests and nonpriests is to fall away. The ground of this will be the forgiveness of sins wrought without any human merits by the grace of God."

Walk Closer to God

What would you think of a contract that offered these benefits without cost?
- Forgiveness of sins
- Eternal life
- A living knowledge of God

That is precisely what the new covenant offers. Think of it—God's love—signed, sealed, and delivered in the person of His Son.

There's not a better offer anywhere.

*W*orship from the Heart

From today's Old Testament reading we see that the new covenant is ratified by the blood that Jesus shed on Calvary for the forgiveness of sins. Praise God that through the power of the Holy Spirit the new covenant empowers you to live the life that the old covenant intended.

*W*alk Thru the Word

New Testament Reading
Hebrews 8
Old Testament Reading
Jeremiah 31:31-34

When that which is perfect is come . . .

The Holy Spirit was showing by this that the way into the Most Holy Place had not yet been disclosed as long as the first tabernacle was still standing (Hebrews 9:8).

Which would you prefer: Seeing the shadow of the Eiffel Tower or the Tower itself?

Seeing a famous person's picture or meeting that celebrity in person?

In each case, the former hints at what only the latter can reveal.

The Old Testament system of sacrifices was an imperfect forerunner of the perfect New Testament sacrifice to come.

B. F. Westcott probes the meaning behind both the old and new sacrifices.

Walk with B. F. Westcott

"The levitical sacrifices expressed the ideas of atonement and fellowship resting upon the idea of a covenant.

"In vivid symbols and outward forms they showed how human beings might yet reach the destiny for which they were created.

"The self-sacrifice of Christ upon the cross fulfilled absolutely all that was thus shadowed forth. That sacrifice had a spiritual, eternal, and universal validity, where the 'shadow' had been necessarily external and confined.

"And when we look back over the facts of Christ's sacrifice brought forward in the epistle, we notice two series of blessings gained for mankind by Him: the one being the restoration of man's right relation to God which has been violated by sin, and the other fulfilling the purpose of creation, which is attainment by mankind of the divine likeness."

Walk Closer to God

What the readers of the Old Testament could only picture imperfectly, we can appreciate and appropriate fully: the perfect sacrifice of Christ.

The picture, no longer shadowy, is perfectly clear. The way of redemption and right standing with God is possible through Jesus Christ.

The question remains: Are you perfectly clear about your standing with God?

Worship from the Heart

Make these words your prayer of praise today: My Advocate appears for my defense on high; the Father bows His ears and lays His thunder by. Not all that hell or sin can say shall turn His heart, His love, away (Watts).

Walk Thru the Word

New Testament Reading
Hebrews 9:1-10
Old Testament Reading
Leviticus 9:23-24

*O*nly one true Sacrifice

The law requires that nearly everything be cleansed with blood, and without the shedding of blood there is no forgiveness (Hebrews 9:22).

A critically ill patient needs emergency surgery. A skilled surgical team gathers; instruments are readied. There is just one problem. The patient has a rare blood type that is not available. Without blood, the surgery will surely fail.

The human race lies critically ill and in need of a similar life-giving transfusion. Only in this case, one blood type suffices for everyone—the blood of Jesus Christ. Nothing else will do, as Martin Luther explains.

Walk with Martin Luther

"This is clearly a sacrifice entirely different from the ones the priests offered, but as those sacrifices demonstrated, God will not grant reconciliation and forgiveness without blood and death.

"Thus the epistle to the Hebrews says that the sacrifice of Christ the Priest had to consist of the shedding of blood. However, it was His own blood, not the blood of a stranger. The cross was the altar on which He, consumed by the fire of the boundless love, presented the living and holy sacrifice of His body and blood to the Father.

"That is the true sacrifice. Once and for all it takes away the sins of the world and brings everlasting reconciliation and forgiveness.

"This sacrifice, which He completed once for all, suffices until the last day. But we are still sinful and spiritually weak. Therefore He must unceasingly represent us before the Father and intercede for us that such weakness and sin will not be reckoned to our account. Rather He must grant us the strength and power of the Holy Spirit to overcome sin."

Walk Closer to God

Blood tainted with sin can only bring death. By contrast, the spotless blood of the Savior brings life and power to all who believe.

By His sacrifice, Jesus took the weight of sin upon Himself. He was "sacrificed once to take away the sins of many" (9:28). As your Sin-Bearer, thank Him for the sacrifice He has made for you.

*W*orship from the Heart

Imagine yourself one of the people to whom this unknown author is bringing the good news. All your life you have believed that your relationship to God depended on your own righteousness. You honor the Law and try to keep it, but always you fall short. Now you learn that God Himself has set you free from sin. Can you do anything but love Him?

*W*alk Thru the Word

New Testament Reading
Hebrews 9:11-28
Old Testament Reading
Leviticus 23:26-32

God's justice satisfied by Jesus' death

By one sacrifice he has made perfect forever those who are being made holy (Hebrews 10:14).

A murderer approaches the final minutes before his execution. His last words are a moving declaration of sorrow and remorse. Yet last words do not change the fact that a capital crime was committed. Justice must be served.

Because of crimes committed against God, every person stands guilty and condemned. Last words or mere remorse cannot change the justice of God. Only God Himself can alter the verdict— which is precisely what He has done through Jesus Christ.

Oswald Chambers examines how God's justice is satisfied in the death of His Son.

Walk with Oswald Chambers

"We trample the blood of the Son of God if we think we are forgiven because we are sorry for our sins. The only explanation for the forgiveness of God and for the unfathomable depth of His forgetting is the death of Jesus Christ.

"Our repentance is merely the outcome of our personal realization of the atonement which He has worked out for us.

"It does not matter who or what we are; there is absolute reinstatement into God by the death of Jesus Christ and by no other way, not because Jesus Christ pleads, but because He died. It is not earned, but accepted. All the pleading which deliberately refuses to recognize the Cross is of no avail; it is battering at a door other than the one that Jesus has opened.

"Our Lord does not pretend we are all right when we are all wrong. The atonement is a propitiation whereby God, through the death of Jesus, makes an unholy man holy."

Walk Closer to God

Hebrews 4:13 tells us that God sees sin. He cannot ignore it. But He also sees His sinful children *through* the blood of Christ. And what He sees is justice and mercy walking hand in hand. "Their sins and lawless acts I will remember no more" (10:17).

Those are words worth remembering!

Worship from the Heart

"Forgive and forget," we say. If the love of God is in our hearts, we can freely forgive. Forgetting is more difficult. It seems that the harder we forgiven sinners try to forget what another did to harm us, the more that memory sneaks back into our minds. Rejoice that the cross of Christ erases the memory of your sins in the mind of God.

Walk Thru the Word

New Testament Reading
Hebrews 10:1-18
Old Testament Reading
Isaiah 53:5-6

Enter the Most Holy Place by the blood of Jesus, by a new and living way opened for us through the curtain (Hebrews 10:19-20).

*C*hristianity can be defined as "life through death." But how do these apparent opposites relate? Paul explains.

"Anyone who has died has been freed from sin. Now if we died with Christ, we believe that we will also live with him. For we know that since Christ was raised from the dead, he cannot die again. " (Romans 6:7-9).

Put it together and you have a picture of Christianity as "life through death—in Christ." He is the One who can make even opposites work together to His glory.

Andrew Murray adds this timeless perspective.

Walk with Andrew Murray

"Christ opened for us a way to walk in, as He walked in it, 'a new and living way, through the curtain [veil, KJV], that is his body.'

"That is the way of the Cross. That way led to the rending of the veil of the flesh, and so through the rent veil of the flesh, to God.

"And was the veil of Christ's holy flesh torn that the veil of our sinful flesh might be spared? Indeed not. He meant for us to walk in the same way that He did, following closely after Him.

"He dedicated for us a new and living way. As we go in through the torn veil of His flesh, we find in it at once the need and the power for our flesh being torn too. Following Jesus always means conformity to Jesus."

Walk Closer to God

Hopes of glory and victory have accompanied many a great military leader's shout, "Follow me to the death!" But only Christ has ever called out to men and women, "Follow me through death to victory!" In Christ, death becomes not a crushing defeat but a resounding victory.

A soldier follows his leader for the fragile laurels of victory and recognition on the field of battle. How much more should a soldier of the cross be willing to follow his Commander-in-Chief.

*W*alking in a new and living way

*W*orship from the Heart

Paul reminds Hebrew Christians not to neglect meeting together. As you meet with other worshipers, ask yourself why it is important to meet with fellow believers. As the Holy Spirit reveals the blessings of being part of a community of believers, thank God for those who encourage and support you. It's wonderful to be part of the family of God.

*W*alk Thru the Word

New Testament Reading
Hebrews 10:19-39
Old Testament Reading
Job 17:9

Staking all upon the venture of faith

Now faith is being sure of what we hope for and certain of what we do not see (Hebrews 11:1).

*I*n some instances, wishful thinking might be a pleasant pastime or a delightful diversion.

But biblically based faith is not simply wishful thinking or hoping against hope. Rather, it is hope grounded in solid evidence. The One to whom your hope and prayers are directed must be worthy of your confidence.

Hebrews 11 spotlights the importance of a well-placed faith. Without it, no one can hope to please God, as John Henry Jowett makes clear.

Worship from the Heart

The most beautiful music, the loveliest scenery, the happiest moments can create a longing ache in your heart. If life on earth were all there is to life, this reaction would be senseless. But if your true and permanent home is heaven, these moments of beauty awaken in you a longing for perfect beauty, perfect joy. You're homesick.

Walk with John Henry Jowett

"Faith substantiates the unseen. Faith takes the energy of splendid ideals and incorporates it into present life. Faith unfolds the eternal in the moment, the infinite in the trifle, the divine in the commonplace. Faith incorporates God and man.

"Yes, faith gives substance to things hoped for; it brings them out of the air and gives them reality and movement in the hard and common ways of earth and time. And faith is also the test of things not seen. By a test faith gains a conquest. By an experiment faith acquires an experience. By a great speculation faith makes a great discovery.

"It is an invitation to humble and sincere assumption. Try it and see that it works! Make a hallowed experiment with the powers of grace.

" 'Lord, incline me to make the gracious test! Let me stake my all upon the venture! Let me dare in order that I may gain all! Let me sow bountifully, and so reap a bountiful harvest.' "

Walk Closer to God

As you read through chapter 11—a list of some of history's faithful saints—ask yourself, "Have I ever faced what they faced?" Mockings . . . scourgings . . . bonds . . . imprisonment . . . stoning . . . torture . . . temptation . . . death by the sword.

It's not a pleasant picture. And yet, the picture of faithfulness painted here is beautiful to behold. Clearly these men and women were living on something more than wishful thinking.

Could the same be said of you?

Walk Thru the Word

New Testament Reading
Hebrews 11:1-16
Old Testament Reading
Joshua 6:1-21

320

The persecution that reveals the power of God

They were stoned; they were sawed in two; they were put to death by the sword . . . destitute, persecuted and mistreated—the world was not worthy of them. . . . These were all commended for their faith (Hebrews 11:37-39).

Through the centuries, heroes of the church have announced allegiance to Christ and have refused to be moved—even in the face of death. One such hero is Polycarp, a disciple of the apostle John and an early church leader whose life ended when he refused to betray his Lord.

Asked one last time to disavow his Christ, the old man replied: "Eighty and six years have I served Him, and He has done me no wrong. How can I speak evil of my King who saved me?"

Here is his martyr's prayer, as recorded by the historian Eusebius.

Walk with Polycarp

"Father of Your beloved and blessed Son Jesus Christ, through whom we have received the knowledge of You, I bless You that You have counted me worthy of this day and this hour, that I might be in the number of the martyrs.

"Among these may I be received before You today in a rich and acceptable sacrifice, as You have beforehand prepared and revealed.

"Wherefore I also praise You also for everything: I bless You: I glorify You, through whom, with Him, in the Holy Spirit, be glory unto You both now and for the ages to come. Amen."

Eusebius adds: "When he had offered up his amen and had finished his prayer, the firemen lighted the fire."

Walk Closer to God

Killing believers has never been an effective way to kill the church. Instead, others see that a faith worth dying for must also be a faith worth having. Persecution merely reveals salvation at work, causing heroes of the faith to rise to the occasion.

Faith in God may not give you a long life—on this earth. But it will give you a powerful life . . . a persuasive life . . . a heroic life—in a day when heroes are in short supply.

Worship from the Heart

Think of Daniel in a den of lions, of Shadrach, Meschach, and Abednego in a fiery furnace, of Jeremiah in a muddy cistern. Their faith brought victory because it was placed in God's faithfulness. Recall a time when you were aware of God's faithfulness to you in a difficult circumstance. Praise Him by telling another person about that experience today.

Walk Thru the Word

New Testament Reading
Hebrews 11:17-40
Old Testament Reading
Psalm 69:9-18

The making of unusual Christians

No discipline seems pleasant at the time, but painful. Later on, however, it produces a harvest of righteousness (Hebrews 12:11).

*W*hen disciplining their children, parents sometimes say, "This hurts me more than it hurts you." And children have a tendency not to believe them.

The momentary pain of discipline is never pleasant. But whether understood or not by the child, the loving action of the parent has a purpose. Explanations can wait; obedience cannot.

A. W. Tozer adds this timely perspective on receiving discipline from your heavenly Father.

Worship from the Heart

"A cloud of witnesses"—who are they? For present-day Christians, they are those in Bible times and later history whose faith endured to the end. For you, they are also those in your life whose vibrant and steadfast faith has shown you the reality of God. Recall each special person and give thanks for them, one by one.

Walk with A. W. Tozer

"If God has singled you out to be a special object of His grace, you may expect Him to honor you with stricter discipline and greater suffering than less favored ones are called upon to endure.

"If God sets out to make you an unusual Christian, He is not likely to be as gentle as He is usually pictured by popular teachers. Saw, hammer, and chisel are cruel tools, but without them a sculptor cannot transform rough, formless stone.

"To do His supreme work of grace within you, God will take from your heart everything you love most. Thus you will learn what faith is; you will find out the hard way, but the only way open to you, that true faith lies in the will, that the joy unspeakable of which this passage speaks is not faith itself but a slow-ripening fruit of faith.

"You will learn, too, that present spiritual joys may come and go as they will without altering your spiritual status or in any way affecting your position as a true child of the heavenly Father."

Walk Closer to God

"To whom much is given, much is required." These simple words fit the challenge of Hebrews 12. Like the parent who loves a child too much to let discipline grow lax, God loves those created in His image so much that He disciplines them.

At times you may feel like responding, "Ouch! Don't love me quite so much, Lord!" But the pain has a purpose that will bring an eternal smile through today's tears.

Walk Thru the Word

New Testament Reading
Hebrews 12:1-13
Old Testament Reading
Genesis 32:24-32

. . . to God the judge of all men, to the spirits of righteous men made perfect (Hebrews 12:23).

*A*fter serving ten years in prison for his crime, the convict walks out a free man. But now a question arises: Has he changed his ways? Or will he return to a life of crime?

Justice may have been served without the criminal's having been rehabilitated. But unless both take place, the criminal will only become more hardened in his unrighteous ways.

In the Christian life, progress results from the twofold action of *justification* and *sanctification*. Charles Spurgeon describes this glorious combination of the working of God.

Walk with Charles Spurgeon

"There are two kinds of perfection which the Christian needs—the perfection of justification in the person of Jesus, and the perfection of sanctification wrought in him by the Spirit.

"At present, corruption remains in the breasts of the regenerate—experience teaches this. Within us are still lusts and evil imaginations. But God shall finish the work that He began. He will present my soul, not only perfect in Christ, but perfect through the Spirit, without spot or blemish.

"Yet let not the hope of perfection later make us content with imperfection now. If it does this, our hope cannot be genuine; for a good hope is a purifying thing, even now. The work of grace must be abiding in us now, or it will not be perfected then."

Walk Closer to God

Jesus satisfied the justice of God by taking upon Himself the death penalty that sinful humanity deserved. Thus, coming to Him in believing faith, you can walk out of the prison of sin a free person.

But the act of declaring you free from the guilt of sin inevitably is followed by the process of rehabilitation. Like a convict tempted to return to a life of crime, you will be tempted to sin. That's when you need to remember that Christ also walked out of prison with you, to help you "go straight." He's the best friend a convict ever had!

Set free to be made perfect

Worship from the Heart

Isaiah 49:8-10 indicates that the Messiah would free prisoners. Indeed the Jews looked for a political or military leader to break their oppression. But this promised liberty is freedom from the prison of sin. Praise God, Jesus has set you free!

Walk Thru the Word

New Testament Reading
Hebrews 12:14-29
Old Testament Reading
Isaiah 49:8-10

The one Friend you can depend on

Jesus Christ is the same yesterday and today and forever (Hebrews 13:8).

The school bully looms just ahead, waiting for another chance to torture and taunt you. Supported by your friends, you decide to take a stand. But just when you have reached the point of no return, you discover that your "friends" have retreated, leaving you to face the foe alone.

With friends like that, who needs enemies? But there is one Friend you can always depend upon when facing a spiritual battle. Jonathan Edwards reveals His identity.

Walk with Jonathan Edwards

"Comfort yourself that you have an unchangeable, constant friend in Christ Jesus.

"How excellent Jesus' friendship is. You may learn from His manner of treating His disciples on earth. He treated them as a tender father treats his children: meekly instructing them, most friendly conversing with them, and being ready to pity them, to help them, and to forgive their infirmities.

"He is the same still that He was then, and He will always be the same. You are so changeable that, if left to yourself, you would soon fall utterly away; but Christ is the same. Therefore, when He has begun a good work in you, He will finish it. Your love for Christ is itself changeable; but His for you is unchangeable. The writer gives this reason why the saints' love for Christ cannot fail—that His love for them can never fail."

Walk Closer to God

No one enjoys fair-weather friends, for when times are tough—when you need a friend the most—that's when they are most unreliable.

When Jesus went to the cross, most of His friends were nowhere to be seen. One "friend" betrayed Him with a kiss, another denied Him three times. But Christ still forgave even His enemies.

How are you at standing by your friends when they need you most? Take a lesson from the Friend who "sticks closer than a brother" (Proverbs 18:24), and stand up with confidence to the bully of sin.

Worship from the Heart

Surely Christians in today's world are not expected to show hospitality to strangers —or are we? The possibility of danger is very real. But the world of Paul and of Jesus Himself was full of such dangers. Meditate on this passage, and ask that the Holy Spirit interpret it for you so that you can in some way reach out with hospitality.

Walk Thru the Word

New Testament Reading
Hebrews 13
Old Testament Reading
Daniel 3:19-25

324

Consider it pure joy, my brothers, whenever you face trials of many kinds (James 1:2).

Questions: Have you ever attended a funeral? (Probably so.) Have you ever attended a funeral you enjoyed? (Probably not.) Have you ever attended your own funeral? (Definitely not.) Yet, strange as it may sound, Christians are commanded to do just that! "In the same way, count yourselves dead to sin but alive to God in Christ Jesus" (Romans 6:11).

Dead to sin; alive to God. The sooner you "count" that to be true, the sooner your Christian life will reflect the reality of it, as A. B. Simpson makes clear.

Walk with A. B. Simpson

"We do not always feel joyful, but we are to count it all joy. The word *reckon* [count] is one of the key words of Scripture. It is the same word used about our being dead. We do not feel dead. But we are to treat ourselves as dead and neither fear nor obey the old nature.

"So we are to reckon the thing that comes as a blessing. We are determined to rejoice, to say, 'My heart is fixed, O God, my heart is fixed: I will sing and give praise.' This rejoicing, by faith, will soon become a habit and will always bring the spirit of gladness and the spontaneous overflow of praise.

"Then, 'Though the fig tree does not bud and there are no grapes on the vines, though the olive crop fails and the fields produce no food, . . . I will rejoice in the Lord, I will be joyful in God my Savior' (Habakkuk 3:17-18)."

Walk Closer to God

Psychologists tell us the last place people can imagine themselves is in a coffin. Instead of dealing with death, most of us would rather look for detours around it.

But death defers to no one. Even Christ in His earthly life encountered death. He was the first to conquer it, and in doing so, made it possible for others to attend their own funeral—to see sin's penalty and power laid to rest.

And that's one funeral you won't want to miss!

*D*ead to sin, alive to God

*W*orship from the Heart

Examine the times when you did not deliberately set out to sin but sinned anyway. What happened? According to James, your own desires entice you to sin. Desires will arise, but you choose which ones to entertain. Praise God that as you set your heart on Him, He enables you to close the door on wrongful desires.

*W*alk Thru the Word

New Testament Reading
James 1:1-18
Old Testament Reading
Psalm 119:71

325

Making progress in a life of holiness

Religion that God our Father accepts as pure and faultless is this: to look after orphans and widows in their distress and to keep oneself from being polluted by the world (James 1:27).

*Q*uestion: What could Florence Nightingale (a famous nurse) and Attila the Hun (an infamous barbarian) have in common?

Answer: The need for a Savior.

"Good" people and "bad,"—all are guilty before a perfect God. But once the Savior has begun His work in the human heart, it will demonstrate itself in works of faith.

Johann Peter Lange explains.

Walk with Johann Peter Lange

"We must not misunderstand this description of pure and unspotted religious service, as if these words contained an exact definition of the *inner* side of true religious service in general.

"Anyone who is somewhat philanthropically inclined, while keeping himself *outwardly* free from worldly contamination, is still far from being able to say that he is practicing what James meant.

"Notice that James refers not to the service, but to pure and unspotted service and states in a general way what is above all things essential to practical religion. The great and principal condition is taken for granted: repentance and faith.

"James uses as examples the duty we owe to our neighbor, represented by widows and orphans, and the duties we owe to ourselves by the practice of self-denial and vigilance. These two points together reveal the true disposition toward God.

"To fulfill God's commands, to progress in holiness, is an ever-growing enjoyment of blessedness, granted more and more to the believer."

Walk Closer to God

Is your response to the Savior a heartfelt desire to serve Him as Lord? If you have any other response than grateful service to your Master, perhaps it's time to see just how "pure and undefiled" your religion really is.

After all, no sinner can afford to mistake himself for a saint when salvation is at stake.

Worship from the Heart

A horse is bridled so that it will not run wild. A tongue is bridled for the same reason. Unbridled tongues have destroyed reputations, severed friendships, ruined marriages, betrayed nations, and dishonored God. Thank your heavenly Father that the power of His Spirit is sufficient to bridle an unruly tongue. And pray that your words will reflect the divine character of the God you serve.

Walk Thru the Word

New Testament Reading
James 1:19-27
Old Testament Reading
Micah 6:6-8

For whoever keeps the whole law and yet stumbles in one point is guilty of breaking all of it (James 2:10).

Only one way to get right with God

*H*ow many violations of the law does it take to make a normally law-abiding person a law-breaker? The answer is simple: only one.

Every broken law carries a consequence. Breaking the law of God—falling short of His glory—carries the death penalty (Romans 6:23), whether the sin is as "big" as murder or as "small" as gossip. And there is only way to escape paying the penalty yourself, as Oswald Chambers reveals.

Walk with Oswald Chambers

"The moral law does not consider us as weak human beings at all. It takes no account of our heredity and infirmities; it demands that we be absolutely moral.

"The moral law never alters, either for the noblest or for the weakest; it is eternally and abidingly the same. The moral law ordained by God does not make itself weak to the weak; it does not excuse our shortcomings; it remains absolute for all time and eternity.

"When we realize this, then the Spirit of God convicts us of sin. Until a man gets there and sees that there is no hope, the cross of Jesus Christ is a farce to him. Conviction of sin always brings a fearful, binding sense of the law. I, a guilty sinner, can never get right with God; it is impossible.

"There is only one way I can get right with God, and that is by the death of Jesus Christ. I must get rid of the idea that I can ever be right with God because of my obedience. Who of us could ever obey God to absolute perfection?"

Walk Closer to God

"Father, I cannot please You in my own power. Even if I were able to 'go straight' from now on, there are still past sins to deal with. I have broken Your law repeatedly and deserve only death.

"I can only throw myself on Your mercy. I admit my need of the mercy found only in Christ. He alone has obeyed the law to perfection; He alone can save. Save me, Lord Jesus, for Your name's sake. Amen."

Worship from the Heart

"Lord, teach me to see other people through Your eyes. My own eyes are often blinded by preconceived ideas and prejudice. You have said that the way we treat the least of Your children is the way we treat You. At times I have treated You rudely or ignored You completely. There is no excuse for my behaving that way. Forgive me. Amen."

Walk Thru the Word

New Testament Reading
James 2:1-13
Old Testament Reading
Deuteronomy 27:26

No secrets from your dearest Friend

And the scripture was fulfilled that says, "Abraham believed God . . . " And he was called God's friend (James 2:23).

"I'm so ashamed. I can't believe I did something so awful."

"I'm your best friend; you can tell me."

"Well, okay, but only if you won't tell anyone."

Confession, they say, is good for the soul. But it is most beneficial to confess your shortcomings to the One who can do your soul the most good.

Alexander Maclaren reminds us that God is a good listener.

Walk with Alexander Maclaren

"If we are friends of God, we shall have no secrets from Him. There are very few people to whom we could venture to lay bare the depths of our hearts. There are black things down in the cellars that we do not like to show our friends.

"But if there is trust and love, we shall not be afraid to spread out before God all our foulness, our meanness, and even our unworthy thoughts and acts toward Him.

"Tell God all, if you mean to be a friend of His. Do not be afraid to tell Him your harsh thoughts of Him, and your complaints of Him. He never resents anything that a man who loves Him says about Him, if he says it to Him.

"What He 'resents' is our huddling up grudges and murmurings and questionings in our own hearts, and saying never a word to the Friend against whom they offend. Out with it all!

"And, if we are God's lovers, He will have no secrets from us."

Walk Closer to God

Perhaps you never realized that God knows your secrets already. "Everything is uncovered and laid bare before the eyes of him to whom we must give account" (Hebrews 4:13).

And if He knows you that well—and still loves you that much—doesn't it make sense to keep lines of communication open with Him?

Confess to Him what He already knows, and you will discover just how good a Friend He is.

Worship from the Heart

As you awake each day, praise God that the laws of nature operate as they do, allowing you to function smoothly in the material world. And praise Him for Jesus Christ, who has awakened you to life in the spiritual realm as well. How exciting it is to live, work, play, and worship in a world that is under God's control.

Walk Thru the Word

New Testament Reading
James 2:14-26
Old Testament Reading
Jeremiah 17:10

If anyone is never at fault in what he says, he is a perfect man, able to keep his whole body in check (James 3:2).

*B*e careful when you open your mouth. According to James, the unleashed tongue is an untamable beast. But with God's help you can "be quick to listen, slow to speak and slow to become angry" (1:19). Wise words for those convinced it is impossible to speak and not sin.

As F. B. Meyer points out, James' words provide insight by which you can examine your own speech patterns and the various ways the tongue can trip you up.

Walk with F. B. Meyer

"The tongue boasts great things. We are all apt to be vain, boastful, exaggerated. We contrive to focus attention on our own words and deeds; even in delivering God's message we manage to let it be seen that we have a clearer insight into truth or a closer familiarity with God than our fellows.

"We break the law of courtesy, and become harsh and uncivil; or the law of purity, and repeat stories that leave a stain; or the law of truth, and practice insincerity; or the law of kindness, and are harsh toward those who are beneath us in station. Or in our desire to stand well with others we are guilty of flattery or servility.

"We disparage other workers; compliment them to their faces and disparage them behind their backs. Alas for us! How greatly we need to offer the prayer of the psalmist: 'Set a guard over my mouth, O Lord!' "

Walk Closer to God

The antidote for misguided speech is carefully guarded silence. The Scriptures are filled with examples of periods of silence that refreshed God's men and women. Silence for worship, silence for thought, silence for prayer. "Be still, and know that I am God" (Psalm 46:10).

"Silence," one teacher has observed, "first makes us pilgrims. Secondly, silence guards the fire within. Thirdly, silence teaches us how to speak."

Do you want to speak well? Learn first to speak not at all as you listen to the voice of your Lord.

*E*ngaging the mind before starting the tongue

*W*orship from the Heart

God considers wise speech so important that there are over forty-three references to the subject in the book of Proverbs alone. As you have time, underline or jot down all the passages in Proverbs that you can find on the subject. As you write, pray that God will make each concept a practical reality in your life.

*W*alk Thru the Word

New Testament Reading
James 3:1-12
Old Testament Reading
Proverbs 15:1-2

Truth that talks in more than one way

Who is wise and understanding among you? Let him show it by his good life, by deeds done in the humility that comes from wisdom (James 3:13).

Arguments tend to bring out the worst in people. Sooner or later, accusations are made that go beyond the search for right and wrong. Anger and bitterness result.

How do you react when confronted with a volatile situation? Conventional wisdom says, "Win at all cost." Godly wisdom suggests otherwise, as the helpful 19th-century commentary *An Exposition of the Bible* describes.

Walk with a 19th-Century Expositor

"How do we bear ourselves in argument and in controversy? Do we desire that truth should prevail, even if that means our being proved wrong? Are we gentle toward those who differ from us? Or are we likely to lose our temper, and become heated against our opponents?

"If the last is the case, we have reason to doubt whether our wisdom is of the best sort. He who loses his temper in an argument has begun to care more about himself and less about the truth.

"He has become like the many would-be teachers rebuked by James: slow to hear, swift to speak; unwilling to learn, eager to dogmatize; less ready to know the truth than to be able to say something, whether true or false."

Walk Closer to God

When Christ admitted to His accusers that He was the Son of God, they feared for their own entrenched positions. In order to silence the truth, they crucified Him.

But notice that Christ did not argue; He didn't need to. After all, truth was on His side—indeed, He was the very embodiment of truth. His enemies may have seemingly won the battle, but He triumphed in the end.

Truth has not been entrusted to you just to be debated. Indeed, the whole world waits for a convincing demonstration of the life-changing power of God's truth.

As Christ showed, the application of truth to life is the most powerful argument of all.

Worship from the Heart

One aspect of wisdom is speaking to others with proper respect. Many of us would never dream of speaking to God the way we sometimes speak to those around us, including our nearest and dearest. Honor God by making your conversations with others edifying and uplifting in both content and tone.

Walk Thru the Word

New Testament Reading
James 3:13-18
Old Testament Reading
Job 28:28

*P*ray with honesty and care

When you ask, you do not receive, because you ask with wrong motives, that you may spend what you get on your pleasures (James 4:3).

*T*he young man rushed up to Jesus with a request sure to warm the heart of the Son of God. "Good teacher, what must I do to inherit eternal life?" But Jesus' reply lacked the warmth that might be expected.

" 'One thing you lack,' he said. 'Go sell everything you have and give to the poor, and you will have treasure in heaven. Then come, follow me' " (Mark 10:21).

That was certainly not the answer the young man had hoped for, and so he went away grieved.

God's open line of prayer doesn't answer every request as expected. A. W. Tozer points out the problems with some prayers.

Walk with A. W. Tozer

"Prayer is usually recommended as the panacea for all ills and the key to open every prison door—and it would indeed be difficult to overstate the advantage and privilege of Spirit-inspired prayer.

"But to escape self-deception, the praying person must come out clean and honest. Grace will save an individual, but it will not save him and his idol. The blood of Christ will shield the penitent sinner alone, but never the sinner and his idol. Faith will justify the sinner and his sin.

"No amount of pleading will make evil good or wrong right. A man may engage in a great deal of humble talk before God and get no response because, unknown to himself, he is using prayer to disguise disobedience."

Walk Closer to God

The rich young ruler wanted the best of both worlds: the mammon of man, and the grace of God. But receiving one means leaving the other behind; you cannot embrace both as master of your life.

Prayer is not meant to give you what you want, so much as to prepare you to receive what God wants for you. Ask for His will, and you will never regret what you receive in return.

*W*orship from the Heart

The best way to pray in accordance with God's will is to seek Him with your whole heart. When you are sure you are doing this, you won't have to worry about your motives. Jesus has given us a pattern of prayer to follow. Thank Him for it—and use it.

*W*alk Thru the Word

New Testament Reading
James 4:1-12
Old Testament Reading
Jeremiah 29:13

Doing good by getting involved

Anyone, then, who knows the good he ought to do and doesn't do it, sins (James 4:17).

A pedestrian is mugged in broad daylight while a dozen spectators look on in detached curiosity. When questioned, the onlookers might justify their behavior by claiming, "I didn't do anything wrong." And they would be right.

But not doing a right action is as wrong as doing a wrong one—a truth James declares and one that Albert Barnes explains.

Walk with Albert Barnes

"It is universally true that if a person knows what is right and does not do it, he is guilty of sin.

"If he understands what his duty is; if he has the means of doing good to others: if by his name, his influence, or his wealth, he can promote a good cause; if he can, consistently with other duties, relieve the distressed, the poor, the prisoner, and the oppressed; if he can send the gospel to other lands, or can wipe away the tear of the mourner; and if, by indolence, or avarice, or selfishness, he does not do it, he is guilty of sin before God.

"No man can be released from the obligation to do good in his world to the extent of his ability. No one should desire to be so released.

"The highest privilege conferred on a mortal—besides that of securing salvation—is doing good to others: alleviating sorrow, instructing ignorance, raising up the bowed down, comforting those that mourn, delivering the wronged and oppressed, supplying the wants of the needy, guiding inquirers into the way of truth, and sending liberty, knowledge, and salvation around the world."

Walk Closer to God

Meeting needs is costly . . . inconvenient. It takes time and energy. It may earn no thanks or appreciation. But it is simply the right thing to do.

Aren't you thankful that when the Father asked His Son to bear the burden of humanity's sin, Jesus didn't say, "No—I don't want to get involved"?

What answer will you give to God's call asking you to follow in His footsteps today?

Worship from the Heart

Regardless of how long life may seem to be, it is like a wisp of smoke when compared to eternity. Praise God that He gives believers the opportunity to make investments with eternal value and "to store up . . . treasures in heaven." Take a moment to examine what is in your "investment account" in heaven.

Walk Thru the Word

New Testament Reading
James 4:13–5:6
Old Testament Reading
Proverbs 21:13

Let your "Yes" be yes, and your "No," no, or you will be condemned (James 5:12).

A mortgage is a promise to pay. Break it, and you may lose a house. A treaty is a promise to protect. Break it, and you may lose an ally.

A wedding vow is a promise to "love, honor, and cherish till death do us part." Break it, and you may lose a partner.

But one thing is often lost when promises are broken: the reputation of the promise-maker.

George Müller laments the fact that even Christians are not immune to broken promises and the damage that accompanies them.

Walk with George Müller

"It has often been mentioned to me in various places that fellow believers in business do not attend to the keeping of promises.

"I cannot but entreat all who love our Lord Jesus, and who are engaged in a trade or business to seek for His sake not to make any promises except those which they absolutely believe they will be able to fulfill.

"They should carefully weigh all the circumstances before making any engagement, for it is even in these little ordinary affairs of life that we may either bring much honor or dishonor to the Lord. And these are the things which every unbeliever takes notice of.

"Surely it ought not to be true that we, who have power with God to obtain by prayer and faith all needful grace, wisdom, and skill, should be bad servants, bad tradesmen, bad masters."

Walk Closer to God

In the pursuit of Christlikeness, don't overlook the importance of letting your word be your honor.

God's word "cannot be broken" (John 10:35). Jesus Christ is "the same yesterday and today and forever" (Hebrews 13:8). "No matter how many promises God has made, they are 'Yes' in Christ" (2 Corinthians 1:20).

Remember, you may have trouble remembering the promises you made. But others will have little trouble remembering the promises you broke.

*K*eeping your word sets your light on a hill

*W*orship from the Heart

What difference does it make to you that Jesus is coming again? Bearing in mind that believers will give an account for attitudes, actions, and words, take a moment to praise God for the many ways He molds, shapes, and conforms you to the image of His Son. As you finish reading the book of James, ask your heavenly Father to make its practical principles a real experience in your daily life.

*W*alk Thru the Word

New Testament Reading
James 5:7-12
Old Testament Reading
1 Kings 8:54-61

Love that brings others to Jesus

Whoever turns a sinner from the error of his way will save him from death and cover over a multitude of sins (James 5:20).

*D*uring the tragic sinking of the *Titanic* in 1912, some selflessly helped others into the lifeboats, then stayed behind with the ship as it went down. Self-sacrifice made it possible for many to live.

Paul also displays this "lifeboat" mentality toward his fellow Israelites. "For I could wish that I myself were cursed and cut off from Christ for the sake of my brothers, those of my own race" (Romans 9:3).

How committed are you to helping others into the "lifeboat" of eternal life? Andrew Murray offers these challenging words.

Walk with Andrew Murray

"When Christ and His love took possession of our hearts, He gave us this love that we might bring others to Him. In this way Christ's kingdom was extended.

"Everyone who had the love of Christ in his heart was constrained to tell others. This was the case in the early Christian church. After the Day of Pentecost, people went out and told of the love of Christ, which they had themselves experienced.

"What a change has come over the church! Many Christians never try to win others to Christ. Their love is so weak and faint that they have no desire to help others. May the time soon come when Christians will feel constrained to tell of the love of Christ. Let us pray earnestly to be so filled with God's love that we may wholeheartedly surrender ourselves to win others for Him."

Walk Closer to God

"Father, I recall when another helped guide me into the safe harbor of Your love. Since then, I confess that I have not always been diligent to watch for those around me who need to be rescued from the shipwreck of sin.

"Give me the attitude of Paul the apostle, and of those who considered their lives expendable on the *Titanic,* so that others might be saved before it is too late."

Worship from the Heart

Describing his early days in a Christian community, a Christian leader writes that he often thanked God for giving him patience with the quirks of those around him. Then one day, as he prayed, he seemed to hear God's reminder: "Don't forget to thank Me also for giving others the patience to put up with you." Thank God now for the friends, co-workers, and family members who lovingly put up with your quirks.

Walk Thru the Word

New Testament Reading
James 5:13-20
Old Testament Reading
Proverbs 11:30

334

Light in the Darkness

A room devoid of light is a good place to stub your toe; a mountainside cloaked in darkness is a likely place to fall off the edge of a cliff. But turn on a light in the room or use a flashlight on the mountain, and the chances of hurting yourself diminish. For the Christian, God's Word is a light to guide you through life (Psalm 119:105), for in it God tells you how to live in the world in which He has called you to serve. But other voices—those of false teachers—contradict what God has said. Their words confuse rather than comfort, and they lead people astray. God has much to say about how to avoid being ambushed by these "wolves in sheep's clothing"(cf. Matthew 7:15). The letters of Peter, John, and Jude can help you unmask error and guard the truth.

Peter's two letters contain practical admonitions for those called to be representatives of God's truth. His first letter reminds Christians that suffering for doing what is right is not a sign that things have gone wrong. Instead, God is being glorified, for Christ Himself suffered for doing good. In his second letter, Peter first calls his readers to consider the virtues of truth as it is proclaimed in Jesus Christ; then he turns his attention to false teachers and their rightful condemnation.

John's three letters are masterpieces of profound truth expressed in simple terms. His overriding concern emerges in his third letter: "I have no greater joy than to hear that my children are walking in the truth" (3 John 4). His first letter centers on the true characteristics of one who trusts in Christ—fellowship, forgiveness, righteousness, faith. The other two letters contain guidelines for dealing with people who do not live according to truth.

The short letter of Jude is a succinct yet passionate exhortation to defend the faith against ungodly men who would subvert the truth.

After reading these six letters, you will see that God's truth is worth defending and applying to your life. Turn the light of God's Word on your life this month and discover that it is indeed truth to live by, truth to die for.

> *The letters of Peter, John, and Jude can help you unmask error and guard the truth.*

Finding the treasures of the King's palace

. . . so that your faith—of greater worth than gold, which perishes even though refined by fire—may be proved genuine . . . when Jesus Christ is revealed (1 Peter 1:7).

*I*f gold could only talk, what a tale it might tell. "Such heat! Doesn't the goldsmith know I might melt under such high temperatures?

"And that hammer! The goldsmith uses blow after blow to shape and mold me into his image. Doesn't he know I bruise easily? The pressure is terrific. I feel as if I am being squeezed into a whole new state of being . . . "

Think of that scene as a parable of the Christian life—a life marked by heat, pounding, and pressure. But the pain is nevertheless purposeful, as A. B. Simpson describes.

Walk with A. B. Simpson

"Our trials are great opportunities. Too often we look on them as great obstacles. It would be an inspiration of unspeakable power if each of us would recognize every difficult situation as one of God's chosen ways of proving His love and power to us; and if, instead of expecting defeat, we should begin to look around for the messages of His glorious manifestations. Then indeed every mountain would become a path of ascension and a scene of transfiguration.

"If we will look upon the past, many of us will find that the very time our heavenly Father has given us the richest blessings has been the time when we were strained and shut in on every side. God's jewels are often sent to us in unexpected packages and by dark servants, but within we find the very treasures of the King's palace."

Walk Closer to God

The brilliance of gold twice refined, then crafted into exquisite jewelry, is breathtaking indeed.But from the comfort of the jewelry store, no one recalls the heat and pressure, stamping and shaping at the hand of the goldsmith that made it possible.

Are you living in the crucible? Then take heart! Something beautiful is about to happen at the hands of your Creator.

Worship from the Heart

Suppose you were in the high priest's courtyard on the night Jesus was arrested. You heard Peter deny knowing Jesus. You understood his terror. Then you see him later in today's reading, proclaiming the resurrection of Christ. Rejoice in the change that knowing the resurrected Christ made in Peter's life—and in yours.

Walk Thru the Word

New Testament Reading
1 Peter 1:1-12
Old Testament Reading
Judges 7:1-8

The dignity and duty of God's children

You have been born again, not of perishable seed, but of imperishable, through the living and enduring word of God (1 Peter 1:23).

*B*orn with a silver spoon in his mouth." It's a figure of speech used to describe a child of position and privilege, one who is heir to estates and earnings, born not to serve but to be served.

The Christian can lay claim to an even greater heritage. His estate reaches to the limits of heaven and earth, for he is a child of God. But the Christian's birthright is not a ticket to a life of leisure. His high privilege brings with it high responsibility, for he is saved to serve, not to be served.

Charles Spurgeon elaborates on the dignity and duty of the child of God.

Walk with Charles Spurgeon

"What is a Christian? If you compare him with a king, he adds priestly sanctity to royal dignity.

"A king's royalty often lies only in his crown, but with a Christian it is infused into his inmost nature. He is as much above his fellows through his new birth as man is above the beasts.

"Surely he ought to conduct himself, in all his dealings, as one who is not of the multitude, but chosen out of the world, distinguished by sovereign grace, written among the 'peculiar people,' and who therefore cannot grovel in the dust as others, nor live after the manner of the world's citizens.

"Let the dignity of your nature, and the brightness of your prospects, O believer in Christ, constrain you to cleave to holiness and to avoid the very appearance of evil."

Walk Closer to God

The first privilege of the Christian is to serve the One whose name he bears—Christ Himself. Those who recognize their high calling will strive to keep that name pure and unsullied. They have a reputation to uphold.

The imitation of Christ is the highest form of honor. As He lived and served, so shall His fellow heirs in the family of God live and serve.

That's how we as children of position and privilege radiate the evidence of our royal birth.

Worship from the Heart

Isaiah 1:16-20 contains an invitation to "wash and make yourselves clean." Through the work of Jesus Christ, that invitation is extended to all who will come to Him. Spend a few moments remembering what your life was like before you experienced salvation, and then thank God for the changes He has made in your life.

Walk Thru the Word

New Testament Reading
1 Peter 1:13–2:3
Old Testament Reading
Isaiah 1:16-20

$\mathcal{G}$od's precious, living stones

You also, like living stones, are being built into a spiritual house to be a holy priesthood, offering spiritual sacrifices acceptable to God through Jesus Christ (1 Peter 2:5).

The vibrant diamonds, rubies, and sapphires worn by royalty make a spectacular sight. But did you know that there is a building being built even now using stones more precious than these?

Yes, the Master Stonecutter is preparing gems for His masterpiece: a holy priesthood built upon the Cornerstone of Jesus Christ. The fire opal is an example of one of these previous "living stones." Isobel Kuhn draws the analogy.

Walk with Isobel Kuhn

"A stone is the embodiment of principle—hard and cold. Fire is the essence of passion—warm and energizing. Put the two together, and we have living stones: principle shot through with passion, passion held by principle. That is the description of a human stone of fire.

"God needs more stones of fire today. He can quarry them anywhere, and He does not need rare materials from which to make them—desert dust, sand, silica—these can be found anywhere. Principle shot through with passion; passion held by principle.

"The stone is only a stone until its heart is broken and the air has a chance to get in. The Christian convert is only a principle until he lets God have His way with him and break his heart, if that has to be. Anything, in order to rip open the hardness and let God in! When the air has filled the fissures, then the stone is no longer a pebble. It is a gem, a precious opal, a living stone."

Walk Closer to God

Britain's Imperial Crown contains some of the world's most valuable gems including a 309 carat diamond, a large uncut ruby, and four huge pearls. But these stones do not approach the value of God's precious living stones—the Christians who will one day adorn His palace.

Will you allow the great Gem Cutter to make you into a beautiful stone of fire?

Worship from the Heart

Engraved with the names of the twelve tribes, the jewels on the breastplate of the high priest were worn over his heart and were taken with him into the very presence of God. Ponder that Old Testament symbol as you realize that this is the same place our Savior takes us as He holds us close to His heart.

Walk Thru the Word

New Testament Reading
1 Peter 2:4-12
Old Testament Reading
Exodus 28:15-29

338

That we might dwell with Him

He himself bore our sins in his body on the tree, so that we might die to sins and live for righteousness; by his wounds you have been healed (1 Peter 2:24).

*P*eople in high-visibility positions often yearn to disappear into the crowd. The rich and royal attract an entourage of onlookers, while bodyguards try to protect them from danger and annoyance. Yet the richest, most royal Person who ever walked the planet enjoyed no such human care and concern for His welfare.

During His earthly life the Son of God attracted attention and sparked animosity. He dwelt among men for a reason, as F. B. Meyer explains.

Walk with F. B. Meyer

"He came into the sinner's world. Himself sinless, He took our nature. He lived the ordinary life of a man. He worked in the carpenter's shed; attended wedding festivals and heart-rending funerals; ate, drank, and slept. He sailed in the boat with His fisher-friends.

"He sympathized with the sinner's griefs. In their affliction He was afflicted. He often groaned and sighed and wept.

"He died the sinner's death. He was treated as the scapegoat, the sin-offering of the human family. He stood as our substitute, sacrifice, and satisfaction. He carried the guilt and curse and penalty of a broken law in His suffering body.

"He is preparing the sinner's home. 'I go to prepare a place for you.' No mother was ever more intent on preparing a room for her boy's return, than Jesus on preparing heaven for His own."

Walk Closer to God

Christ dwelt among sinners in order that sinners might dwell with Him eternally. Unprotected and often unaccompanied by human ally, He always lived to please His heavenly Father.

Are you prepared to do the same today? Rest assured, you'll not be alone. "Surely, I am with you always" were the reassuring words Jesus left with His followers.

No earthly bodyguard could offer any greater comfort!

Worship from the Heart

Recall times when Jesus has lovingly pulled you back when you went astray. Then meditate on the words of William Bradbury: "Savior, like a Shepherd lead us; much we need Thy tender care./ In Thy pleasant pastures feed us; for our use Thy fold prepare. / Blessed Jesus, blessed Jesus, Thou hast bought us: Thine we are."

Walk Thru the Word

New Testament Reading
1 Peter 2:13-25
Old Testament Reading
Isaiah 53:7

Looking your best for your heavenly Bridegroom

Worship from the Heart

A major way to develop the true beauty of a "gentle and quiet spirit" is to sit at Jesus' feet and listen to His words. Read today's Scripture portion with the idea that you hold in your hand a letter from the Person who is most dear to you. Don't read thinking, "I'll learn something today." Read instead thinking, "My dearest and most treasured friend is writing especially to me."

Walk Thru the Word

New Testament Reading
1 Peter 3:1-7
Old Testament Reading
Proverbs 4:5-9

Your beauty should not come from outward adornment. . . . Instead, it should be that of your inner self, the unfading beauty of a gentle and quiet spirit, which is of great worth in God's sight (1 Peter 3:3-4).

*G*od could have created a very functional, very bland, black-and-white world. Instead, He made a universe abounding in luxuriant variety, rich color, amazing textures, and all kinds of shapes and sounds. He created a world for all His creatures to enjoy.

The adorning of creation provides a lesson on which Peter draws in chapter three, and which poet Anne Bradstreet underscores in this insight.

Walk with Anne Bradstreet

If so much excellence abides below,
  How excellent is He that dwells on high,
Whose power and beauty by His works we know?
  Sure He is goodness, wisdom, glory, light,
That hath this under world so richly dight* . . . .

My great Creator I would magnify,
  That nature had thus decked liberally:
But ah, and ah, again, my imbecility!
O time, that fatal wrack of mortal things,
That draws oblivion's curtains over kings,
  their sumptuous monuments, men know not,
Their names without a record are forgot,
  Their parts, their ports, their pomp's all laid in
    th' dust,
Nor wit, nor gold, nor buildings 'scape time's rust;
  But He whose name is graved in the white stone
Shall last and shine when all of these are gone.

* Obsolete word meaning "adorned" or "arrayed."

Walk Closer to God

Outward adornment is nice—but not necessary.

By contrast, inward adornment is more than a good idea—it is a command!

God has called His bride to develop a beautiful inner life . . . a life adorned with the fruit of the Spirit . . . a life colored by the character of Christ.

And, as Peter suggests, putting on the inner beauty of a gentle and quiet spirit is a good place to start "looking your best" for God.

*B*ecoming one in mind and purpose

Finally, all of you, live in harmony with one another; be sympathetic, love as brothers, be compassionate and humble . . . that you may inherit a blessing (1 Peter 3:8-9).

*I*t takes two—husband and wife—to make a marriage. But unless those two become one in mind and purpose, the marriage is in for stormy times.

Peter's instructions in chapter 3 to husbands and wives are not popular in a day of personal rights. And yet, if a Christian marriage is to be marked by compassion, love, and courtesy, both partners must have the mind of Christ.

Johann Peter Lange provides this helpful commentary on turning *discord* into *accord* in marriage.

Walk with Johann Peter Lange

"Let such married persons as God has blessed learn what cause they have to be thankful to God.

"Let the jars and discord that they see between other mismatched men and women be a means to put them in mind of God's great mercy and goodness toward them, and to make them more thankful to Him for the same.

"Since they have received each other from God, let them show their thankfulness to God by endeavoring to bring each other nearer to God, by helping each other forward in the ways of God.

"Do with the other as Hannah did with her son Samuel: As she had received him from God, so she gave him back to God. Return each other back to God, and labor to return each other better than each was received. The nearer you bring each other to God, the more good through God's goodness you will get from each other.

"The more a man and wife profit in the fear of God, the more contentedly they will live together, and the better it will be for them both."

Walk Closer to God

Luther called the family a "school for character." Certainly it is a proving ground for Christianity. If two people, sharing the mind of Christ and empowered by the Spirit of Christ, can produce the character of Christ *there*, then just imagine the impact they can make on a watching world!

*W*orship from the Heart

"Two wrongs don't make a right." That statement is quite logical, but logic flies out the window when someone hurts you. But before you strike back, stop. Remember that the love of Christ in your heart can absorb the hurt and can enable you to bless your would-be adversary. Thank God that His Spirit will give you grace to follow the example set by Christ Himself.

*W*alk Thru the Word

New Testament Reading
1 Peter 3:8-22
Old Testament Reading
Proverbs 25:21-22

Using your talents in the Master's service

Each one should use whatever gift he has received to serve others, faithfully administering God's grace in its various forms (1 Peter 4:10).

*T*he taunts were loud and ugly: "Come down from the cross, if you are the Son of God. . . . He saved others, . . . but he can't save himself!" (Matthew 27:40, 42).

Of course, they were wrong. What He *could* do, and what He *came* to do were two different things. Indeed, He had the power to rally the angelic hosts in His defense, but that was not His purpose.

Self-promotion has a way of crowding out self-sacrifice. Martin Luther points out the right way to use what God has entrusted to you.

Walk with Martin Luther

"A person who boasts of his gifts as if they were part of him and he had not received them makes an idol. He is not at all concerned about what becomes of God's honor or the welfare of his neighbor.

"The apostle Peter reminds us to attend to our occupation and faithfully do whatever is demanded of us. For, as Scripture teaches, no work is nobler than obedience in the calling and work God has assigned to each one.

"Many fickle, unstable believers think too much of themselves to continue in their calling. They stir up nothing but mischief and have no grace to do anything good. For they do not use their talents in the service of their neighbor; they use them only for their own glory and advantage."

Walk Closer to God

Self-promotion says, "Hold onto what you have, and use it to your fullest advantage."

Self-sacrifice says, "Be willing to release what you have, that you might become God's channel of blessing in the life of another."

"He can't save himself," the crowd had jeered. If they had only known . . . What they were seeing was not limited power but limitless love.

"Freely you have received," He told His followers. And you might have expected what He said next: "Freely give" (Matthew 10:8).

Worship from the Heart

Showing ungrudging hospitality to other Christians means more than opening your home to them. It means making room in your busy day to pray for them. It means gladly sharing yourself and all you have and are. Praise God that as you make room in your heart for others, you do so because He has made your heart His home.

Walk Thru the Word

New Testament Reading
1 Peter 4:1-11
Old Testament Reading
Zechariah 4:9-10

Saints in the place of God's choosing

So then, those who suffer according to God's will should commit themselves to their faithful Creator and continue to do good (1 Peter 4:19).

The sense of pain helps to defend the body from injury. People who can't feel pain are physically sick; those who enjoy pain are mentally sick.

In the walk of the believer, pain can come from following God's will, or from fleeing it. Paul obeyed God's instructions to go to Rome and ended up shipwrecked; Jonah disobeyed God's instructions and ended up in a great fish.

Oswald Chambers explores the kind of suffering that earns God's commendation, and the by-products that suffering brings.

Walk with Oswald Chambers

"To choose to suffer means that there is something wrong; to choose God's will even if it means suffering is a very different thing. No healthy saint ever chooses suffering; he chooses God's will, as Jesus did, whether it means suffering or not.

"Be merciful to God's reputation. It is easy to blacken God's character because God never answers back, He never vindicates Himself. Beware of the thought that Jesus needed sympathy in His earthly life; He refused sympathy from others because He wisely knew that no one on earth understood what He was going through.

"Notice God's 'waste' of saints, according to the judgment of the world. God plants His saints in some of the most useless places. We say, 'God intends me to be here because I am so useful.' Jesus never estimated His life along the line of the greatest use. God puts His saints where they will glorify Him most, and we are no judges at all of where that is."

Walk Closer to God

Christ Himself suffered for the purposes of a sovereign God. You as His ambassador should expect no less. Do not fear what others may do to you. After all, what is the Enemy compared to the strong and faithful Keeper of your soul!

With your eyes fixed on Him, you will be ready to face whatever results from doing His will.

Worship from the Heart

If you step out with the love and compassion of Christ, you may well experience the questioning, rejection, and pain that He encountered. The important thing is to carry on with His constancy of purpose. And remember to thank Him for walking right beside you all the way.

Walk Thru the Word

New Testament Reading
1 Peter 4:12-19
Old Testament Reading
1 Samuel 20:31-42

Ample grace for every journey

And the God of all grace, who called you to his eternal glory in Christ, after you have suffered a little while, will himself restore you and make you strong, firm and steadfast (1 Peter 5:10).

When will we be there? Is it much further? How many more minutes?"

What family trip would be complete without a child's impatient questions? And what parent hasn't responded: "Just a little longer . . . not quite yet . . . a few more miles"?

Children tire quickly during long trips, just as children of God tire quickly of the troubles of this world. Yet what is suffering for "a little while" in anticipation of the glory that is to follow?

F. B. Meyer puts the Christian's pilgrimage into perspective.

Walk with F. B. Meyer

"A little while! Compare it with the eternal years, with the far more exceeding and eternal weight of glory, with the compensations that await us.

"There is a limitation to our suffering. It is only for a little while, but every moment has been fixed by the immutable purpose and love of God. You shall not suffer one moment more than is absolutely necessary for your perfecting of God's glory, and for every moment there is an ample supply of grace.

"What a banquet that will be when God will satisfy the expectations of those whom He has called to partake of it!

"And the suffering is being used in ways you little understand to perfect, stablish, and strengthen you. God brings forth His veteran hosts in the day of battle. Think not so much of affliction as of the love of Christ, and the blessedness of being like Him and with Him forever."

Walk Closer to God

Arriving at your destination, the memories of pain and fatigue along the journey quickly fade.

Christian, you have a destination worth the cost of any trip. "Eternal Glory" is the name engraved above the gate. And it's a one-way journey you'll never forget!

Worship from the Heart

Some people seem to clutch their anxieties like trophies that show how important they are. If you are trying to cope with stress by yourself, don't brag about it. God's remedy is the only one that works: "Cast all your cares on God. He cares for you." Freedom from anxiety is a gift you can gratefully accept.

Walk Thru the Word

New Testament Reading
1 Peter 5
Old Testament Reading
Numbers 33:1-49

His divine power has given us everything we need for life and godliness, through our knowledge of him who called us by his own glory and goodness (2 Peter 1:3).

*I*t's a home run!" An experienced ear can tell by the sound of bat-hitting-ball what the outcome will be.

The science of ballistics can describe the speed and curve of the pitch, the angle of impact, and the ball's flight path out of the stadium. Theoretically, a scientist knows more about what happens than the batter. But the scientist doesn't have the practical knowledge or skill to play the game proficiently.

Your knowledge of Christ can also be theoretical or practical. Here, H. P. Liddon describes the results of knowing your Savior personally and practically.

Walk with H. P. Liddon

"Jesus is not set before Christians as a revered and departed Teacher whose words are to be gathered up and studied. He is rather an invisible and living Person who is to be known spiritually.

"This practical knowledge of Jesus is the crowning point of other attainments. It is the result of both faith and practice, and of the intellectual and moral sides of the Christian life.

"In the long line of graces which this special knowledge implies are moral strength, self-restraint, patience, piety, brotherly love, and, in its broadest sense, charity. In this higher knowledge of Jesus, all these excellencies find their completion. For this higher, practical knowledge of Jesus Christ is the means whereby Christians escape from polluting impurities of the world."

Walk Closer to God

Theoretical truth about Christ—*head knowledge*—is vitally important. But it's practical understanding of Christ—*heart knowledge*—that makes faith effective in your daily walk with the Lord.

The Word of God will stir your mind, warm your heart, and transform your life—but only as you combine doctrine and duty, belief and behavior. In the Christian life, to settle for anything less is to miss the "name of the game!"

*P*ractical knowledge that makes faith effective

*W*orship from the Heart

Psalm 112 is a brief, pointed glimpse into practical righteousness. You can even take a short quiz from this passage: (1) Are you gracious (v. 4)? (2) Are you compassionate (v. 4)? (3) Are you generous (v. 5)?(4) Do you give to the poor (v. 9)? (5) Are you an irritant to the wicked (v. 10)? Praise God for the work He does in you as you "find great delight in his commands" (v 1).

*W*alk Thru the Word

New Testament Reading
2 Peter 1:1-11
Old Testament Reading
Psalm 112

Reviewing the basics on a regular basis

So I will always remind you of these things, even though you know them and are firmly established in the truth you now have (2 Peter 1:12).

It happens to everyone sooner or later. You pick up the phone to call home, and you can't remember your own phone number. Or one day you can't remember a verse you've known since childhood.

Reviewing the basics on a regular basis is one way to combat forgetfulness. And for the Christian, the basics of the faith are too important to take for granted. Albert Barnes suggests a helpful way to stay knowledgeable about your Christianity.

Walk with Albert Barnes

"It was important for Peter to bring known truths to remembrance. Believers are apt to forget them, and then they do not exert the influence that they ought.

"Amid the cares, the business, the amusements, and the temptations of the world, the ministers of the gospel render us an essential service, even if they do nothing more than remind us of truths which are well understood, and which we have known before.

"A pastor need not always aim at originality; he renders an essential service to mankind when he reminds them of what they know but are prone to forget. He endeavors to impress plain and familiar truths on the heart and conscience, for these truths are most important for mankind. Though we may be very firm in our belief of the truth, yet it is appropriate that the grounds of our faith should be stated to us frequently, that they may be always in our remembrance."

Walk Closer to God

"I won't forget" are famous last words—even for Christians. It's easy to let the urgent drive from your mind thoughts of the timeless.

Pick a book of the Old Testament you haven't read for some time (such as Proverbs or Daniel), and refresh your memory on some of the vital truths that book contains. Remember, "I have hidden your word in my heart that I might not sin against you" (Psalm 119:11).

Worship from the Heart

People who knew Elvis Presley or worked in Buckingham Palace can name their own price for publishing their memoirs. Television and newspaper reporters flock to interview eyewitnesses of any newsworthy event. Peter, James, and John knew Jesus as friend, teacher, and risen Lord. Praise God that He inspired them to write their own eyewitness accounts.

Walk Thru the Word

New Testament Reading
2 Peter 1:12-21
Old Testament Reading
Deuteronomy 4:9-14

346

The Lord knows how to rescue godly men from trials (2 Peter 2:9).

Staying out of sin's way

*I*t starts with a touch. The touch leads to a punch, the punch leads to a kick. Before you know it, "war" has erupted between preschoolers. The best way to avoid such conflicts? "Don't touch!"

But this advice often falls on deaf ears. After all, what's the harm in one little touch? As with many temptations, a touch is all it takes to trigger the series of events that leads to sin.

Jonathan Edwards offers advice for keeping sin at arm's length.

Walk with Jonathan Edwards

"It is evident that we ought not only to avoid sin, but things that expose us and lead to sin, because this is the way we act in things that pertain to our temporal interest.

"We desire and love to have God's providence toward us so that our welfare may be well secured. No one likes to be vulnerable, uncertain, and in dangerous circumstances. While he is so, he lives uncomfortably and in continual fear.

"We desire that God would so order things that we may be safe from fear of evil. So we do not love the appearance and approaches of evil, but love to have it at a great distance from us.

"We desire to have God be like a wall of fire around us, to defend us, so that no evil may come near us. This plainly shows that we ought, in our behavior toward God, to keep at a great distance from sin, and from all that exposes us to it."

Walk Closer to God

"I won't if you won't." Such shaky endings to childish squabbles rarely last. First one child, then another tries to infringe on the forbidden area or action without actually violating the "agreement."

Jesus' model prayer (often called the "Lord's Prayer") charts a new course: "And lead us not into temptation, but deliver us from the evil one" (Matthew 6:13). With that as your attitude, you are well on your way to becoming a maker of peace instead of war!

Worship from the Heart

In Christ who strengthens you, you are ready for anything. Rejoice today that God will give you power to meet whatever comes into your life, and that He will use it for His higher purposes. Walk in obedience with joy.

Walk Thru the Word

New Testament Reading
2 Peter 2:1-12
Old Testament Reading
Genesis 19

Enjoying your liberty in Christ

They promise them freedom, while they themselves are slaves of depravity—for a man is a slave to whatever has mastered him (2 Peter 2:19).

*F*ishermen are always in search of a better lure. They invest time and money trying to entice unsuspecting fish to take their bait. And the same is true of false teachers: They seek better ways to lure the faithful into a net of satanic deceit.

In chapter 2 of his letter, Peter makes his readers aware of Satan's deadly devices. John Calvin underscores the apostle's warning.

Walk with John Calvin

"Peter strikingly compares the allurements of the ungodly to hooks. As the lusts of humans are headstrong and craving, as soon as liberty is offered, they grab it with great longing; but soon afterwards the strangling hook within is perceived.

"Let us beware, especially after having once been enlightened, lest Satan entice us under the pretense of liberty to gratify the lusts of the flesh.

"Liberty is sweet, and they abused it so that the hearer, being loosed from the fear of the divine law, might abandon himself to unbridled behavior. But the liberty which Christ has obtained for us is altogether different. He has exempted us from the yoke of the law as far as it subjects us to a curse, so that He might also deliver us from the power of sin, as far as it subjects us to its own lusts.

"Thus, where lusts reign and where the flesh rules, the liberty of Christ has no place whatever. True liberty leads those who are set free from sin to a willing obedience to righteousness."

Walk Closer to God

False teachers toss out attractive lures to the untaught and unsuspecting. Their promise of liberty with "no strings attached" lures the unsuspecting—hook, line, and sinker.

But ask the person who has been snagged by their deceit, and he'll tell you what kind of "liberty" they deliver.

Learn to recognize the lures before you take the bait, and you'll enjoy your liberty in Christ for a long, long time.

Worship from the Heart

If you suffer a relapse after recovering from the flu, the second bout with the disease may be worse than the first. So it is with a Christian who has known righteousness but turns away from it, sliding back into sinful habits. Praise God that in Christ we have all we need to live a life of holiness and fruitfulness.

Walk Thru the Word

New Testament Reading
2 Peter 2:13-22
Old Testament Reading
Proverbs 28:10

Do not forget this one thing, dear friends: With the Lord a day is like a thousand years, and a thousand years are like a day. . . . But the day of the Lord will come like a thief (2 Peter 3:8, 10).

She pauses in her work, gazing out to sea. Her sailor husband has been away for many months, and now, every sail on the horizon quickens her pulse. Time after time, as her hopes are disappointed, she returns again to work, to watch, to wait.

She knows he is a man of his word, and her expectations are built on three simple words: "I will return."

For nearly two thousand years, the bride of Christ, the church, has waited for the fulfillment of her Bridegroom's promise: "I will come back and take you to be with me that you also may be where I am" (John 14:3).

Isaac Watts expresses the longing of a watchful bride in this hymn of expectation.

Walk with Isaac Watts

> *Come, for Thy saints still wait;*
>   *Daily ascends their sigh:*
> *The Spirit and the bride say, "Come":*
>   *Dost Thou not hear the cry?*
>
> *Come, for creation groans,*
>   *Impatient of Thy stay,*
> *Worn out with these long years of ill,*
>   *These ages of delay.*
>
> *Come, and make all things new;*
>   *Build up this ruined earth;*
> *Restore our faded paradise,*
>   *Creation's second birth.*

Walk Closer to God

The return of Christ is no mere fairy-tale ending drawn from an imaginative mind. Rather, it is the unconditional promise of the One who is the embodiment of truth. "In keeping with his promise we are looking forward to a new heaven and a new earth" (2 Peter 3:13), knowing that a "crown of righteousness" awaits "all who have longed for his appearing" (2 Timothy 4:8).

*T*he longing of a watchful bride

*W*orship from the Heart

Samuel Wesley says of the church: "From heaven He came and sought her to be His holy Bride; | With His own blood He bought her, and for her life He died." You are His beloved. Read aloud the Song of Solomon 5:6–6:3. Meditate on that passage, as you speak the words to Christ.

*W*alk Thru the Word

New Testament Reading
2 Peter 3:1-10
Old Testament Reading
Song of Solomon 5:6–6:3

Cultivate a Christlike character

Make every effort to be found spotless, blameless and at peace with him (2 Peter 3:14).

A "lean, mean fighting machine" is
(a) a skinny tank
(b) a slender boxer
(c) a well-organized team that has no spare parts, no excess baggage. (Check one.)

When every member of a team has a specific job to do and knows how to do it, when the goal is clear and the enemy is imposing and time is short, watch out! Something exciting is about to happen.

The army of the cross faces a great challenge. Alexander Maclaren suggests a course of action for those who want to be part of an effective "fighting force" in the service of the King.

Walk with Alexander Maclaren

"I offer three simple exhortations. First, be earnest in cultivating a Christlike character. Half-and-half Christians are of no use either to God, to others, or to themselves.

"Second, make it your business to cultivate a character like that of Jesus Christ. If we would approach the work of growing a Christlike spirit with one one-hundredth the diligence we will put into our businesses, there would be a very different condition in most of our hearts.

"Third, make haste to cultivate a Christlike character. The harvest is great, the reckoning is at hand, and the Master waits to count His sheaves.

"There is no time to lose. Set about it as you have never done before, and say, 'This one thing I do.' "

Walk Closer to God

Two armies square off on the field of battle, but only one is thoroughly prepared and properly equipped. Which one would you expect to win?

Two Christians stand toe to toe with their Enemy, but only one has learned about Satan's devices and has put on the armor of God.

Which one do you think will still be standing when the dust has settled and the skirmish is at an end? (Ephesians 6:11, 13).

Even more to the point, which most closely resembles you?

Worship from the Heart

Jesus Himself during His time on earth did not know when the end would come (Matthew 24:36). Rejoice that you do not know either. Whether that time comes tomorrow or long after your death, you can live each day as if it were the last, giving your very best to and for your Savior. Thank Him for that privilege.

Walk Thru the Word

New Testament Reading
2 Peter 3:11-18
Old Testament Reading
2 Kings 3:16-20

That which was from the beginning, which we have heard, which we have seen with our eyes, which we have looked at and our hands have touched—this we proclaim concerning the Word of life (1 John 1:1).

*J*ohn's proclamation is a triumphant statement of faith.

The heretical Gnostic teaching that Jesus did not really have a body had weakened the faith of some, so John wrote to remind the church of the truth of the incarnation.

How like John's audience we are! The foolish philosophies of this world easily take us captive. Robert Murray McCheyne urges us to fix our eyes on Jesus and throw doubt to the wind.

Walk with Robert Murray McCheyne

"Oh, brethren, could you and I pass through these heavens and see what is now going on in the sanctuary above—could you see the Lamb with the scars of His wounds sitting in the very midst of the throne—could you see the thousands, all singing, 'Worthy is the Lamb that was slain'—and were one of these angels to tell you, 'This is He that undertook the cause of lost sinners; consider Him; look long and earnestly upon His wounds and glory'—could you see all these things, do you think it would be safe to trust Him?

" 'Yes, yes,' every soul exclaims. 'Lord, it is enough! Let me ever stand and gaze upon the almighty, all-worthy Savior! Yes, though the sins of all the world were on my wicked head, still I could not doubt that His work is complete, and that I am quite safe when I believe in Him."

Walk Closer to God

John had enough faith to publicly proclaim his Christianity at a time when it brought imprisonment or death. Do you have enough faith to "salt" your conversation with Christ at a time when it might bring scorn?

If you're like most of us, you answered, "Well, maybe." Fortunately, we have a Savior who hears us when we cry, "I do believe; help me overcome my unbelief!" Be encouraged. That is a prayer He will answer.

I know that my Redeemer lives

*W*orship from the Heart

Remember that Jesus is your light and salvation. He is the source of spiritual vision. In times of trouble or need, you can turn freely to Him for there is no one else who cares so much for you.

*W*alk Thru the Word

New Testament Reading
1 John 1:1-4
Old Testament Reading
Isaiah 2:1-11

351

*L*ight we cannot live without

This is the message we have heard from him and declare to you: God is light; in him there is no darkness at all (1 John 1:5).

*P*lants aren't the only living things that need the light of day. Animals and human beings may not contain chlorophyll and perform photosynthesis, but light is still vital for their long-term health. If you stay in the dark for very long you will eventually experience depression and disorientation.

And where there is spiritual darkness, spiritual death cannot be far behind. That's why it is vital that men and women encounter God's healing light firsthand. Andrew Murray adds this timely perspective.

Walk with Andrew Murray

"Children of God, it is the ardent longing of your Father that you should dwell and rejoice in His light all the day. Just as you need the light of the sun each hour, so the heavenly light, the light of the countenance of the Father, is indispensable. As surely as we receive and enjoy the light of the sun, so confidently may we count on it that God is longing to let His light shine on us.

"Even when there are clouds, we still have the sun. So amid difficulties the light of God will rest upon you without ceasing. If you know the sun has risen, you count upon the light all day. Make sure that the light of God shines upon you in the morning, and you can count upon that light being with you all day. Take time till that light shines in your heart, and you can truly say: 'The Lord is my light and my salvation.' "

Walk Closer to God

Let this hymn be your response to God's light:
> *O Splendor of God's glory bright,*
> *From light eternal bringing light;*
> *Thou Light of life, light's living Spring,*
> *True Day, all days illumining.*

> *Confirm our will to do the right,*
> *And keep our hearts from envy's blight;*
> *Let faith her eager fires renew.*
> *And hate the false, and love the true.*

*W*orship from the Heart

As you read Psalm 27:1, remember that Jesus is your light and salvation. He is the source of spiritual vision. In times of trouble or need, you can turn freely to Him for there is no one else who cares so much for you.

*W*alk Thru the Word

New Testament Reading
1 John 1:5–2:2
Old Testament Reading
Psalm 27:1

Work out your salvation

We know that we have come to know him if we obey his commands. The man who says, "I know him," but does not do what he commands is a liar, and the truth is not in him (1 John 2:3-4).

*J*ust mention the word *commands* in our society and watch what happens. Some people bristle and the rest squirm. Sadly, that attitude not only permeates the world, but also the church. But John regards obedience to God's commands as a good way to judge whether we know Christ.

In the first chapter we saw John refute the heresy that Jesus could not have come in the flesh. John also wrote to correct another Gnostic error; licentiousness. Their reasoning went like this: If evil is in matter, rather than in breaking God's law, then breaking God's law is not evil. You can imagine what kind of wickedness followed.

Shouldn't the Christian want to obey God? Listen to Bishop Ryle.

Walk with J. C. Ryle

"Believers are eminently and peculiarly under a special obligation to live holy lives. They are not dead, blind, and unrenewed; they are alive unto God, enlightened, and have a new principle within them. Whose fault is it if they are not holy? On whom can they throw the blame if they are not sanctified? God, who has given them a new heart and a new nature, has deprived them of all excuse if they do not live for His praise.

"This is a point which is far too much forgotten. A man who professes to sanctification (if indeed any at all), and coolly tells you he 'can do nothing,' is a very pitiable sight and a very ignorant man. Against this delusion let us be on our guard. If the Savior of sinners gives us renewing grace, and calls us by His Spirit, we may be sure that He expects us not to go to sleep."

Walk Closer to God

John says God's commands distinguish love from sin and are not burdensome (1 John 3:4; 5:3). The world says God's commands are chains to be broken and fetters to be thrown off (Psalm 2:3). Which attitude characterizes you?

Worship from the Heart

Father, often I find that my desire to do right, to follow Your commands, is not what it should be. Give me a desire to do right, not just because I should but because I want to. In the name of Your Son, my Savior, whose highest aim was to please You. Amen."

Walk Thru the Word

New Testament Reading
1 John 2:3-11
Old Testament Reading
Psalm 119:57-64

353

Charles Spurgeon (1834-1892) Ambassador of God's Truth

*A*sk any person to compile a list of great Christian communicators of the past, and chances are good that the name of Charles Haddon Spurgeon will be included at or near the top of the list.

"Prince of preachers" he was called. "The greatest preacher since the apostle Paul." These are just two of the many accolades Spurgeon has received from his contemporaries and successors.

Spurgeon's popularity—unsurpassed among preachers of his day—has not noticeably diminished after what is now a century after his death. Such praise seems overwhelming for a man who never attended college or formally studied for his profession. But since he was a third-generation preacher, following in the footsteps of his father and grandfather, Spurgeon had good models to observe.

Born in 1834, Charles always excelled in school, even becoming an assistant teacher while still a teenager. During this time he committed his life to Christ, and later preached his first sermon at the age of sixteen. Instead of going on to college, Spurgeon became the pastor of a small church . . . at the tender age of seventeen!

Three years later the New Park Street Church in London asked him to become its pastor. The young

preacher accepted, and in a few short years saw his congregation grow from one thousand to several thousand members. By the age of twenty-two, Spurgeon was already the best-known preacher of his day.

In 1861, the Metropolitan Tabernacle was built, seating six thousand. Eager listeners filled its pews twice each Sunday to hear this gifted young man preach. Here Spurgeon remained for the next quarter of a century, preaching God's Word to the masses of London.

But his ministry was not limited to the pulpit. He also established an orphanage . . . trained young men for the ministry . . . wrote devotional and theological books and pamphlets . . . and edited his sermons for publication. The amount of material that found expression from his pulpit and pen staggers the imagination.

Without a doubt, Spurgeon was the dominant figure in 19th-century British Christianity until his death in 1892 at the age of fifty-seven. An unquestioned master of the spoken word, Spurgeon never missed an opportunity to declare God's truth fearlessly.

Once, after preaching an unpopular message, he was approached by a friend who said, "I hear you are in hot water." Spurgeon replied, "Oh, no. It is the other fellows who are in hot water. I am the stoker, the man who makes the hot water boil."

Heard and read by millions on both sides of the Atlantic, Charles Spurgeon stood tall as a preacher of God's Word. A fellow minister once asked, "Who since Paul has done so much to advance the kingdom of God?" The unspoken but obvious answer testifies to Spurgeon's willingness to place his gifts and abilities entirely at the disposal of his Lord.

You too have talents that God has given you, such as the ability to speak, to write, to serve, or to encourage. Perhaps you have a gift that is as yet undeveloped. Whatever it may be, the best place to use your gift is in the service of the One you call Lord.

God is not as concerned about how many people you stand before as He is about what you stand for! Regardless of who listening, you can still declare faithfully and unfalteringly the timely truths of God's Word.

A Lesson from the life of Charles Spurgeon

When I place my gifts and talents at the Lord's disposal, other lives will be blessed.

*F*irmly planted on the Rock

I write to you, young men, because you are strong, and the word of God lives in you, and you have overcome the evil one (1 John 2:14).

*W*hat would be your reaction to these responses from a job applicant?
Question: "Are you dependable?"
Answer: "Part of the time."
Question: "Do you do good work?"
Answer: "Occasionally."
Question: "Do you make decisions easily?"
Answer: "Well, yes and no . . . "
To put it in Scriptural terms, "A double-minded man [is] unstable in all he does" (James 1:8).

Charles Spurgeon provides this profile of wholehearted commitment.

Walk with Charles Spurgeon

"The spiritually strong man is not halfhearted, torn between two opinions.

"He is for Christ. Whoever may be for the false, he is for the true. Whoever may side with the unjust, he is for the honest. Whoever may adopt crooked policy, he is for straightforward principle.

"He has made up his mind that he is Christ's, and therefore he does not tolerate within his soul anything like a question on that matter. He is decided, not only in his service for Christ, but in his opinions. He is strong in the truth.

"You cannot pull him this way and that. He does his own thinking with his Bible before him. He has grown strong by feeding on a heavenly diet. He is a man with his feet firmly planted on the Rock."

Walk Closer to God

"Firmly planted . . . spiritually strong." Paul supplies the key to that kind of stability.

"Then we will no longer be infants, tossed back and forth by the waves, and blown here and there by every wind of teaching. . . . Instead, speaking the truth in love, we will in all things grow up into him who is the Head, that is, Christ" (Ephesians 4:14-15).

Truth . . . delivered and received in love . . . leading to growth and stability in the faith. Now that's a promise you can sink your roots into!

*W*orship from the Heart

Search the deepest, darkest corners of your mind and heart. Is there anyone you hate? Hatred blinds us to the true light and causes us to stumble. Bring any hidden hatred into the light now. Acknowledge it before God, and ask Him to use you as a channel of Christ's love to that person. Praise God that Jesus Christ, the Light of the world, has allowed you to partake of His life.

*W*alk Thru the Word

New Testament Reading
1 John 2:12-17
Old Testament Reading
Job 1:1-5

The anointing you received from him remains in you, and you do not need anyone to teach you. But as his anointing teaches you about all things and as that anointing is real, not counterfeit—just as it has taught you, remain in him (1 John 2:27).

The Teacher who dwells within

*I*magine your reaction if you heard a teacher announce: "Today is Veteran's Day, so you must take your pets to the doctor's office. A veteran is an animal doctor, and he will look after your pets."

If you were outside a classroom, you would be concerned about the misinformation being handed out. But if the "teacher" was your five-year-old and the students were dolls, you would chuckle and jot this anecdote in the family memory book.

Playing teacher is a common practice among small children, but when it comes to spiritual matters, credentials must be carefully weighed. Matthew Henry explains who the Christian's final authority and Teacher is.

Walk with Matthew Henry

"This letter was written to fortify against deceivers. But true Christians have an inward confirmation of divine truth: The Holy Spirit has imprinted it on their minds and hearts. We should not desire to teach anything except what the Holy Spirit has taught us in His Word; and the same Spirit teaches all who partake of His anointing, though they differ in less important matters.

"The Spirit of truth will not lie; and He teaches all things necessary to our knowledge of God in Christ, and their glory in the gospel. He teaches us to abide in Christ, and He restrains our minds and hearts so that we will not revolt from Him."

Walk Closer to God

It's fine for children to teach dolls. But your heavenly Father wants His children to have the best possible Teacher—the indwelling Holy Spirit.

Abide in the teachings of Christ and "test the spirits to see whether they are from God" (1 John 4:1). And through careful study of God's Word, you will be able to tell if someone is trying to deceive you or is teaching you from ignorance.

Worship from the Heart

Today's Old Testament reading reminds us that God carefully supplied the physical needs of His people in the wilderness. But God, who is a Spirit, also met their spiritual needs. As you ponder the fact that God's love for His children is as great now as it was then, thankfully acknowledge His daily provision for you—in both material and spiritual realms.

Walk Thru the Word

New Testament Reading
1 John 2:18-27
Old Testament Reading
Nehemiah 9:20

As Christ Himself is pure

How great is the love the Father has lavished on us, that we should be called children of God! (1 John 3:1).

*W*hen you see a well-behaved ex-convict, one of two things is true: (a) He is a parolee, behaving well because of fear; or (b) He is a new person, and his behavior reflects his gratitude.

The threat of incarceration can effectively deter further crime. But so can the privilege of adoption into God's family, for being part of God's family involves both rewards and responsibilities.

Isaac Watts draws these twin thoughts together in this inspiring hymn.

Walk with Isaac Watts

> Behold the amazing gift of love
>   The Father hath bestowed
> On us, the sinful sons of men,
>   To call us sons of God!
>
> High is the rank we now possess;
>   But higher we shall rise;
> Though what we shall hereafter be
>   Is hid from mortal eyes:
>
> Our souls, we know, when He appears,
>   Shall bear His image bright;
> For all His glory, full disclosed,
>   Shall open to our sight.
>
> A hope so great, and so divine,
>   May trials well endure;
> And purge the soul from sense and sin,
>   As Christ Himself is pure.

Walk Closer to God

Elsewhere the apostle shares how a child of God can achieve this purity: "Dear children, do not let anyone lead you astray. He who does what is right is righteous, just as he is righteous" (3:7).

Christ has released His adopted children from the prison of sin and has given them a complete pardon. As joint heirs with the Son they now have a responsibility to behave as one of the family. It's no longer the "long arm of the law" that instills fear, so much as the "loving arm of the Savior" that inspires gratitude.

Worship from the Heart

"In him all things hold together" (Colossians 1:17). As you meditate today, remember that when Jesus is both the center and the circumference of your life, harmony reigns. Because He is in control, things do not fly apart or go to pieces. May your heart's deepest desire be for Christ to be the focal point of all your thoughts and activities.

Walk Thru the Word

New Testament Reading
1 John 2:28–3:10
Old Testament Reading
Deuteronomy 14:2

A heart persuaded that all is well

Whenever our hearts condemn us . . . God is greater than our hearts, and he knows everything (1 John 3:20).

*E*veryone can point to errors of judgment and performance that have caused problems for others. But often the memories of such painful moments can linger long after the offense has been forgiven.

No, it's not the harsh criticism of a boss or spouse berating you for a recent blunder, but the silent accusations of your own heart—the inner turmoil of conscience only you and God can hear. Others may forget, but somehow you can't.

As Albert Barnes demonstrates from 1 John 3, self-condemnation can be conquered.

Walk with Albert Barnes

"The meaning here seems to be that we shall allay our doubts and produce a state of quiet and peace by the evidence that we are of the truth. Our consciences are often troubled by past guilt. But, in furnishing the evidence of true piety by love to others, we shall pacify an accusing mind, conciliate our own hearts, and convince ourselves that we are truly the children of God.

"In other words, though a person's heart may condemn him as guilty, and though he knows that God condemns the sins of the past, yet his mind may be soothed by evidence that he is God's child and that he will not be finally condemned.

"A true Christian does not attempt to conceal the fact that there is much for which his own heart and conscience might justly accuse him; but he finds, in spite of all this, evidence that he is a child of God, and he is persuaded that all will be well.

"The heart can be kept calm only by such a course of life that God and our own hearts shall approve the manner in which we live."

Walk Closer to God

Reminders of your sinful past are best remedied by thoughts of your present life in Christ. Indeed, without Him, life would be one dark memory.

When God has forgiven you and has buried your sins in the deepest sea, He also puts up a "No Fishing" sign—and He means it!

Worship from the Heart

The defeating attitude of self-condemnation has no place in the life of a Christian. God knows about your sins and has covered them with the blood of Jesus. Remember that in Christ you are redeemed, forgiven, and made a member of His family. Walk in victory as a child of the King.

Walk Thru the Word

New Testament Reading
1 John 3:11-24
Old Testament Reading
Psalm 147:1-6

Time for a test

Dear friends, do not believe every spirit, but test the spirits to see whether they are from God (1 John 4:1).

"It's time for a test." These words periodically send shock waves through countless classrooms; but without the test, there's no assurance that you've learned the lesson. In chapter four, John gives his readers a series of tests to help them to distinguish between false spirits, evil spirits, and God's Spirit.

Testing your spiritual experiences against the timeless standard of God's Word is another "exam" you can't afford to miss, as A. W. Tozer comments.

Walk with A. W. Tozer

"The seeker after God's best is always eager to hear from anyone who offers a way by which he can obtain it. He longs for some new experience, some elevated view of truth, some operation of the Spirit that will raise him above the religious mediocrity he sees all around him.

"Our Lord has made it plain not only that there shall be false spirits abroad, endangering our Christian lives, but that they may be identified and known for what they are!

"The first test must be: 'What has this done to my relationship with and my attitude toward the Lord Jesus Christ? Do I love God more? Is Jesus Christ still to me the center of all true doctrine?

"Again: 'How does it affect my attitude toward the Scriptures?' Did this new view of truth spring from the Word of God itself or was it the result of some stimulus that lay outside the Bible? Be assured that anything that comes to us from the God of the Word will deepen our love for the Word of God!"

Walk Closer to God

"Father, now is a good time to test myself and see if I am growing in my walk with You.

"When seeking the truth, may I be quick to ask these two questions: 'What will this do to my relationship and attitude toward Jesus Christ?' and 'How does this affect my attitude toward Your Word?' May my answers reflect my deep love for You, Father. Amen."

Worship from the Heart

In Jeremiah 31, the prophet records God's love song for His people Israel. God's love for Israel is everlasting, joyful, comforting, and abundant. Think of seven other adjectives that describe how you perceive God's love in your life. Praise Him that His love for you is tailor-made and personal.

Walk Thru the Word

New Testament Reading
1 John 4:1-6
Old Testament Reading
Jeremiah 23:31-32

If anyone says, "I love God," yet hates his brother, he is a liar. For anyone who does not love his brother, whom he has seen, cannot love God, whom he has not seen (1 John 4:20).

"I love you," he whispers.

"And I love you too, my darling," she replies.

"Cut!" yells the director. And the two actors, who have just spoken so affectionately, exchange glares and march off the stage.

An actor suppresses personal feelings in order to project a persona for the audience. Similarly, a Christian may fool friends and family, but the actions of his heart do not escape God's view.

Andrew Murray points out the implications for those who want to please God.

Walk with Andrew Murray

"What a solemn thought, that our love for God will be measured by our everyday behavior toward others and the love it displays; and that our love for God will be found to be a delusion, except as its truth is proved in standing the test of daily life with our fellow human beings.

"It is even so with our humility. It is easy to think we humble ourselves before God. But humility toward others will be the only sufficient proof that our humility before God is real.

"The lesson is important: The only humility that is really ours is not that which we try to show before God in prayer, but that which we carry with us, and carry out, in our day-to-day conduct.

"It is in our most unguarded moments that we show and see what we really are. To know the humble man, to know how the humble man behaves, you must follow him in the common course of daily life."

Walk Closer to God

The actor on the screen may portray a person of virtue and godliness, but what about the person behind the performance?

Do you put your best foot forward in public, only to act far from Christlike in private? Then remember this: In the final analysis there is really no such thing as "private."

In the unguarded moments of ordinary days

Worship from the Heart

"What wondrous love is this, O my soul?" This love is agape, described in 1 Corinthians 13. It is far more than a warm, fuzzy feeling. This love is a commitment to love unconditionally with no promise of being loved in return. Rejoice that Christ loves you with agape love. And because He does, you too can love others in this way. Wondrous indeed!

Walk Thru the Word

New Testament Reading
1 John 4:7-21
Old Testament Reading
1 Samuel 2:3

*G*od's paternal love made known

And this is the testimony: God has given us eternal life, and this life is in his Son. He who has the Son has life; he who does not have the Son of God does not have life (1 John 5:11-12).

A letter arrives on government stationery. You read carefully, for your future is at stake. Your stockbroker calls about your investments. You listen, for your financial security is on the line. God speaks to you in the pages of His Word about your need for salvation. You listen, for your eternal destiny hangs in the balance. Or do you?

John describes faith as the lifeline every person needs to grasp. John Calvin explores the necessity for belief on the part of the individual.

Walk with John Calvin

"The apostle invites us to believe. It is indeed a reverence due to God to receive without controversy whatever He declares to us. Doubtless the words of the apostle are intended to show that we ought to do more than just reverently obey the gospel, but that we ought to love it because it brings eternal life to us.

"The apostle repeats that life is found in Christ; no other way of obtaining life has been appointed for us by God the Father.

"And he includes here three things: One, that we are all given up to death until God in His favor restores us to life. For he plainly declares that life is a gift from God. Thus it follows that we do not have it, and that it cannot be acquired by merits.

"Two, he teaches us that this life is conferred on us by the gospel, because there the goodness and paternal love of God are made known.

"Lastly, he says that we cannot otherwise become partakers of this life than by believing in Christ."

Walk Closer to God

Strange, isn't it, how quickly we listen to financial advice, yet how slowly we respond to God's warning about the course our life is taking?

Have you grasped hold of God's lifeline in the person of His Son? It's sound advice for those with "ears to hear."

*W*orship from the Heart

As you prepare for worship, meditate on these words: "His commands are not burdensome." Call God's commandments to mind. Have they sometimes seemed burdensome? Probably. But looking back you can see how, time after time, they kept you from getting into serious trouble. Praise God for giving you His law.

*W*alk Thru the Word

New Testament Reading
1 John 5:1-12
Old Testament Reading
Isaiah 25:9

This is the confidence we have in approaching God: that if we ask anything according to his will, he hears us (1 John 5:14).

/t is Christmas morning. The presents have all been opened, but eight-year-old Bobby sits pouting in the corner, mad at Santa Claus.

"Why are you mad at Santa?" his dad asks.

"Because I asked Santa for a real gun, but I got this silly old air rifle!"

Didn't Bobby's father love him? Hadn't he heard his son's request? Didn't he delight to give gifts to his children?

Yes . . . yes . . . and yes! The problem was not an unhearing father, but an immature son.

Prayer was never intended to be a wish list for God's children, as Martin Luther explains.

Walk with Martin Luther

"Here you ask: Do you mean to say that this promise is always true even though God often does not give what we have asked for?

"As His Word shows, it is certainly His will to deliver you from all evil, not to leave you in temptation, and to give you your daily bread. Otherwise He would not have commanded you to pray for these things. If you pray in this way— that all may go according to His will—then your prayer is certainly heard.

"Therefore when in trouble, you should certainly pray for deliverance and help, but in the way the Lord's Prayer teaches you—if it tends to hallow His name and please His will; if not, that He will act as He sees best. If it is not heard according to our will, then it is heard according to the will of God, which is better than ours."

Walk Closer to God

Perhaps you can think of requests you have made of God in the past that now make you cringe at your naiveté. As a wise Father, He knows better than to give a lethal answer to a childish request.

As you pray, always take the time to ask, "What do You think?" instead of rushing on with "God, I think . . ." You will quickly learn to like His replies better than your requests!

*A*sking with confidence in the One who hears

*W*orship from the Heart

As you ponder the well-known words of Psalm 23, let the imagery of the caring, confident shepherd comfort your heart. Regardless of how far you wander, the danger you place yourself in, the enemies you encounter, or the sickness you suffer, your Shepherd is there. He is Jesus who seeks and saves lost sheep. Relax in His love. He will bring you home to the fold.

*W*alk Thru the Word

New Testament Reading
1 John 5:13-21
Old Testament Reading
Psalm 23

Prowling wolves and spiritual swindlers

Many deceivers, who do not acknowledge Jesus Christ as coming in the flesh, have gone out into the world (2 John 7).

*I*t's one of the oldest tricks in the book. Swindlers and con artists prey on the elderly, the innocent, and the gullible, bilking them out of paychecks and life savings. And many of the same methods have worked for years.

Spiritual swindling is equally timeless—and devastating in its impact—robbing people of their peace of mind and soul.

John warns his readers of the dangers of deceit, and A. W. Tozer adds these watchful words.

Walk with A. W. Tozer

"We have gotten accustomed to the blurred puffs of gray fog that pass for doctrine in churches and expect nothing better. From some previously unimpeachable sources are now coming vague statements consisting of a milky admixture of Scripture, science, and human sentiment that is true to none of its ingredients because each one works to cancel the others out.

"Little by little Christians these days are being brainwashed. One evidence is that increasing numbers of them are becoming ashamed to be found unequivocally on the side of truth. They say they believe, but their beliefs have been so diluted as to be impossible of clear definition.

"Moral power has always accompanied definite beliefs. Great saints have always been dogmatic. We need a return to a gentle dogmatism that smiles while it stands stubborn and firm on the Word of God that lives and abides forever."

Walk Closer to God

The best way to avoid being taken in by lies is to take in the truth. And that truth is found in God's Holy Word.

"As you have heard from the beginning, his command is that you walk in love. Many deceivers . . . have gone out into the world. . . . Whoever continues in the teaching has both the Father and the Son" (2 John 6-7, 9).

And that's the truth!

Worship from the Heart

For those who are in Christ, eternal life is not just a future escape from the misery of this world. It is a present possession that changes the complexion of our days and fills us with love and wonder. In Christ we can see ourselves growing up in Him, children who are being molded and shaped to be like Him when we shall see Him face to face. What a destiny!

Walk Thru the Word

New Testament Reading
2 John
Old Testament Reading
Jeremiah 28

It gave me great joy to have some brothers come and tell about your faithfulness to the truth and how you continue to walk in the truth (3 John 3).

O pinion—a belief not based on absolute certainty or positive knowledge but on what seems true, valid, or probable to one's mind.

Fact—a thing that actually happened or that is really true.

What do you think? Is the Christian faith based on fact or opinion? Scholars may argue, but the testimony of Scripture is impressive indeed.

John emphasizes the importance of truth in this postcard-length letter. But don't let its brevity leave the idea that truth is a minor matter.

Robert Law elaborates.

Walk with Robert Law

"John's mind is dominated by the truth. To him Christianity is not only a principle of ethics or even a way of salvation. It is both of these, because it is, primarily, the truth—the one true disclosure, without a competitor, of the realities of the spiritual and eternal world.

"The light of the gospel is the 'true light,' no dim symbolic light, but the light of the Eternal Mind shining out in Christ upon every object in the spiritual world. The God revealed in Christ is the 'true God,' the God who is, and who is the totality of deity.

"No words are more characteristic of John than these: 'No lie is of the truth.' Everywhere we find the same rigorous sense of reality, the same insistence upon squaring conduct with facts—of 'doing the truth'; and of knowing, believing, and confessing the great facts in which all true life is rooted."

Walk Closer to God

John not only encouraged belief in what was true, he exhorted believers to "work together for the truth."

How? By demonstrating truth in their lives. As others saw that faith at work, they became convinced that Christianity was no mere philosophy or creed. A life of faith rooted in the great facts of the faith—ah, now there's a convincing argument!

Having a faith that is rooted in facts

Worship from the Heart

Our society uses the word "friend" to mean anyone from a business connection to a drinking buddy. John makes it clear that true friendship is rooted in a mutual commitment to Christ. This gift from God does indeed bring fullness of joy. Thank God for Christian friends and pray that you will never take them for granted.

Walk Thru the Word

New Testament Reading
3 John
Old Testament Reading
Proverbs 23:23

Truth that makes a difference for eternity

For certain men . . . have secretly slipped in among you. They are godless men, who change the grace of our God into a license for immorality (Jude 4).

When it comes to the truth of God's Word, there are only two kinds of teachers: those who are forthright, and those who are wrong.

Jude's powerful imagery pictures the futility and frustration of false teachers: "clouds without rain . . . trees without fruit . . . wild waves of the sea . . . wandering stars."

They may be spectacular, but as Ulrich Zwingli reminds us, they lack substance.

Walk with Ulrich Zwingli

"Jude foresaw the coming of mockers in the last time who would walk after their own lusts and godlessness, not having the Spirit.

"And by their deeds we see clearly that they have no hope, for they rage furiously and live shamelessly and desire inordinately and persecute arrogantly and seize and grasp everything that they can plunder or steal or gain.

"All these things are tokens of their godlessness and despair. Like their father the Devil, they are harsh toward everybody, refuse the joy and consolation of salvation, and despise every warning that might turn them from error. They will not retain God in their knowledge. So they begin to experience already that perdition that in the world to come they will fulfill eternally."

Walk Closer to God

Thoughts of future consequences can inspire either rage or repentance in a sinner's heart. That's why it is important for the Christian teacher to be on the lookout for those who are searching for God.

"Keep yourselves in God's love as you wait for the mercy of our Lord Jesus Christ to bring you to eternal life. Be merciful to those who doubt; snatch others from the fire and save them; to others show mercy, mixed with fear" (21-23).

Can one teacher, one student, or one concerned friend really make a difference in a world of false teachers and fuzzy thinking?

If only the truth were known!

Worship from the Heart

Never has a life devoted to prayer been more evident than in the Old Testament prophet Daniel. He would rather spend sweet moments in prayer and risk death, than deny his Lord. God was that real to him. Ask God to be that real to you as you live for Him today.

Walk Thru the Word

New Testament Reading
Jude 1-16
Old Testament Reading
Malachi 2:7-8

O worship the King, all glorious above

To the only God our Savior be glory, majesty, power and authority, through Jesus Christ our Lord, before all ages, now and forevermore! Amen (Jude 25).

If you received an invitation requesting your presence at the White House, chances are high that your initial excitement would soon dissolve into a mixture of fear, wonder, and curiosity.

Fear at the power of the officeholder. Wonder over the grandeur of his office. Curiosity about why you were invited!

Attitudes change when God is in view. Thomas Manton describes the attitude of a Christian confronted with the greatness of God.

Walk with Thomas Manton

"It is a comfort to the soul to consider God's glory, majesty, dominion, and power; for this is the ground of our respect to Him and that which encourages us in our service. We need not be ashamed to serve Him to whom glory, and power, and majesty, and dominion belong.

"It heartens us against dangers. Surely the great and glorious God will bear us out in His work.

"It increases our awe and reverence. To whom should we go in our necessities but to Him who has dominion over all things, and power to dispose of them for the glory of His majesty?

"God is glorious and will maintain the honor of His name and the truth of His promises. When we are dismayed by earthly rulers, it is a relief to think of God's majesty, in comparison to which all earthly grandeur is but the dream of a shadow."

Walk Closer to God

If the thought of standing before your nation's president or prime minister causes your pulse to quicken and your vision to sharpen, how much more should standing before the omnipotent God of creation!

He "is able to keep you from falling and to present you before his glorious presence without fault and with great joy" (Jude 24).

And in addition to all the reasons Thomas Manton has suggested for glorifying God, that's one more good reason to live for Him!

Worship from the Heart

Jude closes with one of the most beautiful doxologies of Scripture. These few words capture the essence of worship—declaring God's worth, admiring His character and work, seeing His plan, and celebrating His greatness. Meditate on the meaning of each matchless phrase, then read Jude 24-25 aloud as a prayer of praise.

Walk Thru the Word

New Testament Reading
Jude 17-25
Old Testament Reading
Job 37:22-24

*W*orship Him and Crown Him King of Kings

*B*y reading Revelation your own worship of God will be enriched by the grandeur of His ultimate triumph.

*C*asually mention to a friend that you are reading the book of Revelation and the odds are good you will receive one of two reactions: either a skeptical look and a raised eyebrow, as if to say, "What's the use of inquiring into such mysteries?" or an admiring look of fascination, as if to say, "What secrets are you discovering between the lines?" You may finish the last chapter with more questions than when you began! And if you turn to the commentators for help, you will quickly discover there are about as many interpretations of the book as there are visions in it! But don't allow this to keep you from reading—and responding to—God's final words in Scripture.

The apostle John, who received this revelation from God, introduces the book by saying, "Blessed is the one who reads the words of this prophecy, and blessed are those who hear it and take to heart what is written in it" (Revelation 1:3). That's your challenge: to read it, to understand it, and to live it. Though interpreting this book has always been difficult, certain themes emerge clearly and insistently, regardless of the precise method you use. (1) Faith triumphs over might; all the gathering powers of antagonistic forces are laid low at the end. (2) Divine judgment is inevitable. (3) History will reach a final satisfactory consummation when Jesus Christ returns as King of kings.

The book is, therefore, a book of encouragement and exhortation. To those who combat the great forces of evil with apparently little success, the book brings inspiration. To those tempted to forsake their faith because the odds against them seem too great, the book issues an insistent warning and a powerful challenge to endure. The end is coming. Jesus will return. Inequities will be set right. The victory is yours in Christ.

Your own worship of God, both private and corporate, will be enriched by the grandeur and finality of His ultimate triumph. Your opportunity to broaden your horizon is as near as the first chapter of this powerful book.

"I am the Alpha and the Omega," says the Lord God, "who is, and who was, and who is to come, the Almighty" (Revelation 1:8).

Some people are never around when you need them. When help or encouragement is needed, their phone is out of order.

But you can never say that about Jesus Christ. By His own testimony to the apostle John, He has always been with His people in the past, is with them now, and will stay ever faithful in the future.

Although finite human beings find themselves trapped by time, the Son of Man has time in His capable hands. And that sheds important light on the action taken at the cross nearly 2,000 years ago.

Martin Luther discusses the Savior's act of love that transcends time.

Walk with Martin Luther

"Whoever offered a sacrifice and, while doing so, remembered the true Lamb, who was to be slain for the sins of the world, was saved through faith in the Christ who would come. Whoever did not do this was not saved, even though he had a thousand oxen to sacrifice.

"There is only one and the same salvation from Adam and Abel onward; it is the same salvation we have. It continued until Jesus Himself came. But now, of course, it is no longer faith in the future Christ but in the Present One.

"The teaching has been one and the same from the beginning of the world and shall remain so until the end of the world. There has at all times been one and the same Christ, a Christ who is in the past, present, and future—the One 'who is, and who was, and who is to come.' "

Walk Closer to God

To the past. To the future. Christ reaches eternally in both directions. Yet He also finds time to be an "ever-present help in trouble." That's a comforting thought when present circumstances are difficult and the future looks bleak.

He whom time cannot change has all the time in the world to watch over you—yesterday, today, and tomorrow.

Transcending time, touching eternity

Worship from the Heart

Take a moment to meditate on the descriptions of Jesus Christ in today's New Testament reading. As you seek a sense of stability amid the constant turmoil of the world, don't look to the changes time will bring. Instead focus on the Timeless One who is the Almighty.

Walk Thru the Word

New Testament Reading
Revelation 1:1-8
Old Testament Reading
Psalm 89:24-29

Looking at death from the life side

"I am the Living One; I was dead, and behold, I am alive for ever and ever! And I hold the keys of death and Hades" (Revelation 1:18).

*H*urry doctor! It's a matter of death and life—" Just a minute, something's not quite right. Isn't the issue supposed to be a matter of life and death . . . not vice versa?

Read again Christ's words in Revelation 1:18. Perhaps as you read those words the first time, you subconsciously rearranged them to say, "Christ died; then He came back to life."

But Jesus emphasizes *life* by speaking of it before mentioning His *death* on the cross. As A. B. Simpson points out, the message of life overwhelms the mourning of death.

Walk with A. B. Simpson

"It is not said, 'I am He who was dead and now lives,' but 'I am the Living One; I was dead, and behold, I am alive for ever and ever.' Life is mentioned before death.

"There are two ways of looking at the cross. One is from the death side and the other is from the life side. One is the suffering, crucified Christ; the other is the glorified Jesus with only the marks of the nails and the spear. It is thus we are to look at the cross. We are not to carry about the mold of the sepulcher, but the glory of the Resurrection.

"Our crucifixion is to be so complete that we shall even forget our sorrow and carry with us the light and glory of the eternal morning. So let us live the death-born life, ever new and full of a life that can never die because it is dead and alive forevermore."

Walk Closer to God

Does your view of life and death need to be reversed?

Death appears to be the final certainty, the end of life as we know it. But for the Christian, death is no longer the last word. Because Christ rose to life beyond the grave, life is the final reality for all who trust in Him.

Consider carefully your relationship to Christ. It's a matter of life *after* death.

Worship from the Heart

Recall the wonderful truth of being crucified, buried, and resurrected with Christ. Praise Him for the mighty love which motivated Him to die for you. Concentrate on the fact that His divine life is in you because you are now His child.

Walk Thru the Word

New Testament Reading
Revelation 1:9-20
Old Testament Reading
Daniel 7:9-10

"Remember the height from which you have fallen! Repent and do the things you did at first. If you do not repent, I will come to you and remove your lampstand from its place" (Revelation 2:5).

*F*riends and lovers often find it difficult to keep secrets from each other. They develop a sixth sense that brings a form of communication deeper than mere words.

But the all-seeing, all-knowing Son of God needs no sixth sense to be aware of all that beats in the heart of His bride, the church.

Individually and collectively, His church— those who are His children—can hide nothing from Him, as G. Campbell Morgan notes.

Walk with G. Campbell Morgan

"To each He says, 'I know'; and on the basis of His knowledge He either commends or condemns. To each one also He reveals the way of escape from those things He condemns. He speaks of the possibility of overcoming, and He promises appropriate rewards to those who do.

"There was much in this church at Ephesus which gained His commendation, but it had one serious failing. It had lost the freshness and enthusiasm of its early devotion. It was still loyal and true, but the loyalty lacked passion, and the truth was devoid of flame.

"This is always a serious condition, because it so easily passes on into other phases. How was it to be remedied? By a return to the very starting point, that of repentance and faith."

Walk Closer to God

True love is more than just going through the motions—doing things because of external appearance rather than from an internal devotion. True love is reciprocal, responsive, intimate, devoted, and unconditional.

Have you sensed a lack of inner spiritual passion in your relationship with your Savior? Then turn back now to look Him full in the face.

Remember what He has done for you. Ponder the magnitude of His love. Consider where you would be without Him. Let His love be the spark to rekindle your love for Him.

A passion fired with the flame of truth

*W*orship from the Heart

"O blessed Savior, Your love draws and excites me, calms and comforts me, saves and strengthens me. I rejoice in Your promise that no person or thing in heaven or earth can separate me from Your love. Father, enlarge the passion of my love for You; in the name of Jesus, the Lover of my soul. Amen."

*W*alk Thru the Word

New Testament Reading
Revelation 2:1-11
Old Testament Reading
Genesis 2:9; 3:22

The treasures of a well spent life

"Only hold on to what you have until I come. To him who overcomes and does my will to the end, I will give authority over the nations" (Revelation 2:25-26).

Question: If you had put $100 under a mattress years ago, what would it be worth now?

Answer: About as much as the mattress.

But had the money been wisely invested to build compound interest, that same $100 might be worth many times its original value.

The same principle applies in the spiritual realm. If truth is known but not applied to life, folly is the result. But when God's truth is wisely invested in a life, God's blessing is the dividend.

A. B. Simpson uses the language of commerce in speaking of the wealth of spiritual wisdom.

Walk with A. B. Simpson

"As each day comes and goes, let us put away in the savings bank of eternity its treasures of grace and victory. Let us be conscious from day to day that something real and everlasting is being added to our eternal fortune.

"It may be just a little, but if we invest all that God gives us and pass it on to His keeping, we shall be amazed to see how much the accumulated treasures of a well-spent life have laid up on high, and how much more He has added to them by His glorious investment of the life committed to His keeping!

"Oh, how the days are telling! Oh, how precious these golden hours will seem sometime! God help us to make the most of them now."

Walk Closer to God

Did you know that a sum of money invested at 12 percent annually will double in value in six years? At 18 percent that same amount of money will double in only four years.

Money put to work will accomplish more than money left under a mattress. Truth put to work in a life will be far more beneficial than truth that is heard but not heeded.

What investment have you made with the truth you possess? Invest wisely, and you will find the seeds for eternal rewards compounding daily.

Worship from the Heart

"In You, O Christ, are hidden all the treasures of wisdom and knowledge. Draw me to look to You first and thirst for Your righteousness. For I know that when I seek Your kingdom, You provide all that I need. As a seeker, I come in Your name, Jehovah-Jireh, 'God will provide.' Amen."

Walk Thru the Word

New Testament Reading
Revelation 2:12-29
Old Testament Reading
Psalm 2

"Wake up! Strengthen what remains . . . Remember . . . what you have received and heard; obey it, and repent" (Revelation 3:2-3).

*N*ight watch on a dark night. The moon and stars are hidden behind thick fog and storm clouds. On the ship's bridge, the night watchman strains every muscle to stay awake, for the ship's safety depends upon him. While others are sleeping, he must be vigilant.

Like the watchman, you must be alert and prepared for unexpected dangers. As Matthew Henry reminds you, staying awake means staying on course.

Walk with Matthew Henry

"We must return to our watchfulness against sin, and Satan, and whatever is destructive to the life and power of godliness.

" 'Strengthen what remains.' Some understand this to refer to people, or it may refer to practices. But there is something lacking; there is the shadow, but not the substance.

"Your works are hollow and empty; prayers are not filled up with holy desires, alms-deeds not filled up with true charity, Sabbaths not filled up with suitable devotion of soul to God.

"We must remember the affections we felt under the working of the Word, and how welcome the gospel and the grace of God were to us when we first received them."

Walk Closer to God

Three kinds of sight help you maintain your watchfulness against sin and Satan:

Hindsight includes learning from your past. Don't forget God's goodness to you in former times. Ask Him to help you learn and grow so you won't repeat past mistakes.

Insight comes by saturating your life with Scripture. Study the proverbs, for example, and become a more spiritually discerning person.

Foresight involves preparing for tomorrow's battles. Look ahead, anticipate future needs, then move out confidently in God's strength.

Your vision can't help but improve when you set your sights accordingly.

*S*etting your sights and staying on course

*W*orship from the Heart

"O God and Father, I repent of my sinful preoccupation with visible things. The world has been too much with me. You have been here, and I did not know it. Open my eyes that I may behold You in and around me for Christ's sake. Amen."
—A. W. Tozer

*W*alk Thru the Word

New Testament Reading
Revelation 3:1-6
Old Testament Reading
Exodus 32:32

Faith: reckless confidence in God

"Since you have kept my command to endure patiently, I will also keep you from the hour of trial that is going to come upon the whole world" (Revelation 3:10).

*N*ear the end of a long run, the weary but determined jogger is sorely tempted to ease up, to quit a few steps early.

But the mind has ways of overcoming the muscles, and ten telephone poles later he reaches the finish line. He has done what his body told him it was impossible to do.

In Revelation 3 John speaks of the goal of patience, which seems unreachable to many believers. And yet it is a goal that God is committed to developing in the lives of His children.

Oswald Chambers has insight into the relationships between patience, confidence, and faith.

Walk with Oswald Chambers

"Patience is more than endurance. God is aiming at something that the saint cannot see. Thus God stretches and pushes the saint until every now and again he cries out, 'I can't stand anymore.'

"But trust yourself in God's hands. Maintain your confidence in Jesus Christ by the patience of faith. You cannot see Him just now; you cannot understand all He is doing, but you know Him.

"Shipwreck occurs where there is not that mental poise that comes from being established on the eternal truth that God is holy love. Faith is the heroic effort of your life, as you fling yourself in reckless confidence on God.

"God has ventured all in Jesus Christ to save us; now He wants us to venture our all in abandoned confidence in Him."

Walk Closer to God

God calls you to trust Him even as you are being stretched to the limit—and beyond. Patience comes when you look ahead and see God waiting at the finish line of life. He is the one who controls all the circumstances, knows the limits of your endurance, and will reward you at the end.

Don't lose patience with Him. He will not lose patience with you. You can be confident He'll finish the good work He has begun in you.

Worship from the Heart

Take time to review and meditate on the promises Jesus makes to those who overcome. Tell Him how you would feel to find yourself receiving the rewards promised those overcomers. Praise Him that He has given you the power to be an overcomer.

Walk Thru the Word

New Testament Reading
Revelation 3:7-13
Old Testament Reading
Isaiah 22:20-22

374

*E*xalting the Giver of every good gift

"You say 'I am rich; I have acquired wealth and do not need a thing.' But you do not realize that you are wretched, pitiful, poor, blind and naked" (Revelation 3:17).

A wealthy businessman who had stopped for a shoeshine was moved to pity by the thin, poorly dressed lad who stood before him.

"Here, son," he said as he removed an enormous ring from his finger and handed it to the boy, "use this to buy the things you need."

Moments later, another man took a seat in the chair and commented on the marvelous ring.

"Do you like it?" asked the boy. "I think it makes me handsome."

And therein lies a parable about how easily we deceive ourselves. Martin Luther paints a picture of the sin condemned above all others.

Walk with Martin Luther

"It is the worst kind of vice and the most demonic kind of pride for us to pat ourselves on the back if we see some special gift in ourselves.

"We steal and rob God of His glory this way, and we make ourselves an idol, without seeing the trouble we cause by all this.

"Scripture addresses the person who thinks he is more learned and better than others: 'You say, "I am rich; I have acquired wealth and do not need a thing. But you do not realize that you are wretched, pitiful, poor, blind, and naked.'

"If it is true that your gift is greater than somebody else's, this is as God intended. But when you use your gift as a mirror in which you admire yourself, you spoil it completely and make this sublime ornament filthier than everybody else's faults."

Walk Closer to God

What do you see when you look in the mirror? A person who has the outward marks of success but can only see himself . . . or a person who sees in each success or disappointment the face of Christ?

If God is the Giver of every good gift (and He is), then He should be praised for what He has done in your life. Is He?

*W*orship from the Heart

Realizing that God desires truth in the inward parts, quietly ask the Holy Spirit to search your heart and cleanse you from secret faults. As character failures and specific sins come to mind, recognize that God is answering your prayer and confess any uncleanness He reveals.

*W*alk Thru the Word

New Testament Reading
Revelation 3:14-22
Old Testament Reading
Isaiah 55:1-6

*E*mblem of mercy, picture of peace

The one who sat there had the appearance of jasper and carnelian. A rainbow, resembling an emerald, encircled the throne (Revelation 4:3).

*T*he sky is dark and sinister with rain clouds boiling and thunder rolling. Suddenly a thin ray of light appears, then another, and yet another. As the rain ends, the sun breaks through and the dark clouds melt. A shimmering rainbow appears, heralding fair weather and hope.

The appearance of the rainbow has a special significance in many cultures, but Albert Barnes probes its meaning according to Scripture.

Walk with Albert Barnes

"The rainbow was probably designed to be symbolic as well as beautiful. From its own nature and associations, it has always been an emblem of peace. It contrasts beautifully with the tempest that has just been raging.

"If the rain has been gentle, the leaves and flowers appear clothed with new beauty; if the storm has raged violently, the rainbow is a pledge that the war of the elements has ceased.

"Therefore the rainbow around the throne is a beautiful emblem of the mercy of God and of the peace that is to pervade the world as the result of the events disclosed to John in his vision.

"True, there were lightnings and thunderings and voices, but there the bow abode calmly above them all, assuring John that there was to be mercy and peace."

Walk Closer to God

You can count on it: Life will have its share of lightning and thunder; many a parade will be rained out; tragedy and sorrow will touch every life. But this too is a fact you can count on: For the Christian there will surely be a calm after the storm that makes the storm pale by comparison.

So take heart. The bow in the clouds is a divine reminder from the God of the universe that all is under control. As God's own dear child, look to the day when you will see God's heavenly rainbow emerge to signal the peaceful reign of Christ and the fulfillment of all His promises.

*W*orship from the Heart

First given when God promised never again to destroy the world by water, the rainbow is a symbol of our promise-keeping God. As you come before God in prayer, remember that He is enthroned in the circle of the rainbow. Praise Him for His faithfulness to His promises and His people yesterday, today, and forever.

*W*alk Thru the Word

New Testament Reading
Revelation 4
Old Testament Reading
Ezekiel 1

The sacrifice of love enthroned

Then I saw a Lamb, looking as if it had been slain, standing in the center of the throne, encircled by the four living creatures and the elders (Revelation 5:6).

*B*y earthly standards, the lion may be king of beasts, but the Lamb of God is the Lord of heaven and earth. Ultimately every knee will bow before Him. Nowhere is this truth more clearly proclaimed than in the chapter you read today.

F. B. Meyer expounds on the unique qualities that brought your heavenly Lamb to this throne.

Walk with F. B. Meyer

"It is a marvelous combination, the throne with the Lamb, the Lamb and the throne, the Lamb in its very midst. How does the Lamb come here? Surely meekness, humility, and gentle submissiveness are not the characteristics that win thrones!

"Perhaps not in our world, but they do in God's. In the eternal world sufferers wield more might than wrestlers; to yield is to overcome; to be vanquished is to conquer. It is because He was God's Lamb that He is now God's anointed King.

"The marks of suffering, of agony and death, of sacrifice, are stamped upon His flesh. The redeemed ones that stand around tell the story. He purchased and cleansed them by His blood; He is worthy to fill the throne and rule forever. He who could make Himself the supreme sacrifice and offering for the sins of the world is worthy to be the world's King."

Walk Closer to God

Who is more worthy to be enthroned in your heart than the One who willingly humbled Himself to the point of death?

Without Him, every day would become an agony of guilt and sin leading to hopelessness and despair. With Him, every day becomes an opportunity to experience anew God's grace and forgiveness and to reach out to others with love.

The Lamb that was slain. The Lion no enemy can vanquish. Truly He is worthy of the title "King of kings."

Is that the title by which you address Him? Is that the position you give Him in your heart?

Worship from the Heart

Jesus is the culmination of redemptive history, the Savior of all who believe, the all in all. As a child of the King, you are seated with Him in heavenly places. As you tell Him of the situations that concern you today, stay in His presence until you see your cares from His perspective.

Walk Thru the Word

New Testament Reading
Revelation 5
Old Testament Reading
Isaiah 53

377

Seeking truth from the One who is true

I watched as the Lamb opened the first of the seven seals. Then I heard one of the four living creatures say in a voice like thunder, "Come!" (Revelation 6:1).

The young mother suppressed a grin as her five-year-old made this announcement: "I'm going out to dig for diamonds. I learned how in school."

Later than afternoon he came back inside with a bucketful of common, red rocks. "I didn't find any diamonds," he reported seriously. "I guess I didn't look long enough."

Whether you are five years old or fifty, looking for the right thing in the wrong place will never bring success. Jeanne Guyon examines that truth from a spiritual standpoint.

Worship from the Heart

Ask God to give you wisdom that will apply to a specific situation in your life, realizing that "the way of the Lord is a refuge for the righteous" (Proverbs 10:29). Praise Him now for His timely answer and the wisdom He unveils for those who seek Him.

Walk with Jeanne Guyon

"The Lamb begins to open one of the seven seals that has kept the book shut. One of the four living creatures is begging John to come and see.

"We, too, must go to Jesus Christ before discovering the wonder of His truth. We do not find His truth except as we discover Jesus Christ. Seek it in Him, and abandon yourself to Him for that.

"We must go to Jesus Christ to have truth; seeking it elsewhere is seeking error and lies. These living creatures invite us to come to Jesus Christ and discover truth in Him."

Walk Closer to God

In our fast-paced world, all kinds of people and organizations stand ready to offer advice, sell hot tips, and provide services to change your life. Some are beneficial and have much to offer. Others have no substance and no basis in truth.

Where do you seek truth? From whom do you take counsel?

Think about the areas in which you need wisdom—personal relationships, finances, career, education, and others.

When problems arise, you will find the best help available by turning first to God. As you meet Him in the pages of His Word and through prayer, He will give wisdom as He has promised—"generously . . . without finding fault" (James 1:5). It's yours for the asking.

Walk Thru the Word

New Testament Reading
Revelation 6
Old Testament Reading
Zephaniah 1:14-18

378

*A*n earthly apprenticeship for heavenly service

After this I looked and there before me was a great multitude that no one could count, from every nation, tribe, people and language, standing before the throne and in front of the Lamb (Revelation 7:9).

*H*ave you ever wondered what Christians will do in heaven? Have you speculated about the duties and pleasures that will occupy our time?

Believers don't often think about work in connection with heaven, but Scripture seems to indicate that while heaven will be a peaceful place, it will also be a busy one.

God has much for His people to do once they get to heaven—and much to do in preparation for their arrival—as Alexander Maclaren explains.

Walk with Alexander Maclaren

"The caricature of heaven as an eternity of idleness has no basis in Scripture. Instead, the New Testament conception unites the two thoughts of being *with* Christ and of service *for* Christ.

"This blending is definitely set forth in the last chapter of Revelation where we read of 'those who serve Him, and see His face.' Here the life of contemplation and the life of active service are welded together as being not only compatible, but absolutely necessary for completeness.

"But remember that if there is to be service there, the exercising ground is here. I do not know what we are in this world for unless it is to apprentice us for heaven. Life on earth is a bewilderment unless we are being trained here for a nobler work which lies beyond the grave."

Walk Closer to God

How much do you enjoy your work? Do you dread the daily drudgery, or are you disappointed when closing time arrives?

Whether your work is menial and routine or of world-changing proportions, its most important aspect is that it is a tailor-made environment in which you can draw closer to God.

View your work as an opportunity to praise God, to serve others, and to prepare you for heaven. That's work worth doing, and doing well, as befitting a faithful servant.

*W*orship from the Heart

As you go about your daily work, focus your interior gaze on God. Take delight in His presence and carry on little conversations with Him as you go about your tasks. You'll find your load lighter and your Companion very precious and ever present.

*W*alk Thru the Word

New Testament Reading
Revelation 7
Old Testament Reading
Isaiah 49:10-13

Alexander Maclaren (1826-1910) The Priority of Preaching

If Charles Spurgeon is acknowledged as the most widely read preacher of his time, then Alexander Maclaren deserves recognition as one who stands not far behind. His *Expositions of Holy Scripture* remains one of the finest collections of sermons ever compiled.

Other preachers have openly admitted that reading Maclaren's comments on a particular passage of Scripture often caused them to forsake their own outline and to follow his because of its clarity, originality, and power.

For Maclaren, the minister's great priority was the preaching of God's Word. But Maclaren gave no evidence early in life that he would go on to become a well-known preacher.

Born to godly parents in Glasgow, Scotland, in 1826, he became a Christian at the age of fourteen. His father wanted him to enter the ministry, but there was some question whether the young man had the necessary aptitude for the profession.

After moving his family to London in 1842, Maclaren entered college, where his hardworking nature propelled him to the head of his class. His shyness, however, still left others doubting if he could be successful in the ministry.

Graduating in 1846, Maclaren took a position as the pastor of Portland Chapel, a small church that was teetering on the brink of collapse. Over a period of a dozen years, Maclaren built the church into a thriving congregation, an achievement that received little notice because Maclaren disliked publicity. But his obvious abilities did not escape the notice of the Union Chapel in Manchester, England, where Maclaren was called as pastor in 1858. Thus began a 45-year ministry that made Maclaren's name synonymous with Manchester.

His reputation soon spread to other cities and counties. Speaking tours resulted that brought thousands to hear this devoted student of the Scriptures.

Maclaren retired as pastor of Union Chapel in 1903, but continued to travel and speak until his death in 1910. What enabled Alexander Maclaren to excel as a preacher of God's Word when his early years seemed to offer so little promise?

First and foremost, Maclaren was a man of the Word. He let nothing interfere with his time of study and preparation in the Bible. He refused to attend social activities or accept speaking engagements if it meant forsaking time in God's Word. It was not uncommon for Maclaren to spend sixty hours in preparation for one sermon!

The message Maclaren preached was the Word of God. He spent two hours a day in the original languages of the Scriptures absorbing the sense and substance of every "jot and tittle" of God's revealed truth. His preaching was thoroughly biblical. He simply took a passage of Scripture, explained its meaning, applied its truth to himself, and then to the lives of his hearers.

It was Alexander Maclaren's deep conviction that godliness and God's Word go hand in hand. As Paul told Timothy, "All Scripture is . . . useful for teaching, rebuking, correcting and training in righteousness, so that the man of God may be thoroughly equipped for every good work" (2 Timothy 3:16-17).

Are you ready to follow Maclaren's profitable example?

A Lesson from the life of Alexander Maclaren

The priority of time spent in the Scriptures will insure the primacy of God's rule in my life.

The divine fragrance of heaven

Another angel, who had a golden censer, came and stood at the altar. He was given much incense to offer, with the prayers of all the saints (Revelation 8:3).

*P*erspective. It's which end of the telescope you look through when you pray to your heavenly Father about your earthly problems!

Seen one way, your problems appear enormous, and your Father far away. And from that perspective, your prayers can't help but sound like this: "How long, O Lord, will I have to . . . ?"

But there is another perspective which Horatius Bonar investigates in this perceptive comment.

Worship from the Heart

The intercession of the saints is directly related to God's judgment—and His blessing. Personalize the words of Psalm 135:5-7, 13-14 and return them to God as the prayer of your heart.

Walk with Horatius Bonar

"Let us pray always. This is the day of prayer, the day of the answer's coming.

"Our prayers—'the prayers of all the saints'— are lying now on the altar, presented long ago in much weakness, imperfection, and unbelief. They are waiting for a fresh application of the divine fragrance which will make them irresistible. The fragrance is on its way. It is at hand.

"The church is on her knees. The burden of her cry is, 'How long?' Earth is not improved, and its guilt is accumulating. The unrenewed heart works in defiance of God's sentence against us.

"But when the righteous King arrives He will break His enemies in pieces with His iron rod and sway His holy scepter over an earth which, passing through the fires of judgment, will be fit for the habitation of the just."

Walk Closer to God

Your part now is to prevail in prayer until God answers. You may have to wrestle in prayer or come with tears of intercession. But your prayers, along with those of all the saints, are God's weapons against the Enemy. When the question on your lips is "How long?" rest assured your Savior knows and will not tarry needlessly.

When the angel took the incense and prayers from the altar and cast them to earth, the result was "peals of thunder, rumblings, flashes of lightning and an earthquake" (8:5). The answer came. The prayers of God's people were heard.

Walk Thru the Word

New Testament Reading
Revelation 8
Old Testament Reading
Ezekiel 38:18-23

Under the weight of eternal wrath

During those days men will seek death, but will not find it; they will long to die, but death will elude them (Revelation 9:6).

When dulled by the passage of time, humiliating moments can become the funny stories you tell your children and grandchildren.

But this is not so when sin has been the cause of the embarrassment. Then the guilt and shame are real. They will not be a matter for laughter when the time comes to stand before God.

Jonathan Edwards urges repentance from sin by describing the magnitude of God's wrath.

Walk with Jonathan Edwards

"The wrath of a mere king is the roaring of a lion; but this is the wrath of Jehovah, the Lord God Omnipotent. How dreadful must be the wrath of such a Being when it comes without pity or moderation or merciful circumstances.

"What must be the uttermost of God's wrath, He who made heaven and earth by the word of His power, who spoke and it was done, who commanded and it stood fast! What must His wrath be who commands the sun not to rise, seals up the stars, shakes the earth, and causes the pillars of heaven to tremble!

"What must His wrath be whose majesty is such that no one could live in the sight of it! What must the wrath of such a Being be when He makes His majesty appear! And what is a worm of the dust before the fury of this wrath!

"Therefore it behooves all to flee for their lives, to get into a safe condition, to get into Christ."

Walk Closer to God

"Flee from the wrath to come." This is not an outdated admonition as some would suggest. Instead, it is a clarion call to safety.

As long as sin exists, expect God to wage war against it. As long as sin is tolerated in your life, expect God to wage war against you.

Indeed, it is a fearful thing to fall into the hands of the living God. Fall instead at His feet and seek His mercy while it may be found. He has provided safety through Jesus Christ.

Worship from the Heart

Bow before Him and adore Him; He is the King of kings! On your knees before God, express your deepest gratitude that He has brought you into fellowship with Him and has delivered you from the peril of His wrath. Praise Him for the robes of righteousness you now wear.

Walk Thru the Word

New Testament Reading
Revelation 9
Old Testament Reading
Jeremiah 8:3

Saints under scrutiny for sin

I took the little scroll from the angel's hand and ate it. It tasted as sweet as honey in my mouth, but when I had eaten it, my stomach turned sour (Revelation 10:10).

*Q*uestion: What do the senior voted "Most likely to succeed" who turns to crime instead and the pastor whose ministry is ruined by immorality have in common?

Answer: Both are examples of high expectations going wrong and ending in sinful circumstances.

Individuals as well as the entire church are under close scrutiny from many sides. William Milligan offers this observation to encourage holy conduct among believers.

Walk with William Milligan

"We have good reasons to suppose that the little scroll John mentions contained indications of judgment about to descend on a church that had practically disowned her divine Master.

"When we look at the judgment of the world as the vindication of righteousness and the beginning of a divine and righteous order, the thought imparts nothing but joy.

"But to think that the bride of Christ shall be visited with judgment and be compelled to admit that the judgment is deserved, to think of the selfishness which has prevailed where love ought to reign, of worldliness where there ought to have been heavenliness of mind—these are the things that make the Christian's reflections bitter. They are his burden, his sorrow, and his cross.

"The world may disappoint him, but from it he expected little.

"When the church disappoints him, the foundations are overturned, and the honey of life becomes gall and wormwood."

Walk Closer to God

It's easy to grow bitter when you see sin running rampant—especially in the church where, of all places, Christ should be exalted.

But do you care enough to grow concerned and committed in dealing with the problem?

Remember, no one ever moved from *bitter* to *better* until the "I" moved out.

Worship from the Heart

Worship God by acknowledging that you trust Him in all circumstances. Thank Him for every adversity and trial in your life that He uses to give you a deeper thirst for His presence. Rejoice in the ways He demonstrates His faithfulness to you, His child.

Walk Thru the Word

New Testament Reading
Revelation 10
Old Testament Reading
Daniel 12:4-9

They heard a loud voice from heaven saying to them, "Come up here." And they went up to heaven in a cloud (Revelation 11:12).

The fear of flying can actually prevent some people from enjoying the freedom and convenience of jet travel.

In a similar way, some people would rather keep both feet firmly planted on this earth than take off for heaven. Even Christians are not immune, as Charles Spurgeon explains.

Walk with Charles Spurgeon

"In due time there shall be heard 'a loud voice from heaven' to believers saying, 'Come up here.'

"This should be the subject of joyful anticipation to the saints. Instead of dreading the time when we shall leave this world, we should be panting for the hour of our emancipation.

"We are not called down to the grave but up to the skies. Our heaven-born spirits should long for their native air.

"Yet the celestial summons should be the object of patient waiting. Our God knows best when to bid us 'Come up here.' Patience must have her perfect work.

"God ordains with accurate wisdom the most fitting time for the redeemed to abide below. Surely, if there could be regrets in heaven, the saints might mourn that they did not live longer here to do more good. Whether our Master shall say 'go' or 'stay,' let us be equally well pleased."

Walk Closer to God

Paul had to correct some of the Thessalonians who had become so heavenly minded that they were no earthly good. "We hear that some among you are idle. They are not busy; they are busybodies" (2 Thessalonians 3:11).

His counsel in such cases was clear and compelling: "If a man will not work, he shall not eat. . . . Never tire of doing what is right" (2 Thessalonians 3:10, 13).

Don't be content to stay in your comfortable surroundings rather than fly to do the work that waits in the harvest fields.

Joyfully anticipating the celestial summons

Worship from the Heart

It has been said that music is the language of heaven, and certainly heaven is the subject of much of our music. Choose one of your favorite hymns about heaven, and sing it to the Lord with praise and anticipation in your heart.

Walk Thru the Word

New Testament Reading
Revelation 11:1-14
Old Testament Reading
Zechariah 14:9-11

*T*he blessed hope of Christ's return

"The kingdom of the world has become the kingdom of our Lord and of his Christ, and he will reign for ever and ever" (Revelation 11:15).

*C*hristians today, like those of old, are prompted to ask, "Where is the promise of His coming?"

Patience, Christian. God is working out His purposes. Sometimes visibly, sometimes invisibly, He is patiently gathering the sons and daughters of the kingdom from every tongue, tribe, and nation.

Hymnwriter Charles Wesley knew this truth well. In one of his inspiring compositions he proclaims the hope of every Christian—"Christ the Lord Returns to Reign."

Walk with Charles Wesley

Lo! He comes, with clouds descending,
    Once for our salvation slain;
Thousand thousand saints attending
    Swell the triumph of His train;
Alleluia, alleluia!
    Christ the Lord returns to reign.

Every eye shall now behold Him,
    Robed in dreadful majesty;
Those who sat at naught and sold Him,
    Pierced and nailed Him to the tree,
Deeply wailing, deeply wailing,
    Shall the true Messiah see.

Yes, Amen! let all adore Thee,
    High on Thine eternal throne;
Savior, take the power and glory;
    Claim the kingdom for Thine own:
Alleluia, alleluia!
    Thou shalt reign, and Thou alone.

Walk Closer to God

Someday the kingdom of God will come and God's Son will enjoy ultimate victory over the forces of evil. Every eye will see Him, and every knee will bow before the One who shall reign for ever and ever.

Let the coming of His kingdom encourage you to readiness and expectancy. Someday you too will "swell the triumph of His train."

*W*orship from the Heart

Tradition teaches that when Handel's Messiah *was performed, the king and his entire entourage would stand when they heard the words, "And He shall reign forever and ever." Praise the Lord God that one day worldly kingdoms will be subdued and He will reign forever and ever!*

*W*alk Thru the Word

New Testament Reading
Revelation 11:15-19
Old Testament Reading
Psalm 40:10

386

The great dragon was hurled down—that ancient serpent called the devil, or Satan, who leads the whole world astray. He was hurled to the earth (Revelation 12:9).

*W*hen you're caught in a storm, there's nothing quite as secure as a place of shelter.

When an angry dog bares his teeth, there's nothing more reassuring than the fence between you.

When a bully makes fearful threats, there's nothing quite like having a big brother who will come to defend you.

And when Satan attacks you, you can find protection, shelter, and security in the arms of the Lord—and in the fellowship of His people.

Satan may bluster, but he can never destroy the house that God has built. Johann Peter Lange celebrates the strong hand of the Master Builder.

Walk with Johann Peter Lange

"As the church triumphant is now established in heaven, so, in correspondence with it, the church on earth also has a place that is purified from all satanic influence—the sphere of pure Christian spiritual life, the communion of saints.

"The foundation of the holy church, the communion of saints, is an infinitely glorious achievement. A great voice pronounces the hymn of victory; it is a single, common triumphant consciousness of all the heavenly throng.

"Now there is founded, with Christ and through Him, a pure church with three attributes: salvation—the perfect and final redemption from all evil, power over redeemed souls, and sovereignty in the current of world affairs."

Walk Closer to God

Jesus Himself said it best in the prayer He taught His disciples: "Deliver us from the evil one. For Yours is the kingdom and the power and the glory forever. Amen." (Matthew 6:13 NKJV).

When Satan prowls like a roaring lion, don't take matters into your own hands. Find shelter and protection in the presence of your sovereign God. Like the psalmist, you'll discover that "He will cover you with his feathers, and under his wings you will find refuge" (Psalm 91:4).

*H*eld in the hand of perfect protection

*W*orship from the Heart

"Father, God, thank You that You indeed 'hem me in—behind and before; you have laid your hand upon me' (Psalm 139:5). There is nothing in the present or in the future that I need fear. No circumstance or person comes into my life unless it comes through Your strong hands of blessing and protection. Amen."

*W*alk Thru the Word

New Testament Reading
Revelation 12:1–13:1a
Old Testament Reading
Psalm 91

*H*idden in Christ is the safest place to be

If anyone is to go into captivity, into captivity he will go. If anyone is to be killed with the sword, with the sword he will be killed. This calls for patient endurance and faithfulness on the part of the saints (Revelation 13:10).

*T*o say that something has "boomeranged" means that what you intended to send somewhere else has instead come back to haunt you.

In the case of the enemies of God and His people, all the enmity they can muster against the forces of righteousness will "boomerang." They will suffer at the hands of their own weapons.

William Milligan offers words of comfort for Christians threatened by suffering and opposition.

*W*orship from the Heart

Never forget: The God we serve is a victorious God. He provides the courage, the strength, and the armor for the battle we are in. Praise Him as you spiritually and prayerfully clothe yourself in each piece of armor listed in Ephesians 6.

Walk with William Milligan

"Nothing can harm the life that is hidden with Christ in God. But the saints may still be troubled, persecuted, and killed—as were the witnesses of chapter 11—by the beast that was given power to make war to conquer them.

"Such is the thought that leads to the words which we now consider: 'If anyone is to go into captivity, into captivity he will go. If anyone is to be killed with the sword, with the sword he will be killed.'

"In the great law of God, consolation is given to the persecuted. Their enemies would lead them into captivity, but a worse captivity awaits themselves. They would kill with the sword, but with a sharper sword than that of human power they shall themselves be killed. Is there not enough in that to inspire the saints with faith and patience?

"Well may they endure with unfailing hearts when they remember who is on their side, for 'God is just: He will pay back trouble to those who trouble you' (2 Thessalonians 1:6)."

Walk Closer to God

"If God is for us"—and He is—"who can be against us?" (Romans 8:31). The Enemy's efforts will boomerang to his own destruction; the believer in Christ will enjoy a well-deserved rest.

So take heart! "Hiding with Christ in God" is the safest place to be.

*W*alk Thru the Word

New Testament Reading
Revelation 13:1b-10
Old Testament Reading
Daniel 7:21-28

No one could buy or sell unless he had the mark,
which is the name of the beast or the number of his
name (Revelation 13:17).

A world that ignores God is a world that
rejects Christians. In the eyes of the world,
the only thing worse than a Christian who lives
like Christ is a Christian who doesn't live like
Christ.

When John writes of the mark of the beast, he
speaks of the unholy fraternity that confronts
Christians.

F. B. Meyer shares two resolutions for you to
consider as a person devoted to Christ.

Walk with F. B. Meyer

"Christians must resolve that they will not trifle with their consciences, but will obey the law
of Christ in all respects. For everyone there is an
inevitable choice to be made and maintained,
whether a clear conscience of a fortune is to hold
first place in their business careers.

"Second, they must be content to bear poverty
as part of the cross of Christ. We admire and can-
onize martyrs, but are strangely unwilling to face
the disgrace of poverty, the dens and caves of the
earth, which they endured for principle. Our religion will cost us something, or we may fairly
question its vitality and worth. What one will not
suffer for, one does not value."

Walk Closer to God

If it might cost you your livelihood to take a
stand for your living Lord, would you sway in
your commitment? Consider these sobering—
and challenging—words of Jesus:

"If anyone would come after me, he must deny
himself and take up his cross daily and follow
me" (Luke 9:23).

"Anyone who does not carry his cross and follow me cannot be my disciple" (Luke 14:27).

"In the same way, any of you who does not
give up everything he has cannot be my disciple"
(Luke 14:33).

Dare to obey Christ—regardless of the cost—
and He will give you a contentment and confidence no earthly career or profession can supply.

*S*uffering for what you value

*W*orship from the Heart

In the final days of
history, attacks
against believers will
intensify as Satan
mounts his last-ditch
effort. Praise God
that He, and we, have
triumphed through
the cross. Though the
mark of the beast is
as yet unrevealed, the
"mark" of the Cross
is burned deeply into
the spirits of those
who have died with
Jesus. Rejoice that
you are sealed to the
day of redemption.

*W*alk Thru the Word

New Testament Reading
Revelation 13:11-18
Old Testament Reading
Jeremiah 26:2-8

Singing melodies of joy before the Lord

And they sang a new song before the throne (Revelation 14:3).

From the first century to the twentieth, believers have sung about their joy in the Lord. Christians sing when they are joyful; and when they are discouraged, spiritual songs renew their joy.

A song to the Lord can lift your spirits. Find a quiet room, or a group of sympathetic friends! Sing in the yard, in the kitchen, or as you drive to work—but sing!

"Shout for joy to the Lord" (Psalm 100:1), and let Albert Barnes's description of the language of praise inspire your singing.

Walk with Albert Barnes

"To appreciate fully the songs of Zion and to understand the language of praise, a person must have known what it is to be a sinner under the condemnation of a holy law and to be in danger of eternal death. He must have experienced the joys of pardon in order to understand, in its true import, the language used by the redeemed.

"One who is saved from peril, rescued from long captivity, pardoned at the foot of the scaffold, or recovered from dangerous illness, will have an appreciation of the language of joy and triumph which can never be understood by one who has not been in those circumstances."

Walk Closer to God

Thoughts of Zion will keep you humming with these words from "He Keeps Me Singing":

There's within my heart a melody,
Jesus whispers sweet and low;
"Fear not, I am with thee—peace, be still"
In all of life's ebb and flow.

Feasting on the riches of His grace,
Resting 'neath His shelt'ring wing,
Always looking on His smiling face—
That is why I shout and sing.

Jesus, Jesus, Jesus—
Sweetest name I know
Fills my ev'ry longing,
Keeps me singing as I go.

Worship from the Heart

God has made us to praise and adore Him, to fall down before Him and worship Him forever. Imagine what it will be like to be part of the throngs of the redeemed singing before God's throne. Worship then will be your highest joy. Let it be so now.

Walk Thru the Word

New Testament Reading
Revelation 14
Old Testament Reading
Psalm 33:1-3

DECEMBER 21 ❏ DAY 355

[They] sang the song of Moses the servant of God and the song of the Lamb: "Great and marvelous are your deeds, Lord God Almighty. Just and true are your ways, King of the ages" (Revelation 15:3).

The Bible has been likened to a before-and-after picture.

The Old Testament is the before side, depicting the desperation of sinful humanity.

The New Testament is the after side, showing how Christ dealt with sin and brought salvation for who would believe.

Jesus is indeed the hub on which to place all the spokes of God's inspired Word. Alexander Maclaren highlights the unity of God's timeless message.

Walk with Alexander Maclaren

"The one broad lesson to be drawn from this is the essential unity of the revelation of God in the Old Covenant and in the New.

"Men pit the Old Testament against the New; the God of the Old Testament against the God of the New. They sometimes tell us that there is antagonism. Modern teachers want us to deny that the Old is the foreshadowing of the New, and the New the fulfillment of the Old.

"This text asserts, in opposition to all such errors, the fruitful principle of the fundamental unity of the two testaments. It bids us find the blossom in one and in the other the fruit.

"The God who brought the waters of the ocean over the Egyptian oppressors is the God who has mercy through His Son Jesus."

Walk Closer to God

"The New is in the Old concealed; the Old is in the New revealed."

Those who were born before Christ . . . and those born after Christ—both find the needs of their lives met in the person and work of Jesus Christ. He is the fulcrum of history and the focus of the Scriptures.

Before and after, B.C. and A.D., old and new—all find their center and circumference in Christ.

If you have never done so, invite Him to assume the pivotal place in your life as well.

*S*cripture's focus, history's fulcrum

*W*orship from the Heart

In Psalm 142, David voices the petition of all persecuted saints: "Set me free from my prison, that I may praise your name." As you read today, praise God that He will administer justice and will reveal His righteous acts.

*W*alk Thru the Word

New Testament Reading
Revelation 15
Old Testament Reading
Psalm 142

391

Subtle attacks and spiritual dangers

"Blessed is he who stays awake, and keeps his clothes with him, so that he may not go naked and be shamefully exposed" (Revelation 16:15).

Throw a frog into a pan of hot water and it will quickly leap to safety. The danger is apparent.

But place that same frog in a pan of cold water, and slowly raise the temperature. The frog will not realize the danger until he is on the verge of being boiled alive.

In similar ways, believers easily recognize Satan's frontal assaults. But Satan also has subtle ways of attacking from the blind side.

Charles Spurgeon alerts us to the danger of Satan's schemes.

Walk with Charles Spurgeon

"The tests of the Christian life, though outwardly not so terrible, are even more likely to overcome us than those of the fiery age. We have to bear the sneer of the world—that is little. Its soft words, its oily speeches, and its hypocrisy are far worse. Our danger is that we grow rich and proud, give ourselves up to the fashions of this present evil world, and lose our faith.

"Or if wealth is not the trial, worldly care causes difficulty. If we cannot be torn by the roaring lion, we may be hugged to death by the bear. The Devil little cares which it is, as long as he destroys our love for and confidence in Christ.

"We must be awake now, for we walk on dangerous ground. We are most likely to fall asleep to our undoing unless our faith in Jesus is a reality and our love for Him a fervent flame."

Walk Closer to God

C. S. Lewis once said, "The safest road to hell is the gradual one—gentle slope, without sudden turnings, without milestones, without signposts."

A trip downriver can be peaceful—until you hear the roar of the waterfall. By then, it may be too late to return safely to shore.

In the spiritual warfare, the believer's best safeguard is to abide in Christ and remain alert. Don't be deceived; the fire is hot and many are in danger. But a special blessing awaits those who make watchfulness their byword.

Worship from the Heart

"O, Father, when the works of Satan rage around me, deepen my understanding of the victory that You've won on the cross. Help me to experience the cross inwardly that I might meet any and every attack with a sense of destiny and place my confidence in Christ. Amen."

Walk Thru the Word

New Testament Reading
Revelation 16
Old Testament Reading
Joel 3:13-16

A battle in the war God has already won

"They will make war against the Lamb, but the Lamb will overcome them because he is Lord of lords and King of kings—and with him will be his called, chosen and faithful followers" (Revelation 17:14).

Some wars have been fought for noble causes; others for selfish gain. Some men have gone to war believing their destiny was to rule the world; others fought to make the world a safer, saner place.

At times it may be difficult to determine just who are the heroes and villains in warfare. But there is no mistaking the good guys for the bad guys in the war between Satan and God.

It is a fight to the finish, but God will emerge triumphant. By the way, whose side are you on?

That's the question Isaac Watts asks in this penetrating hymn.

Walk with Isaac Watts

> Am I a soldier of the cross,
>   A follower of the Lamb?
> And shall I fear to own His cause,
>   Or blush to speak His name?
>
> Must I be carried to the skies
>   On flowery beds of ease,
> While others fought to win the prize,
>   And sailed through bloody seas?
>
> Are there no foes for me to face?
>   Must I not stem the flood?
> Is this vile world a friend to grace,
>   To help me on to God?
>
> Since I must fight if I would reign;
>   Increase my courage, Lord;
> I'll bear the toil, endure the pain,
>   Supported by Thy Word.

Walk Closer to God

"Father, when it comes right down to it, I would often rather quit than fight.

"But I remember that Your Son endured death on the cross so that I might enjoy His triumph.

"In my own battles, Father, keep me mindful of the Savior who stands with me. Amen."

*W*orship from the Heart

When the Holy Spirit alerts you to pray for a specific situation or person, recognize that as a call to battle. Present yourself before the Commander-in-Chief and let Him reveal the prayer target. You never know how many of His warriors the Lord of Hosts is marshalling to fight a battle in prayer. Your call is simply to obey—and pray.

*W*alk Thru the Word

New Testament Reading
Revelation 17
Old Testament Reading
Deuteronomy 7:9-11

A sword drawn against sin

I heard another voice from heaven say: "Come out of her, my people, so that you will not share in her sins. . . . For her sins are piled up to heaven, and God has remembered her crimes" (Revelation 18:4-5).

*T*he Gospels portray the Savior in the company of swindlers, idolaters, and adulteresses—not to participate in their sin, but to identify with them in their need.

If the Babylon described in Revelation 18 had been close by, Jesus might have paid it a visit.

In the pages of Scriptures Babylon is used as a symbol for the domain of sin and corruption, a domain inhabited by all who do not put their trust in Christ. G. Campbell Morgan describes how Christ came to recapture enemy territory.

Walk with G. Campbell Morgan

"The ultimate purpose of God is to dwell with men. Man is to be blessed in God; God is to be glorified in man.

"Here is the picture of God's final methods in the world; the tabernacling of God with men; the city of God coming out of heaven; the realization of the divine purpose on earth.

"The progressive purpose of God is that He is at war against sin. He is destroying sin. The book of Revelation clearly presents God, the Alpha and the Omega, at war with sin, a picture full of comfort.

"Persuade me for a single moment that God is going to make peace with sin, and I become a most hopeless man. Let me see God with drawn sword fighting against sin. Then I see a God of such infinite love that I know the kingdom of this world shall become the kingdom of our God."

Walk Closer to God

Where God is present, sin trembles and flees. Sin cannot stand in the face of the Holy One.

Therefore, "Resist the devil, and he will flee from you. Come near to God and he will come near to you" (James 4:7-8).

All the resources of heaven are available to help you stand firm against the Enemy of your soul. And as you do, you will be blessed and God will be glorified.

*W*orship from the Heart

"Father, I acknowledge that following You separates me from the world. I praise You that Your power is sufficient to keep me from the counsel of the ungodly. Open my eyes to see 'Babylon' around me and keep me from its evil influence. Keep me in Your Word that I might be clean through the words You have spoken. Amen."

*W*alk Thru the Word

New Testament Reading
Revelation 18
Old Testament Reading
Jeremiah 51:49-58

394

Then the angel said to me, "Write: 'Blessed are those who are invited to the wedding supper of the Lamb!' " (Revelation 19:9).

*W*hat would a marriage celebration be without feasting and festivity? Jesus' first public miracle took place in Cana at a wedding—and involved an embarrassing emergency.

The marriage of Christ to His bride, the church, is not an afterthought. It is instead the glorious culmination of all God's plans and promises.

F. B. Meyer looks ahead to that great feast, the celebration called the "wedding supper."

Walk with F. B. Meyer

"Now we see the church of Christ unveiled and visible to heaven and earth. She has laid aside her tears and stands forth a monument of grace, the joy of the Bridegroom's heart.

"The wedding supper, it has been said, is the arrival of that time which the redeemed of every age have anticipated. It has been the longed-for day of patriarchs, the glowing prediction of prophets, the theme of songs, the hope of the church, the era for which creation groans and the children of God pray.

"But there must be a present character to fit us for this future celebration. Who are they that are called to the wedding supper?

"They are of every kindred, nation, people, and tongue who have accepted the invitation of the everlasting gospel. They have washed their robes and made them white in the blood of the Lamb.

"Let us now pass on that invitation. Let him that hears say, 'Come.' "

Walk Closer to God

Little girls dream of the day they will walk down the aisle to join hands and lives with their devoted groom. Some even rehearse the vows of commitment they will speak on that day.

Do you look forward to meeting your loving Bridegroom? As part of the church you will be dressed in bridal finery to meet your Savior.

And what a feast for the soul there will be on that most wonderful day!

*B*eholding the beauty of our Bridegroom

*W*orship from the Heart

United as a single voice of praise, the voices of those around God's throne blend into one harmonious chorus of praise. In anticipation of that day, worship now with your own Hallelujahs as you sing a praise hymn or chorus to God who gave His Son for our salvation.

*W*alk Thru the Word

New Testament Reading
Revelation 19:1-10
Old Testament Reading
Isaiah 11:1-9

The thrill of victory

On his robe and on his thigh he has this name written:
KING OF KINGS AND LORD OF LORDS *(Revelation 19:16).*

"*O*h, the times, they are a-changin'." The successes of atheistic humanism read like a devil's litany: God has been expelled from the public schools; abortion is still a legal "choice"; pornography is viewed as harmless, homosexuality as healthy. Christianity is ridiculed in the media.

In times like these, the temptation is to withdraw in silence—become a "secret agent" for Jesus. But do you know how God reacts to those who conspire against Him? He laughs (Psalm 2:4).

B. B. Warfield encourages us to take comfort in this: Christ is going to win.

Walk with B. B. Warfield

"The section opens with a vision of the victory of the Word of God, the King of kings and Lord of lords over all His enemies. We see Him come forth from heaven girded for war, followed by the armies of heaven. The birds of the air are summoned to the feast of corpses that shall be prepared for them. The armies of the enemy—the beasts and the kings of the earth—are gathered against Him and are totally destroyed.

"It is a vivid picture of a complete victory, and entire conquest, that we have here; and all the imagery of war and battle is employed to give it life. This is the symbol. The thing symbolized obviously is the complete victory of the Son of God over all the hosts of wickedness. Christ is to conquer the earth: He is to overcome all His enemies."

Walk Closer to God

Surrounded by wickedness, the psalmist asked, "Why, O Lord, do you stand far off?" (Psalm 10:1). Yet he took courage in God's coming victory: "The Lord is King for ever and ever; the nations will perish from his land" (Psalm 10:16).

Likewise, the apostle Paul wrote: "God is just: He will pay back trouble to those who trouble you . . . when the Lord Jesus is revealed from heaven in blazing fire" (2 Thessalonians 1:6-7).

Do you have this same confidence? Meditate often on Christ's victory, and you will be thrilled!

Worship from the Heart

God has made us to praise and adore Him—to fall down before Him—to worship Him forever. We have been gathered from among the nations to give thanks to His name and to triumph in His praise. Therefore "From everlasting to everlasting, let all the people say, 'Amen!' " (See Psalm 106:47-48).

Walk Thru the Word

New Testament Reading
Revelation 19:11-21
Old Testament Reading
Psalm 10

The glory that makes burdens bearable

They came to life and reigned with Christ a thousand years (Revelation 20:4).

Although some passages of the book of Revelation are difficult to understand, many verses—like small diamonds of encouragement—shine brightly with comfort.

As John switches his focus from the present to the future; from this world to the next, he discovers encouragement to face each fresh challenge to his faith.

Martin Luther also had these encouraging observations for those facing unjust suffering.

Walk with Martin Luther

"If we consider the great glory of the future life, it would not be at all difficult for us to bear the vexations of this world. But when Christ comes to judge the living and the dead and we experience these blessings, everyone will have to say for himself: 'Shame on me!'

"If I believe the Word, I shall on the last day not only gladly have suffered ordinary temptations, insults, imprisonment, but I shall also say: 'Oh, if I had only thrown myself under the feet of all the godless for the sake of the great glory which I now see revealed and which has come to me through the merit of Christ.'

"Paul well says, 'I consider that our present sufferings are not worth comparing with the glory that will be revealed in us' (Romans 8:18)."

Walk Closer to God

Remember Stephen, known as the first martyr of the New Testament church. Even as the rocks were hurtling toward him, Stephen looked up to heaven and saw Jesus at God's right hand. Then, like his Lord, he died praying for those who were taking his life.

Chances are you won't be stoned for your faith, or even persecuted in any physical way. But don't be surprised if you feel the heat as you live out your faith.

One message permeates nearly every chapter of John's book: Victory is assured. So take heart . . . look up . . . wait patiently. The glory to be revealed in us makes any burden bearable.

Worship from the Heart

When the King comes, His bride will be clothed in "fine linen, bright and clean . . . (Fine linen stands for the righteous acts of the saints.)" (Revelation 19:8). But John is careful to point out that this clothing is "given" by the Lamb, not earned by the wearers. Praise God again for His mighty grace. He does for us what we can in no way do for ourselves!

Walk Thru the Word

New Testament Reading
Revelation 20:1-6
Old Testament Reading
Daniel 12:1-3

The death of death and Satan's doom

I saw the dead, great and small, standing before the throne, and books were opened. Another book was opened, which is the book of life. The dead were judged according to what they had done as recorded in the books (Revelation 20:12).

"*H*ave you come to a verdict?" the judge asks the somber jury after their deliberations.

"Yes, your honor," the foreman responds. "We find the defendant guilty on all charges."

The jury has done its job; guilt has been established. It remains for the judge to set the sentence.

In the case of *Holy God v. sinful man* humanity's guilt has been established, but the sentencing comes later, as William Milligan explains.

Walk with William Milligan

"In previous chapters, three great enemies of God have been introduced to us—the dragon (or the Devil), the beast, and the false prophet. These were the main opponents of the Lamb, in one way or another stirring up all the efforts that had been made against Him by the kings of the earth, their armies, and their followers.

"For a time they had appeared to succeed. They had persecuted the saints, overcome them, and killed them. However, the final triumph remains with those who have suffered for the sake of righteousness. In chapter 19 the beast and false prophet perish. The destruction of the third is reserved for chapter 20.

"Then is described the judgment of those who had listened to these enemies. They had been defeated but had not yet been consigned to their doom. Thereafter all that remains to complete the triumph of Christ and His saints is for death and Hades to be removed from the scene and cast into the lake of fire."

Walk Closer to God

The penalty paid by Christ on the cross makes it possible to enjoy the full benefits of a pardoned criminal. Pardon comes only through Him.

To avoid the sentence of death, you must throw yourself on the mercy of the court and allow Jesus Christ the righteous Judge to become your merciful Savior.

Worship from the Heart

Praise God that He has made a way of escape through the blood of Jesus Christ. Praise Him that the cross of Christ is indeed the bridge over hell and the door to heaven. Consider what it meant for Jesus to be totally separated from His Father so that you might be forever present with Him.

Walk Thru the Word

New Testament Reading
Revelation 20:7-15
Old Testament Reading
Isaiah 61:6-7

"Now the dwelling of God is with men, and he will live with them. They will be his people, and God himself will be with them and be their God" (Revelation 21:3).

*I*mmanuel: God is present with His people

*I*n the presence of a king, soldiers snap to attention and civilians bow or curtsy. Even the members of his family show the appropriate deference to his rank.

In the presence of God, similar behavior is in order. But there's more to enjoying God than merely knowing when to bow before Him. Allow Matthew Henry to explain.

Walk with Matthew Henry

"The presence of God with His church is the glory of the church. The presence of God with His people in heaven will not be interrupted. He will dwell with them continually. They shall be His people. God Himself will be their God.

"This new and blessed state will be free from all trouble and sorrow. God, as their tender Father, shall wipe away the tears of His children with His own kind hand. All the causes of future sorrows shall be forever removed.

"The truth and certainty of this blessed state are ratified by the word and promise of God. He has committed it to writing for perpetual memory and continual use to His people.

"We may and ought to take God's promise as present payment. His titles of honor are a pledge of the full performance—Alpha and Omega, the beginning and the end. As His power and will were the first cause of all things, His pleasure and glory are the last end.

"The greatness and the fullness of this future happiness are declared to all the saints."

Walk Closer to God

Great . . . free . . . full.

These powerful words describe an eternity in the presence of God.

Meeting the King face to face would be honor enough. But He has also given you the authority to become an heir to every heavenly blessing.

And that's a promise to cherish while you're in the present—awaiting His presence.

*W*orship from the Heart

Praise God for faithfully fulfilling His plan. Read Leviticus 26:11-12; John 1:14; 14:1-3; Revelation 21:3. Praise God for all the events of history which have carried forward His plan to be with His people. Express to Him your confidence and joy that you will be with Him throughout eternity.

*W*alk Thru the Word

New Testament Reading
Revelation 21:1-8
Old Testament Reading
Isaiah 25:6-9

A city resplendent with God's glory

And he carried me away in the Spirit to a mountain great and high, and showed me the Holy City, Jerusalem, coming down out of heaven from God. It shone with the glory of God (Revelation 21:10-11).

*H*ome Sweet Home. Those comforting words have greeted countless weary travelers who have returned at last to the place where they truly belong.

The Christian too longs for home, in this case a place he has never seen. Bernard of Cluny's words express the believer's desire for heaven.

Walk with Bernard of Cluny

> For you, O dear, dear country,
>   Mine eyes their vigils keep;
> For very love, beholding
>   Your happy name, they weep:
> The mention of your glory
>   Is unction to the breast,
> And medicine in sickness,
>   And love, and life, and rest.
>
> O one, O only mansion!
>   O paradise of joy,
> Where tears are ever banished,
>   And smiles have no alloy!
> The cross is all your splendor,
>   The Crucified your praise;
> His laud and benediction
>   Your ransomed people raise.
>
> You have no shore, fair ocean!
>   You have no time, bright day!
> Dear fountain of refreshment
>   To pilgrims far away!
> Upon the Rock of Ages
>   You raise the holy tower;
> Yours is the victor's laurel
>   And yours the golden dower.

Walk Closer to God

Though heaven may seem far away, remember that you are a stranger and pilgrim on the earth. For you—and all the saints of all the ages—heaven is your heart's sweet home. Your Savior has gone to prepare a place for you there. Rejoice!

*W*orship from the Heart

Jesus said, "I go [to] prepare a place for you" (John 14:3). As you read today's Scripture, let your imagination soar and your spirit lift. Even if the treasures of this world were heaped together, they would be nothing compared to the place God has prepared for you and the joy of being with Him forever.

*W*alk Thru the Word

New Testament Reading
Revelation 21:9-27
Old Testament Reading
Ezekiel 43:5-12

*L*iving forever in perfect light

There will be no more night. They will not need the light of a lamp or the light of the sun, for the Lord God will give them light (Revelation 22:5).

*H*istorically in many parts of the world, a solar eclipse was cause for fear and trembling. The appearance of night in the middle of the day prompted animal (and even human) sacrifices.

Even those who know the eclipse's true origin are still awed by the sight of midday darkness. But there is one place where you will never have to worry about the lights going out.

God dwells in unapproachable and inextinguishable light. Albert Barnes explains what this means for you now and in the future.

Walk with Albert Barnes

"It will be a world of perfect light. There will be literally no night there. Spiritually and morally there will be no darkness—no error, no sin.

"Light will be cast on a thousand subjects now obscure; and on numerous points which now perplex the mind, there will be poured the splendor of the perfect day. All the darkness that exists here will be cast away. All that is now obscure will be made light.

"In view of this fact, we may well submit for a little time to the mysteries which hang over the divine dealings here. The Christian is destined to live forever, and he will be permitted to know all that is to be known in those worlds that shine upon his path by day or by night. Well, then, may he bear the darkness and endure the trials of this world a little longer."

Walk Closer to God

"Father, I praise You that You are the light of the world. Truly You are the light of my life. I discover what is true by the clarity of Your light. My heart is softened by the warmth of Your light.

"When I cannot see Your eternal purposes, help me to trust. When the light of Your Word reveals only the next step, give me patience not to run ahead.

"In the name of Your Son, who came as the Light of my world. Amen."

*W*orship from the Heart

At last, faith becomes sight. In prayer, praise God for each step of your pilgrimage; thank Him for His provision along the way, and raise the eyes of faith to your heavenly destination. Let your heart cry out with joy, "Even so, come, Lord Jesus!"

*W*alk Thru the Word

New Testament Reading
Revelation 22
Old Testament Reading
Psalm 36:7-9

Indexes

Credits

The editors wish to express appreciation for permission to reprint excerpts from the following works:

Renewed Day by Day, by A. W. Tozer. © 1980, Christian Publications. Used by permission.

Specified excerpts from the works of C. S. Lewis reprinted by permission of Collins Publishers, London.

Commentary on Mark, Lectures on the Book of Acts, Commentary on Galatians, Second Epistle to the Corinthians, by H. A. Ironside. Used by permission of Loizeaux Brothers, Inc., Neptune, New Jersey.

The Gospel According to Matthew, © 1929; *The Gospel According to Mark*, © 1955; *Searchlights From the Word*, © 1977; and *An Exposition of the Whole Bible*, © 1959, renewed 1987; by G. Campbell Morgan. Used by permission of Fleming H. Revell Company.

*I*ndex
of
Authors

*T*his index of authors gives a brief statement about each Christian leader who is quoted in *Closer Walk* as well as the page numbers where their quotations can be found.

Peter Abelard (1079-1142)
French philosopher and theologian who attracted students from all over Europe. Page 14

Ambrose (c. 339-397)
Church leader and spiritual father of Augustine. Page 94

Augustine (354-430)
Theologian and leader of the early church. Page 50

Albert Barnes (1798-1870)
American preacher and commentator. Pages 9, 40, 95, 115, 122, 136, 156, 169, 185, 186–87, 207, 236, 248, 259, 270, 295, 308, 332, 346, 359, 376, 390, 401

Donald Barnhouse (1895-1960)
American radio preacher and magazine editor. Pages 195, 199

Richard Baxter (1615-1691)
Self-taught English Puritan preacher who wrote more than 100 books. Page 23

Bernard of Clairvaux (1090-1153)
Known for his hymn "O Sacred Head Now Wounded." Page 81

Bernard of Cluny (12th century)
French poet and hymnist about whom little is known. Page 400

INDEX OF AUTHORS

INDEX OF AUTHORS

INDEX OF AUTHORS

INDEX OF AUTHORS

INDEX OF AUTHORS

Subject Index

*T*his subject index will direct you to *Closer Walk* devotions covering a wide range of issues, concerns and topics facing you in your daily walk with God.